CLOUDLESS MIND

Volume 3

CLOUDLESS MIND

Conversations on Buddhahood

with

Daniel P. Brown, PhD

SENTIENT PUBLICATIONS

First Sentient Publications edition 2025

Transcribed and edited by: Susan Pottish and Scott V. Anderson MD

A paperback original
Book design and cover design by Laura Waltje

Library of Congress Control Number: 2024952907
Publisher's Cataloging-in-Publication Data

Names: Brown, Daniel P., 1948-2022, author.

Title: Cloudless mind : conversations on Buddhahood , volume 3 / with Daniel P. Brown, PhD.

Description: Includes bibliographical references. | Boulder, CO: Sentient Publications, LLC, 2025.

Identifiers: LCCN: 2024952907 | ISBN: 9781591813545 (vol. 1) | 9781591813569 (vol. 2) | 9781591813583 (vol. 3)
Subjects: LCSH Buddha (The concept) | Buddhahood. | Buddhism. | Meditation--Buddhism. | Spiritual life--Buddhism. | BISAC RELIGION / Buddhism / Tibetan | BODY, MIND & SPIRIT / Mindfulness & Meditation | PSYCHOLOGY / Psychotherapy / Spiritually Integrated
Classification: LCC BQ7612 .B76 2025 v. 3 | DDC 294.3/923--dc23

Printed in the United States of America
10 9 8 7 6 5 4 3 2 1

Sentient Publications
A Limited Liability Company
PO Box 1851
Boulder, CO 80306
www.sentientpublications.com

Contents

May the knowledge, guidance, and wisdom shared by Dan Brown in this collection be helpful to all in understanding their path to wellbeing and freedom in this life.

Editor's Foreword

Daniel P. Brown, PhD was known professionally as Doctor Brown, but in his interactions with students and colleagues, as in the question-and-answer sessions making up this book, he was always addressed simply as Dan. He spent forty-six years as a clinical psychologist, and researcher; he was also an expert witness on trauma and the veracity of children's memories and testified in courts across the U.S. as well as at War Crimes Tribunals in eastern Europe. This deep expertise gave him a unique perspective on and a depth of knowledge of human potential—both positive and negative. His forty-five years as an authorized teacher of Buddhist practices to Westerners gave him an opportunity to integrate his psychological knowledge with the wisdom of the Buddhist path to spiritual awakening. The ultimate principle guiding him, in all areas in which he worked, was to enhance the wellbeing of others.[1]

In 2008 Dan began inviting students, friends, and associates to join him at a meeting room in a small two-story building in Newton Center, Massachusetts, to explore spiritual and psychological understandings of healing, positive growth potential, and flourishing for human beings, including the path to spiritual awakening and enlightenment as presented in Tibetan Buddhism and as Dan had been teaching for decades by then. The recordings of these sessions by students began in 2012.

---

1 For a fuller picture of Dan's work over the years, please see his biography and C.V. at the end of the book.

There were no guidelines given for questions. People were invited to ask questions about "whatever." Thus, neither Dan nor anyone else knew what the topics would be on any given night, and yet Dan often gave his answers to the myriad subjects raised in rather astonishing detail.

The pointing-out style of teaching that Dan developed was not something he did on his own. First, at the direction of H. H. the Dalai Lama, Dan hiked to a remote area of Tibet and sat with a yogi practitioner who demonstrated "rainbow body" (physically dissolving into light and then reappearing) to Dan, while describing in words what he was doing at each stage of the way. The yogi also told him specifically never to practice or teach what he saw. The question in Dan's mind remained, "Why did His Holiness send me there? What was I supposed to learn?" After nearly two years, he understood that the benefit of that encounter was to have the experience of learning from a teacher who was teaching him by "pointing out" each stage of a practice. After that, and after fifteen years of teaching meditation in the traditional manner with Denma Locho Rinpoche, a high lama in the Gelugpa lineage (assigned to teach with Dan by H. H. the Dalai Lama), Dan proposed an innovative method using "pointing out" instructions when they taught together to increase efficacy in learning by students. The increased efficacy was demonstrated so well to Denma Locho Rinpoche that he gave Dan permission to continue teaching in that pointing out way on his own. (Dan published *Pointing Out the Great Way: The Stages of Meditation in the Mahāmudrā Tradition* in 2006 as an homage to his teachers.)

In 2009 Dan partnered with his longtime spiritual friend, Rahob Tulku Rinpoche, and they agreed that Dan would prepare students for the higher transmissions to be given by Rinpoche. Rahob Tulku was viewed by H.H. the Dalai Lama as an emanation of Guru Padmasambhava for our time. Although living quietly at a small center in Petersburg, New York, Rinpoche became well-known and beloved by many of Dan's students as he met them individually to give them guidance in their practice either in retreats with Dan or at his small center in upstate New York. When Dan mentions "Rinpoche" in the Wednesday Night talks, it is Rahob Tulku Rinpoche to whom he is referring.

Also, Dan made it clear that he would never teach alone, meaning he was always overseen and held accountable by a lineage master. While he often had to be the sole teacher at his retreats, he preferred to have a co-teacher whenever possible. There were multiple reasons for this, including the understanding that teaching by oneself could easily lead to a sense of "self-importance," which, in

Dan's view, was a disastrous failing.[2] Thus he taught his wife, Gretchen Nelson (a physical therapist and yoga teacher), to teach his pointing-out way, and they taught together internationally for nearly thirteen years.

His commitment to being accountable and overseen expanded later when Dan discovered and began studying and practicing teachings from the Bon tradition that preceded Buddhism in Tibet. At that time, Dan became a heart-student of H.H. the 33rd Menri Trizin, whom Dan recognized as his Root Lama in 2014 and who encouraged Dan both to teach and to translate texts never translated before into English. This he did in collaboration with Geshe Sonam Gurang, a Bon Geshe also accountable to H.H. Menri Trizin.

Because Wednesday Night sessions rarely focused on a single topic, the titles given to each chapter in this collection consist simply of the date each took place and a subheading of "themes," attempting to capture something of the range of that evening's questions and answers. Also, as the talks often included conversation, the conversational style has been preserved throughout, with no attempt to edit Dan or questioners into something like "written" material. On occasion, if it seemed like Dan left out a word accidentally or because a word was inaudible on the tape, the most likely missing word has been put in brackets [like this] or indicating a group response like [Laughter]. Also, because the names of people asking questions were mostly inaudible or unknown, the people who asked questions are identified simply as Student 1, Student 2, etc.

When Dan does mention someone's name, it has been changed to honor their privacy.

On another slightly technical note, Dan often used Tibetan words in his responses to people, particularly when explicating the Tibetan Buddhist interpretation of a given topic. Instead of using a formal glossary that gives Wylie transliterations (which does not convey pronunciation), the approach chosen here was to give the best phonetic rendering of the words Dan spoke as heard on the recordings, just as he said them.

---

2 He cited the declaration by one of the early Christian Desert Fathers that self-importance, or pride, was "the eighth deadly sin." Nevertheless, several of Dan's students, both in the U.S. and abroad, have chosen to teach on their own. Dan would not have approved of this, giving his wife, Gretchen Nelson, sole authority to train and approve new teachers. For information on approved teachers, please contact admin@pointingoutthegreatway.com.

Another aspect of Dan's later work included pioneering neuroscientific research using EEG measures in relation to levels of mind. His goal was not to show that the brain was the cause or the source of mind nor of its awakening, but rather to show that as awakening progresses there are also detectable changes in the brain's activity. Some thirty of his students were assessed by Dan and an assistant teacher for their capacity to shift into and out of a number of what he called the "basis of operation," or well-established and continuous states of mind, including "awakened awareness," and then, in a laboratory environment, participants underwent brainwave evaluation while making those shifts.

This research was sponsored by the Fetzer Foundation and performed in the neuroscience lab of Judson Brewer, MD PhD in Boston at UMass Medical School. (See the Wednesday night talk #65 of July 19, 2017 for a basic description of the study.) The results reported by Dan were "stellar" because they showed uniquely high levels of activation of specific centers in the brain when the subject shifted through levels of mind they had learned from Dan, and most especially when shifting to the level of awakened awareness.

To our knowledge, this kind of research had never been done before. In a meeting to review the results of the study, a representative of the Fetzer Foundation and a representative of the National Academy of Sciences found the outcomes to be highly valuable and worthy of further research funding. Unfortunately, that additional research didn't happen because the lab was closed during the Covid pandemic, and Dan passed away in April of 2022.

It has recently come to our attention that there are several new initiatives in contemplative neuroscience (CN) to investigate deeper levels of practice than have been the focus (of CN) previously. Among these initiatives are the Harvard Meditation Research Project,[3] and the initiatives reported in a recent article in *Scientific American*—"Advanced Meditation Alters Consciousness and our Basic Sense of Self"[4]—that provides a link to Dan's innovative study.

In the Wednesday night conversations, Dan describes steps, stages, levels, and ranges of spiritual development. He describes the spiritual path according

---

3 Mass General Meditation Research. "Research." Massachusetts General Hospital. https://meditation.mgh.harvard.edu/research/.

4 Zanes, Anna. "Advanced Meditation Alters Consciousness and Our Basic Sense of Self." Scientific American, Joe 24, 2024. https://www.scientificamerican.com/article/advanced-meditation-alters-consciousness-and-our-basic-sense-of-self/.

to three progressive maps, with explicit instructions along the way, and also warning practitioners against trying to jump ahead. He made it clear that just because the map is there, if a particular location is not where you are, it's better that you don't focus on that location. Why? Because if you're not there yet, you will be thinking about it, using ideas, images, or concepts; and such thinking about it, he says, actually hardens the mind and makes it more difficult to experience awakening. So, even though Dan discusses the full range of experiences, it is not to encourage people to imagine them, but rather to know that there is a path that leads to their natural and spontaneous appearance.

Finally, at the start of each Wednesday night meeting, Dan would routinely ask for people attending for the first time to identify themselves and speak a bit about how and why they came to the meeting. Sometimes those conversations went on for quite a while. Then, at the end of the introductions, Dan would clarify for everyone the purpose and structure of the meeting, which was, first, to create a completely open forum for questions that anyone might have about literally anything; and second, once the question and answer period was over, there would be a bathroom break and people would reassemble for a guided meditation—what Dan called "meditation improv"—in which he created on the spot a novel guided meditation to give people some direct experience of what had been spoken about earlier in the evening. (Those meditations were not transcribed and thus are not part of this collection.)

Because the opening conversations were often personal, and also repetitive, rather than repeat the introductory descriptions by Dan for each Wednesday Night meeting, one very simple version has been included at the beginning of each talk, namely, "Welcome everybody. You have a question?"

The reason there is no introduction for the first talk presented in this text is that on that particular occasion Dan did something unusual, introducing the topic for the night without asking for questions, and then offering a summary of the Buddhist path to enlightenment. While not planned by anyone, of course, it does seem to be a wonderful introduction in this publication to the scope and depth that Dan presents throughout the Wednesday Night talks, and thus also seems a perfect opening. We hope you will delight in the experientially derived scope and depth of Dan's unique integration of Eastern Wisdom traditions and Western psychology.

Susan Pottish & Scott V. Anderson, M.D.

October 5, 2016

Themes: Constructs Are Clouds; Three Maps; There's No "Out There"

Dan

Welcome everyone. You have a question?

Student 1

There's one pith instruction that I'm not sure how to do—the one about when we're not partializing or just going big and not seeing any boundaries. I'm not, like how to not see boundaries, but go way beyond, and it sounds straightforward but it's also very difficult.

Dan

[Smiling] You want me to go over the very most advanced stuff that there is?

Student 1

That's where I'm struggling. That's where my edge is right now.

Dan

There are no edges.

Student 1

All right …

Dan

That's the answer. [Laughter] That's the answer.

Student 1

Yeah, but I don't know how to do it other than just sense it. I don't know maybe that's all there is to do but ...

Dan

The ordinary mind, by its nature, constructs. And it constructs representations for the world. It constructs external visual forms. It constructs sounds. It constructs smells, tastes. It constructs the body, the sensations experienced in the body. Within the field of the mind, it constructs thought, memory, emotions. So, from a practice perspective everything is merely a construction.

From a practice perspective what you're seeing, hearing, smelling, tasting, sensing, thinking, emoting are the mind's own constructions. We don't even know if it's an out there. What you see is not a world out there, what you see is the mind's representation of whatever's there, if anything. What you're hearing is the mind's representation of that in terms of sound.

Everything is a construction. And because that's the nature of how the ordinary mind works, it constructs everything. And in that sense, Buddhism is very similar to modern, Western constructivist psychology. In the old logical positivist view of the universe, and Western psychology, we used to think that it's a world out there. And the function of science was to measure that world and to observe constancies and to see how things are created by various interactions and variables. So that the old logical positivist view of perception was that the eyes, for visual perceptions, are like tape recorders. We make an image of the world out there. We just record it, and then we send that to the brain that makes another image.

Then, in the 1960s, by a man named [Alex] Huk in J. Gibson's work, that [old view] got challenged. He said, "If you look at it from the system's perspective what you have is the sense system that's interacting with whatever's there (we don't even know what that is), and then it constructs representations. So, what you're seeing really isn't the world out there. What you're seeing is the mind's construction of an out there, representing an out there, and representing visual forms, and what you're seeing, hearing, etc. is your own mind's representations. Because that's all we can see, hear, taste, smell, and sense."

And in that sense, it's very similar to Buddhism, and the theory of emptiness is that everything is just a construction. It's not that it doesn't exist. It exists because that's what the mind does in relative reality, it makes constructions. And in that sense, to say that everything is interdependent in Buddhism, that relative reality appears that way because everything is depending on everything else, is very similar to the concept of interaction effects in science. We make a world of constructions. And that culminated in a holographic theory. When you go to the science museum you see something very vivid that you can put your hands through, and you know it's not real. But what if the whole world is a holograph like that—vivid, but not substantial, not independently existing, as the Buddhists would say?

That's what the word emptiness means. It doesn't mean that something doesn't exist. It means that it exists in relative reality because that's what you're seeing as your own constructive nature. External reality is constructed, thought is constructed, memory is constructed, the sense of self is constructed. Self-psychologists in the West tell us we didn't come into the world with a developed sense of self. I didn't come into the world with Dan-ness. Dan's a construction. And the construction of a psychological sense of self comes in about twelve to eighteen months, roughly equivalent with the capacity for human representational thinking. When we can represent, we can represent the self as a construction.

In a relative reality, constructions are useful. Dan becomes a central organizing principle in my life. I organize a lot of my action plans and needs around Dan. Another big construction is time. And I organize a lot of my social calendar around time. That's why we can start class on time and end on time. But what if those are all just constructions of mind? Empty. Then I start seeing Dan as not something real but something as just a construction. It's useful. Time isn't something real but just a construction. And by looking at all those as empty constructions through a practice of emptiness meditation, I see beyond them, into the deeper nature of the mind.

So, when you do emptiness practice you look into the fact that everything is constructed. And the trouble is that each one of those constructions of mind, once we develop it and it becomes a habit, there's two problems from a Buddhist perspective. One problem is called *dzin-pa*, grab. Things have grab. Emotions have grab. The sense of self has grab. If I'm caught in traffic, time has grab. And the grab of all these constructions is what causes suffering. Secondly *mümpa*. These constructions of mind become like clouds that obscure. *Mümpa* means to obscure the mind. We get layer upon layer of empty constructions of mind. And we live in those constructions and we think that that's all there is. So, we never look deeper. And all those constructions obscure the real nature of the mind.

So, from a great Great Completion, Dzogchen point of view, the real nature of the mind's radiance, awakened awareness, is always here. You are never apart from that. So, everybody experiences awakened awareness all the time. But you don't recognize it. And the analogy that's used in Dzogchen is it's like the sun. The sun shines all the time. And if it's cloudy and the cloud's clear we say, "The sun just came out." But that's not true. The sun shines day and night. But from your perspective, only when the clouds clear you could see the sun shining forth. And as long as the mind is clouded over by one solid construction after another, layers and layers of thought, sense of self, time, and the solidness of emotional reactions. All that stuff is like layers and layers of clouds. So, the radiance of the infinitely vast awakened awareness, an ocean of awakened awareness-love that's always right here, is obscured like the sun. So, if you clear away all those clouds, the sun becomes more obvious.

That's what the Heart Sutra mantra is all about. It's a description of the stages of emptiness practice. It goes like this in Sanskrit ["*gate*" here sounds like gah-tay]:

Gate gate pāragate pārasamgate bodhi svāhā

Gate gate pāragate pārasamgate bodhi svāhā

Gate gate pāragate pārasamgate bodhi svāhā

Now here's what it means literally from Sanskrit. *Gate* (gone); *gate* (gone); *pāragate* (gone beyond); *pārasamgate* (gone way beyond); *bodhi svāhā* (Ooohh, what a realization).

Now the first layer of clouds is all your conceptual thought. It's like a massive clouding over of the real nature of the mind's awakened awareness. So, if you concentrate through practicing concentration meditation, thought becomes calm. After you get skilled in concentration you get longer periods of stillness. And when you get longer periods of stillness, at some point you figure out that you're operating not out of thought anymore because there isn't any thought. So where does your operation come from, if there are no thoughts going on? It comes from the intention of awareness. And the intention of awareness is much quicker than thought. But it's only when you can separate out thought enough that you can go beyond it.

That's the first *gate*: awareness, *rigpa*, beyond thought. You've shifted what we call *chulya*—you've shifted your basis of operation. *Chulya* means where you're coming from. Usually we're lost in thought; we're coming from thought operations. But if you calm thought enough you can't be coming from thought anymore because there aren't any thoughts happening at that moment. So. where you're coming from is you're operating out of the intention of awareness. You've gone beyond thought. You've separated out the solidness of thought from the pure radiance of awareness. If you want a good Tibetan metaphor, you separate out the solid curds from the yak milk and get the sweetness of the milk.

But it's likely at that point in the meditation you're still operating out of self. Dan still seems to do the meditation. And if I do emptiness of self, I don't get rid of Dan, I just get rid of its capacity to cloud things over. And I shift my [basis of] operation. I go beyond Dan. That's the second *gate*—awareness itself gone beyond self-representation or personal identity to a bigger field of awareness. Now Dan's not doing the meditation anymore. It's awareness itself doing the meditation.

Now I'll linguistically mark that *rang rigpa*, awareness itself, just to show that it's a different level of awareness. But still, that awareness will come and go in the convention of time. And if I do the emptiness of time meditation and go beyond time, I'll locate, as my basis of operation, a level of awareness that's absolutely constant and changeless beyond coming and going in time. And because time and space are related, it's a level of awareness that's vast and boundless. We call that ocean-like, changeless, boundless awareness. So, I learn to operate out of that. Now that's a much bigger change. So, that's why in the

Heart Sutra it's called *pāragate*, it's linguistically marked, gone way beyond the convention of time to ocean-like, changeless, boundless awareness.

But I've still got one big cloud left. And that's my information processing system. So, here's the issue. The whole thing is set up like a video game. You've got to solve the puzzle. Always right here is an infinitely vast ocean of awakened awareness-love. You are never apart from that. But you don't realize it. And the reason why you don't realize it is that that unbounded wholeness of awakened awareness-love cannot be apprehended by a partialized stance. The partialization can't recognize the whole. Every operation of your information processing system partializes, from slowest to fastest operations. So, the slowest operation is thought.

If you take a tachistoscope of Western psychology, a high-speed electronic board that can measure the speed of the mind, thought is rather slow. Most thought occurs from about 3,000 milliseconds to about five hundred milliseconds, or half a second. That's pretty slow. Directing our attention to this or to that takes about two hundred fifty milliseconds. The lightning speed of the intention of awareness is as fast as a machine will measure. Now ordinarily we mix up thought, directed attention, and the intention of awareness as if they're all the same. But a good yogi learns to separate them out, and learns to operate out of the intention of awareness rather than operating out of thought.

If you want a practical example of that, since it's the baseball playoffs, think about a major league baseball player. When you're standing up there trying to hit a fast ball, the fast ball comes down to the plate at ninety miles an hour. That's four hundred milliseconds. So, if you're thinking, you can't locate that fastball because thinking's too slow. Thinking is slower than the ball is actually going to reach the plate. So, if you're thinking to locate where the ball is and match it with your bat speed, it's impossible. That's why batters get in a slump because they think too much.

But, if the ball comes down at four hundred milliseconds and you're directing your attention, not using thought but pure attention, two hundred milliseconds, you should be able to direct your attention to the location estimated and hit the ball. But if you wanted to become a great baseball player, what you would do is you would train yourself to operate out of the lightning speed of awareness. And wherever that ball comes in to you, with lightning speed you would pick it up and match it with your bat speed.

That's what Tony Gwynn did, who had the second highest average batting career of any player. He figured it out by himself. He would stand up at the plate and have the pitching machine throw in tennis balls at a hundred and fifty miles an hour—no bat speed can match that. But he wasn't trying to hit them. He was trying to locate them with awareness. And after a hundred and fifty, two hundred and fifty balls he could just "tchh," just like that, high speed, lightning speed. Then when he had the pitching machine throw in hard balls, baseballs, at ninety miles an hour, they seemed slow to him. One after the other. One after the other. He's a hitting machine.

I once had a friend who was a part owner of the Pirates when they weren't a very good team. So, when my youngest was eleven and he was totally into his little league, as a treat I said, "I've got a surprise for you." So, I didn't tell him where we were going and I got him on a plane and we flew to Pittsburgh, and I didn't tell him what we were doing because it was a surprise. And we showed up at the ball park for a double header with the St. Louis Cardinals. And my friend had arranged that we could go on batting practice. And we got to sit, and I got to stand right behind the batter's box, this distance away from Albert Pujols, and he was in the flow that day and hit about fifty home-runs in batting practice.

When you're standing that close and you're watching his bat speed and the crack off the bat, it's awesome. I think I got more out of it than he did actually. But it was an unforgettable event to watch somebody like that because he was using his mind. With lightning speed. You could see it. Not a thought in his mind. Just like a little machine, chuu, chuu, one after the other. It was remarkable. Because what he had done was train himself to shift his basis of operation out of thought mode, out of attention mode, to pure awareness mode. He had gone beyond thought, the first *gate* in the Heart Sutra.

The great Dzogchen scholar, Mipham, said, "The function of thought is to delineate." When you have a concept, if it's this, it's not that. And as soon as you have a concept about anything you're operating out of a partialized stance. And the partialization of thought can never apprehend ultimate reality, the unbounded wholeness of awakened awareness. You can't think your way into awakening. But you can realize awakening when thought has cleared away long enough to get a window of opportunity to see what's right here.

Secondly, directed attention: if you're attending to this, you're not attending to that. So, no instant of directed attention can ever apprehend the unbounded wholeness of an awakened mind.

And the highest information processing operation is called particularizing. We don't even have a word for it in the West because in the West, Western psychology starts with stimulus perception. I see something, I react to it. Buddhist psychology is pre-stimulus, the tendency of the mind towards something. The outcome is a stimulus perception. And that's called, in Tibetan, *yila jepa,* which literally means the tendency of the mind towards something, the outcome of which is something particular. A particular stimulus. It comes close to what in Western psychology we call an action potential. I like the word particularizing for that. In every moment the mind's doing this. [Dan moves his hands first in one direction than another and another.]

If I take a panoramic view of this room and try to take in everything all at once—go ahead and do that—everything all at once. Nothing in particular. "Like a child viewing a temple for the first time," seeing nothing in particular and going, "Ah!" at everything. Try and do that. And you see you can't do it. Because as soon as you try and hold a panoramic perspective, you watch your mind picking out things. And every one of those instances of picking out something obscures the unbounded wholeness. So, the entire video game of your information processing system is set up to obscure awakening—unless you get special instructions that help you to see beyond it. Those are the pith instructions. And if you see beyond it, even if for a short time, you shift out of that particularizing, that partialized mode, to being the unbounded wholeness of the radiance of awakened awareness.

So, emptiness, we say, is the path because it clears away the clouds enough to get a taste of awakening. But once you have a taste of awakening it's usually not very stable. It clouds over because of all the habits of the mind. A Dzogchen Mahāmudrā lama who is in Seattle for many years who's got a good sense of Western humor says, "Many people when they awaken, they put the snooze alarm on many times." Like that. It keeps clouding over. But if you get a taste of awakening it changes everything because that longing for your true nature is now solved. You've got that one done. You know your home base. And that longing doesn't come up again, ever. So, in that sense getting a taste of awakening, however unstable it may be, we say is the end of the path. From another perspective it's the beginning of the path.

So, that's the first map. It takes you from the beginning of these practices up to a taste of awakening, however unstable. Then there's a whole other set of practices that helps you to stabilize awakening so you have it all the time on the pillow and off the pillow. You keep setting up that view in the right way so that you can have that taste of awakening more frequently, on the pillow for longer duration and more and more immediately. And the *tak*, the sign of progress that you're looking for, is that just the intention to look shifts your basis out of ordinary mind, shifts your basis of operation out of ordinary mind to awakened mind.

So now, at least on the pillow when you set up your view, you are stably staying in awakening more times than not. That's a good time to take it off the pillow. So, when you shift to awakening in a stable way on the pillow, you intentionally get up and mix it into daily activities. Most people at that point can get up and try and mix awakening into being out in nature without losing the awakening. If you lose it, go back on the pillow, set up your view again, re-shift your basis again, and then get off and try it again.

But most people would have a hard time stabilizing it in other situations. I did this for a whole month with my teacher. I didn't meditate on the pillow at all, hardly. He's very busy because he's the Dalai Lama's meditation teacher, so he's got a big audience. And my entire practice for the month consisted of sitting outside of his room and there'd be a stream of people, and the task was I had to converse with them while I maintained awakening. Then I had to go translate and work on my computer and think while I maintained awakening until I could get to the point of maintaining awakening—the ideal is at all times in all situations. It doesn't go away anymore. And after a while you develop what's called *dengwa*, confidence. Even if it clouds over, it's like a thin veil—it seems perfectly ridiculous to you—you can never lose what's always right here. That changes everything, when you're confident you can never really lose it again. And that finishes the second map.

The third map starts with transforming karmic memory traces. You hold the view of what we call the inseparable pair—the vast expanse of empty awareness space and simultaneous to that, whatever arises as nothing but the liveliness of an awakened mind expressing itself to itself. So, you hold both those views simultaneously—the vast expanse and the liveliness—and you don't engage anything that comes up. But non-engagement isn't a strategy because that's engagement; it's part of the view. And if you're that advanced, everything that comes up in that field is left completely in its own way without engaging it. Engagement means we move towards it to process it further or we move towards it to stop processing it and dismiss it so we can go on to something else. Both of those types of mental engagement are what form karmic memory traces.

So, if you set up a practice where you do not engage anything in every moment that arises within the vast expanse, it comes up in its own way; and as soon as it comes up, since it's not being engaged, it doesn't form a new karmic impression, so it immediately disappears leaving no trace. We say, like writing on water. Or like snowflakes merely melting in a vast ocean and disappearing. And if you set that up as your practice, everything that comes up, just like a leaky sieve, it just runs right through your mind automatically and disappears. And because you're not forming any new karmic impressions, it forces the mind to dip into its reservoir of many previous karmic impressions that would otherwise ripen, and rapidly release them at an accelerated rate. And that's called *dharmadhātu* exhaustion. Within that vast expanse you're exhausting the storehouse of all karmic memory traces.

The average time if you do that practice 24/7 is about six years. If you supplement it with energy-drop practices you can get it down to about two years. And then you achieve what in Buddhism is called *sangye*. In Indian Mahāyāna Buddhism, the ultimate outcome is called buddha, realized one. *Budh* means realize. But when the teachings came to Tibet, that's not how they translated the term. Tibetan word for buddha is *sangye*. It's a compound term. *Sangwa* means complete purification of all negative states. And *gyewa* means the flourishing of all positive states. So, the outcome of *dharmadhātu* exhaustion is you don't have any negative states of mind left.

We say the mind is stainless—I like to translate *drime* as clean, the field of experience gets cleaner and cleaner. Imagine the implications of that for mental health. No negative states whatsoever. And what comes out when they're no longer obscured are eighty positive qualities of mind that flourish, come out all at once. So, you achieve the epitome of mental health which is all positive qualities of mind and no negative states left for the rest of your lifetime. Except if the Patriots lose. [Quiet laughter] If the Patriots lose that's still a negative state. Short of that, it's relative, relatively speaking. That's my best practice, right?

Then, at that level of practice, all karmic memory traces are eradicated. At that level of practice, ordinary perception changes and is transformed. Everything changes into light rays and the sound of awakened awareness expressing itself to itself. So, you live in a world of light and energy. The body isn't solid anymore. It's what we call clear light body. It's like an empty glass bottle filled with light, and there's only two other things to open up.

Next step, you have to come to see that the mind is limitless. And one of the residual things that the mind does is it constructs boundaries. So, that's the practice you're referring to. You had to get this whole context because what you're asking for is something fairly advanced. Okay?

So having mastered that, the next step is limitlessness. You see, out here there's a bubble of external reality, seeming external reality. And each of you imposes an edge, a boundary to that bubble. Where's the edge of that? Sometimes it's in this room. Sometimes it's the edges of Newton. Maybe it's the surroundings of Boston. Maybe it's the Earth. But wherever you put that edge or boundary or series of boundaries, that's the end of your universe. It's like in the old days when people thought the world was flat and you'd fall off the edge. We construct like that. Still do.

We think there's an end to the seemingly existing world. But what if all those edges and boundaries and the delineation of that space is just another residual construction of mind the same way that thought is and self is and everything else we talked about. It's one of the last things to go, the demarcation and delineation of space. So, the practice is rather simple. Wherever you see the boundaries, open right into those as empty space, as if you're pouring space into space. And those boundaries dissolve. If you think there's a front to that space, open into the front of that space. If you think there's a back to the space, open to the back of the space.

If you think that space has directions, north, south, east, west, cardinal directions or intermediate directions, wherever you think there's a direction, open into it as basic space. If you think there's a larger space beyond that and that space has an edge, go right into the edge and open right into that as basic space and pour the space into the space beyond. And if you keep doing that, what do you think is going to happen? It's going to dissolve all the constructions that articulate that space, and the space gets more and more huge and limitless.

There's no space "out there." It's the space of awareness mind. And that awareness mind becomes absolutely huge and limitless. Now, if you directly experience that in the meditation, which is what you're asking, that's the prerequisite state for basis enlightenment. You build upon that limitlessness with certain special instructions that will open up enlightenment, which is the full experience of *dharmakāya*, *sambhogakāya*, and *nirmāṇakāya*. And I'm not going to go into that at this point, because then you'll think your way through it. But you're asking for the penultimate of practice.

Student 1

I'm at the level of practice where I'm trying to stabilize. That's where I'm at in my awakening, what I have is just getting more frequent ...

Dan

So don't look ahead, stay with what you're doing.

Student 1

Oh, I would, because we follow that instruction sometimes when we do awakened awareness …

Dan

Sometimes I add that instruction, a limited version of that instruction, for people who are spatializing because when they take the view of the Lion's Gaze to open up awakening it won't work because they've imposed too much structure on that space.

Student 1

Okay. So, I shouldn't worry about it too much.

Dan

There's a simple instruction that Nagarjuna uses for that: if you think the space is vast, take a view that it's localized; when your experience is localized, take a view that it's vast; when you experience it as vast, take the view that it's localized, and keep doing that until it's neither vast nor localized and those distinctions collapse. They're very powerful and simple instructions. And if you do that it will open it up because sometimes when people set up the view of Lion's Gaze, which is the unbounded wholeness, it's not really the unbounded wholeness; it's this narrow little thing that they're doing with a panoramic view.

And that residual habit of spatialization will interfere with awakening. That's why it's done. So, usually we give people two or three times the classic crossing over instructions or slightly different instructions. And if they don't get it, then I'll add the spatialization instructions in one form or another. At that level of practice, it's useful because some people will get it. But this other instruction you're asking for is a much more detailed systematic version of that as a main meditation. So, that's not the level you do it at. That's why I had to set the context.

Student 1

So, basically, I shouldn't worry about that much, right? At this point in time worrying about it …

Dan

No, but it's okay to intellectually understand what we're talking about.

Student 1

Okay, no, it was a great answer.

Dan

It's okay to set the context for it, but just don't try and do it tonight. [Dan smiles]

Student 1

Yeah, I got it. Well anyway, it sets my mind at ease about where it is …

Dan

If you think your way to it, you harden the mind and it makes it harder to awaken.

Student 1

I won't.

Dan

That's why the pith instructions are not given out, to protect you from misusing them. They won't work if you try and think your way through them. You've got to clear up all thought before you use the classic crossing over instructions.

Student 1

It also just ... but the other thing I took away from it was ... just as a lot of trust that it'll work just the way other things have opened things …

Dan

Yeah, there's a path here. There's a path here.

Student 1

You kind of do each thing and I get some results and I'm like, "Oh well that really does work. I better just keep doing it."

Dan

You've got to just follow the instructions. That's all.

Student 1

Yeah. Okay.

Dan

It works. They've been around for a long time because they work.

Student 1

They do.

Dan

It was a good question.

Student 1

Thanks.

Dan

Anything else? [Silence] Noble silence. Everybody's content with their practices. Think of that. Oh. Or they're terrified to ask a question. Okay. It's okay. You're missing new opportunities. You get precious opportunities in life.

Student 2

Cool. This is also not just, well, I've been, to supplement my regular practice I've been going to the sensory deprivation flotation tanks in Somerville and sitting for like ninety minutes and I feel like it's really having a really very positive impact on my practice, and I was wondering is there something special about that environment or is it just that I'm practicing for ninety minutes in a row frequently or what is your experience with those modalities and your recommendations around that?

Dan

That's a very interesting question. In 1971—that's a long time ago—I worked at Maryland Psychiatric Research Center. In the summer that I went there to work, the dolphin guy, John Lilly, had just left and he left behind his lab which he closed which had the first sensory flotation tank, and all this commercial stuff came from that. So, we had two summers where we got to play in the tank a lot. And it was nice because the way the flotation system works is you can move around anywhere. And no matter how you moved around your head was always out of water. And it's completely dark and, and it was somewhat warm water, and it was comfortable and womb-like. And if you stayed in there for, on the average, of five to six hours, that was the time that you dismantled your perceptual system. You have to wait. It takes about five or six hours, and you dismantle your whole perceptual apparatus. The whole thing fragments and everything turns to light. Now that's my experience as a Westerner. And we weren't just trying to float for an hour to relax. We were trying to see what the mind was like when you experienced the extremes of sensory deprivation which meant dismantling your perceptual system after five or six hours.

A similar thing happens in Dzogchen in what's called dark retreats. The average retreat is forty-nine days in complete darkness. You seal up the meditation place. There's no light whatsoever. You have to grope your way around. There's an outer door that they can put food in and then close it so that when they open the outer door the light doesn't get into the inner door. They can put food in once a day for you and then you can reach the inner door when the outer door is closed and it won't let any light in, because if you let light in it ruins it.

So, imagine seven weeks of complete sensory isolation. It's a little bit longer than six weeks. And it's not like you just sit there in the dark hallucinating for seven weeks. I translated one of the dark retreat manuals. It's very detailed. And basically, what you do is Inner Fire practice and central channel practice. You go through the different levels of bypassing visions where you dismantle perception in a much more systematic way than the Western research. And having dismantled ordinary perception completely you begin to see in your direct experience that all that seeming "out there" stuff is internally generated. So, after a while you can see things just like this world except there's no light, and you realize that this whole thing is internally generated. It doesn't come from out there because you're seeing the same world perfectly clearly in the dark.

So, once you get that started and it opens up the levels of visions, you enhance the practice in that time frame by using central channel practice. So, the first five weeks you go through each of the five buddha families. You have a trip to each of the five buddha fields. You know, the Lotus family, the Vajra family, etcetera. You go through all the five buddha fields, enhanced by Inner Fire practice. So, it's all of what we call *sambhogakāya* practice. And in the sixth, you do all the five buddha fields simultaneously with different copies of yourself, and then the seventh you dissolve everything into *dharmadhātu* with black energy drops. So, everything turns to formless realms. And then you end up with just the experience of clear light. Everything is clear light in the midst of that darkness. It all becomes the clear light with the brilliant radiance of awakened awareness, all the time; in its sheer blazing splendor, as we call it. So, it's quite a ride.

So, they use the sensory deprivation to enhance the practice, but of course the magnitude of sensory deprivation in that environment is far beyond what we were doing in the West with five to six hours, and certainly far beyond the one or two hours that you're in the range with these commercial things. So, it's not really sensory deprivation. It's more like floaty-relaxy stuff—this is big league.

You have to watch if you go into that short range, five or six hours, or ten hours or something like that, because there's a lot of fragmentation of your perceptual systems. It can be very unsettling. And you tend to see the fragmentation more than the pure visions at that point. So, the trouble with the Western stuff is it doesn't go long enough to start to see the purity of the visions. Generally, you're not given a lot of guidance.

[For dark retreat] you memorize the text for each week ahead of time because you're not going to be able to read it in the dark. There's no flashlight there. But usually what happens in a good retreat is the lama will come by once a week, outside your dark retreat place, and he will give you the detailed instructions about how you use the central channel practice and how the visions are going to come up. That way he can give you the whole thing, and you've got to memorize it; and obviously you're in the dark so you can't take notes. And then you do it for a week.

And the reason for the forty-nine days is that it matches the forty-nine days of the *bardo* practices because you go through the same states. The visions are similar to after death states. You get all the peaceful deities and all the wrathful deities and all the realms, buddha realms and things like that, so it's the same trip. But it's not something that the Western research on sensory deprivation really has unpacked because we never did it for that long. We were mostly getting the fragmented dismantling effects of ordinary perception.

The commercial stuff doesn't do it long enough to get into any of those effects usually. And that's done intentionally for liability purposes. I mean some people don't handle their mind fragmenting very well. So, in the total dark it can be pretty scary for some people because you've got to deal with your own mind, all of it. And either you deal with it or you don't. You learn a lot about yourself in the process.

Student 1

Okay, so is that something that, if a commercial place would let you be in there for six more hours, and you got your teacher to give you good instructions, is that something you think would be beneficial?

Dan

You're not going to do anything with dark retreat in six hours.

Student 1

You have to do it a lot longer.

Dan

The minimum is about two or three weeks.

Student 1

That long? Okay.

Dan

The ideal is seven weeks.

Student 1

Yeah, that's a good point. Yeah.

Dan

At the monastery they have a special place for dark retreatants, and it's a little hard to do because they tend to like to do it when the sun is lowest, which means they tend to do the dark retreats in January and February. There's no heat in the dark retreat places. So, you have to generate your own Inner Fire.

There's no blankies. Either you can generate enough heat from your Inner Fire practice or you're not comfortable enough to survive it.

Student 1

So, basically, if I'm getting benefit out of this just because I'm meditating for ninety minutes mostly?

Dan

Yeah, but you have to watch, because you're floating in water, you have to watch that your meditation, the concentration doesn't deteriorate. There are two things that you have to watch for. It's hard to explain it.

One is subtle dullness. You're staying on the object, but the object gets more and more vague. And there's this background noise of all the little subtle stuff that comes with the sensory deprivation, dismantling of imagery and stuff like that. So, there's a little chatter in the background, but basically the object, your concentration object remains vague. You have to watch for that, because you're at a disadvantage in that environment.

The second thing is hard to explain. The word is *dangwa*. The closest I can come to it in English is "cut adrift." One of the problems that comes up in concentration is, if you're deeply concentrated and very still and quiet, then all of a sudden you realize that you're just drifting, and you've completely lost the meditation object.

It's like, oh, I remember going fishing once out in Gloucester, and the anchor didn't hold. We're just sitting there, cod fishing, and all of a sudden, we're right next to the shore. The tide's pulled us in; and how did we get from here to there? Because, we had the illusion that we were stationary and staying on where we were, but we had moved quite a bit because the boat had caught a drift, and that's what happens in meditation sometimes.

You think you're very still, but you're just off, drifting. You've got to watch for that, *dolwa*. Particularly in sensory deprivation when you're floating around. It's easy to get caught adrift. So, you have to watch that you're not being dishonest with yourself and thinking that you're deeply concentrating, because you're relaxed, but really, you're dull and you're adrift.

Student 1

I know exactly what you're talking about. They actually have two different kinds of tanks in some of them. They have one that's just like a coffin, that's totally dark, and they've got these new tanks that go way up to the ceiling. You can also turn on some lights like stars at the top, so it's not total sensory deprivation, but sometimes I'll turn on the stars, because exactly what you're saying, it's easier to not do what you just said. Yeah, so you can get luminosity better in that way, keeps you on track, but anyways.

Dan

But we're not looking for luminosity, we're looking for staying on the object. I think you're putting yourself in an environment where it's very difficult to concentrate. It's not the ideal setting for concentration. It's like saying the same thing that, well, try and concentrate while you're lying down. Well, how's that going to work for you? It doesn't work very well, does it? And here, you're lying down, you're in warm water, and you're floating around. It's all those things that are going to make you dull and have your mind doing wandering. So, it's not the best for concentration—unless you're a great yogi, you're developing the illusion of concentration.

So, a counter argument would be if you're training dull, drifting meditation, maybe it's better to not meditate when you're in a sensory environment such as the deprivation environment. Maybe it's better to just enjoy the relaxation effect for what it is. Then keep the meditation, when your body posture is better, outside of that, and you can do better concentration. That's a legitimate point of view. I'm not convinced that the tank is going to enhance your practice. It's going to enhance your delusion of the practice, but I don't think it's going to work unless you're a great yogi and can meditate any place, in any environment.

Student 1

I feel like my practice has gotten better from doing it, but, anyways, but I'm ...

Dan

I know, but that's exactly what I'm concerned about.

Student 1

Right.

Dan

Because you're convinced that it's okay. So, I can't tell you anything about it.

Student 1

I heard everything you said, I'm just …

Dan

Look for the drifting.

Student 1

Okay.

Dan

See for yourself. Remember, dullness is hard to recognize. Drifting is easy to recognize.

Student 1

I'll pay attention.

Dan

Look for it. All the deck is stacked against you in that environment to concentrate.

Yes?

Student 2

I feel like, I mean, some I might have shared before, that I've gone through a lot of deaths, and, just, my husband, my best friend just passed, and I lost my job. So, when we talked last time, when we did the ...

Dan

Grief protocol.

Student 2

Yeah, which was incredible. I feel like life, I don't know quite how to say this, but I feel like I'm in a situation where, I certainly get impermanence now, but none of the constructs that I had, like everything has changed, gone, but I'm happy. I mean, I've been through very, I would say, heavy grieving, but I also had the benefit of being with my friend and my husband through their dying process. But I feel like life has put me in a situation where, because I'm just, I've always been a dabbler of meditation. So, I feel humbled to the point that my, I don't really have a stable practice.

Dan

Nothing like death to sort of impress upon you the nature, the reasons for doing spiritual practice.

Student 2

Exactly, but I'm amazed, also. So, I don't feel that the practice is at the point to support me in terms of the experience in front of me, of life, but it's a commitment.

Dan

That's good.

Student 2

Yeah, but it's more that it's, I do find it harder to really do the practice, because I do still feel that there's this, the grieving is there, but it's different. I don't know, it's almost a gratefulness. I feel like it pushed me through to this other experience of life. There's no denying it anymore, this is what I'm trying to say. I'm just wondering if you …

Dan

Well, we try hard to do that, don't we?

Student 2

So, I don't know, is there a particular practice that would help to stabilize that part of it?

Dan

Impermanence. Meditate on the impermanence of everything. You imagine the stages of your own aging process. Of course, when we're at this age, it's not hard to do. Then, you imagine your own dying process. That'll do it.

So, those are basic practices to impress upon you the necessity for changing your priorities and developing a spiritual practice, because amongst other things, spiritual practice prepares you for the process of dying. So, that's what you do. It goes very quickly.

I just had lunch today with two old friends that I haven't seen for years. We're from that same generation when we were doing the sensory deprivation research, some forty-five years ago. I mean, he's the same age as me, almost unrecognizable, not healthy—in the last three years he recovered from cancer, lost lots of weight, and recently fell down the stairs.

And then, he told us of our other old friend who he just visited, who formerly had a 170 IQ, and now he's completely demented. These are people my age. So, that impressed upon me the shortness and preciousness of what we've got here. It was a stark—not escaping—look at the nature of what we're looking into here, which is that we age and die.

Somebody once said, "You know you're getting old when you read the obituaries and see all your friends in it." It's true. We have this remarkable ability for denial of that. We think that we're going to go on forever.

Now, if you understand that with impermanence, you don't waste a single moment, because every moment counts. So, think about how much time we waste. Then, at some point, there isn't much left to waste anymore. I'm sorry for your losses, but it seems like you've seen some benefit in all that's happened, so that you wake up to what's necessary here. It's a good thing.

November 30, 2016

Themes: Trump's Election; Compassion; Overcome Greed and Selfishness

Dan

Welcome everyone. You have a question?

Student 1

My friend and I were having dinner together saying he's got to talk about Trump. This is the first time that we gather since then. And so, there's not a specific question, but please guide us.

Dan

[Dan laughs] Good luck.

Student 1

To Australia, I think you said last time

Dan

I was in Israel at the time. And I stayed up all night to watch the election results with considerable horror, and it didn't look good from the get-go. Somebody sent me a, I have it on my computer, which I'll make sure I show you during the break. It's Trump dressed up in a monk's robe saying, "I'm the most spiritual person in the world. I know everything about spirituality and I'm the most spiritual person in the world." It's basically his approach to everything. I don't know what to say. I think it's a time of great discouragement. I don't think it's just an American phenomenon; I think it's a phenomenon around the world. What's happening is basically selfishness. We have a world now… we've created a world in the last twenty years where 1.5 percent of the population owns 95 percent of the wealth. If you divide that down further, sixty-three powerful families own 98 percent of all the wealth in the world. So, the inequality is so profound that it's way out of proportion.

Student 2

So much grief.

Dan

Yeah. But the grief comes from greed. There's a small group of people who own everything and everybody else is envious of that. So, they developed this kind of morbid fascination with people who have power and money because they all want it. That's not a good working combination, especially in the face of what the unfortunately consistent evidence is of a profound disrespect for so many different types of individuals—from Hispanics, Blacks, to all minorities, all Muslims, anybody who was not part of the aristocracy. We've now created that. In Israel, the next morning in the Tel Aviv Times there was a cartoon. There's a picture of the United States, and the Northeast, Minnesota and the West were painted blue, and it was called America. And the rest was painted red and it was called "Dumbfuckistan," which sort of spells it out you know, so I don't know what to say.

It's stunning, and it means we all have to work harder to make a better world against the considerable adversity of these times. So, this is wherever your spiritual practices come in, and this tests your strength. Now is the time to call on whatever you learned, because nothing is going to go well. Just look at the decisions in the last couple of weeks. The mouthing off and the disrespect of the bullies; it looks like it's going to be consistent. The fantasy that somehow he would become more presidential isn't going to happen. That's not his nature. He's still going to be disrespectful to many people, and mouth off impulsively. The environment's basically fucked. Look at the decision so far, the one who was chosen for his cabinet for the environments: the person who's most opposed to the idea of global warming. That's not going to go in a good direction. His attorney general is basically racist, so that's going to intensify racial strife. And what you saw today and yesterday was this whole thing about people who burn the flag get jailed for a year.

Yeah. So, what you're seeing here is essentially this kind of rigid nationalism that occurs in countries when the culture is failing. And we're failing economically. We've sold this country to corporations. That's the truth of the matter no matter what you want to call it. This is the long-term results of the Reagan deregulation. I have a small business as a private practitioner. I pay 48 percent in taxes as a small business. Apple, Google, Microsoft, and Facebook paid no taxes in any country, except Apple now was sued by Ireland and they all pay 3 percent.

Those four companies alone, if you calculate the money that they owed for twenty years of taxes just in the US, that's our entire national debt. So why should I have to pay that? Why should anybody as a hardworking citizen have to pay that? But if you challenge them, they just go to another country. The corporations have taken over the world and they can do whatever they want, do whatever they want to the environment, and then everything is outsourced. So, we've sold this country in the last twenty years to corporations. I understand that's where this profound dissatisfaction comes in that won him the election.

People are stupid enough to think that he's going to be their friend. He's not a friend of the blue-collar white population that's out of work. It's not going to happen. It's total marketing hype. So, we're in big trouble. And I don't know what the way out of that is. I've always thought that the way out of it is you have to go back to regulating the runaway train of Wall Street. It's out of control and you have to rope in all of these corporations and make them pay their fair share of the tax burden in the US. That's the only way you're going to build back the middle class again. And we're going farther away from that.

So, we're in for the dark times. How bad that will get, I don't know. Most of my European friends where I teach a lot, who are much more politically concerned than we are, see this as the next Mussolini. And it could go in that direction. We don't know. When the world gets worse, it means you have to work all the harder to do what's right. So, this is the time that all your spiritual practice matters. There's no place for discouragement. There's only place for hope and working harder for whatever that means to you in your own practice.

Student 1

So, a specific question about that, a couple of specific questions about that?

Dan

Sure.

Student 1

A very practical question—I want to stay informed and so I read some print media and yet I also need to have time for meditation every day. I need to have time for actual physical exercise almost every day and just basics of self-care. And lately the balance at that has been really difficult.

Dan

It's difficult.

Student 1

If I read the paper in the morning, a kind of post for part of the day, if I read the paper before bed, I've got insomnia for one or two hours at night. And there's this thing that I'm experiencing in meditation. It's almost like there's a layer of anxiety that I need to take this …

Dan

Yeah, it's fear.

Student 1

In some ways I'm finding myself ...

Dan

It's fear.

Student 1

Yes.

Dan

And you're responsible for your own state of mind, so that means working with the fear, holding that larger view, working with your own states of mind. You have plenty of opportunity to practice now.

Student 1

I'm not quite there.

Dan

There are some people who don't know that story, but Bob Thurman, who is very funny, a translator for the Dalai Lama for ten years, he wrote a book on why the Dalai Lama is necessary politically in terms of compassion for the world. And one time, Debbie Solomon, when she was in the New York Times Book Review Department, she interviewed Bob and she asked him, "What do you do for compassion meditation?" He said, "I imagine I'm a young mother and I'm suckling the baby Dick Cheney at my breast." He said, "That's ultimate compassion." And he meant that as a joke, but it wasn't really a joke. We have to be compassionate towards Trump, as hard as that is. You have something you want to add to that?

Student 2

I just want to talk a little bit about the theme of what I thought was, the theme that went on for me throughout this whole thing and the word that kept coming up for me was contempt.

Dan

Contempt, yeah.

Student 2

On so many levels in so many areas, and what I had to do was to look inside myself, and see my own contempt and try to understand what that meant, where that was coming from, and where I had contempt, you know, that was mirrored by everything that was going on, and what I found was that it was, I think the basis of that for me was fear. And at times out of that arises compassion for others for whom there is fear as well. I certainly can't maintain that view, but that's I think what was going on for me for a number of weeks.

Dan

Well, you have plenty of reasons to practice compassion at the moment, for all the people who feel forgotten and unnoticed, the economy has passed them by, for Trump himself, for his profound limitations, in terms of how he treats people. But the time will exercise your true practice. Difficult times. As the Daoist once said, "Crisis is opportunity." This is the best time for your practice.

Student 3

This is just really a continuation of what she was saying, that when we were with Rinpoche last, he was asked about all the anger and he just said, "It's in your mind. Look for it there." And went on to talk about how in *rigpa* there's no loneliness and that loneliness …

Dan

And there's no despair.

Student 3

And that loneliness is the fundamental ignorance. Right? So, all the other poisons flow from that. And it seems to me that's the biggest challenge is to stay, to let go of what we need to let go of so that we aren't coming from that place.

Dan

I'll remind you of a famous line from the Gandhi movie, "The only real enemies are those within our own hearts." That's the only thing you have control over here. What's that?

Student 4

Another quote: "I've met the enemy and they is us."

Dan

Yeah, same thing. So, whatever this stirs up for you, that's your practice. It means dealing with the fear, the despair, the hopelessness. And if you've worked all that through in yourself, then in a very difficult time you become an exemplar for what needs to happen. You're showing everybody else the path. So that's important. it's not a time for fear, despair—there's no place for it. There's too much work to do.

The days following the election, I did three things. Some of you know I've worked on the Bobby Kennedy assassination for eight years. We now have a three-way contract with Sundance, Showtime, and Netflix for a four-hour series, to expose the government cover up. We have a big budget. It will be shown June 2018. That's one of my ways of responding to this kind of stuff. And we'll cover, we'll expose everything.[1] Most of the filming is already done.

---

1 Not finding this anywhere, we reached out to the producers at Sundance about this, but have received no reply. If you get one, kindly let us know.

Then I negotiated with a group of doctors who work with Physicians for Human Rights. We did two things. One was we're going to work with refugees in Israel in the West Bank. Most of the doctors who work or volunteer there are traumatized by all the awful stories of the violence all the time, so we're going to bring in a UN team of specialists in PTSD to prevent secondary PTSD in the doctors. We were working on getting together all the families who have lost family members to violence, both the Palestinians and the Israelis, in the same room to grieve together. That's what I'm doing in response to this situation.

Do whatever you can within your expertise to make the world a better place. You don't stop your vision of that. There's no time for all these negative states. There's no time for despair. There's no time for fear. There's too much work to do. Work through your own fear, work through your own despair, do the best you can to help out in whatever ways that you have your expertise in. That's my message to you.

Student 5

That partly answers what I was struggling with …

Dan

How so?

Student 5

That it has felt that the meditation has been the only real place that I can really become calm and get, and …

Dan

But it's not about being calm. It's about putting yourself in the thick of *samsāra*. All these teachings are coming to the West at this time for a reason.

Student 5

Yup.

Dan

This is the time that you learn to use the practice off the pillow in the midst of all this mess.

Student 5

Yeah. And what I've been struggling with is how to get to the clarity of the determination of what to do in this world.

Dan

Work through your negative states and the vision will come internally. It'll arise spontaneously from awakened *dharmakāya* space. You don't have to figure it out; it's not a concept. It will come naturally.

Student 5

Yeah, I guess so. It has felt that it has to do with …

Dan

All comes from awakened *dharmakāya* space.

Student 5

Yeah.

Dan

You're not going to do this one conceptually. What's necessary to do will occur to you. If you have the level of realization, then you'll just do it.

Student 5

Well, I think I've begun to get it. It's beginning to form and maybe that's where I can leave it.

Dan

Yeah, just trust. Do your practice and trust will become clear.

Student 6

I'm a very practical person. At first, I cried. My daughter cried after the election, and I thought about how I was going to get through my days, and one of things I thought, which I knew wasn't going to work, is if I was like an alien looking down at this experiment saying, "Let's see how this is going to work." But I can't do that. So, all I could come up with was compassion. So, I spent more time, because I'm a physician, just spending more time being compassionate, and it helped me. And I think it helped other people. And it was a simple approach. I didn't have to overthink it.

Dan

That's good. You act in a profession where that becomes a calling. There is some research on primary care docs showing that those who view their work as a calling more than something that they necessarily have to do, are much more resilient, they have greater well-being, they're much more satisfied with their job, and they don't feel the stress of it. So, it's all about the view you take of what you're doing. The view matters.

Student 7

Let's see. I wanted to make a brief comment on this thread, and then I wanted to ask a question that had nothing to do with what we're talking about. So, I would just say that I'm actually kind of optimistic because as Dan was saying, it's just these are going to be hard times whether Clinton or Trump was going to be president.

I think this is an opportunity for us to grow. I think the universe is saying you've got to take over this world. You can't let these psychopaths, corporations and leaders keep leading and we've got to step up. And I'm looking at it as an opportunity to help people grow. You know sometimes you've got to get kicked, society gets kicked, to take it up to a new gear.

So, I'm reframing it like that for me and I'm just seeing it as an opportunity, for what it's worth. Also, I would … One observation about the media. I think the left and right media it's kind of a paradigm to keep people in fear, keep people fighting with each other instead of uniting. So, you might want to look at it from that perspective and try and find the commonalities with people with our differences.

On a completely unrelated note, I had a question. Have you ever read the book by Julian Jaynes, *The Origins of Consciousness in the Breakdown of the Bicameral Mind*?

Dan

Yeah, a long time ago. This was in what, in the 1980s?

Student 7

I found that was a fascinating book and I'll just say what it's about succinctly for the people who haven't read it and ask a question about it. It's this guy who did this really integrative research and he was trying to figure out when our modern consciousness came online. As we are, we're reflective beings as opposed to like amazon warriors or worshiping gods.

And he, I'm not going to go through all the analysis because it's pretty complicated. But it is ultimately his theory is that way back when they were worshiping idols that man actually had two parts of their brain and one was, he called them bicameral or one part of the brain was telling the other part of the brain what to do. And then there was some society changes that changed that.

So, I guess with that in mind, I guess Dan, I have two questions. One, I was just wondering if you had any take on that history and how that related to the Bon or if that was, if you thought it was true or part of the population.

Then I know we're also talking a lot about direct, clearing our minds and having direct experiences, and I feel like the world is going on an evolutionary path, and I see, I don't know, I see these direct downloads as a tool for us to help us be better selves.

But also, I don't think if the bicameral thing is true, I don't think the universe wants us to go back wayward. Our universe is always telling us what to do. So, I was just … I don't know what you thought about that. Is that looking at direct knowing as a tool? I know cognition is not something we're supposed to do all the time but it's another tool. So, what are your thoughts on those?

Dan

Well, that book came out at a time that right and left-brain function was popular, but most of the neurobiology in that book is completely wrong from the modern perspective, because I read most of the neurobiology stuff. It's not correct.

But it represents a larger theory of theories that are part of the evolution of consciousness. Some people, proponents of those theories think that we are, if you look at the larger picture, evolving our minds here. And you can make a compelling argument that we are evolving our minds in certain ways, certainly the social anthropologists talk a lot about how humans are different from primates and there's been a lot of studies on that.

Primates can only collaborate in very limited ways, but humans have skills built into the species. So, primates will collaborate on getting food together and won't share it very much but they'll at least collaborate on how to get it. Whereas humans are the only species that will actually collaborate on work projects that have nothing to do with food intake. So that's a huge evolutionary step.

But critics of those theories, the de-evolutionists will say for every step forward we tend to make a step or two back. If you look at it from an economic point of view, we're not evolving. We're evolving into an oligarchy where smaller numbers of people have everything and nobody else has anything, and that's not going to work.

So, from a *dharma* perspective, the main issue there is that as a species we have to work with our own minds and overcome greed and selfishness. It is destroying the planet. We have to work through our own fears of difference because the intolerance of difference is destroying the planet.

You know, if we're going to destroy this planet it will come in three forms. It will come in the form of destroying the environment substantially; the greed of accumulating more and more resources for a smaller number of individuals at the expense of everybody else; and fundamentalism in any form of religion. Those are the three forces that will militate against moving forward with our evolution.

Until we solve those issues, we keep moving one step forward and three steps back, and that concerns me. That's where spiritual practice is necessary, because if you learn anything from spiritual practice, it's the fundamental lesson that self-importance isn't terribly important. If you master that lesson, then you move beyond trying to accumulate more for yourself and you start thinking more in terms of other people.

That's one of the reasons why I spend a lot of time in Switzerland because a lot of our students are Swiss bankers. If we can give them a taste of awakening, then some of them actually start thinking about sharing resources and collaborative banking rather than money laundering for wealthy individuals, which fundamentally changes how they view the world. We do that one person at a time. It makes a difference. I don't think we can make a dent in Wall Street, but at least the European culture is more open to this.

So, it ultimately comes down to what in Buddhism is called self-grab. All this selfish grasping for more for ourselves at the expense of everybody else. On an evolutionary planet, as a species that doesn't work, but at least the practice gives us the tools to work with that.

So, that's where emptiness of self as a practice is important. That's why compassion as a practice is important. So, you learn to get out of yourself and think about a larger world. Most people who find a larger vision in life and get out of themselves, they're happier.

Bob Emmons did a study called *The Psychology Of Ultimate Concerns*,[2] and he found that people who had developed and articulated a larger vision of their life, what matters, their life is more meaningful, they have greater well-being, and they're more resilient in the face of stress, just by shaping that vision and operating out of that vision.

I teach a course in performance excellence and stress reduction for judges, and that's the single exercise that's most popular with the judges. If I can [help them] shape that for themselves, they can then hold on to that larger vision of why they're doing the work, they're more resilient on the stand, they're much less bored, they can manage the courtroom better, and they're happier and more resilient in the face of that stress, which is a lot, just by shaping that vision.

---

2 *The Psychology Of Ultimate Concerns: Motivation and Spirituality in Personality*, Robert A. Emmons, 2003, Guilford Press.

Then it becomes good work. It's not a thing you do, it becomes a calling. And they're always operating out of that vision. You can do that with any profession like what I was saying with primary care docs. The ones who develop that vision as a calling are much happier in what they do with the considerable stresses of what it takes to do that job in this climate in this country.

So, there are simple practice things that one can do that go very far. After the break we'll work on shaping that vision. If you get out of yourself and think about a larger world and compassion towards others, you're happier.

Howard Culter, a psychiatrist, asked the Dalai Lama if he would be open to being interviewed about compassion and they did a series of filmed interviews together and he wrote a book on it with the Dalai Lama.

The Dalai Lama said, "When I'm practicing compassion, I don't think about myself and I'm generally happier." That's not just a statement of his experience; it's true for anybody when they practice compassion. You get out of yourself.

Anybody ever read the Lapierre book or see the film *City of Joy*? Anybody know that? It's a wonderful thing to read. The book's better than the film but the film was the first film I think that Patrick Swayze did that made him famous as an actor.

The story is about a very talented young, very idealistic, driven, pediatric neurosurgeon who watches one too many children die on the operating table. He's a brain surgeon, and he loses it. He gets disillusioned and can't work anymore. If you lose faith in life, what do you do? You go to India. Lost.

And the first thing he does when he goes to Calcutta is he gets mugged and robbed, beaten up rather badly by some street thugs. So, he has to go to a local free medical clinic to get care, and he gets to be, over time, friends with the person who runs the clinic, and they of course want him to help out, but he is too self-absorbed and too angry to ever work in medicine again. That's the main text.

The subtext is that there is a local tension between the rickshaw-wallahs and their families who make nothing, who are on foot carrying people around on the streets all day in crowded Calcutta, and the slumlords who own the rickshaws and extract all the money from them. So, there's a pending strike amongst the rickshaw-wallahs and the slumlords who run them. He gets caught up in the drama of these hardworking, decent people, and helps them organize a strike against the slumlords, and it turns out the slumlord is one of the people who beat him up. He didn't know that at the time.

In the course of that, he slowly comes around to helping people in the clinic with absolutely no medical supplies and no resources, just working with what he knows. And he's working impossible hours and in impossible conditions, and you watch the evolution of him becoming happy. He likes what he is doing and he finds deep meaning in his life just by practicing compassionately under the most difficult of all life circumstances. It's a wonderful story about extending oneself compassionately and getting out of oneself. That's what needs to happen now for everybody. In whatever ways you bring your resources and talents.

I do a lot of work in the courts, that's how I do it. It's my skill. Right now, I'm doing a lot of work with the special-victims unit in Southern Florida for young kids who were severely abused, mostly in poor ethnic families, to give them rights in the courts. When I do that work, I'm happy and I'm fiercely protective. But it's meaningful to me. You have to find what's meaningful to you within your own talents. Get out of yourself, get out of your despair, get out of your fear and do something that matters now. That's my message to you.

Student 7

Dan, I just got that part of my question … I was wondering, you had mentioned when you talked about the evolution of consciousness and I feel like these pith instructions and meditation teachings are helping all of us and I'm very grateful for them.

And I have kind of been taking a step back and I'm feeling like, I don't know, I feel like the universe is actually optimistic, is giving us a lot of abundance and there's just all these things out there that …

Dan

Lots of opportunities.

Student 7

Yeah, opportunities that, I don't know, it's just like everything is out here but the universe isn't teaching, telling us exactly what to do. We have to figure it out. I feel like it's a big puzzle and that's part of our evolution.

Dan

That's where trust in your own resourcefulness and intelligence comes in. Each of you has to figure it out.

Student 7

Yeah. Thanks.

Dan

That's why trust is so important as a quality. It's the cornerstone of all positive qualities of mind. You trust your own intelligence and your own resourcefulness and you have within you what you need to figure this out and where to take it. If you do that without doubt and without fear, then you'll find your way.

Student 7

Wise words.

Dan

It's not a time for doubt and fear. There's no place for it. So much work to do.

Student 7

Agreed.

Dan

It's not an accident that this is the time in history that all these great spiritual teachings are being dumped on the West. That's a good thing, but we have to take them up and use them because if we don't, we're not going to survive. So, there's a larger game plan here. If your practice is sincere, you get what you need along the way. But not usually in ways you expect. That's the deal.

Yeah.

Student 1

I often say "what's outside is inside and what's inside is outside," and I don't completely know what that means, but it occurs to me that I sort of feel like my own personal experience of fear and terror and the direction of anger that I could go into, the direction of collapse that I could go into is, you're right, I must tolerate holding the space for that. So, this compassion that people are talking about, for me when that comes from my head as an intended practice that's, for me it's different from when it comes from me starting right here with my own fear. So, thank you for this. My own fear.

Dan

Don't start with your fear. Start with your strengths.

Student 1

No, but what I mean is in order to start with my fear I need to, number one, recognize that it's there. Number two, go into my practice because in my practice is, what I find there is I find the resistance to my fear, and then what I find is that if I'm approaching that from my practice, what happens is the fear melts and …

Dan

Because you're taking a larger vision.

Student 1

Yes, and from there there's this immediate connection, this direct connection to … You're right, what I need to know, right? It occurs to me that on some level I'm, you know, it's like once I get there I start picking up on my view of other people's pain and fear, not only the ones with pain and fear about the result of the election, but the ones with pain and fear that led to the result of this election.

Dan

Yeah, equally compassionate.

Student 1

And in that space, it just happens.

Dan

Let me ask you a question, because you and I come from the same neighborhood. Personally, everybody that I grew up with in that neighborhood is either dead or in jail. Very few people made it out of that culture. I did. You did. You always knew that you would get out of that, as I did. Where did that come from? Look into that. That's the same quality that's needed now. It's just a view that you're really not part of that. There's something more, that you always look for, and you had as a kid, as I did. We're not different. You understand exactly what I'm saying. It's the same quality that you need now. That's the way out of this mess. You know what I'm talking about. There's your answer. And that single-mindedness is uncompromising, but it's also a good place to have come out of, because you can't be anything else than compassionate for all those who are not going to make it easily, because those are your roots.

All those failing blue-collar families who have nothing left and are scared of the world, who voted for Trump, those are our roots. You know these people intimately and you have something to offer them because you chose a different path, and that path has much greater hope in it. Don't ever look back from that. Just keep looking forward. You understand. So, in that sense, you see you've got everything you need. It's good.

Student 1

Thank you.

[A few minutes of dialog is deleted here where students raise questions about how they might work together in a political way. No decisions were reached.]

Student 10

Seven or eight years ago, I first met you when you were teaching hypnosis, and at the break, I think the question was, "Can you hypnotize someone to do something against their will?" And you started to tell the story of Sirhan Sirhan, and the work you were doing then, on Robert Kennedy's assassination. And I said to myself, "God, not only does this guy know about hypnosis, but he's really politically active too and I think I want to continue to hang around with him." So, I really appreciate that this project has come to fruition for you.

Dan

Eight years later.

Student 10

Eight years later, because it's big, I think that's a huge accomplishment. I don't want to give you false praise or anything, but I think it's worth noting that that in itself, a lot of off-the-pillow practice. So, I just didn't want that to go by without an acknowledgement that you've been working on this for a very long time, and the first time I ever cried about somebody dying was Robert Kennedy. So, it means a lot to me that you did this, Dan, so thank you.

Dan

I'm not sure how or if it's going to go over well at the government, because we're exposing the cover up, but it's all going to come out. And for the record, I don't just work in remote places like Tibet and Nepal, but personally I pay more than twice a month of my mortgage for affordable rent for homeless people to get them off the street; done that for a number of years now. It's much harder to help homeless people in this country, for lots of reasons, than it is to help kids in Nepal. But we're committed to doing that too. So, I'm not just attached to the dharma cultures. Everybody has to do that in their own way.

January 4, 2017

Themes: Learning to Move Beyond Negative Beliefs in the Background; Metacognition

Dan

Welcome everyone. You have a question?

Student 1

One of the things that has been coming up for me again is the prevalence of stories in my life and my tendency to want to follow them. And depending upon what my view is, sometimes I follow them. But as I've been taking the view of looking into them more deeply and seeing, not the content, but that I have stories and that everyone has stories—my patients have their own stories, their families have their own stories, my siblings, each of them has her own story. And the more I look into it and I see them for what they are, the field seems to open up and there seems more of a connection with all people and their stories.

Dan

Oh, that's a really good question. Hmm. I have to answer that both East and West because the answers are a little different.

From a Western perspective, we're talking about cognition and cognitive therapy that, in the West, got popular in the late 1970s and early 1980s, largely with the work of Aaron Beck and David Burns and others, where they discovered patterns of negative self-talk. These are incessant, habitual, somewhat automatic ways that people, moment to moment, negatively evaluated their experience. And they were so incessant and so automatic that it seems like that's all that there was that dominated consciousness. And what they were disturbed about is the fact that these stories were so incessantly negative that people could actually think themselves into major depressive states or major anxiety states.

So, they began to develop a whole way of trying to look at the stories that people were telling themselves, and it was called "the patterns of negative self-talk," or ATs, "automatic thought." And the treatment method that was developed in the West was called "triple column technique." In the first column, you list the negative things you persistently say to yourself, the evidence, just the way it is; and in the second column you list the categories of negative self-talk; and in the third column was you sort of get a perspective on it and you challenge the evidence, you test the evidence. So, if I'm depressed, I would say something like, "Why does this always happen to me? This is the worst ever. Nothing will go well." So that would be the first column, just a list of the negative things I would characteristically, over and over again, say to myself.

The second column is categorizing the types of negative self-talk. Personalizing. Why does always this happen to me? This is the worst ever. Catastrophizing. Nothing good ever happens. Over-generalization. And the third column would be the correction. "Wait a minute. It doesn't always happen to me. Sometimes things happen to me that are bad and sometimes things that happen are good, and sometimes it happens to other people. I'm not unique in that sense. This is the worst ever, catastrophizing. Maybe it won't turn out to be that bad this time. Other times maybe it has been, but there are a lot of times that it didn't."

That was basically the approach, and they found that if they helped people be metacognitively aware of their patterns of negative self-talk and got some perspective on it and got some distance on it so they weren't so extreme, that their depression and anxiety states would relatively clear up. And that was the beginning of, not really the beginning, but they thought it was the beginning of cognitive therapy. After it had gotten very popular, about a decade later, the same group—Aaron Beck and David Burns and others at U Penn—started to apply that model to other clinical areas, and it didn't work out so well. They tried to apply the model to people with a diagnosis of personality disorders, and they tried to apply it to people with major addictions like alcoholism and drug addiction and eating disorders.

And the method of testing the evidence and correcting the negative self-talk didn't make a dent in working with personality disorders or working with people with addictions. So, they got curious about why the model was so effective for certain conditions and so ineffective for other conditions. And what they began to see is that underneath that moment to moment negative self-talk was another layer of much more stable and somewhat impervious to change negative beliefs and schemas. And they're not moment to moment things that we say to each other. They're relatively stable. And they had rediscovered something that was really popular ten years earlier than the discovery of negative self-talking. It was what Albert Ellis talked about, where they're irrational beliefs. But he never got full credit for what he was talking about, that, as cognitive psychotherapists say, beliefs and schemas develop slowly over time, but once they develop, they're relatively intractable to change.

So, the common human tendency is, if you develop a negative belief, and you come up with new experiences that would run contrary to that belief, the natural human tendency is to dismiss the new experience and to leave the negative belief intact, so you never learn from new experiences anymore. And that's what Ellis was trying to get at by saying that beliefs have a certain irrational component to them. So, if you have a belief that you're not smart, that that's what you were told because you had a sibling who would constantly tease you as being dumb, or you had parents that sort of put you down all the time and didn't think that you were smart and never encouraged your education or something like that—so there's lots of reasons you might've developed that belief.

But then you have some experience where you draw upon your natural intelligence and you accomplish something quite important. The tendency would be to dismiss that important experience and say, "Nah, it doesn't make a dent in my not being smart," and leave the belief intact. So, one of the things that happens after a while, these beliefs develop and they don't change very much. In fact, it takes a lot to blow up those stable negative beliefs. Not easy to change. But another thing happens, and that is that those negative beliefs, once we develop them, we lose awareness of them, metacognitive awareness, so they operate in the background of our awareness. So, negative beliefs are deeper than the negative self-talk that you can sort of observe in your mind. They're not easy to get access to.

Beck and Burns in that group developed this technique called "the downward arrow." You start with the negative self-talk and you trace it down to the deeper structures of negative schemas and beliefs and see what you can infer about what those negative beliefs might be because they're hard to get at. But the most important point to remember is that once you develop certain negative beliefs, they operate by having an influence on our outlook, our experience of ourselves, and how we experience others. So, they have a profound influence in a negative way, but we don't even know it, so that most adults have a whole network of limiting beliefs and schemas. Sometimes we use the word schema to talk about those deeper structures that might not be just beliefs because they're not just entirely cognitive. They also have a strong emotional component and they form under conditions of strong emotional valence in families early in our lives, and they don't change easily, and we don't listen to new information that would allow us to change those beliefs.

Now there are many limiting beliefs, and the best work on this was done in the West by Jeff Young in a book called *Schema Therapy*. And Jeff was the head of the research division under Aaron Beck's work, but he eventually broke with Aaron Beck and went out on his own because when they started applying this model to personality disorders and drug abuse and found out the negative self-talk treatment method of testing the evidence didn't make a dent, then Jeff was feeling that they needed to develop a whole new approach, and Aaron Beck having developed the method, didn't want to make a new approach, they wanted to try and find ways of applying the old approach. So they couldn't agree. So, he developed a whole new thing called schema therapy, which is based on not just testing the evidence rationally, but what he calls "emotion-focused" techniques. Because these deep-seated beliefs are, he calls them "schemas" because they always have a strong emotional component to them.

When you say, "I'm not smart. I've never been smart in anything I've done in my life," that's not just a belief. That's a strong emotional statement. Right? There's a charge to it because it affects everything in your life. And sometimes we say that the most important negative schemas and beliefs that we have are what we call "core beliefs and schemas," and there are three categories of core beliefs and schemas from a Western point of view. First are beliefs about the world or what we call outlook beliefs, how you expect the world to be. The second are beliefs about the self, what you think the possibilities are in a positive sense, and in a negative sense, what you think the limitations of the self are.

So, every time you say, "I can't do," that's a limitation. Whenever you say, "I'm really able to," that's a possibility. Or "maybe I'll be able to."

And the third set of beliefs which are important core beliefs are beliefs about what we expect to happen in relationships, how we expect people to treat us both as work relationships and friendships and in intimate relationships, and we develop the whole fabric of those beliefs. And we even select relationships based on our beliefs, not necessarily what's best for us. We select them to prove that those beliefs are accurate even though they're not. So, if you have a strong belief that you're not smart, you keep selecting intimate partners who will put down your intelligence, or you vote for a president who does that, as we have just done. [Dan chuckles] So, the idea is that you have to identify these deep core beliefs and bring them into metacognitive awareness and find some way of distancing yourself from these. So that's the heart of schema therapy. You can google this, just google "schema therapy," and on that website there'll be a thing called the YSQ, which stands for Young Schema Questionnaire. It's very complete. He designed it for working with people who have a diagnosis of personality disorders, which means they have a lot of negative schemas. And in that questionnaire, there are beliefs presented that you rate regarding whether they are characteristic of you, not at all characteristic, somewhat characteristic, or very characteristic of you. There are 232 different negative beliefs on that questionnaire and they're divided into eighteen domains, schema domains, or categories. And the way it works is as you score it up so you can see the individual negative beliefs.

What I like about doing that is that most of these things you'd never think of because they're not in your awareness. But when you see it in print and you say, "Yeah, that's really something that applies to me." it's all in one place, so in half an hour of filling out this questionnaire, you're going to get your own diagnosis of the beliefs that most get in your way. It just brings it all into your awareness. And everybody has some negative beliefs. But what characterizes people with a diagnosis of personality disorder is they have many maladapted beliefs. So, in the empirical testing of that, of the eighteen schema domains, people with personality disorders usually score very high or high in six or more of the eighteen domains. That's a lot. So, they're off the charts with that. So, the first step is to bring into your awareness what your negative beliefs and schemas are, and then to find ways in Western therapy terms of how to change them so you don't operate out of them anymore.

Now, from my point of view in the work that I've done on this, the trouble with the schema questionnaire is that it's based on the presumption that at a certain point in your life, these are the negative beliefs that you've developed at various points in your life and this is what you now have. It's a cross-sectional view. But it doesn't allow you to appreciate that beliefs and schemas, including negative and positive beliefs and schemas, change over the course of our life depending on experiences that we have. So, if you want to see how that works and what your core beliefs are, we'll do a little exercise around that after the break called "constructing a belief map," and you'll see how this works.

But what I'll ask you to do essentially is to go through the various periods of your life and map out what you think the main beliefs that you had were about the world, yourself and the world of others, and look at the critical events that shaped those beliefs. For example, and for myself, when I did that, I grew up in the 1950s, so the great belief system in terms of outlook of life was science. I grew up in the Cold War, so science was the most constructive and the most destructive thing, but science was religion in the 1950s, so that was a strong belief I had and the commitment to becoming a scientist. But then that belief changed and I got profoundly disillusioned with science because I had spent three years on a science fair project when I was eleven years old. I entered the science fair and I won the first prize in biology, but I didn't get the grand prize. The kid who got second prize in biology won the grand prize.

I was an innocent kid, had worked hard on my project, but all these people kept asking me, "How could they? I don't understand the logic of this. How could somebody win second place when they won the grand prize?" And I said, "Well, a different set of judges." And then six months later I get this phone call from the head of the science fair offering me an apology because the science fair was fixed, and it was fixed by the Catholic Church. It was rigged because their kid had to win because the kid who won the grand prize got a lot of money for the school. And since they supplied the support staff to register all the people for the fair, they had to win and they got caught, and that was profoundly disillusioning to me. It shattered my world. I don't suppose it's any accident that I've done seventy priest abuse cases against the Church [laughter] and the Church has a bounty of unlimited funds to take me out and discredit me, and I take it as a great compliment that I pissed off the Church.

But you see where that comes from. You see how that influence is there? I mean, it's not that I'm unaware of it. I actually enjoy the influence of it. (Laughter) But it's not something that's foreign to me. But in my own work on myself, at some point I mapped out where all those beliefs came from and the critical incidents that helped shape those.

Either [of] two things shape beliefs: Critical incidents, and that [aforementioned] case is an example of that, or family messages, family and cultural messages.

A lot of times we internalize the messages from our families or sub-cultural or cultural messages. But you want to identify those stories because we live in a life of stories. They have such profound influence on everything we do. What if you were completely free of the stories? And there weren't any stories anymore? And all the stories revolve around the sense of self and what we think is possible, and what limits what's possible for the self. What the Sufi master and poet Hafiz once called "the tiresome project of maintaining the self through its stories." Nice quote. It's tiresome to live in all these stories. We live in a prison of our own stories.

So, how do we change the stories? It's not so easy, but it's possible. There's a Western, and there's an Eastern answer to that. The Western answer is that there are methods that help you to get distance from the stories. In the old psychodynamic tradition, the idea was to come to see that all stories are conditioned. So, if you had some fundamental belief that "I'm not lovable, no one could ever love me," that's a pretty common story, okay?

Then what you would do is you'd take that story and see how it's operated in your everyday life currently, and then once you're familiar with it at a conscious level in your current life, you trace it back. Trace that story back to earlier times in your life to incidents that were involved in either developing the story or reinforcing it, and tracing it back to some other incident in your life that was important in developing the story or reinforcing it. So, you telescope back through all these critical incidents and you can see how the story is essentially conditioned. And when you can see how it's conditioned, you get some distance from it. That was the traditional approach—a more psychodynamic approach to working with stories, but it works, more or less.

The most important way of working with it I think is something that clinicians don't use enough, and that's an old method that's been around for seventy years now. It's the concept of cognitive dissonance. But clinicians don't use it very much because it was developed in social psychology and clinicians don't read that stuff. But here's the original experiment that was done in the 1940s, post-war World War II: Studies were done at Yale with a well-to-do undergraduate population. And they would have students who volunteered for this research rate their political beliefs, zero being the midpoint, and then it goes from one to ten in the direction of more and more liberal beliefs or one to ten in the direction of more and more conservative beliefs. And if they did that with a large population of the college campus in post-World War II, what do you think the ratings would be? The majority of the ratings would be about seven in the direction of liberal beliefs after the war.

Then the students, once they rated their beliefs from liberal to conservative on the continuum, were given what was called a counter-attitudinal behavior to enact. They were given the following task: They would get paid for the task—not a lot of money, but some modest payment the researchers give students. We call them volunteer research. They'd have to go around the campus and recruit members for the Young Republicans, which, in the 1940s, that was sort of like the Tea Party. So, the behavior that you have to enact is completely counter-attitudinal for you, contradictory to your political ideology. And they have to do that for a whole month, and they'd have to produce results, so they have to recruit people, so they have to talk it up. And what do you think happened at the end of the month when they re-rated people? They rated themselves zero or one in the conservative direction, or two in the conservative direction. They regressed to the mean or they went slightly in the conservative direction.

So, the explanation of that observable behavior was that by having established what the baseline belief was, and then having the people behave in a way that was completely contrary to that belief, they induced a state of cognitive dissonance. There was a disconnect between the belief and the behavior that they had to enact, and the only way that they could reduce that intolerable dissonance was to shift away from the original belief position to something more neutral in the direction of the behavior.

Now that research was done originally around attitude change, but it's very clear that it applies to limiting beliefs and schemas in the same way, and clinicians never exploit that enough. But here's the issue. The more extreme the belief or the behavior, the more leverage you have because there's more dissonance. So, the best way, in my opinion, of changing limiting beliefs is through using or evoking dissonance.

Let's take extreme behavior, okay, and what in the health field we do wrong with that. Somebody goes to the primary care doc. Their drinking has increased to the point that it's now a drinking problem. They're out of control where they're drinking at times. And the doctor's aware of that and tries to counter the patient, and what do you think the primary care doctor's going to say, not having much sophistication in psychology? They're going to say, "You've got to stop drinking." And what do you think the patient's going to do when the doctor says, "You have to stop drinking?" They're going to resist it. And now you've taken the struggle and you've made the struggle between the patient and the doctor. Does that ever get anywhere useful? Never. Never.

But, if the primary care doctor had some sophistication in cognitive dissonance, he'd talk the language of parts. He would say, "You know, there's a part of you that knows you're out of control with your drinking and you can't stop it, and that part actually believes that there are things you get out of it that are beneficial. And yet there's another part of you that knows that this is really harmful to you and you're going down the tubes with it, and there's a deep conflict within you, within you, between the part that wants to continue doing it and won't stop and doesn't want to stop, and the part that knows you've got to stop."

Now, you see the way that that sentence is worded? It frames the dissonance. It keeps the dissonance within the patient and it highlights it. So, if you understand the seven years of research on cognitive dissonance, what choice does the patient have [about what] to do if you highlight the dissonance to them? They have to shift behavior out of the extreme, just like shifting away from the liberal to a more conservative perspective.

It forces the issue if you keep the dissonance in their face and don't let them minimize it. And what will happen is, if you keep doing that, every time you see the patient, the patient will say, "At some point, I've got to stop," and they'll bring it up. "This is killing me." And if you bring up the other side, you can do what's called "leveraging." You bring up the other side and you emphasize the adaptive function of the drinking. "Yes, but there are things you're getting out of it." The patient will keep saying, "No, no, no. I've got to stop." And you keep saying, "But you continue because, see, you still continue because there's something you're getting out of it." And they keep saying, "No, no." And what do you think that's going to do? You can structure it so that it leverages some amount of the behavior. We call that leveraging. And they do the entire thing themselves, and you never get into this power struggle, because it's a complete misunderstanding of how dissonance works.

Here's the key. The more extreme the behavior—like drinking that's out of control—or the more extreme the belief, the more likely the dissonance will leverage it. So, it's not so hard if you understand the principle involved here. It works.

I'll give you an extreme example of it working. I had a clinician come to me. She was seeing a woman in her early twenties who had complex trauma and a major dissociative disorder and had multiple parts [of her personality]. The therapist was a good therapist, had done all the stabilization work, and the patient started to uncover memories of sexual abuse by her father. Only trouble was the patient was still living at home with her father, and the abuse was still going on in her twenties. Now, perpetrators act like perpetrators, right? They tend to do that thing. So, what the father did was the father illegally wire tapped. The patient would call the therapist on a number of occasions, many times. The father wire tapped all the phone conversations without letting his daughter know that. And to protect his butt, he then filed a complaint to the licensing board that the therapist, using regression therapy, was fostering, creating false memories in the patient.

The board did their review. The therapist was very careful, and the therapist had many consultants on this case. They all conferred and agreed. And the finding was that the therapist didn't do anything wrong. And they dismissed the charges without prejudice, and then they told the therapist, "You have this thing called rights. You have a chance to take criminal action against what the father did because it's totally illegal." But here's the problem. Therapist sues the father. The patient's still living at home with the father and father's paying the bills for the therapy. That's a little bit of a conflict of interest. But the patient is attached to the father because that's what trauma bonding is about. The more abused you are, the deeper the bond. A faithful dog is a beaten dog. Right? That's what trauma bonding is about. So how do we get out of this extreme situation?

So, I consulted with the therapist and said, "I want you to leverage it. I want you to say there's a part of you that needs the relationship with your father and there's something you're still getting out of it, even though you know there's another part that's damaging and abusive and it's degrading on an ongoing basis. Nevertheless, there's a reason why you stay."

We scripted it. "We know it's abusive to you, it's degrading, but there must be something you're getting out of it because you're still staying in it. Let's look at what you're getting out of it that's positive." "No, no. There's nothing positive about it. You don't understand." Well, we never really understood. All we had to do is continue to hold the dissonance. Two months later, she moves out. It lasted a week. Therapist says, "See what I mean? You went right back. There's something you need in the relationship." "No, no, no. You don't understand."

Four months later, she moved out for good, got her own job, paid for her own therapy, got better.

And the whole thing was done with cognitive dissonance: creating the dissonance between the part of her that was getting something out of the relationship, however abusive it was, and the part of her that knew it was quite abusive and degrading, and just holding that dissonance so it has to shift the extreme behavior, which is overdependence on an abusive trauma bonding relationship. It works.

The outcome was actually creative. We made a deal with the DA to suspend the case for a year so that there wouldn't be any live prosecution until the patient got better. And once the patient got better, the DA's position was that if anything comes up in the future, we're going to prosecute right away, but for now it's suspended, and gave the chance to the patient to get better. The patient got better, finished treatment. Clear enough example? You can do that with any belief.

So now I have to do that with our current situation in the world, you know—the belief that everything's going to go down the tubes under Trump. And there's some subtle, other part of me that believes there's some hope, so I have a lot of dissonance at the moment. And I hope that will move me away from my extreme pessimism about this. But it's the same process, right?

Now, more recently, there are other Western ways of handling extreme beliefs, and you can handle them through attachment imagery. Jeff Young does a type of therapy, schema therapy, which is what he calls "reparenting." So, if a patient comes in and says, "I'm never lovable. I've never been lovable. I never will be lovable," he will present a series of hypotheticals off the therapy relationship. "If it were different, how could I possibly be with you here that would change that idea that you're not lovable, that you would feel deeply cared for and loved in this relationship? What would have to happen for that to be something that would actually change your belief? Just as a hypothetical?"

Now as you know, we play it off of the ideal parent figures. "Imagine you grew up in a family different from your family of origin, with a set of parents ideally suited to you and your nature. Imagine being with them in a way that this negative belief about yourself as not being lovable would never come up. That they would've been with you in a way that you felt deeply lovable and cared for, and it was never a question in your mind." The extreme opposite. We call that positive remapping, and if you do that over and over again, you start to operate out of the positive map and the negative map gets irrelevant. It works.

Six months, two years later, you've remapped all that. So, attachment-based imagery, both my work and Jeff Young's work, have been pretty good with that stuff. The outcome studies are looking good with it. It works.

Another strategy is future time orientation. "Imagine yourself at some hypothetical time in the future when you're no longer operating out of this negative belief system, but whatever the positive opposite of that is." And get the person to try on something more positive. "Imagine a time in the future when you have no question in your mind that you're completely lovable, and imagine all the details of your life," and get them to remap it. So, what I'm saying is that there is, in the history of psychology over the last hundred years, we have evolved a series of methods that actually fundamentally change these seemingly intractable negative beliefs. We know how to do that.

Now, the main problem from a Western point of view is bringing these beliefs into a person's awareness. What's missing is metacognitive awareness, the capacity to step back and look at your own state of mind and say, "These are what the beliefs are," because by definition, they operate in the background of your awareness. So how do you know what they are? It's a little tedious by starting with the negative self-talk and saying, "Well, let's go through all this negative self-talk and let's get to follow this downward arrow to the deeper structure." It's not as easy as Beck and Burns make it seem. It's not obvious to us. That's why getting something like having it all spelled out in a questionnaire and say, "Oh, this one applies to me and this one applies to me," it makes it easier. That's why I like this questionnaire a lot. There are several of them, but that's the better one, I think.

In Buddhism, there's a similar problem. And as you know, if you follow the stages of the Level 1 course, you concentrate. Why do you concentrate? Well, one, because it makes the point of observation stable so you can look at how the mind constructs experience. What's the purpose of concentrating? It stabilizes the point of observation. So, if I went to, well, soon I'll go to Australia. I like to go to the outback and go to the cave art. If I go to one of the sites for the rock art and I hold up a candle and there's a wind blowing, I can see what's on the wall, but I only get fragments because the candle's flickering too much and I get little pieces of what's there. I'm still seeing what's there, but I get bits and pieces of it and it's not very stable. But if I hold up a candle and there's no wind, I get to see everything in vivid detail that's on that wall. Our ordinary mind is like a flickering candle. It's unsteady. It's highly distractible. But if I train concentration, then the mind is stable and I can see everything in the mind from that stable vantage point.

That's what the word *samādhi* means. *Dha*, the root *dha* in Sanskrit means to stay. *Sama* means evenly. It means that if you've concentrated enough, you reduce all that distractibility and you've made that concentration a steady state, or what we call "making the mind serviceable." But in the course of focusing on one thing and tuning everything else out, you've also calmed all that other extraneous thought activity, all that noise in the system. So, when there isn't all that incessant noise of conceptual thought, you can see the deeper structures of the mind. So, from the Buddhist perspective, we'd say you can't possibly look at your negative beliefs if your mind has got all that noise in it, all the thought. You can't find that downward arrow and sift through all the surface thought to the deeper layers of thought because there's just too much noise. It's not so easy to do that.

Even the Western cognitive therapists say that, too. It's not so easy. But if you develop concentration strongly, you develop a quality of mind called *shinchong* in Tibetan, mental pliancy. Whatever the mind's awareness intends, it goes just to that and only that and nothing gets in the way of it, with lightning speed. We call that making the mind serviceable. So, if you have that metacognitive awareness, at that point, when the mind is calm, when most of that extraneous thought activity, all that noise is calm and it's quiet, with your awareness you can actually look at the deeper structures and they come up more clearly. So, there's a certain point in the path, usually much further along, when you develop that metacognitive awareness strongly after you've done emptiness of self and emptiness of time that you can actually look at those belief structures.

In Buddhism we say you can't look at those belief structures until you can look so quickly that you can catch thoughts at their head, before they form. When you can catch thoughts at the head before they form, quickly, that's when you can now step back and look at those belief structures, and they're obvious. So, there's a certain point in the overall path where it's obvious how to do this, and it's crystal clear what those negative beliefs are. So, as you know in the basic course, for those of you who have gone through it, at some point, that's called "sealing practice." You seal all the negative beliefs. And there are beliefs that are core beliefs about your own practice. For Westerners, their main beliefs are around capacity. The assumption is that there is something about your spiritual practice that you'll necessarily have a problem with and you can repeatedly have that problem with it. Something won't go well, or the problem is too big to really overcome. So, Westerners make a lot of assumptions about problems that they think they're going to have and they won't overcome.

The other thing that Westerners do a lot is they think they're not deserving of it. They're not deserving of the gains of the practice. I remember, I mean, a good example of how cultural messages become beliefs … I was teaching a course in London and half the group was from the UK and the other half was from the Netherlands. And it was during the World Cup, so we had to reschedule some of the actual meditation sessions around the World Cup because that's important for the sake of all sentient beings. [Laughter]

Student 2

No. This isn't as important as football.

Dan

Not as important as American football. That's right. Go Pats.[3] [Laughter]

So, the Brits would look at their states of mind with this kind of wry, distant humor; and the Dutch would just work so hard at it and they would beat themselves up when they couldn't get the meditation practice quite right. And halfway through the week we were looking at negative beliefs, and one of the Dutch said, "But you have to understand. We have to do it this way because we're from a Calvinistic culture. We have to work hard and they're never supposed to work out." [Laughter] I said, "Damn right. That's where it came from." It was so obvious. He hit the cultural nail on the head. And we all have these cultural and familial messages of where this stuff comes from; and it's about everything in our life, including our practice. So, part of the interesting question here is what are your limiting beliefs about your own spiritual practice, you see? It's important.

The big one for the Tibetans, because they have this idea of reincarnation and rebirth, is that it takes lifetimes to do this practice, so don't even bother to try in this lifetime because you can't do it in a single lifetime. That's just an idea and it's hugely limiting. Why not? The practices were designed to do in

---

3 Short for Boston Patriots, Dan's favorite (American) football team.

this lifetime, including full enlightenment. So, they have their own share of limiting beliefs.

So, there's a certain critical point in the practice when you develop metacognitive awareness enough that you can actually step back and see this stuff clearly, and you can find a way of moving beyond the influence of any negative beliefs. Think about being totally free of the influence of any negative beliefs. That's profound. Now we're talking about freedom, real freedom, with no influence of any of these things.

Yes?

Student 3

I have a couple of questions about direct knowing. So, I guess the first thing I'm kind of wondering is, is direct knowing, would it be the same for every vessel or is it contingent on the development and knowledge of that vessel?

Dan

No. Direct knowing—see, this is where I'm going to use brain metaphors. Okay?

Student 3

Okay. And if you could include also, whatever your answer is, how we validate this.

Dan

Metacognition. The first paper on metacognition in the West was by John Flavell, the Piagetian scholar at Stanford in 1979, an American psychologist, and he defined it as thinking about thinking. That's an unfortunately poor definition of this. Because if you look at the development of metacognition in neurocircuitry, using brain metaphors here, the right dorsolateral prefrontal cortex, this piece right here, is your metacognitive piece of the mind. It has nothing to do with the secondary association cortices or Broca's area that has to do with thought and sub-vocalization of thought. It has nothing to do with "thinking about thinking." It's direct awareness of seeing into and being able to monitor your state of mind.

But sometimes we recruit other areas. We can recruit thought instead of using awareness. It's the same way if you're practicing a new exercise routine in Pilates and you use the surrounding muscles, not just the muscles that you need to isolate for that exercise, until you get used to how to isolate that muscle group. So thought becomes an overlay to metacognition, but it's not really part of it. If you're really seeing the mind, you can monitor your state of mind and see it just the way it is with pure awareness. Okay? It's much quicker. You can have what's called *jeshe*, afterthoughts about that, after you see into it. But if you have forethoughts into it, you won't see into it with awareness. You just have ideas about it, and those become their own beliefs. Do you see the problem here? You've got to look into it and see it.

But that's why in a Tibetan point of view, they don't work on beliefs until you've got fairly advanced in your practice because you need that speed of awareness, because thought's too slow. And that's an outcome of pure old concentration practice. Once you get concentrated enough, you pick up the speed of awareness and the marker that you're ready to look at beliefs is that with the speed of awareness, you can pick up the thought at the head as it's beginning to form before it is already elaborated and breaks. It's like picking up a wave at the beginning of its forming rather than when it's already broken.

Student 3

So, you're saying direct knowing, it sounds like what you're saying is you're seeing …

Dan

You just see it.

Student 3

You're just seeing what's there without thinking about it.

Dan

You just know it. You just know it. And you can see all the stories in stark relief just as being stories. It's like a house of cards.

Student 3

Okay. Yeah, so it's seeing clearly. I got that. Okay. Because, I don't know, maybe I thought it was like you're getting a direct download from some source. It is just about seeing clearly and getting rid of obfuscation. That makes more sense, actually.

Dan

But it's still not easy.

Student 3

No, I know.

Dan

So, there are three answers to your question. How do you get to see those deeper, underlying stable beliefs? One is you have to sharpen your metacognitive awareness to see it. That's the first Buddhist answer. The second is, even if you do that, sometimes you still won't be able to do it, so that's why if you run your practice by your teachers, they can hear what the limiting beliefs are and feed them back to you. You get feedback from your teachers or from a therapist, or sometimes use aids like a questionnaire. We don't have a limiting belief questionnaire for spiritual practice, but it'd be fun to develop one. We could develop one. I mean, we've seen thousands of people go through this stuff. It's not like we don't hear these things over and over again. It's always the same set of limiting beliefs. We all have the same stories, not quite the same, but there's a finite set of stories about practice, spiritual practice.

And the third is you get help from your friends. You ask for the gift waves of influence, and you let the *ḍākinīs* and the other non-ordinary beings in the lineage activate the stories in your mind and put them online so you can see them more easily. You ask them to help you. *Ḍākinīs* will do that.

So that's how you bring it into your awareness, and you just see it as what it is. It's just an empty structure of mind. It has no grab to it anymore. You don't have to get rid of it. It just loses its grab. It's just insubstantial and you move beyond it.

January 18, 2017

Themes: *Dukkha* Means Reactivity; Your Mind Affects the Field

Dan

Welcome everyone. You have a question?

Student 1

I have a question about types of practices you would recommend during the waking hours, whether it's walking, things like that, so not necessarily on the cushion, but sort of off the cushion. I'm sure there are types of practices that help with general mindfulness and other things, not just necessarily when you're practicing.

Dan

That's a good question. What do you do off the pillow?

Well, mindfulness is very popular in the Burmese style that we saw. So, it depends on what the overall intention of the practice is. Mindfulness is about, in everyday life, the discontinuities of awareness. We have great moments of mindlessness in our everyday life. We have lapses in our attentiveness; most people do. So, when you practice the Burmese style of mindfulness, you're trying to approximate the condition of continuous uninterrupted awareness with no gaps in it, no lapses.

So, in the Mahāsī Sayādaw method, which is popular in this country, what you do is you simply label what the activity at the moment is. If you're thinking, you say [silently] "thinking," you don't think about the content of the thing, it's just that thinking is going on. If you're looking at something, "looking"; if you're hearing, "hearing," and if you're sensing something, "sensing something." And if you use those labels, you approximate the condition of continuous, uninterrupted awareness in contrast to the ordinary state, which is big chunks of awareness missing. And that's a legitimate goal within the domain of what you try and do with mindfulness. But there are many practices you could do in the daytime, even within that tradition, in the Theravāda tradition.

I once studied with a Sayadaw called Tumpalow Sayadaw, and what he would do is he would have you every moment use different labels, not seeing, thinking, sensing, walking, whatever. He had four labels: "mind moving towards something to make more of it," "mind moving away from something to make less of it," "mind oblivious to what just happened and catching it after the fact," or "pure awareness of that moment without doing anything to it and moving towards or away from it." Those are the only four possibilities. And if you start labeling the reactivity of your information processing system, at first you see a lot of mind movements away and a lot of mind movements toward, and a lot of moments being oblivious to what just happened, and every now and then moments of awareness. But if you keep observing it continuously, what do you think is going to happen over time? You're going to start moving in the direction of pure awareness, absent of doing anything, reacting to it by making more or less of it, and absent of all those chunks missing.

Now that's a very different goal because now it's not just training continuous mindfulness, but at a more subtle level it's training yourself to drop the reactivity, number one, and to drop all the missing moments number two. That's a superior practice within the Theravāda tradition, but not popularly practiced.

In fact, what Tumpalow Sayadaw was trying to do was something close to what Buddha tried to describe in his first teaching. When he got enlightened under the *bodhi* tree and he walked to the next town, Sarnath, and gave his first teaching having just been enlightened. It was on the Four Noble Truths. And the first one was on reactivity, the truth of *dukkha*, reactivity.

Now unfortunately in Nepali, *dukkha* has been translated as suffering. So, we think of that as the "Truth of Suffering," and that he was trying to tell everybody that everything is suffering. That's not what *dukkha* means. It means reactivity. The outcome of the reactivity is suffering. But the trouble is, if you translate *dukkha* as suffering rather than as reactivity, you miss the method, which is the amazing main thing he was trying to convey. He was saying, "You can watch your mind and watch how this happens. You watch the mind moving towards, you watch the mind moving away. You watch the mind being oblivious and picking it up after the fact, or you watch the mind in pure awareness without doing anything to anything." There's your method. And what Tumpalow Sayadaw was trying to capture was the original teaching of the Four Noble Truths as something that anyone can do by observing their mind that way.

Now that's a very different practice than simply being aware and trying to get continuity of awareness through Burmese mindfulness. But, in the Indo-Tibetan tradition or Mahāyāna Buddhism, you get a very different answer to what you do in daily practice because there the practice is all centered around the theme of emptiness meditation. Emptiness means seeing things as insubstantial, not as real. They still exist in the relative reality, they're just not real. So, you see them as not independently self-existing and you see them as not substantial.

So, if you make the mistake of taking things as too solid or too real, there are two experiential consequences. One in Tibetan is called *dzin-pa*, grab. It's similar to the notion of reactivity in Theravāda Buddhism with one twist. The difference is that what they say is, "Yes, the mind moves towards everything it likes to make more of it, and moves away from everything it dislikes to make less of it, but all that becomes organized over time around the concept of self."

So, the cause of suffering isn't the mind moving away and the mind moving towards. The cause of suffering is that all that activity, or reactivity, better, is organized around the self-system. So, it's about self-grab. We move towards what we like, the self; we move towards what we dislike, also related to the self. So, it's a little bit more specific explanation. It's not like it's definitely built into the information processing system that you're reactive every moment. That reactivity over time gets shaped around sense of self. So, Dan likes this and he wants more of this, and Dan doesn't like that and he wants less of that. And it's incessant variations on the theme of self-grab.

So, from that perspective, if you did a daily practice, and you went about your daily life, you wouldn't try to be aware of walking when you're walking. You wouldn't try to be aware of thinking when you're thinking. You'd simply follow episodes of self-grab. Grab is perceivable. If you like what I'm saying and you praise me, grab. If you don't like what I'm saying and you criticize me, grab. Either way I get grab, right? Mind moves towards what it likes, moves away from what it dislikes. It's all organized around "the tiresome project of self." Dan likes this. Dan doesn't like that. He doesn't like to be criticized; he likes to be praised.

So, grab: Most emotions have a lot of grab. Thoughts that are important to us have a lot of grab. Things that we like in the perceptual environment, sights, sounds, have a lot of grab. Things that we dislike in the perceptual environment have a lot of grab. So, from a Tibetan point of view, you go about your daily life and every time you notice some variation on the theme of grab or reactivity, at the time that you notice it, you look right into it; you roam around in high-speed awareness and do an emptiness search task. And the more you look for the solidness of that, whatever that was grabbing you, it would keep slipping away as unfindable because when you search into things from an emptiness perspective, what you search for keeps slipping away as unfindable.

The Dalai Lama says the essence of emptiness meditation is *nyerme*, unfindability. You have to look into it. You can't just say, yeah, this is empty. You can't do it conceptually. You've got to roam around with high-speed awareness in the field of experience and find what's substantial about that.

So, I was down the street at the restaurant and they served my meal at twenty-five after, and I'm looking at my watch, and there's a lot of grab. [Laughter] So I roamed around in all of that, and then there wasn't a lot of reactivity. So I gulped down my food for five minutes, came five minutes late. There's a lot of grab to the time thing there. Now if I wasn't so caught up in the time thing, I would look at all the reactivity with that, just roam around in it until there was no grab left whatsoever.

So, if you do that, it's like doing an emptiness meditation in daily life at the points that you most need to do it, which are the points of the biggest grab. So, it's always applied to what is needed most. So, the practice becomes very powerful because it's not using abstract moments and doing sitting on the pillow once a day for twenty minutes. Things are not going to come up on the pillow because you're quiet. This is when you're using it when you most need to use it. So, it's a very powerful practice. But if you do that, after doing that, after doing that for several weeks, with your metacognitive awareness, you're going to notice patterns. You'll notice that you get caught up in some things over and over again and other things you don't get caught up in. It's what one of my students calls, and I like the term, "my favorite clouds." It's a good term.

So, your task is that after you get caught up in the grab, look into the patterns that occur over the first couple of weeks you're doing that and say, "What do I get caught up in the most?" Do you get lost in thought a lot because you over-Identify with thought? Is that where your most grab is? Do you get caught up in out-there-ness? Do you get caught up in the construction of time and always race around like the rabbit in *Alice in Wonderland*?—"I'm late, I'm late for a very important date." Do you get caught up in external perceptions? Do you get caught up in emotions in general? Do you get caught up in specific emotions more than other emotions? Look at the patterns of where you're most reactive. And then, once you find those out, we would ask you to do a dedicated emptiness practice. If you get caught up in thought, you do emptiness of thought. If you get caught up in emotions, you do emptiness of emotions. If you get caught up in time, you do emptiness of time.

So, you're always working on looking right into the face of where you get most reactive or have the most grab because that's the cutting edge of your practice, where you most need it. Now that's going to remove all the situations in your life that you're most reactive to. And in my opinion, that's a much stronger practice than simply trying to be more continuous with your awareness. People in mindfulness approximate continuous, non-reactive awareness, but when things catch them up, they're very reactive. But in this case, the instructions are to look squarely into the things that you're most reactive to. So, I think it's a better practice myself, having done both of them quite extensively. I think it's a better practice quite honestly, because with mindfulness, you have to watch out. It doesn't lead to the actual experience of being more aware, but the representation of being more aware. That's not the same. That's a thought, and you have to watch out for that.

My wife who teaches the Level 1 courses with me told me the story of when she once broke her leg and was on crutches. That was just before she was going to a ten-day mindfulness retreat. And at the mindfulness retreat she was hobbling along on crutches, and at the lunch line or dinner line, she couldn't juggle her food on the crutches. Everybody in the room was so mindful nobody could help her. Everybody was so mindful and they couldn't open the door. They would just mindfully go through the door and the door would close right in her face when she was on crutches. And she said, "This mindfulness is crap because it's not mindfulness, it's the representation of 'I'm being mindful' and you're being completely oblivious to what's happening in your immediate environment."

And I think the difference is the view, because in the older Theravadan Buddhism, where the stage model is the *Visuddhimagga*, or The Pathway of Purification, which is the stages, step by step in that system, there was a stage when you get really refined, and there isn't any solid content left in the mind. It's all quick bursts and energy and movement and light in the mind, what are called "mind moments," or what in that tradition is called *dharmin*, the simplest observable elements of your mind after there's not much content that gets elaborated anymore. And it begins to flash like strobe lights. And if you watch the arising and passing away every moment, after a while everything starts to break up and fragment. The simplest observable elements in your mind break up and fragment. It's not very pleasant. So, it's called *bhanga ñāṇa* in Pali, or dissolution experience.

But the issue is that if even the simplest observable elements, the most rudimentary products of the mind that are observable break up and disappear, what's left is this vast expanse of mirror-like awareness. And if you look into the nature of that awareness, that becomes the platform for awakening in that tradition. And there are different stages of that awakening. But then Nagarjuna came along in the Mahāyāna tradition and said, "Wait a minute. The idea that things are arising very quickly and disappearing quickly presumes the construction of time. What if time is an illusion? What if that's just an empty construction of mind?" So, he developed this funny thing called the "Nagarjunan dialectic." So, when you look at things arising in time, you take the view that they don't really arise in time because they're already here. And when you look at things disappearing in time, you take the view they don't really disappear in time, but stay here. That's going to flatten out time. So, if you keep looking at everything like that, what happens is it busts the whole thing open and you see beyond the convention, the construction of time, as an empty construction, and you open up simultaneous mode, a level of functioning where everything is here all at once within this ocean-like, changeless, boundless awareness. That's a huge shift. In Western terms we would say you're going from temporal or serial processing to parallel or simultaneous processing. Within that experience, everything that possibly exists is in one huge, interconnected field, and everything is interconnected, and everything affects everything and everyone affects everyone else.

Opening up simultaneous mind is not something that you're going to find in any experiences in the Theravāda tradition. It doesn't exist. It's a different experience of mind. And then your progress from there is different degrees of all-at-once-ness. If you open up that experience of mind, it changes your ethics because in everything that you do, you can't be oblivious to the fact that it affects everything else in the field. That's where the notion of "*bodhisattva* activity" comes from. And what you do in life matters. What you do with your mind and your thoughts, what you do with behavior affects everything else in the field. So, you can have a positive effect. But if you develop that, then you develop an awareness of everything in the field and everyone in the field because we all share the same field of that bigger nondual awareness. Then, that's a very different level of awareness than simple mindfulness, which is caught up in the notion of the self, trying to be mindful.

Then, if you're being mindful and you're doing your walking meditation, or you're in the lunch line, you'd be aware of everybody around you. And if somebody was struggling, you couldn't be oblivious to that. It would pain you. You would be compelled naturally to respond. You see the difference? Because the level of awareness is so vastly different from just ordinary mindfulness. You couldn't do something like that. So, the level of mind that you're operating out of and what kind of practice you do in your everyday life makes all the difference in the world. And not all these practices are the same thing.

There's no concept of levels of awareness in Burmese mindfulness. Either you have a non-judgmental field of awareness, which is usually caught up with self—the self, trying to be mindful—or, in Tibetan Buddhism, you have a level of awareness that's beyond self, that's beyond time, and each level of awareness is cleaned up of all those things. So, your practice is more naturally oriented towards the larger field in which we're all interconnected. And that drastically affects how you view the world and how you act towards others. You can't not respond to people because it then becomes your duty to consider everyone and your needs in balance with everybody else in your interpersonal field, whether you know them or not, because you're all part of the same field. It makes it hard to act selfishly at that point. Our President Elect needs these realizations, quickly, before Friday. [Dan chuckles]

So, I hope I'm conveying to all of you that there's a huge difference in what you do in daily practice. But it does require some understanding of these differences and some intention about where you want to take the practice. It's not enough to say, "Well, I'm going to practice in my daily life." You've got to be clear about what type of practice and where each takes you, and be confident and trusting about where you want to go with this.

Now, the best practice, beyond simply being aware of everybody in your interpersonal field and trying to balance your needs against their needs and seeing that we're all interconnected, which is the practice of *bodhisattvas*, the best practice is to have awakened awareness and the practice off the pillow, where it becomes seeing everything as the liveliness of awakened awareness. That's the best practice. All thoughts are lively, awakened awareness. They're insubstantial. All emotions are lively, awakened awareness. All sights, all sounds. The body. Body sensations are lively, awakened awareness. The whole thing is a continuous uninterrupted flow of lively, awakened awareness in its magical splendorous display. And that's quite remarkable, if you see everything like that. It's all quite splendorous.

There's a little Milarepa song that's rather simple, and it goes like this. [Dan sings]

E-ma, the phenomena
Of the three realms of *samsāra*.
While not existing, they appear.
How incredibly amazing.

It's all amazing. So, if you see everything as a continuous flow of liveliness, it's magnificent; you walk around in a state of chronic wonder. That would be the best practice. But that presumes a teaching that allows for different levels of experience, and learning to shift to different levels of experience so you know what you're getting at each level.

Mindfulness practice is like the bottom floor of the elevator. You want to go up the elevator to explore the different floors beyond that because you get a better view. Each view is more panoramic than the others. But I have to say that if you have the view of the larger field of ocean-like, changeless, boundless awareness where everything and everyone is interconnected, then daily practice isn't just holding the view, it becomes about your behavior. Because what you come to realize is how you act matters, because it influences everything and everyone in the field. And that's where *bodhisattva* activity comes in.

So, if you hold that view as your daily practice all the time, if you're holding the view of ocean-like, changeless, boundless awareness, then it's profound because you start to naturally view the world more in terms of our interconnectedness, and all our propensities towards selfishness begin to drop away. And we begin to naturally think about the needs of others and being basically helpful. You start to think about not what you want to accumulate for yourself, but you start to think more about the greater social good. And if we don't do that, we won't survive, because that's the way out of this mess. So, the view matters.

Yes?

Student 2

So, I have a practice question also about off the pillow. I had recently purchased the Level 1 MP3s, which were extremely helpful, and I was able to compare my practice to what was said in the MP3s, which gave me some new awareness on potential areas of growth. And I was noticing that my weaknesses were particularly in the automaticity of *samādhi* and emptiness. And I've been trying to practice those off the pillow. And I'm finding it's still pretty intermittent, and I'm trying to figure out whether it's more of a focus on the *samādhi* or the emptiness. And I guess how do I know when my automatic emptiness and *samādhi* on the pillow are good enough? Are there certain markers, like a certain amount of time to hold it? I was just wondering if you could give me some guidance on where to focus it and what kind of markers to look for.

Dan

That's a good question. You need to practice more. In the overall path, there are three automaticities. The first one, when you're concentrating, there comes a point when the concentration becomes automatic. And it means that the concentration goes on by itself without your need to do anything to set it up or without your need to do anything to remedy it. Some of the texts define it in terms of the dropping away of any need to apply any strategies or antidotes. It just stays that way. The approximation of that is what's called *samādhi*, or in Tibetan, *nyamjak*. *Nyam* means to stay, *sama* means evenly, and *jak* means to set up, in Tibetan, and *nyam* means evenly. So, the two translations are very close to each other. We like to translate *nyamjak* or *samādhi* as "concentrated evenness." And what it means is if you get deeply concentrated and a lot of the thought activity drops away and you stay on the object for long periods of time, at the beginning of that, when you drop into these periods when the background noise of thought is mostly calm, so there's a lot of stillness, and you're staying completely and continuously on the object, nevertheless, there'll still be a lot of variability in that at the beginning. But over time it becomes more like a steady state. There isn't a lot of variability. That's what concentrated evenness means.

When you start approximating concentrated evenness, you get glimpses of the concentration sort of going by itself. It has a flow to it. And you just let it go. I like to think about it in our car analogy. When you have *samādhi* or automatic *samādhi*, essentially, it's similar to cruise control in a car. You have to set up a certain speed range to get the cruise control, and then you set the settings and then it just goes by itself. And you need very little adjustment to keep it on track beyond that. And even if you step on the accelerator, or take your foot off the accelerator, it still stays pretty much within that range, despite your adjustments. So automatic *samādhi* is like that.

Now, if you're not getting that automaticity, it's probably because there are too many fine-tuned adjustments to try and stay on the object or not stay on the object, and/or it's because there's a little residual fleeting thought. We call that the subtle monkey mind. There are little fleeting thoughts. There's no thought activity in terms of elaborated thoughts, but these little minor things, little blips on the screen that you say to yourself to try and keep it on track. And you don't realize that that stuff is actually destabilizing getting to automaticity. But what you learned earlier is that by intensifying, that's what stops all that coarse level thought activity.

But at the subtle level of mind, the rules are different. So, what you have to do is ease up a little bit, not intensify, but the opposite of that. When you ease off a little bit, all that subtle stuff drops away, and then you notice it starts to go by itself. You go, "Ooh, this is sort of neat." And you ease up a little bit more and it goes all by itself. You say, "Wow." And that's why that fourth tier of the elephant path is called "enthusiastic perseverance" because you get excited that it actually works and you want to pursue it to get it to get fully automatic.

Okay. So, the error with that is making too big adjustments. At the subtle level of mind where you open up automaticity of *samādhi*, the rules of engagement are different. At the coarse level of mind, big output for small effect. At the subtle level of mind, the opposite, small output, bigger effect. So, at the coarse level of mind, it's like a space capsule with three booster rockets to push it out of the atmosphere. But once you get out of the atmosphere, the slightest overshoot of the rocket goes for miles into space beyond the space capsule. You can't dock it. So smaller is better. So, what most people do is when they get to that range where it starts to go by itself, they overshoot the mark. Ease up a little bit, just a little bit, just ease up, just slightly, the intention of easing a little bit.

It starts to go all by itself. Ease up just a little bit more, just a little, little bit. It starts to go all by itself. Then you get it. It's trial and error. You have to see that.

Now, automatic emptiness, that's different. You have to set up ocean-like, changeless, boundless awareness and let everything arise as emptiness liveliness. But then you have to look more quickly, with the lightning speed of awareness, so you're catching everything arising at the head, not when it's already arisen and become elaborated. And way over here you say, "Yeah, that really interesting thought that's gone on for the last five minutes, that's empty." [Laughter] You catch it at the head. And just as it begins to come up, maybe there's not even much content there. You already know it. You know it is empty because you're looking at everything right at the head, as it begins to form. It's like catching a wave that begins to form rather than after the fact that it's already arisen.

So, if you catch every moment like that, it starts to come up by its own momentum and it starts to come automatically already expressing itself as empty. So, it has to do with the speed of realization. If you're not getting automatic emptiness at all, there's not enough speed. If you're getting it and it's variable, you have enough speed, but there's some underlying story, a limiting belief that's like a stable structure of mind that's interfering with the automaticity. So, then you've got to step back with your metacognitive awareness and say, "Okay, what are my assumptions here? What's getting in the way?" And you've got to figure that out.

And when you see that as just an empty house of cards, that it's just a construction of mind, and you're not caught up in the story anymore, then you get automatic emptiness that's not variable, but stable. Now you get emptiness cruise control; and everything comes up all by itself, automatically as empty, and everything will come up quick, quick, quick, and doesn't get expressed very much. There's only two possibilities. Most things, as soon as they come up, are automatically expressed as empty liveliness. So, they immediately dissipate and they disappear. We call that *shīla jepa*, made calm as empty. Or they come up, sometimes, and they continue to get more and more and more elaborated and there's no grab. You just watch the whole thing come up in that spaciousness and there's no grab. We call that *rangdröl*, set free as empty. Those are the only two possibilities. Most stuff dissipates as soon as it comes up. Sometimes it elaborates, but there's no grab. Either way, it's all automatic and goes by itself. There's your emptiness cruise control and everything will come up with a kind of softness to it and a buoyancy. We say like snowflakes falling in a great ocean and immediately melting. Gentle snowflakes. It's very soft and sweet, but don't look for the sweetness. That's just a side effect.

Now there's a third automaticity. It's the last one. When you have pretty much continuous awakening and you can see everything as an infinite, vast expanse of empty, limitless awareness-space, and everything that arises within that is no more than the liveliness of awakened awareness, it's all lively awakened awareness, the whole show is awareness. It's very awake and very lively. When you have what we call "the inseparable pair," you just hold the view and let everything arise. And the key is that when you hold that view, there's no mental engagement to anything.

Mental engagement, the mind moving towards or the mind moving away to make more or less of it is what causes karmic memory traces to form. So, if you can hold the view in just the right way, you're not forming any new karmic memory traces for the first time in your life. And if you continue to hold that view, it forces the mind to release all the previous storehouse of karmic memory traces at a rapid, accelerating rate. We call that process *dharmadhātu* exhaustion because it clears out all the storehouse of karmic memory traces before they ripen and influence your behavior and state of mind.

So, if you do that process, say 24/7 all the time, which becomes completely automatic, just watch it go. Everything releases itself. The average time is six years. Then there's no negative states. You completely exhaust the bin. You completely change the content of your mind. There's no substrate of negative states. And because the negative states mask the positive states, you get *gyewa*, the flourishing of all positive states. There are eighty positive states to a buddha mind.

And that process shows itself to itself by itself. It's all fully automatic. Just don't get in the way. Let the show show itself to itself, because it has its own intelligence. Once you have *sangye*, the complete purification of all negative states and the flourishing of all positive states, that's where you'll connect directly with the threefold embodiment of enlightenment and lock into the structure of ultimate reality and become that. So, it's the platform for buddhahood.

So those are the three options. Each one has a particular fault, and each one has a specific remedy to correct it.

Student 2

The markers for those are a certain amount of time. How do you know when you're, let's say just take the first one, the *samādhi*, when it's good enough? How do you know when it's strong enough? I definitely …

Dan

When it's strong enough?

Student 2

Yeah, I mean I can do all those things, but they're not always happening. They're more …

Dan

If it's variable, then there's either subtle destabilization, or it's fleeting thought, that's interfering. Those are the only two possibilities. And then if it's automatic emptiness and it's not happening at all, you don't have the speed of the intention of realization, you're not looking quick enough. If you have some degree of automatic emptiness, but it's variable, there's some limiting belief that's getting too solid, that's getting in the way. If it comes up automatically, and it's not variable, but continuous, then you have it correctly. And the marker there is the snowflakes, the softness, buoyancy.

If you are doing automatic *dharmakāya* release or everything self-arising/self-liberating, the marker there is you shift the ratio of unfolding states from impure to pure states. So, what you'll notice is what's called *drime*, which is often translated as stainless, but I don't like that translation; I like to translate it as clean. Your field of awareness will get squeaky clean. So, the calming of even the subtlest thought activity is the marker for automatic *samādhi*. The buoyancy and quickness of expressing the emptiness is the marker for automatic emptiness. And cleanness or stainlessness is the marker for automatic *dharmakāya* release. They're very specific markers.

Student 2

So, I guess let's just stick with the automatic *samādhi*. What's a good test to know when you've kind of mastered automatic *samādhi*? Like I am a hundred percent staying for thirty minutes, or I'm just trying to … Is that too specific?

Dan

Well, a good marker for all three is you have no more doubt. [Laughter]

Student 2

Okay. I'll examine that.

Dan

I've given you very clear markers. I can't give you any more clarity about the markers. If you're still asking the question beyond the clarity of the markers, then you're not trusting the markers because you have doubt. The cure for that is to trust in your own intelligence and resourcefulness to figure it out.

Student 2

Fair enough.

Dan

See, there's two issues here. The doubt's getting in the way, or what we call *jeshe*, like second guessing yourself after you have a realization, and you think your way out of it. We're very skilled at that, right? We call that *jeshe*, afterthoughts.

Student 2

Thank you.

Dan

It's good. You saw it right away. That's quick. That'll serve you well. Anything else? Yes?

Student 3

A technical question. So, when I was doing concentration meditation and I felt that I got to this automatic concentration, this state, but it wasn't stable. So, after a while, then I detect basically my mind drifts away. So, I use this little strategy basically telling myself, I would think that's my metacognitive awareness, telling myself, "Stay. Stay here. Stay here. Stay. Then we'll come back." So, after another five minutes, my mind went off again. Then I said to myself, "Stay." It's not. Okay.

Dan

At the sixth stage of the Elephant Path, what you come to see is that the very subtle fleeting thoughts, which are typically associated with reminders to yourself to keep the meditation on track, that's actually destabilizing the *samādhi*. So, if you keep reminding yourself with little instructions, however quick they are, to stay, you're actually getting yourself into a loop you can't get out of, because it won't lead to automaticity because that fleeting thought is interfering with the automaticity.

So, what you have to do is remember the two conditions for subtle level of mind. Remember them? Brightness of the field of awareness; brighten the mind up so there's no subtle dullness. And second, you have to intensify and look so closely into the object that it all becomes energy and light. It's not solid anymore. So, if you look at the light on the ceiling, when you first look at it, it looks solid, but if you look really carefully, it's all dancing energy. You look at the meditation object, the breath, the body, that closely, so it's not a solid breath and not a solid body. It's all dancing energy. Then you're going to open up all that dynamic energy and vibrancy and aliveness, but it won't be stable. Once you open it up and it's variable, ease up, a little bit—if you ease up too much, it doesn't work. Just ease up just very slightly. And if you do it correctly, smaller is better. Like the little booster rockets trying to go beyond the gravitational field, you're trying to get the capsule to line up with the space station. Smaller is better. No big booster rockets here. Smaller is better.

If you ease up very slightly, no more than the intention of easing up, two things happen. The first thing that's more noticeable is all that fleeting thought activity drops away. So, intensifying calms most thought activity except for fleeting thought. Then the rules of operation change, and easing up, the opposite of intensifying, is what calms the fleeting thought. So, you've got to let go of it and trust that the thing will go by itself.

Secondly, when you ease up in the right range, a little is better, you get a glimpse of it starting to go by itself. Then you wait a minute. If you ease up too much, you get a burst of thought activity; and then intensify again and let all that stuff calm down, come back at it. Ease away, ease away, and keep easing your way until in fact it's completely automatic. The strategies, the little labels you're saying to yourself will not work. That's why you're getting into a loop. You see there's a way out of it, and it is counterintuitive.

The exact opposite of what you're doing, which is to let go of all the reminders is what causes you to get it to be automatic. You don't realize that the reminders are not stabilizing the *samādhi*. It has the opposite effect; it's destabilizing it, because it's thinking—however fleeting it is. And it causes destabilization. You understand what I'm saying? Okay.

There's all these little things. You know this, but there's so much to keep track of, you forget it. But you know what to do when you're reminded of it. So, just go back and do it. Then you'll see it working. You know how to do this. Actually, you're quite good at it. You just have to trust yourself. We're back to that same old thing again. Trust that you know how to do this and you've done it before and you'll do it again. You've got to trust yourself. You're good with the practice. That metacognitive awareness is your best strength. Your worst enemy is your doubt. Right? You know what to do. No doubt. No doubt, fearless, just do it. You know how to do it. Just do it. You'll see the difference right away.

It's not a big adjustment. It's not going to take a lot of work to get this right. You've just got to do it right. You've got to set just the right conditions and you'll surprise yourself that it's actually easy. You're making it into a big project. It's not a project. It's easy now. Okay?

January 20, 2017

Themes: Ask Yourself Why You Are Doing This; *Bodhicitta*

[For some reason, there was no gathering on this Wednesday night; however, Dan was there and sat in his usual place at the front of the empty room to give this talk:]

Dan

In Dzogchen, or Great Completion practice, the primordial buddha state is epitomized by Kuntuzangpo in Tibetan, and Samantabhadra in Sanskrit. And Kuntuzangpo means "everything good." *Kun* means everything, *zangwa* means good. So, it's the expression of ultimate reality. And the primordial Buddha Kuntuzangpo has a property of mind called *gongpa*. It's difficult to translate it. The closest translation in English is intention. But it would have to be continuous, uninterrupted, eternal intention—it never stops. And the intention of the enlightened mind of the primordial Buddha Kuntuzangpo is to express reality for the sake of wisdom and compassion.

Every moment of the expression of an awakened mind, fully awakened mind, is a gesture. It's an invitation. And since Kuntuzangpo has a mind that operates encompassing and saturating all levels of being, all realms and all times, then that intention, from our perspective, appears in the form of the way we see this world, how it appears to our mindstream. And to every being, it appears a certain way as a gesture, as an invitation. So, the world looks this way to you as an opportunity, and as an invitation, as a gesture to see it right. And it will patiently and inexhaustibly keep presenting itself, basically to itself, over and over again until you get it.

That's why the word Mahāmudrā means "great gesture," or great invitation, because every moment is another gesture, another invitation to you to see it correctly, and through that, to evolve your own mind. That's the wisdom side of the equation. And every moment the seemingly ordinary world of samsāric existence appears the way it does, it's an opportunity to develop in your depths your own compassionate mind.

If there were no suffering beings, there would be no compassion development. So, from an ultimate perspective, there are no suffering beings—from Kuntuzangpo's perspective. But from our perspective, caught up in *samsāric* existence, it appears like there's an entire array of enormous suffering, and that's an opportunity to train your own compassion. And when you develop your wisdom and compassion to its ultimate condition, your mind and the fully enlightened mind of Kuntuzangpo are inseparable, they're one and the same. At that point, there's no suffering. There's no delusion. And you have the full enlightenment of Kuntuzangpo's mind as the same.

With respect to cyclic existence at that point, game over. Finished with that. But in so far as we're still caught up in the web of cyclic existence, the world will still appear the way it does and every moment is another opportunity. That's from the side of awakened Kuntuzangpo space.

Now, for those who aren't familiar with the terminology here, in *bodhicitta*, *bodhi* means realization, and *citta* can mean mind, but it's the honorific for mind, so it means, it's close to intention again. So, when you practice *bodhicitta* at the very beginning of your meditation practice, before you sit, we can call that relative *bodhicitta*. You're practicing from the perspective of an ordinary mind that's caught up in *samsāric* existence. But the first thing that you do is you set the intention. You set the intention towards awakening.

Now, that has several effects. The first thing that happens is if you set the intention of your practice towards awakening, there's going to be a reaction against that. You're going to bump across all those limiting beliefs, [like] awakening isn't something that you can get. The Western beliefs say you don't have the capacity, or you don't deserve it. The Tibetan limiting belief is that it takes lifetimes, so don't bother to do anything this lifetime because it takes lifetimes. It's slow. And all of those are just ideas, and ideas don't define ultimate reality. They're just interferences.

So, the first thing you do when you practice is you set aside those limiting beliefs and set the intention, because it's like if you're trying to shoot an arrow at a target, if you want the arrow to hit the target, you have to aim the bow. If you want your meditation to go in a positive direction towards awakening and ultimately towards full buddhahood and enlightenment, you have to start by aiming your practice and setting the intention.

If you start your meditation practice with that intention, it serves like a kind of central organizing principle in the backdrop of your awareness. So, you make every moment of your meditation count a little bit more carefully, because any one of those moments could be a moment of awakening to your true nature, because awakening isn't measured in the convention of time. So, you practice a little bit more carefully, and you take yourself more seriously because the practice matters. It's not good enough to just sit if it's aimless sitting. What is the goal? You think the goal is to be quiet? To reduce thinking? That's just a very mundane goal that's never going to get you out of cyclic existence. So now you can be a little bit quieter and more still within the realms of cyclic existence. So what?

You have to start with, "Why am I doing this?" And set it right. Most people today never think about that, because in the Western culture, meditation has become an end in itself. It's our way of relaxing. We never think about the goal of what these practices were designed for; so, we've lost the heart of it. I remember my first Root Lama, Geshe Wangyal. He was very unusual and I lived with him nine years in the summers while I was in college and graduate school. And what I liked about him is he rarely played the guru game. He lived his life. He very rarely gave public talks or public teachings. He had a small group of students, and that changed everything.

And I remember once, he actually accepted an invitation to a talk. It was somehow in the mid-1970s, I think it was, and I think it was in Chicago, if I remember. It was the first international conference on yoga and meditation, way back when in 1975. And there must have been about four or five thousand people who attended this thing, and it was like one sideshow after another of different meditation demonstrations and yoga demonstrations; all sorts of weird yogis were there. And he came to it and accepted an invitation to talk. Although his talk was unforgettable, because he got up on the stage and he said, "I'm not going to give a talk about meditation. Most of you came here to learn how to meditate and there are many people who will show you how to meditate. But what's more important than just meditating is that when you start to meditate, the first thought that should come to your mind is, 'Why am I doing this?' Make sure you know how to answer that question right. Think about your motivation. And if you're doing it for the sake of your own realization, and better, if you're doing that for the sake of how it will help others, that's a good way to start your meditation. It's the most important point."

That was the end of the talk and he walked offstage. And because it was so brief, it was unforgettable. And with all the yogis and the self-importance of the yogis, what struck me is the simplicity and utter truth of his message. He didn't care what people thought about him, but he said what needed to be said, because nobody at this conference was talking about the end point, awakening the mind and developing that awakening to enlightenment. So, he had foreseen what would be very much the heart of how we go about that in this culture, aimlessly. It made the point. At least it did to me.

But the second part of that is that when you set the intention towards *bodhicitta*, and the intention towards awakening, you're practicing and doing this not just for your own realization in the Mahāyāna vehicle, where you open up simultaneous mind where everyone and everything is interconnected. If everyone and everything is interconnected, then that changes the way you treat people, because you can't live in a vacuum anymore. And it's not your practice. You're doing it for the sake of how it helps others. And ultimately, if you evolve your own mind, that has influence, because in the field of big mind, awakened mind, we are all interconnected and everything that we think, feel, and do affects everyone around us in the field.

It's not like if you awaken then everybody on the planet wakes up along with you. But it is like … the strength of your realization is like planting a seed in every mindstream. And it will ripen eventually into the eradication of all negative states and the flourishing of all positive states. Everyone's practice affects everyone else. So, from that perspective, we never practice in isolation and it's never about personal gain. It contributes to the greater good.

February 1, 2017

Themes: *Phowa*; Importance of Lineage; Stabilize Awakening

Dan

Welcome everyone. You have a question?

Student 1

Dan, a number of weeks ago you spoke a little bit about the whole *phowa* training and ... well, here's the question, I have a card that has me being an organ donor.

Dan

Yeah.

Student 1

And the whole idea of preserving the body for three days is for its dissolution, and what you taught us, has made me wonder is that something I should be concerned with in terms of ...

Dan

No.

Student 1

No?

Dan

No.

Student 1

Okay.

Dan

For those of you who don't know what she's asking, *phowa* means shifting from one location to another. It's often translated as consciousness transference. And it's about how you shift your location during the dying process, voluntarily. So, ordinarily when you're dying and the body is crashing and burning, and all the perceptual and conceptual mind is dissolving, and whatever your previous momentum of your karmic tendencies is, that determines the nature of your experiences. And there are three *bardo* or intermediate states.

The first is the *chikhai bardo*, which is the *bardo* of the dying process itself. As an end point to that, the body systems systematically shut down and the perceptual systems (sight, sound, etc.) systematically shut down. Action plans and conceptual thoughts shut down. And the mind's consciousness gets more and more subtle. And then there is a series of physical changes in the body until all the systems shut down, and then you achieve what in Western terms would be called physical death. Physical death in Buddhist terms doesn't equal spiritual death.

There's an indestructible essence which is like a computer chip that's lodged in your heart at conception, and that contains the signature, the unique signature of all your previous experiences from all your lifetimes. And that indestructible essence is tied into your heart area by four energy knots, channel knots.

And during the dying process those knots loosen and the indestructible essence is dislodged from the heart area, makes its way into the central channel, and stays in the central channel for up to three days, not three days. That's the maximum point. It could leave immediately. And there's no guesswork in terms of when it leaves because as long as it's still in the body, there's a subtle, very subtle consciousness. There are different experiences of that very subtle consciousness. Once it leaves the body, that's the point of spiritual death. So that's why physical death and spiritual death don't equal each other.

During that time, whether it be one to three days or hours or up to three days, when the indestructible essence is in the central channel, then ideally you don't want to disturb the body too much because it will impact which orifice of the body the essence leaves by. So, if you leave by the crown, which is desirable, you get a human rebirth. If it leaves by your butt, you get a birth in the hell realm. The location of how it leaves is important, but not the only determinant. What determines the location by which it leaves is really your karmic memory traces from this lifetime and previous lifetimes. That's the first stage of dying.

The second is the *chönyi bardo*. I like to call that the sound and light show, a series of forced choice. Different lights appear, two at a time, and different sounds. It's like a video game that's set up and you choose all the wrong ones; and the ones that you choose determine which kind of rebirth you're going to get. But if you see all the sound and light show as just empty visions, as the liveliness of awakened awareness, and you don't see them as substantial and out there as real, then at that point, if you get the message, game over, you become a buddha; you don't get reborn.

If you miss that show, then you develop what's called the *bardo* of becoming, *sidpa bardo*. That's the one that has a lot of mental content associated with it. The nature of what content emerges tells you which of the six realms of existence—hell realms, hungry ghost realms, animal realms, god, demigod, or human realms—you're going to be born in. Why that's important in Tibetan Buddhist terms is that we say all creatures, even the smallest of insects, have awakened nature, but only humans have the metacognitive capacity to recognize awakening. So, only humans can be realized and develop not only awakening, but develop that to full realization or enlightenment.

So that's why in Buddhism, a precious human birth is considered so precious because it's the only existence that you can have where you can get off the cycle of *samsāric* existence and become enlightened. Then you have voluntary control over how you come back, and you can emanate any form you want on multiple levels of reality that help guide people along the path.

So, now as for what's called *phowa*; there are different kinds of *phowa*. The common kind of *phowa* is taught typically after you do your 100,000 preliminaries. And it consists, essentially, of using a visualization and sound to widen the upper central channel. The central channel goes from four fingers below the navel to right out of the crown of the head. It's shaped like an upside down Tibetan trumpet—it's tapered, so it's wider at the top than at the bottom.

The central channel is relatively inactive in most daily life. The only time it gets active is either during the dying process or if you do deep concentration and can perfect *samādhi* in this life. Short of that, the central channel isn't utilized in most of our waking lifetime. And because it's not utilized, it largely collapses and remains somewhat closed. So, after you finish your preliminary practices, you do a kind of *phowa* where you take an energy drop, a *thigle*, or your seed syllable, which is a protective energy drop about the size of a quarter. You visualize that at the level of your heart chakra and then you imagine successively pushing it up the upper part of the central channel by making a sound, which propels that little energy drop up the central channel. So, by sounding "hik, hik, hik, hik, hik," with each one you push it further and further up. It's like roto-rootering the central channel, the upper central channel.

And when you get it to the top, it's going to hit the [skull] plate; and if you keep forcing it up with the sound of "hik," eventually it starts to move that plate aside. The average time it takes is two weeks. And as you move it aside and open that opening, that aperture, it will result in some local inflammation of the tissue and some edema, some fluid buildup, so you end up with a little bump and some reddening of the tissue due to the inflammation that's caused by shifting that plate around. And if you do it correctly, the test that the lama gives you is he takes a piece of straw from a, say a broom, and he can stick it in there, and it'll go right through the plate. There's a hole there. It sticks straight up. If you've done that, you've done it correctly. The average time is two weeks.

Once you widen that upper central channel by repeatedly practicing this every day, it remains widened, but here's the danger. You have to put a plug on that spot and you have to plug it correctly with a seed syllable, usually an upside down *ah* or *ha*. If you're not given those instructions and you try and do it on your own and you don't know that, then there's a risk of prematurely dying because if you get hit in the head, like if you got rear-ended in a car accident, the jolt could knock your indestructible essence right out of the body, and at that point you'd die. But if it's plugged up, it can't get knocked out.

So, you have to do the practice correctly. If you do it correctly, much later in your life, when you're dying, hopefully much later when you're dying, then it's sort of like an ejection seat in a jet plane, so that when the body's crashing and burning you just take the plug out and with the sound of "hik" you compel the indestructible essence. [As the dying proceeds] and the energy knots start loosening around the heart, you can dislodge that indestructible essence from its location, compel it up the central channel and propel it out the head. If you do that, at the point that it leaves the crown, because there's no perceptual delusion or no conceptual mind to get in the way anymore, because that's gone, then not only would you become awakened, you'd become enlightened, you'd become a full buddha. Game over. You repopulate yourself into awakened *dharmakāya* space. You can either stay there indefinitely in something like storage of the potential of a realized being, or, through intention, *gongpa*, you can emanate yourself in any form or as many forms as you want on different planes of reality to help beings out. That's called a tulku or an emanation.

So, you basically gain voluntary control over the rebirth and dying process, the dying and rebirth process. Then you can come back any way you will. Now, that's the ordinary type of *phowa*, and it's called internal *phowa*, which you as a practitioner will do sometimes. And there's a controversy, at least in the Bon tradition, about whether it should be taught or not.

For example, I'm happy to say that our book on the Pith Instructions for the Akhrid Dzogchen system of Bon, is now listed on amazon. It came out today, I'm happy to say. And there, there are fourteen lessons from beginning practices up to enlightenment. Each lesson takes about a week or so to do, so it's their quick path. And then there's a fifteenth lesson that was, there was some controversy within the tradition about whether they should add it or not, and that's the *phowa* practice that we're just talking about. And some people had the view that since in this book there is what's called a *sentab*, an intense means to realize full buddhahood during a single lifetime, then don't water that down by giving them *phowa* practice as a backup plan, because it gives a mixed message. The message you want give is that you can reach buddhahood in this lifetime.

So, from that perspective, it's not included in the main instructions. Some people felt, well, not everybody has that capacity, so they won't get awakened. And therefore, as a backup plan, they should do *phowa*, and they won't get awakened in this lifetime, but during the dying process, they can become enlightened.

So, there are two schools of thought. Both have a legitimate argument. In that book it was originally not included because the view that was taken by the author was to go for it now, use the intense means for full awakening in this lifetime alone. Don't water it down. But representing both schools of thought, we found a *phowa* text and translated it and put it in the English version of this so people would have the whole set of instructions that was intended.

So, if you do your meditation and get awakened, it'll be fine; in awakening you don't need *phowa*. If you think that that's not going to be something that you're likely to do, then, in the best way, you should examine your limiting beliefs about what's possible. But if you so wish, feeling you need phowa practice, then you can do that *phowa* practice. There are many versions of that available. It's not hard to do.

There's another version of *phowa*, which is very rare, called external *phowa*. And Rahob Tulku, who we teach with, his monastery is the only monastery that's known for that. There, when a person dies, particularly if they die under some unusual circumstances, if you make a request for the lamas, out of kindness at that monastery, they will do an external *phowa*. So, let's say a person dies of suicide or they die a violent death because of a car accident or something like that, or murder, the negative states that are going to come up from the karma of that are going to highly cloud over the stages of the *bardos* of dying. So, you'll end up not going to a good place usually. Particularly if you suicide.

So out of kindness, if you petition the lamas of this particular center who know this kind of practice, which isn't very common, they can use sounds to pull the indestructible essence of that person who's already left the body out of the air like a cell phone number, using the sound of "hik," and then they bring it down into the palm of their hand, and they use sounds to soothe and comfort it, and strip it of all the negative karmic emotions, saying, "siu, siu, siu, siu." By doing that, you clean it up. And then like a bird flying, you let it loose, [Dan makes a short blowing sound, then] "hik," you compel it into awakened *dharmakāya* space.

So, you can actually intervene in what would be a bad series of recyclings—of rebirths—and out of kindness, put that person in awakened *dharmakāya* space. It's kind of like a grace experience.

Rinpoche, who's the emanation of Padmasambhava, is one of the rare people who knows how to do that practice. So, being a clinician over the years, whenever I have one of my supervisees—and that happened, myself, to one of my own clients—or if I hear of somebody who suicided, I usually talk with Rinpoche and say "let's see if we can fix this." That's called external *phowa*.

Then the other *phowa* is called *phowa chenpo*, "great consciousness transference." And that's very different. That's essentially a synonym for rainbow body. So, a realized being still looks to others as if they have a physical body. But the more they refine their realization, then the residuals of the ordinary body and mind, their hands and their fingers and toes will not be fingers and toes, they'll be streaming light rays. And the body more and more turns to light as perceived by you as the practitioner. Then there are certain practices you do during the dying process that will not only dissolve the body into light as you practice it, but it will be perceived that way by others, too. But there's a lag time there in which you change to light and nobody else sees that. That's called rainbow body. It's only a practice by great masters who have reached full stable enlightenment, and only by those who do these special rainbow body practices at the dying process.

And the reason why it's done is for inspiring trust and faith. There's a distinction that's made between practices that a teacher does to inspire the actual practices of their students by teaching what are called *sentab*, intense means, clearly. Then there are students who don't get those, no matter how much you go over it and how clear and lucid the instructions are, they still don't get it—they're lesser capacity students. The best that they can do is practice with devotion and faith, which they're not strong on. You can improve their devotion and faith with rainbow body practice.

Great masters, when they know they're dying—because a great master can know pretty much the time of their death—can tell when the dying's going to happen. By looking at certain signs, as in *The Tibetan Book of the Dead*, where these are well listed, particularly looking at breathing, you can tell exactly when the dying's going to happen. You can tell your students when you're going to die. Then a great master will say, "Okay, I'm going to die tomorrow, so put me in an isolated place in the tent or a cave and don't touch me for three days." And then what will happen is that in that practice he'll transform the residuals of the elements of the body into elemental energy and then into light. So, at the end of three days, all that's left is the inanimates of the body, which are nails and hair. And their bones and the rest of the body are all transformed into rainbow light that floats in the air and stays in the air for maybe a couple of hours and then just disappears. That's rainbow body, and it's used by a great teacher to inspire faith in lesser capacity students, because once they see that, then they take their practice more seriously.

The guy who told me the pointing out instructions, when he finished doing that, he popped into rainbow light and then popped back into his body again. That got my attention. He died three weeks later, so obviously he was doing rainbow body practice. So, I went to see some of this and somebody was practicing it. That's the rainbow body and it's used specifically to inspire faith in people. And there are many documented recordings of that in history.

Yes?

Student 1

So, to allow organs or pieces of my eye or my heart or liver to be taken …

Dan

Well, that's the exception. What the Tibetans will tell you is that ideally, because there's a difference between physical death and spiritual death, it's best not to disturb the body for up to three days, but there are signs. It's not three days. If it happens in a day you'll know. The signs are that at the point the indestructible essence leaves the body, shortly thereafter, there's blood that congeals on the tip of the nose and from the sides of the mouth, and the body gives off a death smell. When it starts to smell bad and you can see that dried blood, that means that the indestructible essence has left the body. The body's nothing anymore. If that happens in the first hour, then it's already happened. So, there's no guesswork in this. You know exactly when that process happens.

Now, here's the issue. In the Buddhist and Bon systems, compassion supersedes the dying process. So, there are exceptions here. You would not normally want to disturb the body because that disturbance could cause the indestructible essence to leave through the wrong orifice. That's why it's good when a person is going through the process of dying physically, you don't touch the body—don't hug them, don't hold their hands, because you're going to pull the consciousness out of the wrong orifice. Even though you think you're doing them a good turn, it's not a good thing to do. If you want to do anything at all for a dying person, don't touch them at all. That would be ideal. Or, you know, you can take your finger and go like this [Dan flicks his index finger gently onto the top of the skull]. It will remind them of what they know. Just flick it. Short of that, you're not helping them. Now, ideally you want to leave the body alone until the indestructible essence leaves by its proper orifice and then goes its way into what the next is, which is the *chonyi bardo*.

But there are exceptions, and compassion is the exception to the rule. If you've decided ahead of time that you are giving your organs for organ transplant, then the overwhelming compassion from that act of selflessness supersedes the dying process. The positive karmic impressions from that are much stronger than the overlay of the negative karmic impressions. So, it's okay; it won't hurt your process of dying. In fact, it will enhance it. So, we don't care what happens with the body.

Student 1

So, the right orifice will still be available if you will.

Dan

It supersedes the whole process.

Student 1

Even if the heart itself is ...

Dan

There's a precedent for this in Tibet, which the Chinese have tried to outlaw, but they haven't been very successful, at least in the mountain regions. But, most great practitioners, out of compassion, don't do rainbow body practice. That's rare. Only a few of them know how to do it or will do it for certain reasons.

The common practice for a cave and hermitage yogi is that when you die, you tell your students to take your body, bring it up to the top of the mountain, take a machete and chop it up into little pieces and saw it up into little pieces and feed it to the buzzards and the jackals, because it's over. And out of compassion you want to feed them because they're always hungry, because that's what animals are; they're always searching for food because they're incessantly hungry. So, you're softening, out of compassion, you're softening their misery, which is hunger, by giving up the body. So, if you do that, you don't have to leave the body because you're giving it out of compassion. And that wider purpose of compassion supersedes the normal rules of karmic unfolding during the *bardos*. This is no different than that, you see.

Now the Chinese have tried to sort of outlaw that practice as some sort of primitive thing, but it's still, well, we went to Mustang in Nepal. We were pretty high in some of the places, way up, and we found some places where they still had bones around. It was clear that there were still practitioners doing this thing, which is outlawed in old Tibet, but I don't think successfully. So, you have the wider purpose of compassion, and those rules don't apply. Does that make it clear?

Student 1

It does. I hang out with somebody who's very interested in the whole *phowa* world and so I've had this conversation and left with that question about it still, so thank you.

Dan

It's not a question. It's well documented that there are higher rules of compassion that supersede the ordinary rules of the rebirth process.

Student 1

Okay. Could I ask something to follow on to that with regard to that essential nature? Having come from originally a Christian background and then sort of made my adolescent declaration into refusing all of that, and then studying other things, it's all about …

Dan

I suffer from Post-Catholic Stress Disorder. PCSD. [Dan laughs]

Student 1

It seems like just a huge linguistic issue to talk about essential nature, and spirit, and God, and guidance, you know, angelic guidance or … So, I'm trying to settle all of that in my mind, and maybe it's a mistake for me to reduce it to just a linguistic discussion, and maybe not. I want to bring that to you, that's all, to see if I'm being too simplistic about it or if there really is a commonality in the discussion from all those angles.

Dan

That's a very good question. There are certain paradoxes that are built into spirituality, if you look at the two great systems of meditation in Patanjali's Yoga Sutra (the Hindu system) and Asanga's nine stages of concentration, the nine stages of staying. Many years ago, I lined them all up—the Patanjali Sutras in Sanskrit, the stages of Mahāmudrā in Tibetan, and the older Theravadan Buddhist Stages of the Path of Purification in Pali. And I discovered that the stages were pretty much identical, but that the experiences of each stage were not. And the difference was perspective. The Hindus and the Buddhists debated each other for three hundred years, and they couldn't agree. And it came down to a simple principle, what was called in the Yoga Sutras, the Hindu Yoga Sutras, *citta-vṛtti*, the continuous unfolding of the same mind stuff. In Buddhism there's *kṣaṇika*, momentariness. So, I began to understand why that was an irresolvable debate by segueing into contemporary physics.

In classical Newtonian physics we view light as a continuous phenomenon, a continuous wave propagation. In quantum mechanics, we view light as a discontinuous momentary emission of a photon or a particle, a packet of energy called a photon. You can site as many experiments that show that it's a continuous phenomenon as experiments that show it's a discontinuous phenomenon. And what physicists tell us is that you can't get around the issue of perspective. The perspective that you take makes it appear to be either continuously unfolding or discontinuous, like a momentary particle. And it may be that light is a unitary phenomenon. It may be neither a wave nor a particle; it may be a "wavicle." But we can't see it. We can either see it as a wave or a particle because we can't get around the issue of perspective.

And it's the same with the light of the mind. What the Hindu Yoga Sutras assert is the wave phenomenon, and the discontinuous phenomenon is the quantum mechanics view in Buddhism. And they're both right. So, if I was doing Burmese mindfulness and I was labeling everything that came up, there'd be a thought, and I'd label it "thinking." While I'm having that thinking then there'd be a gap in between and then I'm seeing something, so I'd label it "seeing."

Then after seeing that, I hear a sound and I label it "hearing." And then I have another thought. They're all discreet acts of consciousness with a little gap in between. That's the discontinuous perspective. Whereas when I'm doing it from the perspective of the Indian system, then as I'm having the thought, a sound comes in, and while I'm listening to that sound, I have another thought, and each unfolds out of the other like an Escher-like transformation. It's a continuous transformation of the same mind stuff. See the difference? They're both legitimate. You can look at it from either way depending on the perspective that you take. So, one of the paradoxes in the spiritual path, even though the stages are identical, is whether the path is continuously unfolding or whether it unfolds in these mind moments, discontinuously.

The other paradox that's built into the system is whether the ultimate state of the universe is conscious and personal like a god, or whether it's conscious and impersonal, just knowing. That's the paradox between the Judeo-Christian tradition and, say, the Buddhist and Hindu traditions. It depends on the perspective you take. From one perspective it seems more like the ultimate state of the universe is conscious like the god or godhead. From the other perspective it seems like it's just built into the equation; it's impersonal, brilliantly knowing awareness.

So, take your pick. They're all legitimate perspectives. Neither one is wrong nor right. You go through the same stages and they all lead to compassion; they all lead to freedom from suffering. So, if they all get you to the same place, the ultimate realization, the perspective may be a little different so I'm not sure the ultimate state is always the same with each of these traditions, but it all leads to the same consequences, which is freedom from all suffering, the manifestation of all positive states, compassion towards others. So, in that sense, you see, they're not so different.

Student 1

So, then it would make sense to just read what I am drawn to read and enjoy that paradigm in whatever it is, to the degree that it brings me further in my point of view?

Dan

Well, yes and no. Some readings are more detailed than others. I think the huge difference between Christian mysticism on the one hand and lineage traditions like the Bon and the Buddhist traditions on the other hand, is lineage. In other words, in Buddhism, you have several thousand years of an unbroken lineage and in Bon you have something like nine thousand eight hundred years of unbroken lineages. So, the precision of the instructions is like nothing else. One of my mentors when I was in graduate school was the great philosopher of science Stephen Toulmin. And Stephen talked about the difference between tight disciplines and would-be disciplines in science. Tight disciplines have an evolved precise technical language, often formalized. So, a tight discipline would be physics because a lot of its language is mathematical, it's formalized. Whereas a would-be discipline, which is not really quite a discipline yet, would be something like contemporary psychology, clinical psychology, where we have thirteen different uses of the term "borderline personality," and nobody can agree on what it means because we don't have tight terms. You see the difference? It's not as evolved, and not as precise.

So, when you have the evolution of a lineage, what gets evolved is the precision of the teachings and the preciseness of the technical terms and the languaging that works to get people there. And those are constantly being revised and then improved and passed down for future generations so that the technical precision is remarkable. Look how much precision is involved in just the process of dying, and that's just a little bit of what I'm talking about. It would take me another week just to unpack that for you in anything but broad brushstrokes. That's a lineage tradition.

Whereas in something like Christianity, that never really happened. You've got two problems. One is that mystical experience was always a threat to the Church, so you got Anthony and the early Desert Fathers starting at around the year 50 A.D. and lasting about 200 years. And on two occasions, when people were leaving the Church to go off to study with the Desert Fathers, the Church got threatened by that because they were losing their constituency. So, they hired two great scholars of the day to go out to live with the Desert Fathers systematically to debunk them and they didn't debunk them. They gave them positive billing, which made it worse. And then Saint Augustine was a great yogi, but his mother, Monica, was very ambitious for him. He had to be the big bishop of the day and she forced him to give up his meditation practice. And then after he gave it up very ambivalently and hated his mother for giving it up, he basically trashed mysticism thereafter because it was too painful a topic for him. So, it was never officially allowed in the Church after Augustine when he became the great bishop of the Western Roman Church.

And then you get pockets that occur like the Spanish mystics, like John of the Cross and Teresa of Avila, or German mystics like Suso and Tauler. If you look at Saint Teresa of Avila, it's sloppy because if you read her three books, at different points the language is completely different because she can't decide on the terms because it's all a new discovery for her. It's quite sloppy, and you can see the difference between reading her and reading a lineage tradition like in Indo-Tibetan Buddhism, because the language is very precise.

It's like what Stephen Toulmin was saying about scientific disciplines. Western mysticism is a "would-be discipline" because it never lasted long enough as a lineage to really develop its practices or its language, where in Indo-Tibetan Buddhism it did. And even within that domain of Indo-Tibetan Buddhism, some lineages are more clear than others. So, it's not so much what approach you're taking; it's more about what gives you the best instructions and the clearest instructions. That's not so established in the West because most of it didn't survive. The little that we have of the Desert Fathers is basically notes from students, and not necessarily the most reliable source.

In Indo-Tibetan Buddhism, you have to have a lifetime of proven teaching before you get asked. You have to be petitioned to write a great commentary or a new text about a certain practice. In other words, they only take the people who have proven track records at being the best at what they do to write those things. So, it preserves the best of the tradition and carries on innovations in that way. You don't get that in the West. It never really caught on to develop.

And that was one reason that the Church was threatened by losing its constituency. But the other reason was that it has to do with theology. When they sent out Johannes Cassian to live with the Desert Fathers for two years, and he came back and gave a very positive billing, the Church suppressed his book for thousands of years because they didn't like his theology. He was saying look, if you look at Saint Anthony, the first of the Desert Fathers, and all the meditators around him, he was saying that if you did these practices like the Prayer of Quiet, you became Jesus. Everybody had the potential to be Jesus. And Jesus wasn't limited to a historical figure. Now, of course, the Church didn't like that idea because if you restrict it to a historical figure, you can collect power and money and the importance of the Church and the priests, whereas if everybody can do it, it's a new movement that's part of the populace. And that was terribly threatening to the Church.

But what if it's true? What if everybody has Jesus nature and it's no different than buddha nature? What if those practices were all shared? Because there's some evidence, at least in the Bon tradition, that goes back to an ancient kingdom before Tibet called Zhang Zhung, which included western Tibet, Kashmir, the lower part of Tajikistan, Afghanistan, Pakistan, and the eastern two-thirds of Iran. That was all one kingdom. That was the original Silk Road. And Palladius, who was the guy who they hired first to debunk the Desert Fathers, the Church did, he wrote about all the miracles he saw like people rising from the dead and flying through the air and living for months without eating food. It was fantastic. And the Church suppressed that. So that's why they got Cassian because they needed a second person to debunk it, and neither one debunked it.

What I later found out is Palladius hitched a ride on a camel train because he heard that there were similar practices done by yogis in the Far East, and he ended up in what we now call Rishikesh. And he wrote a second book. This was a Catholic priest in almost 75 A.D. writing about what he observed in India in what we now call Rishikesh with all the yogis and the miracles. And there's one Bon teaching center and a text from Iran that talks about a man who stayed there for ten years called Yehus. Now it's interesting when you look at the old shamanistic Bon and find out that they have books in terms of how you raise people from the dead and how you change to rainbow body, which is essentially the same as the resurrection, and that maybe we have a source for where Jesus learned all these things because all those practices were shared. They weren't broken up into Christianity and Buddhism. They were all yogi practices and they all did them and they shared them. They all traveled along the Silk Route and they traded them with each other like trading baseball cards.

Student 1

That helps tremendously. It just makes the question even bigger than I thought it was.

Dan

Oh, it's a big question. And modern scholarship it's just about coming around to this. But the issue is where are you going to get the depth of the teachings, and there you're going to have to look at lineage traditions because that's where the language is more evolved, and the techniques are more evolved for getting people there.

Student 1

What occurs to me is that it's up to me to choose places that I listen. You know, and I come here, I listen, and that if something I read or something somebody else is teaching me does not make sense, I have to leave it behind.

Dan

From an Indo-Tibetan point of view, it seems like it's up to you to choose and you do have free will, but that's not how the Tibetans would describe it. The Tibetans would describe it as from your previous karmic propensities there are certain things that you don't really choose, you just resonate with. So, when you hear it, it sounds familiar to you because you already have a karmic connection. So, if you are gravitating towards these teachings, you would be called a *kalden*, one who has a fortunate karmic connection to the teachings of this lineage, which is from previous lifetimes. It's not the first time you've done it.

Yes?

Student 2

I don't know if this is exactly related to *phowa*, but I had an experience recently where it felt like my head almost was going to explode. I was doing a meditation that was concentrating on the head, and now I have all this unresolved tension in the head center.

Dan

What was the meditation you were doing on the head?

Student 2

I don't think it ... It wasn't sanctioned or anything by anyone; it was just I noticed a subtle pressure in the head center and I was concentrating ...

Dan

On what?

Student 2

On that locus.

Dan

Just focusing?

Student 2

Just focusing on it.

Dan

Nothing else?

Student 2

Nothing else.

Dan

And then? What happened?

Student 2

It resulted in a lot of tension and …

Dan

Increased when you focused on it?

Student 2

Yeah. And at one point it felt like it was almost going to explode. I don't know if that was related to something like premature *phowa*, but now …

Dan

Premature *phowa*?

Student 2

Yeah. But, at this point I just feel there's a lot of tension at the head center I may've done something really bad. I don't know.

Dan

Yeah, bad doggie. Don't try things on your own like that. Simple to fix. Okay, take your fist [Dan makes a fist and places it against his navel], push very hard and make circles [about six inches in diameter, up on the right side, down on the left]. Like this. Hard. Do it thirty-six times [circling] one way and thirty-six times [circling] the other way and practice that on a regular basis until you bring all that energy back down, in Chinese medicine terms, into your *dachen*. You let the winds move up the upper part of the central channel and blew out the top; so now you have to bring the winds back down to the navel area. Otherwise, you're going to continue residual effects and you'll be spacey.

Student 2

I do feel better.

Dan

So just bring the energy back down. That's all you've got to do. It's not hard to fix. If you have continued difficulty, contact me apart from this, and we'll go over it, how to fix it. But that should work. Do it for a week.

Student 3

I had a practice question about stabilizing awakening, and one part of the question would be, what are your thoughts on using King of Samādhi off the pillow?

Dan

If you can do it from an awakened mind, the vast expanse, it's superior practice to anything.

Student 3

OK. You mentioned that Akhrid book. Who is that appropriate for? Is that a good book for stabilization or which people should consider that?

Dan

It has two chapters that you want to look at for stabilization of awakening, which are unique. You want to look at chapter nine. Let's see. Nine and ten. Nine is how to set up the view of Lion's Gaze so you shift your basis out of ordinary mind to awakened mind. The task is to do it on the pillow. Don't do this Lion's Gaze thing until you have the natural state. If you don't, you're just going to think your way through it and you're going to harm yourself. If you have the natural state steady, then do the Lion's Gaze. Your task is to shift to awakening more frequently on the pillow, for a longer duration, and more and more immediately. The *tak*, the sign that you're looking for, is just the intention to look shifts your basis to awakening. That's how quick it gets. Okay?

In that text, what it will tell you is that if you keep setting it up repeatedly, each time you shift from ordinary mind to awakened mind, you are *chikba*, you are dismantling the residuals of the ordinary mind until there's no boundary between localized individual, ordinary consciousness, and awakened ocean-like mother consciousness, *dharmakāya* space. You dissolve that boundary. And then ultimately, the maintenance of awakening becomes, you learn to cultivate it so it stays automatically, so it never goes away, at which point you take it off the pillow. And there in chapter ten is a series of structured exercises you do on the pillow, [to] shift with Lion's Gaze to awakening. Once it's stable you get up and you do something else. You make a hierarchy of situations from easiest to hardest to maintain awakening off the pillow, which means like staying in nature quietly, to difficult situations to maintain awakening.

When I was doing that with His Holiness, he had me do that for an entire month. I never meditated on the pillow. The whole time, because his schedule is as busy as the Dalai Lama's, there'd be a steady stream of people outside of his room. So, I would have to sit outside his room and converse with everybody while maintaining awakening while I was conversing with them. Or I'd have to work on a computer and translate, and while I was thinking I had to maintain awakening. That's called *drewa*, mixing practice. So that will supplement what you're trying to do, those two chapters.

Student 3

We've talked a lot about the map that takes us all the way through to get to awakening. Is there a map that stabilizes awakening or is it …

Dan

There are three maps. The first goes from the beginning of the practice up to a taste of awakening, but it's not stable. The second is all of the teachings of how to stabilize awakening on the pillow and off the pillow so you have it continuously, all the time.

Student 3

Is there a specific path within that second one, I guess, is what I'm …

Dan

No, there's a bunch of teachings, all the conglomerate of teachings that have been pulled together from different places.

Student 3

All right, so it's kind of contextual …

Dan

The third is continuous awakening up to enlightenment.

Student 3

Okay.

Dan

There are three parallel tracks where you can purify karmic memory traces in emotions. That's one track. That's the easiest track. You can purify perception through the bypassing visions. That's a harder track, but quicker, where you can purify the residuals of the physical body through the inner fire track. Any one of those will set up a connection to the three-fold embodiment of enlightenment. You can do all three; you can do any one of them. They all lead you to the same place. That's the whole path.

Student 3

Are a lot of the students getting to that path or …

Dan

We have about three hundred students who have pretty much continuous awakening while working on that third map now. We have probably about thirty who can do all-at-once. No buddhas yet, but some close.

Student 3:

So, it's a third map. Is that what includes like the special powers like where you …

Dan

That's a consequence, but not taught.

Student 3

Not taught.

Dan

I have two students who are just opening up *sambhogakāya*, so they're close to buddhas.

Student 3

Wow.

Dan

And I think it's important that they're both women, so we're going to have girl buddhas in the West. You want as many girl buddhas as boy buddhas. This is an egalitarian culture, different from Tibet, which is much more hierarchical. It's happening.

Student 3

Wow. I asked that question, but when you're talking about the ... like the special skill where you open up the space. Is that like the third part of the third map where you …

Dan

You're opening. That's part of the third map. That's how you open up all-at-once-ness. Don't jump ahead.

Student 3

I'm not jumping ahead. I'm just contextualizing. Anyways, just curious.

Dan

It's what you do with that curiosity that matters. [Dan chuckles]

Student 3

I’ll stick to where I’m at.

Dan

Good.

April 12, 2017

Themes: Neuroimaging Research Into Four States Up to Awakening

Dan

Welcome everyone.

So, rather than questions tonight, I have something I want to talk about. Because about a year ago, well, you know I'm somewhat critical of the popularity of mindfulness, and I think that we should be studying the heart of the tradition which isn't a technique like concentration or mindfulness. But what we really need to be studying is the nature of awakening.

In this tradition, awakening is the confluence of all the teachings. All the different skillful means are about awakening. So, I had a student take this meditation retreat about two years ago who was a post doc in neuroscience in UC Berkeley, and he came out here to work at the neuroscience lab at U Mass Medical School. He convinced the head of the lab there, Judd Brewer, to take the course and he took the course at the same time that one of the foundation officers from the Fetzer Foundation also took the course.

So, I had lunch with them and tried to convince them to do a study on the neurocircuitry of awakening. So, we did that, and what we did is we took some of our extensive student population, so we wouldn't spend a lot of money on travel, we tried to find students who were around here. We identified forty students who we thought would have at least on and off the pillow some of the time, have a taste of awakening and think it was relatively stable but not all the time. So, we eliminated students who either didn't have awakening or had awakening too much so that we couldn't get a contrast of the waking state. Then having identified a population of students, we developed rating scales to rate the quality of meditation in four different states: [first] the Ocean and Waves, automatic emptiness; and the natural state was the second condition. The third was Lion's Gaze and setting up the view to awakening. The fourth was stable awakening.

The study involved a 128 channel EEG. It wasn't an MRI study because you can't do things in real time with MRI. With 128 channel EEG, if somebody gives you a report and says, "I just shifted to awakening," you can look at what's happening at that point in time. So, the resolution is a little less refined, not that much less than MRI, but it allows you to listen to the verbal report and mark what's going on in the brain. And it was valuable to make these rating scales because they allowed us to be more precise in terms of how we see the students. We had very high inter-rater reliability.

Of our ratings, there were three students that we couldn't agree upon because we both felt that those students were somewhat conceptual about their descriptions, so neither one of us was confident, but one of us would rate higher and the other lower. But we had cutting scores, so everybody was rated for those four conditions of meditation on a one to ten scale; and they had to get a minimum rating of six on all four measures to be in the study. By having rather strict criteria we could select people who we knew were, who had a high probability of being awakened some of the time, and then we could contrast it then when they weren't. Because the whole point was to try to come up with identification of the neurocircuitry of awakening, and we got some answers. So, it worked.

There was a meeting at U Mass, Mindfulness Neuroimaging Center, yesterday, Tuesday. Judd Brewer was there, and his staff who had done the study itself, and then Bruce Fetzer from the Fetzer Foundation was there, and he brought in one of their top science advisors from the National Academy of Sciences to give an opinion upon what the research was. And I'm happy to say that the results are stellar. They're pretty much what we would expect to happen. We found two things in all four conditions, Ocean and Waves, natural state, Lion's Gaze, and stable awakening.

We got very high activation in all thirty subjects on the ACC, the anterior cingulate cortex. But the frequency bandwidth was very high—it was in the gamma range, and that usually means intense concentration or intense focus or intensity of some sort. Because the frequency of the brain activity is the highest it can get, it's peak. So, since the anterior cingulate cortex is generally associated with effortful concentration, and it's what gets activated when you're doing the Elephant Path, my interpretation of the reason we found the ACC activation in all four conditions was that people had been highly skillful in maintaining the view stably through all those conditions, whatever that view was. They could hold the view with a certain intensity and precision. That was the first finding. There's nothing highly unusual about that.

But the second finding which is specific to awakening is that we got very high activation in the inferior and superior parietal lobes. The inferior parietal lobe, the posterior parietal lobe, is important in the development of attention in children. Neonates and infants will orient out in space, and they'll coordinate that with the gaze and taking in the world. When infants have what we call the orienting system developing, it's all superior parietal activity and inferior parietal activity. It's sort of looking out into the expanse. It's consistent with not only what young children do, but it's consistent with how the instructions are set up for awakening. You take the view of the vast expanse and hold that view and look into space, like sky gazing, or just looking at the vast expanse, the totality of awareness.

So, it's not an accident that the gaze is important and the way of looking is important. It seems to be the activation of that parietal system in setting up awakening. But the most interesting part is that awakening itself activates the superior parietal system. Animals have the inferior parietal system, but only humans have the superior parietal system. There are a couple of sub components to it. One is there's an area of the superior parietal system that has to do with perspective taking. So, if you take perspective on things, it's also the same area of the brain that gets activated when you're empathic. So, when you shift perspectives, you activate that part of the brain. There's another area connected with that where you shift from either local to global awareness or global awareness to local awareness. And that seems to be unique to awakening. So, when you set up that view of the vast expanse, at some point you recognize that you've shifted your basis to a rather different perspective because individual and localized consciousness drops out and you are the unbounded wholeness. You're operating out of this vast expanse of the totality of awareness rather than anything localized.

So, [from] what we know about brain activity, it's not surprising that the parietal system is in the neurocircuitry of awakening because it pretty much fits the instructions pretty carefully. And that you're shifting out of that localized self-operating mode to being the unbounded wholeness. So, the results are stellar. And I think it will go far to establish some credibility for what we're trying to teach. I mean, we put everything on the line with this because if we didn't find anything, of course, it raises questions about the credibility of what we're doing. But now we know this is not all just people's beliefs and subjective report; they're actually doing something quite unique and it's consistent with what we expect to be happening here.

The only thing they didn't measure was the dorsolateral prefrontal cortex, which is the metacognitive part of the brain, because you have to recognize awakening; you have to recognize that shift. I asked them to go back and mine the data and see if they can see something there, and they're going to go back and do that. They didn't think of it. I had volunteered myself as a pilot subject a couple years ago, and when I was setting up the Lion's Gaze and shifting to awakening it was mostly parietal activity, so I told them what to look for. Otherwise, it takes years to analyze the data pool because you have to take one hypothesis at a time and test it, and I said, "start with this." and it was the right one to do. So, we had some cuing about why it was important.

The scientists there were very happy with the results as was the Fetzer Foundation for putting up the money for this. They were quite amazed with the precision of the instructions and how everybody seemed to do the same practice quite consistently. Thirty for thirty of the subjects on this, but that's partly because we spent some time and care in terms of trying to get the right subjects. But they hadn't seen anything like that before. So, I think we convinced them that there's something they've got to look more into here. So, this is the start of something important I think, because it's important.

So now maybe people won't say, "Awakening, what's that?" There's something to it that's going to be a source of curiosity for people now.

Yeah.

Student 1

It is?

Dan

The natural state.

Student 1

Of those four different ones, would you see a difference in the readout depending on which state the person was in?

Dan

Not much. In terms of brain functioning in the regions of interests that we looked at, there wasn't a lot of difference. The differences were more between the first three states and awakening than those three states themselves. And that makes sense to me. But there are things that we didn't find like, there was, in mindfulness you get a deactivation of the PCC, the nonjudgmental part of the brain, and that there was some tendency for that in non-meditation meditation in the natural state, but not in the other conditions. But in mindfulness, you get a deactivation of the medial prefrontal cortex, which is self-representation. We didn't get a change in the medial prefrontal cortex in this meditation in any states. So, I interpret that as in the older Buddhism the problem of no-self comes up, you're actually shutting off the medial prefrontal cortex which is the sense of self. But in this meditation, you're going beyond self, so it's still operative; it's just irrelevant. So, you're not shutting off the circuitry. It's just not where you coming from. So, it's just irrelevant to the task at hand. You're just not operating out of it.

The findings were completely different from mindfulness. They overlap with concentration in the sense that the stability of the view seemed to be important. But there was not a lot of specificity in the neurocircuitry for those states. Everybody gave fresh descriptions of what they experienced for each of those states, and they did a linguistic analysis of that. And the difference seems to be that in Ocean and Waves, and the natural state, and Lion's Gaze they were anticipating awakening. So, a lot of the language is about awakening. Whereas when they're in awakening, a lot of the language is more conceptual because they're thinking about how to describe it. It's what we call *jeshe* in Tibetan, or afterthoughts. So, you have to figure out how to put it into words. That was the distinction in the phenomenology of the findings. But no, there were not a lot of distinctions between states.

Any other questions about it?

Student 1

Actually, I guess the reason I asked that question is because sometimes I think as I'm meditating, I'm sometimes not clear myself, which one of those I'm in.

Dan

Yeah, well that's where your metacognitive awareness comes in. You learn to sharpen that so you can tell the difference between the states. We could select students that we thought could do this, and that if it was not clear, then we wouldn't have had the confidence in how we rated them. So, it's an issue of using your metacognition to sharpen the discrimination between these things.

Anything else?

Student 2

In the test, you asked people to identify while they were in the meditative state when shifts occurred?

Dan

We did a couple of things.

Student 2

How did that work out?

Dan

We felt that the best way of getting consistent results would be to standardize the procedure integrity because a big thing in research is procedure integrity. Is everybody doing the same thing or just saying they are doing the same thing? So, we handle that two different ways, three ways: one was we were confident in the selections because we both agreed about who we thought would be in the pool. The second thing that we did is that when they had the 128 Channel EEG cap on, and they closed their eyes or opened their eyes depending on the instructions, then they had a ten-minute guided meditation that I made exactly in ten minutes. So, they had a ten-minute guided meditation in Ocean and Waves, and all thirty subjects got the same ten-minute guided meditation on Ocean and Waves.

Then there was a five-minute rest period, and they had ten minutes of guided instructions for how to refine the Ocean and Waves into automatic emptiness in the natural state. Then they rested for five minutes. Then they had another ten minutes of setting up the view with Lion's Gaze for awakening and crossing over. And then they waited five minutes, and then they continued with the crossing over, and they indicated when they were shifting to awakening. Then we measured them for ten minutes in awakening and reminded them to use their pathways of recognition in a recorded way by opening up the non-localization pathway of their lucidity pathway. So, all thirty subjects had the standardized meditations that I had made.

Then, during that rest period, they were asked to describe what they just experienced, and it was recorded and transcribed and then they analyzed the fresh transcription. So, everybody had a description of what the state was ahead of time; then they actually had a guided meditation, but then they had to describe when just coming out of that state what they experienced that state to be like, so it was fresh. And most of their descriptions as a language were from the fresh descriptions. There is a strong correspondence between the language of the first descriptions and what they actually had experienced on the tapes. It wasn't a lot of deviation and partly that's because of the nature of the teaching, because we asked people to, we used two meditation bells and have them review it just as they come out of it to make sure that they're staying on track, where they're being guided rather than going off somewhere to Never Never Land.

So, we had good confidence that they were actually experiencing what we were describing to them. And that's because we tried to select subjects that could do it. If you're spending that much money for this kind of neuroscience research, then you want to make sure that your subjects can purportedly do what you want to measure; otherwise, it's a huge waste of time and money. This is a year of the research team's work. It's a big study—thirty people; a lot of people are around them. The data analysis is infinite. But we had the advantage of knowing something about, you know, I know the practices and I know how the brain areas function, so I told them what to look for. And we were spot on with what we told them. But there are other things we want them to look into a little bit more now.

So, we now have identified the neurocircuitry of awakening, which is exciting. Then we'll probably take another three to six months to sort of put it all together, but I think it's highly likely we'll put it in some place like the proceedings of the National Academy of Sciences because it will put it on the map, and in a good way then, because everybody will want to be awakened.

Judd, I don't agree with. We have a respectful disagreement. He wants to develop a biofeedback technique to sort of train people to use the circuitry, but I'm not sure that's going to distort what we're trying to do or not. I think the feedback, actually, they had me do feedback when I went into pilot this in the lab and I found the feedback frankly to be a waste of time. It actually interfered with taking the view. Because it gets you to focus in duality and it gets you to particularize. So, it was much harder to shift to awakening when I was doing the feedback—just dump the feedback and just do what I know how to do.

But we decided the way that we would handle that is to do research the way we did it without the feedback and then identify people who either had not been able to awaken or whose awakening we rated as likely conceptual, and then see if feedback will help those people. So that's a better way of handling it than just feedback for everybody.

Student 3

It seems in some ways it could also build spiritual pride. I've got X number of whatever, however it's measured?

Dan

"I can do that." Of course, anything you can do with spiritual pride.

Student 3

Yeah. No, but when you look at the after effect, like, you know.

Dan

Yeah, I remember somebody in the early years of the biofeedback field and he had spent six years turning his gray hair back into brown hair again. He was very proud that he could do that. I said, "Well you just wasted six years. Why wouldn't you do something more important, dude?"

Student 4

So, the brain is going to be mapped for awakening, and that it could be the first …

Dan

First. Yeah. All the neuroimaging studies have been on either concentration, somewhat rarely, and largely on mindfulness.

Student 4

You may have started them.

Dan

That's what I'm hoping. Otherwise, we lose the heart of this. It just deteriorates into a technique and we lose the main essence of this tradition. The heart essence is awakening and refining that to enlightenment. If we're not doing that, we're not doing the practice. It's important.

And it's like, since the main circuitry is the parietal system, which is how infants start out in the world, it is like the child viewing the temple, taking in everything all at once for the first time. That's exactly what the parietal perception is like, so it turns out to be a very apt metaphor. Because once the executive attention system develops, we don't use the parietal orienting system of attention very much anymore. So, this allows you to redo it and modify it in a way that has a very important outcome.

Student 5

After the study is possibly published is there a next step that you are already imagining or possible, another study?

Dan

Well, I think this will establish some depth of credibility for Dzogchen or Great Completion practice. It will make the idea of awakening and crossing over to awakening very real for people. So that should, even for scientists who have no interest in the practice, it will invoke a certain curiosity, I think, about what all this is about.

But my task is to try to bring the full extent of these teachings here to the West. So, what I'd like to study is *sangyé*. If you set up the view of the inseparable pair—the vast expanse of empty awareness space and the continuous uninterrupted automatic liveliness, whatever arises within that state—and you set up that view with no engagement of whatever arises, it just runs its own course; and by not mentally engaging, you establish the conditions by which you're not forming any new karmic memory traces; therefore it forces the mind to rapidly release the whole storehouse of karmic memory traces, which is the key.

That particular practice is the key that opens the door to the third map to buddhahood. Once you open that practice up, if you do it all the time, day and night, it takes on the average six or seven years to, along the path of what's called *dharmadhātu* exhaustion. You exhaust the bin, the reservoir of all karmic memory traces. The consequence of that is the mind gets clean. And the ultimate consequence is *sangyé*. It's a compound term that means "purified flourishing," literally. So, when Mahāyāna Buddhism made its way to the north from India to Tibet, the original term for enlightenment was buddha, which means realized one. But that's not how the Tibetans translated the word *budh* from Sanskrit. They translated it into a compound term, *sangyé*, which means "completely purified and flourishing."

What it means is that if you initiate that process of self-arising/self-liberating—*rangnang rangdröl*—and you do that process all the time, then you open the pathway of *dharmadhātu* exhaustion, and at some point, you exhaust all negative states. There's none left in your field of experience. And because the negative states obscure the positive states, you get all at once all eighty positive properties of a buddha mind flourishing.

I think more important than awakening is to study the implications of *sangyé* for mental health. What would it be like to have no negative states at all for the rest of your life and have only positive states, and to be flourishing in that sense? We have students who are far along that process though no one has fully completed it. But we have students that are far along that process of what's called *drime*, or stainless, or clean mind. And that would be for me the next step, to convince them to do a study of that level of practice and its implications for knowing the neurocircuitry of that. What happens to the amygdala and fear arousal if there's no fear left in your experience, for example? What happens to the limbic system if there are no negative emotional states left? And you've eradicated what Buddha has called the five poisons. What happens to the medial orbital prefrontal cortex, which is the positive emotions and prosocial behavior part of the brain if you have flourishing?

There was a single case study done on Matthieu Ricard, who was a French molecular biologist who in his twenties left molecular biology and became a Gelugpa lama in the Dalai Lama's lineage. He, for thirty years, has mostly practiced compassion and has become much more light hearted and funny, and very warm and compassionate. They did a neuroimaging study of him in Richie Davidson's lab when he was pre-post compassion meditation. And he showed very strong activation of the medial prefrontal cortex, which is the positive emotions and pro-social behavior part of the brain, when he was doing compassion meditation. And relative to norms for that brain, the size of the medial prefrontal cortex was significantly larger and more developed after thirty years of compassion meditation.

That's the *gaywa*, the flourishing part of *sangyé*. So, we have a little data on that. I think that in Western psychology we take as a goal the eradication of negative states. If you can reduce your intrapsychic conflict in the psychodynamic tradition, or reduce your maladaptive cognitions and behaviors in cognitive behaviorism, or overcome developmental deficits and develop a new form therapy, we think that's a legitimate goal. But, the absence of a negative is not a positive; it's just the absence of a negative. Personally, I think that the development of positive states has much more important implications for positive mental health, yet we don't study them.

So, to really look at a tradition where the goal is not only no negative states but the flourishing of all positive states as dual goals, I think we need to step back and look at the larger implications of that for mental health because I think they are profound and will go far beyond what we're now doing. That's what I'd like to study next.

When Jack Engler and I did the Rorschach study at various stages of practice some decades ago, we had a couple of subjects who had achieved that level of what we're calling now *sangyé*. Their Rorschach's were like nothing we've ever seen before. They were absent of any negative states, particularly aggression related states. And they were deeply positive. So, they had completely transformed the content of their mind. But what was striking about them was not the content of the Rorschach, it was who they were when we administered the tests. They were the most present, loving people I've ever met. One of our subjects was Dipa Ma, and she had the most unusual Rorschach that I've ever seen. These were the great saints of the tradition.

But now, the good part of this is that these teachings are now readily available here. We have many students who are on that path now. We could look at that now amongst ordinary people who have developed this practice. That would be for me the next step. If we move people along the path and we have buddhas, then we look at the neurophysiology of buddhahood. We have more girl students than boy students approaching buddhahood. I suppose that says something for the West. Well, it's a healthy competition in there. Yeah. So, I thought it was worth sharing because it says something about what we're trying to do. I'm happy that we got the results because it makes it more real.

Some years ago, we did work with a tachistoscope, a high-speed electronic board that can flash events in thousandths of a second. We were looking at the speed of the mind in meditators. We worked with Western mindfulness meditators first and then we brought the equipment over to Dharamsala, and the Dalai Lama gave us his best concentration meditators, the Elephant Path meditators. And then we would determine what their visual threshold was. We would show blips of light on the screen in thousandths of a second and we would vary the duration from ten to forty to a hundred milliseconds, and we could determine the exact ratio with the critical threshold of how long we had to leave it on the screen so they would have a high probability of recognizing it. It's called a recognition threshold.

And having done that and showing that meditators could pick up and then process things much quicker than ordinary mind people, we did an interesting experiment where we held the blips of light at their threshold and repeatedly showed them the same thing at exactly that threshold. We asked them to describe what they could see, just at the point where they could begin to recognize it. It was an interesting study and a lot of the things that came out of it were that for most people they reported that the field of perception was nondual at that point. But that was the last study I did and that's why I stopped doing research. Because, well, first of all, it was very difficult in those days to do research. It was all out of pocket, there was no grant money, and professional peer-reviewed journals wouldn't accept meditation stuff.

I remember we did a study on cold pressure pain. You take your hand in circulating ice water and generate a certain pain quickly from that. And Jack Hilgard had done a study on giving people hypnotic suggestions so that they would put their hand in the ice water and they'd rate the pain from 1 to 10, 10 being maximal, and in five seconds or ten seconds they'd give you a report of the pain. And in the waking state they go 1, 3, 5, 7 and in about a minute they take their hand out. But, if they were given a suggestion that they would still feel something but it wouldn't be painful, then under hypnosis they would go 1, 3, 0, 0, 0, 0, and leave it in for five minutes, and they wouldn't take it out. So, you could block the conscious perception of pain with hypnotic suggestions.

So, we repeated the exact same paradigm research that Jack Hilgard had done with mindfulness meditation, people who had meditated on a three-month retreat before and after. And we found that they could leave the hand in the water a long time, but unlike in the hypnosis where people would say that they wouldn't feel anything, in the mindfulness they would still feel sensations, there were strong sensations, they just didn't interpret it as pain. So, it was an interesting finding, and we looked at the difference.

So, I submitted the paper to the *Journal of Abnormal Psychology*, which is where Jack published all of his hypnosis papers, and they sent it back, un-reviewed, saying "not appropriate for this journal." And the only difference was that it was on meditation rather than on hypnosis. So, I replicated the study the following year with three times the sample size and much better statistics and sent it in to the journal again. The same person sent it back without reviewing it and said, "Not acceptable."

So, I waited a year, figuring he wouldn't remember, and by then I took the computer and I crossed out the word "meditation" and I put in the word "hypnosis" and submitted the same paper, and they accepted it with no revisions. Then I wrote them again. I pulled the paper and wrote them a letter of protest and explained what they had just done, that this is journal bias. That's how hard it was to get anything accepted in those days.

So that was frustrating. But the thing that changed it for me was when we did this threshold experiment. They had a woman who had very strong, stable, not just awakening but enlightenment, and she said, "I can do what you want, and I can hold the mind at threshold, and when there's a blip on the screen I can tell you at lightning speed when that blip occurs, but you have to understand that when you ask me to respond to the blip on the screen you're pulling me back into ordinary reality and duality, as if there's a blip out there. And I can do that at any speed you want. But tell me, can your machine measure awakening?" And I thought about it and I said, "You know, we're not going to be able to get at what we want to get at with this research. It's just not going to do it." And that was the last day I did research. And I thought it would be more valuable to teach people how to do it as an experience instead. That's why I hadn't done any research beyond that.

So, again, it's important, the science. If anything, it helps people with their doubt, and makes them a little more trusting. But, ultimately, it's about practice. The science isn't going to make people practice. It might make people more curious about the practice, but there's no substitute; they've got to do the practice.

Anything else on this topic? Anything you want to talk about before we take the break, other than this topic?

Student 6

I'm thinking of someone who I see in therapy, who tries really, really hard. She definitely adores her children and she tries very much to be a good mother. But she's divorced and her husband is really difficult. And the kids go back and forth, and given the whole dependent nature of all this, I guess that's something, as a therapist, I find really difficult because you're working with the one person, and the other people are still into what they're into …

Dan

Mm hmm.

Student 6

And it's hard for that person to just barely make a step at a time to maintain that, given all their circumstances.

Dan

Yeah, well, all you can do is focus on coping enhancement in the face of the difficulties.

Student 6

It's like she can make progress but then given the force of the other people's reactions …

Dan

If she makes progress, it will affect the kids.

Student 6

Yeah.

Dan

That's the best you can do.

May 17, 2017

Themes: Spiritual Duties; Lineage; Practice and Protect

Dan

Welcome everyone.

So usually what we do is we leave this open for discussion of whatever questions get raised about either your meditation practice specifically, or spirituality in daily life, and then we discuss that for the first hour and then in the second hour we translate that into a practice.

But I'm going to make an exception tonight, a rare exception. I want to bring up the topic tonight. I want to talk about spiritual duties. In Tibetan it's *damchik*, or in Sanskrit it's *samaya*. And the reason why I want to bring it up is because in a couple of weeks I'm going to do a very advanced course, the first time we've done it, with Asonam—Geshe Sonam—on inner fire practice, teaching all the levels of inner fire practice, in Switzerland. And we have almost fifty advanced students coming.

All the students know the rules. The rules are that if you're an advanced student and you want to take an advanced course, you have to be followed up with your teacher and get their permission to attend the course. And recently, I got the list of participants, but 70 percent of the people never cleared the course with their teacher, even though it says on the website, "Don't sign up." So, we're getting lazy here about spiritual duties, and it's not acceptable to me. If you don't follow basic simple rules, then all the teachings disappear. So, I thought it was important that we have a refresher course on what *samaya* means, or what *damchik* or spiritual duties means.

It's a term that's misunderstood in the West. A lot of times it's seen by some distorted understanding of a relationship with a tantric master: they take on your weird karma and do crazy things, and whatever they ask you to do, you just do. That's a complete distortion of the tradition. It has nothing to do with that. And often times it's used as a rationalization for poor behavior. So that's not a good understanding of spiritual duties.

I like to think about spiritual duties much like in the West where the closest thing we have is legal ethics—duties owed to different parties in a fiduciary relationship. In a fiduciary relationship in the West, the senior party owes a duty to the junior party to put the junior party's welfare and their growth above everything else, and to not bring their own needs into the relationship. So, parent-child relationships are fiduciary relationships. Doctor-patient relationships are fiduciary relationships. Spiritual directors and spiritual followers are fiduciary relationships. Teacher-student relationships are fiduciary relationships. So, as the senior party you owe duty to the junior party to put their welfare before anything else, and not get your own needs messing it up.

In the West, the idea of spiritual duties, viewed in legal ethics terms, are duties owed in fiduciary relationships, each party owing a duty to the other party. So, for example, as a psychotherapist, I owe a duty to my patient to use the very best and updated techniques that I know, and to keep up with the field so I bring them the best methods to get them better. I owe them a duty of using everything that I know, and not bring my own personal needs into the relationship. And I owe them the duty to be transparent and honest. Those are the fundamental duties of a therapist towards the patient. Meanwhile, the patient owes duties to the therapist. The patient owes the duty that they show up physically and emotionally, and they work consistently at what's being recommended. They owe a duty of honesty, that they don't lie about their condition, and that they are honestly disclosing. If there's deceit in the relationship, it's not going to work.

So, as you can see in something like doctor-patient relationships, there's an exchange of mutual duties owed. And it's like that in the Essence traditions. The Essence traditions are the *tantras*, Great Seal or Mahāmudrā (*Chaggyachenpo* in Tibetan), and Great Completion or Dzogchen. Those are the three Essence traditions in Indo-Tibetan Buddhism. And what's unique, particularly in Dzogchen, or Great Completion, as the name implies, is that the techniques complete the path to full buddhahood, to enlightenment. And the fundamental experiences that all the teachings are designed to lead you to [is] the direct experience of awakened awareness, in your own experience, and to stabilize that awakening, and to develop that awakening to full buddhahood.

So, special methods are used to explicitly point out to you the true nature of the mind so that you can directly realize it. Without that set of instructions, most of these things would never occur to you. So, the likelihood of you encountering awakening on your own would be almost zilch. But with these precious detailed instructions, for every level of your practice, that guide you to awakening, we basically use the relationship to walk you through the practice to awakening. That's why all the meditations are guided. That's a very unusual approach to meditation.

Then, if you use those techniques for awakening, that's the first map. There are three maps here. There's a set of methods that guide you to awakening. There are the methods that stabilize awakening so that you have it all the time on the pillow, all the time off the pillow, waking state, deep sleep, and dreaming, so you're awake all the time. That's the second map. And then there's a third set of teachings that take that continuous awakening up to full enlightenment. That's the third map. And in each one of those maps, there's a whole set of explicit teachings that you would never otherwise encounter, that bring you along, that guide you along very precisely along the path, as you know. Or, as one of our students said, "This is GPS for the mind." If you make a wrong turn, we will immediately tell you that and keep you on track. Sometimes these are called *sentab* in Tibet, intense means. They single mindedly keep the focus on you getting the direct experience of awakening, developing that awakening, and then bringing it up to enlightenment.

So, that you get such detailed explicit instructions is a gift. They say it comes from the kindness of the lineage holders of these lineages. But there's an exchange. There are duties owed. Each party owes a duty. That's where this notion of spiritual duty comes in. If you're given special teachings that open up levels of mind that you wouldn't even know existed without the teachings, then there are certain duties that you owe. You're not given them for free. And that's what I want to review tonight, because it's an exchange.

There are certain things that in giving you these precious teachings—they work, you know they work—we expect certain things back. And, if you're given precious teachings that open up things like moving beyond time, and Ocean and Waves, and opening up the natural state of the mind, and if you're given explicit crossing over instructions to shift your basis to awakening, that's a gift. That's a very precious gift. And without these instructions, in this lifetime, you'd probably never encounter anything that would come close to this. So, the best students understand the preciousness of what they're getting.

So, the first duty is to listen and take what you've heard and practice it. There's a famous passage from the Bon master, Ri khrod, whose nickname means "the great hermit," because he liked his hermitage site. First you must hear the teachings, *derpa*. It's not enough to hear the teachings, you then have to listen to them. It's not enough to listen to them, you then have to reflect on them, *sampa*. It's not enough to reflect on them, you have to develop a general intellectual understanding overview of them, *gowa*. It's not enough to have an intellectual understanding of them, you then have to put it into meditation practice, *yamsu lempa*. It's not enough to put it into meditation practice, you have to see the signs of the progress of your meditation in your direct mindstream, *takpa*. It's not enough to see the signs of progress, you have to develop the realization, *tokpa*. It's not enough to develop the realization, you have to integrate that realization into your mindstream. It's not enough to integrate the realization into your mindstream, you have to practice it, you have to manifest it in your conduct towards the welfare of all sentient beings.

Those are the steps of what it means to take the teachings and put them into practice. Listening, *derpa*, [rather] first hearing them; [then] listening to them, *yempa*; reflecting on them, *sampa*; come to a general intellectual understanding of them, *gowa*; *yamsu lempa*, put them into meditation practice; practice continuously until you see the signs of progress, *takpa*; thinking about [or developing] the realization, *tokpa*; integrating that realization so you have it all the time in your mindstream, *kindu*; manifesting that realization as conduct, *trinlé*.

That's the expected duty. In other words, if you have something that's given to you that's very precious, it's like being given a seed. You don't throw it away. You plant it in good soil. You water it regularly and give it nutrients. You give it sunlight. You develop it. And it blossoms.

So, if you're given the precious seed of the teachings, you have to develop it in your own practice, especially if the realizations lead you somewhere. We've kept stats for about ten years now. In all the Level 1 retreats that we do, about one out of three people will get a taste of awakening, however unstable, in their first retreat. That's not bad. It means the teachings mostly work. But, of the people who come to the retreat, about 20 percent actually follow up with being followed by a teacher. That's not a very good track record. Most people take another workshop, another meditation course, and they manifest what Rinpoche calls the *dharma* flea market. They can't see the preciousness of the lineage teaching. It's just another meditation workshop. We've had people who've had strong and stable awakening who never practice. They just throw it away. It's unfathomable to me.

I remember seeing a student from Europe who came to our course for the first time after twenty years of Zen, who got a stable awakening in the course. It lasted for about six months, and she wanted to take an advanced course, the one that we were doing in Europe. She couldn't fit it into her schedule, so she wanted to take one we were doing in California, but the course was full. So, she called me and asked me as a special favor to see if I could get her into the course. There was no trouble fitting her into the room, but there was no bed space. So, it was a lot of work to arrange for her to come. And since she was coming from Europe, she wanted to go see Rinpoche, so I arranged a special audience for her to visit Rinpoche. Two days before the workshop, she canceled. Didn't see Rinpoche, didn't take the course, dropped out of everything because she met a Western person who claimed they were from the Sufi tradition, and she found her true teacher from a past life—no credentials, no lineage. Western arrogance. That became her teacher. And threw away her awakening and threw away the chance to develop it. Stories like that break my heart. People can't see the preciousness of what they're getting. But, what to do? There are many stories like that.

So, if you get something that's precious that comes from a lineage tradition, then your primary duty is to listen to it, and to put it into practice, and develop it. The Tibetan word is *chungwa*, which we often translate as "develop it," but it really means to nurture it like a baby, like a precious baby. That's your primary duty. If you don't put into practice, whatever you got is lost not so long thereafter. So that's your primary duty. And the texts are very clear on this. I mean, there are other duties, but if you're given something that's young and fresh in your mind, if you get even a little flame of awakening, then your duty is to take care with it, be careful with it, nurture it. Set up the view so you have it repeatedly. Develop it so you have it more frequently, for longer duration, and more immediately, until after a while it doesn't go away. It's always here. That's your duty. I can't do that for you. No teacher can do that for you.

So, that's the primary duty. And some people think this issue of conduct is more complicated, you see, because we want you to be kind towards others. We want you to not be selfish in your practice. But we don't want you to go off and take an unstable awakening and then immediately go out and devote your life to serving people. The primary duty is to develop the practice so it's stable. Then, it normally develops into conduct towards helping others. But you can do that too prematurely. The main conduct that you have if you're given precious teachings is to develop the precious teachings that you were given and put them into practice, and to get the realizations in a stable way, to integrate them into your mindstream. That's your primary duty with what you're given.

There are other duties that come with this. These teachings are often kept secret. Most Dzogchen teachings are secret. It's very rare to get explicit details about crossing over instructions to awakening that you get in these courses. It's very rare to get the core instructions that open up the map to awakening, the self-arising self-liberating instructions. They're just not given out. And the reason why they're not given out is because if you try to think your way through them conceptually, it hardens the mind and actually precludes awakening. And precludes enlightenment. So, they're not given out, so that they don't lose their potency. But if you take the time and care to concentrate the mind, to go through the stages of emptiness practice, to develop Ocean and Waves, and a sealing practice so you have automatic emptiness, and to refine that automatic emptiness to the natural state, when you have the natural state, any conceptualization as soon as it arises is expressed as empty. Any kind of doing anything is expressed as empty. So, you're not going to will your way into awakening; you're not going think your way into awakening. It's the first time, if you have the natural state, that automatic emptiness is like a clearing agent for all conceptualization and all kinds of doing. So, it's the one time you can actually use the instructions and get them to work. Then the instructions work.

So, your duty is to follow the path carefully and to put it into practice. But you have a duty to protect the instructions. They're not for sale. If you're given these precious instructions, it's understood that they're for your own personal use. They're given to you from heart-to-heart, from generation to generation. They're not commodities for sale. And we have trouble with that in the West. Look, we've destroyed the entire music industry in the West by free downloads. Precious crossing over instructions to awakening, precious instructions that open up the third map to enlightenment, precious instructions for the threefold embodiment of enlightenment, those aren't given out to be disseminated. They're given out because we have a special relationship with you as part of a lineage, and for you to see the preciousness of them and use them accordingly.

They're not to be recorded. They're not to be used for personal gain or for self-importance. We get all sorts of twisted understandings of that.

We've had people try and secretly tape this stuff and we catch them on that. Even though they can't tape it—we tell them not to—they do it anyway so they can use them in their own teaching, whatever they want to do. It's not like ordinary stealing. If you try and take these instructions and use them for personal gain, you will piss off the *ḍākinīs* and you do not want to piss off *ḍākinīs*. That's your karma. All I can do is warn you about that. Don't piss off the *ḍākinīs*.

We've had people try and take the material, transcribe it and teach from it with no teaching ability whatsoever. One guy we caught recently. At least some of our students are protective of us. So, if they find people trying to steal the material, then they come back to us, mostly. One guy tried—he was in a different country so he didn't think we'd find him. So, he was going to do a day on the Elephant Path and another day on Lion's Gaze in everyday life. What is Lion's Gaze in everyday life? The most precious crossing over instructions he was going to use in a trivialized context because it was a neat new thing he'd found. Now, this guy had signed two forms saying that he understood that the teachings were for his own personal gain, and not to be used in any other context. What about "no" do you not understand here? So, his defense was he claimed that he didn't learn them from me, he learned them somewhere else. We said, "Well, you signed two forms here and if you want to go before a judge and argue that case, I'd be happy to do that, and donate the profits to the Tibetan causes we're funding." He decided not to do that. That was a lot of work. A lot of wasted time. And I find I spend a lot of wasted time doing this kind of stuff.

Now, because 70 percent of the people didn't [get approval to] sign up for the inner fire course, I have to take most of my time this week and next week, which is mostly full, and pack in all these extra interviews. Why am I working so hard? What is your spiritual duty here? It says on the website, if you want to take an advanced course, don't sign up for it. You have to get permission from your teacher. What about that is not clear? These are the residuals of self. The arrogance of self to think, "Well, I'm entitled to do this because I've taken other courses. I don't really need to follow with my teacher." Where's that going to get you? If that's the attitude, your practice will bottom out at some point, develop the illusion that you're actually getting somewhere, but you're not going to get anywhere real. Because it won't work.

So, the main duty is put it into practice. The second duty is don't disseminate the teachings in a way they lose their potency. They're not for sale. They're given freely from heart-to-heart. It's a special relationship. It's based on a karmic connection. We are all *kaldens*, ones of fortunate karma. Don't reverse that, because if you sever the spiritual duties, they're not repairable. It breaks my heart. And it's all about self-interest, the same thing that gets in the way of everything.

When Guru Pema, Padmasambhava, gives a precious instruction that's secret, he ends it by saying, "*Gya, gya, gya.*" "Seal, seal, seal." And Rahob is the emanation of Padmasambhava for this generation, as you know. So, what does "seal, seal, seal," mean? It's means seal your lips about it. Shut up and practice. Don't use it for other things. But the best Western translation of "seal, seal, seal" is, "Don't fuck it up." You've been given something precious. Don't fuck it up. Because if you misuse it, you lose it. Doesn't come back again.

If you try and use it for selfish reasons, that's completely contrary to the spiritual ends of these practices. So, the practices automatically bottom themselves out, and these teachings have a way of protecting themselves. I remember once, we were having a private dialogue with a Western scientist who had done a lot of work on paranormal ability, particularly psychokinesis, how the mind can move things in visual space. And I had set up a private dialogue with him and the Dalai Lama. And the Dalai Lama wanted to see if Western scientists would study paranormal abilities and was willing to supply people who could fly through the air and walk through walls. And of course, very few scientists wanted to put themselves, their careers, on the line by saying they were studying these controversial things. Except one, who had done a lot of good work in the area, and he was Bob Jahn, the head of the engineering school at Princeton.

And then during that day, I said to the Dalai Lama, "Look. Look what the West did with the atom bomb. They used nuclear power for destruction. If you open up these psychic powers through Western science, why wouldn't that happen in the same way? Why wouldn't people, who are unprepared for this, misuse these psychic powers for destruction of this planet?" And the Dalai Lama laughed. He said, "You don't understand. These have a way of protecting themselves. It's built in. If somebody has developed some of these abilities and they start misusing them, then they lose the abilities. It's automatically built in."

You can't do these things out of self, operating out of self-mode. So, if you try to take the teachings and use them for self-interests, so you can use them in your teachings or use them for whatever self-importance you're trying to get, you lose the realizations. And they don't come back. That truly breaks my heart.

So, I'm asking you not to get lax in your spiritual duties. They're not hard. Practice sincerely what you've got, understand the preciousness of what you're getting, put it into practice diligently, don't disseminate the teachings, don't use them for personal gain. That's it. Protect them. And follow with your teacher on a regular basis. What's complicated about that? That's not a hard requirement. But I've been noticing more, as we do more advanced courses, a tendency to get more lax, to follow less, because you think you're advanced. That, my friends, is spiritual pride. And the further, not the less, you get along the practice, the more at risk you are for spiritual pride. Because you think you're beyond being followed by a teacher. That's not going to go anywhere good. It's a problem. And if that persists, and that's the general consensus of the community, then the teachings disappear, my friends. You've got a precious opportunity here. Don't fuck it up.

We're going to give you everything, all the way to buddhahood, in this lifetime. Use it wisely. Use it with heart. That's my advice to you. And no matter how you think you're advanced in your practice, continue to honor your relationship with the teachers who gave it to you. Then you'll get everything you need with nothing held back. It's a simple contract of exchange. Honor the teachings, you'll get more. Disrespect the teachings, they stop.

The inner fire course is like the Lamps course. It's the most advanced course that we're doing. We've not done it before. It took a lot of work translating the texts. It took a lot of work getting some convincing credibility and trust that they would actually allow us to teach this. Like the Lamps, it's probably the most advanced course we've done, even maybe more so. It's taken three or four years to set up to do this, and 70 percent of the people don't get permission to do it? That, my friends, is not acceptable to me. You've been given a great gift. These practices aren't given out usually without a hundred thousand preliminaries. Because of my relationship with the teachers, they've exempted you from that. Out of kindness. You've already got a great exemption here. Don't push the limit.

What we're asking you to do is something really simple. Follow with your teacher regularly. But don't have the arrogance of just signing up without following because that's not going to work. Because as soon as that starts to happen on a regular basis, the teachings will disappear. So, it's up to you about how this moves forward. All of you. Not just in this room, the whole *sangha*. I've done this at great personal sacrifice. It takes all my time and most of my health these days. Meet me halfway. Do the practice, follow with your teacher. If I don't feel that that kind of output is coming, I won't do it. It's up to you now.

If you follow and listen to what I'm saying, you will get everything you need, all the teachings up to buddhahood. There's a plan here. But I'm not going to open up the rest of the teachings in the third map until I get a better response in terms of spiritual duties. Take what I'm saying seriously. And until I see that really happening in our community in general, I'm not going to open up the rest of it. So, mind my words carefully. Because your practice and what you do or don't do in your practice is my karmic debt. I've chosen to open these practices up to the West. What you do is on my head. That doesn't matter to me. It's not important. What matters to me is that you have the realization. It's the only thing that matters.

Please understand what I'm saying. It's bordering on not good enough anymore. Each advanced teaching, we get less and less involvement of people following with the students. But the trend has got to turn around. It's probably not the best place to say, here in Boston, because I'm here more, so you follow more consistently here. So, I'm not blaming you as students here, the ones that are here tonight. But I'm speaking to the larger community.

So, it's important. This is a relational based way of teaching. We've given something special in the relationship, but you're expected to do certain minimal things with it. Practice, use it, don't misuse it, and manifest better conduct in your life. Those are the three duties. They're not hard. And follow with your teacher. They're not hard.

See, this is an unusual experiment. I've worked with the Tibetans for forty-five years now, and we've been able to convince some great teachers to exempt you from the hundred thousand preliminaries in exchange for the promise that you could actually do these practices without doing that. But when you stop seeing teachers on a regular basis and you think you can do it on your own, it's not going to be very convincing to the people that we've asked for the exemptions. So, you put me in a funny position with that. Because the minimum requirement was at least you're being followed on a regular basis so the teachers can correct some of the things that would otherwise get in the way from you not doing the hundred thousand preliminaries. I'd like this experiment not to fail. They're simple requirements and they're not hard to do. Let's open it for your reactions and discussions about it. Please use the microphone.

Student 1

I really appreciate what you're saying. And I think in my life, personally, I have noticed an interaction between character development, the practice, and conduct that evolves out of that and I really appreciate that. And I don't know if, I'm wondering if there's anything more that you want to say about that.

Dan

Well, yeah. Most of you know this, but some of you don't. Maybe in the early 1970s, that's a long time ago, Jack Engler and I gave Rorschach ink blots to people at various stages of practice, mostly in the mindfulness tradition, the Burmese mindfulness tradition, though not entirely. And what we found was that when people, before they did any practice, when they looked at the ink blots, they saw bats and butterflies and people and they projected images, content. When they got deeply concentrated, they saw ink. They stopped making content. They saw the color and the shape and the shading and they didn't make it into anything. When they got to Ocean and Waves practice, the Rorschachs went on indefinitely, we had to stop them at six hours. And the next day, they gave us completely new content. And when you open up the all-at-once simultaneous mind, it's infinite content. When they had a taste of awakening—in the Burmese system, there are four gradations for awakening, there are four levels to it. And the thing that drops off in the first level is reactivity to experience, *dukha*. Those Rorschachs looked like ordinary Rorschachs. But, if we scored them with the Holt system, the defense, demand defense effectiveness, which is another way of saying what we found is that they still had a full array of conflicts, but they were not reactive as conflicts, they were not defensive, it just was right out there. But what was disturbing was that [with] some of those people who had a legitimate taste of awakening, the Rorschachs in Western terms we would say represent personality disorder. Even though they had a genuine spiritual realization, it hadn't changed their character structure one bit. And that helped Jack and I understand the guru game a little bit. You can get teachers coming over here from the East or Western self-realized teachers who can have legitimate spiritual realizations, but they haven't transformed the character structure of their mind, so they can still have a lot of problems and sometimes some of them are personality disordered. They may not suffer by virtue of being less reactive but their behavior is going to make lots of other people suffer.

But then when we got to looking at people who had achieved some degree of *dharmadhātu* exhaustion—where you eradicate all negative states and only have positive states left, much further up the path in that third map between stable awakening and enlightenment—then those Rorschachs were like nothing we'd ever seen before. They were completely absent of any negative states, especially aggression related states. And what was memorable wasn't the content. What was memorable about it was the delivery. They were the most present, loving people we've ever met. They were the great masters of this tradition.

So, what Jack and I realized is that even a taste of awakening doesn't necessarily change personality structure. And for people who have a full array of context, awakening gives you a perspective on how you might begin the path of changing all that. But it's much further along the path that you actually eradicate all negative states and cause the flourishing of all positive states. That's a much more difficult attainment.

So, the disturbing realization is that spiritual realizations at that level of practice don't necessarily change people's problems. And that's why the issue of spiritual pride is even more problematic. Because then people can use their spiritual realizations and claim something from that; and that leads to spiritual pride, self-importance.

I remember once we were teaching at Kripalu—and I like the Berkshires—Gretchen and I taught there for three or four years. We showed up to do another Level 1 course, and they told us that the faculty residence was taken, that we're not going to stay there. They didn't tell us ahead of time. It's a nice building where the faculty stay and they can talk with each other and it overlooks the Berkshires. It's really nice. So, they put us in a regular room without telling us. And the room wasn't even clean. There was a broken glass on the floor, so we are walking on our bare feet and cut our feet up. And I say, "What happened to the faculty residence?" "Oh, that's for such and such a teacher and her attendants." "Who is this person?" "A Western teacher, self-realized teacher."

Her whole realization was going to the Ganges and looking in a *sadhu's* eyes. And that was her whole practice, ever. And she wrote a couple books and got famous from her books. No lineage, no practice. And she took over the faculty residence for her attendants—she had six attendants—and squeezed out myself, someone who represents the Tibetan lineage, and a Tibetan Zen master from Japan. They didn't have room for us because of her attendants. And I said, "What kind of spiritual pride is this?"

Now, I taught morning, afternoon, and night myself, personally, in a relationship. Her teaching was you watch video tapes of her talking about her realizations. And then she comes in once a day with some self-importance and gives a two-hour question-and-answer period. That's the teaching. So, I said to Kripalu, "If you can't tell the difference between a lineage tradition and this Western garbage, you'll never see me again." I haven't been back since.

But, see as Westerners, we can't tell the difference often. You get people who are self- realized and they talk about their own realizations, but they don't have a method. Because they didn't learn it in a lineage where they learn the methods. There's nothing wrong with their realizations. They're probably legitimate. But you've got to watch that they don't go off in the prideful direction. I have to watch for that all the time.

I remember going in and seeing Menri once. I think it's convenient working with a teacher who reads minds because I walked in, I didn't say anything, and he said, "You're doing a lot of teaching. Watch out for the spiritual pride." And I said, "Busted! Thank you." If you learn one thing in spiritual practice, one thing, it's that self-importance isn't terribly important. If you learn only that lesson, your practice is good. Until you start thinking it's good, then you've got spiritual pride on your back again. [Dan laughs]

So, in answer to your question, you see, it doesn't change personality structure that much at that level of practice. It's much further along and then it changes everything.

Student 2

I'm humbled by what you're saying, for sure. I don't know that I have a teacher to follow me. Is that because I haven't done Level 1 yet?

Dan

Yeah.

Student 2

So, I'll get one. And then I'll be in trouble. Then I can be in even more trouble. [Laughter]

Dan

Look what you have to look forward to. [Laughter]

Student 2

So, the other question I have, it's very relevant. I was invited to, I live in North Kingstown, Rhode Island. There's a senior center. A request was made that I come and teach meditation. I don't feel qualified to teach at all what you teach, but I could tell seniors the basics that I learned even before I met you. Posture, breathing and focus. Is that something I should not do?

Dan

Should not do.

Student 2

Okay.

Dan

They're lineage teachings. They're not done that way.

Student 2

Okay.

Dan

But we have a network of people we've trained. Certainly, if you ask, we will find a way of accommodating going there.

Student 2

Well, Ann is local. And maybe I'll let her take that on instead. I don't know if ... In any case, it was timely that you brought this up. But regarding the spiritual pride, since having met you guys, I have far more confidence in the identity, it's almost touching for me that I actually have an identity that is an essential nature [voice quivering with emotion].

Dan

Ah. Good for you. You're understanding something here.

Student 2

It's brought me a level of confidence in living. Is that a slippery slope?

Dan

No.

Student 2

No.

Dan

No, it comes from the heart. Your realization just that moment was very genuine. It moved you.

Student 2

Oh, definitely moves me.

Dan

So, you see it's clear, it's crystal clear. It's also important that you came to this realization just by coming to the Wednesday night classes and not by doing the full retreat.

Student 2

That's right.

Dan

You got it through the instructions anyway.

Student 2

I never saw myself as precious and now I do, and the notion that I can do the practice [gives me confidence].

Dan

And also, if you know the realization strongly, then the teachings are rather simplified because everything comes from that state.

Student 2

Yay.

Dan

When we were with His Holiness Menri Trizin in May, he was healthy enough to follow through with a teaching. He did something rather extraordinary ... so how many of you were there? You were there, right? You were there. It's very extraordinary because what he did was give a teaching where there is sort of a lesson plan from the beginning of the practice with the preliminaries up through full buddhahood in fourteen sessions. Sort of like the managed care of enlightenment. Quick. And I'd never heard him do that before. He started out by talking about how important preliminaries were and he was going to give the teachings even if you didn't have them. Which is unusual.

Student 2

What are the ...

Dan

A hundred thousand preliminaries.

But then he said, in that case you use a seed syllable, A [pronounced Ah], that you take as a visual form in front of you, the Tibetan letter A. And he said the following. He said, "If you keep staring at the A, you concentrate the mind. But after a while, when you stare at it, you realize that you're not looking at the target, the seed syllable A; you're really looking at the mind. And when you come to the point of seeing that you're not really looking at the target but you're looking at the mind, that's when you can ask yourself the question, 'Where is the mind?' and search for the substance of the mind. And then if you look for the substance of the mind and it's unfindable and you keep roaming around looking for that, then you are opening to how there are no boundaries and limits to the mind. And wherever those limits and boundaries are, it keeps getting more and more limitless." So, what he said was, basically, you go from the concentration, it naturally arises that you see you're looking at the mind rather than the concentration targets—what he's doing is emptiness practice—and then from emptiness practice, you go right into limitlessness, and there's your enlightened buddha bodies. You've reduced all fourteen stages to one lesson. You can do the whole thing in one lesson. That's profound! It's not even hard to do. But it takes somebody at that level of realization to say, "This is how you look at it." But he also prefaced it with saying, "I'm giving this to you, even if you didn't do your hundred thousand, but you still have that duty." He didn't say he's going to make you do it, he's saying, "I'm just saying ..." [Student laughs quietly.]

Which is an interesting way of putting it, because to give a clear explanation for how in one session you can go from nowhere to ordinary mind to full enlightenment, that's an extraordinary teaching. I've never heard that before, ever. But it takes that kind of clarity, you see. You don't need to sit; you don't need to do a retreat. You just need the precision and clarity of the instruction. That's why this is so precious.

Anybody else?

Student 3

I just simply want to say I thank you for your clarity and I'm probably speaking for many of us who just want to say sorry to have put you in the position of having to say it so clearly but thank you for just laying it down.

Dan

It's my duty to be fierce.

Student 3

Yeah, and it's helpful. Thank you.

Dan

It's protective. There isn't anybody in the room who can't do these duties. They're easy. It just means to not let yourself get lax with it. That's all it takes.

June 21, 2017

Themes: Relationship Problems: Attachment, Core Conflicts; Positive Maps

Dan

Welcome everybody. You have a question?

Student 1

So, this is of a little bit of a personal nature. I'm hoping, though, that other people might be able to relate to it. And that is that I've noticed that for me in relationships and also with friendships, certain patterns keep coming up. And one of the things that I've noticed is that when conflict arises, even though I'm trying to keep the lines of communication open, I find myself frequently acquiescing. I think it's probably out of fear of taking a risk, of losing the friendship, the relationship.

So, what I've been wondering about is where is that line between on the relative level standing up for myself, maybe perhaps risking something in a particular way, in a friendship; and maybe also, if I were to do that, perhaps that gives the other person an opportunity to look at something in a different way as well, versus on the more ultimate level, looking at it as all stories and all emptiness awareness.

Dan

Well, that's a great question. It really merits a Western as much as an Eastern answer, because from a Western perspective, what you're really talking about is the kind of problems that come up in relationships, intimate relationships, friendships, work relationships. And from a Western point of view, there's a lot of research on what we would call relational disturbance. In fact, Larry Beutler, when he was the editor for the *Journal of Consulting and Clinical Psychology*, which is the flagship APA journal where all the outcome studies go—he was the editor for over two decades—and in some of his research that he did in the early '90s, he found that 52 percent of people who come to therapists don't come in for psychiatric conditions a la *DSM*. They come in for dissatisfaction with relationships or problems with self-development. Over half.

Of course, since managed care, we got into this thing about treating relational problems isn't medically necessary. But if you look at the statistics, it's about half of what people come into therapy for. Of course, it's necessary, because it's one of the major contributing factors to life not being happy. If you're not happy in your relationships, you're really unhappy.

In Western terms, there are two major domains of relational disturbance. The first is attachment disturbance. That comes from the quality of the early childhood relationships with parents, infant-caregiver relationships. And there are four prototypes: secure attachment, dismissing attachment, anxious-preoccupied attachment, and disorganized attachment.

Kids who are secure, when they are close to the parents, the more they can look to the parents as a safe haven, as a secure base, the more exploratory they get, the more independent they get. So, the paradox built into human attachment is the more attached kids are in a healthy way, the more independent they become. They grow and they develop in new ways.

Kids who are dismissing because their attachment needs which are normal were repeatedly rejected, blow off attachment. So, they become sort of pseudo independent, and they deactivate attachment, so they just don't connect in relationships easily. So, they deactivate attachment and they have a kind of exaggerated form of exploratory behavior, whereas kids who grow up to have anxious-preoccupation do exactly the opposite. They inhibit the exploratory system and then they have kind of a clingy, exaggerated attachment. They get very anxious so much about holding on to the relationship that they can't explore. So, they have poor self-development. And kids who are disorganized deactivate both the attachment system and the exploratory system. So those are the four possibilities.

There's a standard paradigm called the Strange Situation paradigm where it's a twenty-minute scenario where you bring a mother and a child into the play lab, and for three minutes you observe the mother and the child in the playroom. There are two chairs in the playroom. There's a bunch of toys on the floor and there's a big box filled with toys. Secure kids will constantly reference the mother, and when they feel secure, they'll get more and more organized exploratory and play behavior in the presence of the mother. And the more secure they feel, they'll check in, and they'll get more independent, and more exploratory.

Then in this Strange Situation paradigm, there's three minutes with the mother alone and with the child. Then a stranger comes in who is a confederate to the research. And you see the child's differential response to the stranger and how that affects the exploratory behavior. And after three minutes, the mother leaves and the stranger is in the room alone with the child for three minutes. And you see how that affects exploratory behavior. You see the child's behavioral response to the mother leaving. Then after three minutes, the mother comes back and the stranger leaves. And you see the reunion behavior. Then, the mother leaves a second time and the child is left alone in the room and you see how that affects exploratory behavior. Then the mother comes back and there's a second reunion for three minutes.

It's a standard paradigm. There's been fifty years of research on this. And it's no accident that it's done with kids who are between ten and twenty months because that's when representational thinking develops. In that period, the child develops an internal representation, a map, for the quality of the relationship. And those maps remain relatively stable throughout preschool years, school years, and adulthood. 70 percent of those maps don't change once they're formed. And they form at about eighteen months.

Kids who have dismissing attachment, they go for the toys. They don't care whether the mother's there, whether the stranger's there, whether they're alone. They just do the toys, because they deactivated attachment. So, there's a kind of exaggerated form of exploratory behavior. Anxious-preoccupied kids are terrified of the unusual situation because it's ambiguous, so they can't play with the toys. They keep clinging to the mother and they need a lot of coaxing. And once the mother leaves, they get disorganized. They get clingy to the mother. Anxious-preoccupied kids do both, they show either at the same time or alternating clingy behaviors and dismissing behaviors. Those are stable patterns. And they're all in place by the second year of life. But, if later in childhood or where there's a healthy extended parent figure or a teacher, or in adulthood a therapist or a child therapist, you can remap that, and develop the attachment system and redo it. We call that "earned security." So, these maps could change under the right conditions.

But that's only one map. There's a second map that develops between the third and fourth year of life. That's at an age where the child has emotional ideas, complex belief systems, a complicated defensive system. And when that cognitive development is much further along, they develop a second set of maps, and they internalize into those maps family messages and cultural messages about what's expected in relationships. That's the second map. It's much more complicated. And that first map that develops at eighteen months is before metacognition develops, so we don't know that we have difficulty with attachment. And the second map is after metacognition develops, so we can sort of get some sense of awareness that we have some conflict in relationships.

To put it simply, someone once said that the difference between these two types of relational disturbance is either you have problems with relationships or you have problems within relationships. If you have attachment problems, it's not easy to connect. If you have problems with core conflicts in relationships, then you can connect but you keep connecting to the wrong people. In that second map, or what we call CCRT maps, and this goes to your question, core conflict relational theme maps are much more mapped out. They're very explicit. And they have to do with internalization of cultural and family messages about what you think is and is not expected in relationships. If there's something you want out of the relationship, we call that the wish. If it's something you expect to get instead, we call that the reactions of others, how you expect them to react instead of giving you what you wish. And then the third is the reaction of self, how you characteristically react when you don't get what you wish in the relationships.

And that research came up because if you ask people to, in an intake, in therapy, if you ask them to give you a history of relational episodes, not facts in their life, like, "Tell me about an intimate relationship. What was the promise? How did it start? What was the attraction? How did it unfold over time? What made it fail? How did it end?" If you ask that in some detail, and you get, say, ten relationship stories, you step back and you read them like a musical score. And what you'll see is that there's an underlying theme and infinite variations of the same one or two themes, that people's relationship behavior is purposeful. We're not all over the map. We keep doing the same old same old over and over again.

There's one famous Boston analyst in the 1940s, Felix Deutsch, who once said, "Each new relationship is an attempted solution to the previous one." It is like that if you think about it. In other words, what's unique about the CCRT research is that relationships are patterned. They're not accidental.

So, you remember what you said about the relationship? Let's go through it again. Just repeat what you said about it, the pattern.

Student 1

That some conflict comes up.

Dan

And the conflict is ... how do people act?

Student 1

Hmmm.

Dan

There's an expectation there. And instead?

Student 1

Instead, what happens is the person pulls away.

Dan

They reject you and abandon you, or something like that. That's what you said.

Student 1

Mm-hmm.

Dan

And the characteristic reaction that you have is?

Student 1

To want to draw them back in again, and to not challenge what's going on for fear of loss.

Dan

So, you said a lot in that. And there's your CCRT formulation right there. What you want are people who can be responsive to you. It's important to you. And what you get and what you expect to get instead is that people will abandon you, and the characteristic response that you make when people abandon you is to get acquiescent, trying to give them more what they want. You see how much is in that statement? It's highly specific. So, if you gave me ten relational episodes, and we went through that, we would see that it all comes down to maybe one or two themes, sometimes three, but rarely more than that. It's like a complex piece of music. There's an underlying theme, or themes, and there's infinite variations of the same one or two themes. And we keep playing out the same old over and over again.

So, in CCRT research, what you do is you take a history of relational episodes. You figure out the pattern as a therapist. And once you get the whole pattern down, you get the deep structure of that, and you spell it out to the person. What you keep looking for over and over again is this, this, and this in relationships. That's the wish. It's usually two or three things, and very specific to what you need to be fulfilled, which you don't get. And what you characteristically get instead is this, this, or this. And the way you characteristically react to that is by being this way, this way, and this way.

When you do that in an intake, it takes about an hour, or half an hour, to get that information. And if you're seasoned with that—I've done thousands of them—then you can spell it out to the patient. Mostly, they'll have the experience of feeling really deeply seen, like "how did you get all that?" Then you know you're on the right track. How do you know you're on the right track? If you're on the right track, they'll give you more information that will support what you just interpreted. If they get diffused, you didn't get it right; it goes all over, it gets scattered and doesn't have a direction, you didn't get it right.

What I'm saying is there is a lot of very sophisticated research on this, and we pretty much know how to determine and formulate what that relational stuff is and feed it back. But it's a different map. That's at a time that metacognitive awareness is fully developed and narrative memory is fairly developed. So, if you have CCRT problems, I can tell you what the core conflicts are and what you expect in relationships and how that doesn't work out and get to the essence of that. If I get it right, you'll say, "Yes!" And then you're going to start seeing it everywhere, because there are infinite variations in every relationship of the same thing.

Now, if I got you to do a visualization practice, where you actually actualize the wish, and change that map so that people reacted the way you needed them to react, rather than what you expect them to do instead, and you kept changing that map in a positive sense, and you change your reaction so they were more healthy, the research shows that somewhere between thirty and fifty sessions, you actually change the map and do it differently. And the sign of doing that correctly is you select differently. In other words, you don't go for the same old same old anymore. You actually select somebody who's going to be not rejecting and abandoning. And if you try and put out your needs in relationship, they're responsive.

I remember working with a woman who came in. She was in her early fifties and she was in a number of therapies, a number of relationships, and she was single, never married. And we did a formulation the first time around and I said, "What you need in relationships or expect in relationships is that somebody will be present to you and attuned to your needs; and when you express your needs, that's not a source of conflict for them." Two ROs, reactions of others, one of them, the negative patterns, is they won't see you, they're not attuned to you, and the other is if they do see you, then there's going to be a source of conflict between the two of you. So, I spelled that out to her, and her characteristic reaction in both cases was to withdraw. I spelled it out to her. She felt seen. But she came in the next hour and I said, "How did you feel about the last session?" She said, "Well, I felt really deeply seen by this, but there's some things I didn't think were quite right."

And I said, "Well, and you can't tell me those, because if you tell me those things, we're going to have a conflict, and that's the other part of the same formulation. You see how we're playing it out right between us right now." She got it. And we worked on that in our relationship and how she imagined it would go, and also by having her imagine a relationship [where] she was both deeply seen and it wasn't a source of conflict but a source of validation. And I had her do those visualizations repeatedly. Then pretty much right on schedule, about thirty sessions later, she came and she said, "Well, I met this guy, and I don't know. He's different!"

"What's different about him?"

"He's an engineer. And he's German."

And I said, "Well, what's the problem here?"

"Well, when I tell him my concerns in the relationship, he listens. And the next day he comes back and he says all these things that he's thought about, and he's thoughtful, and they're helpful, and we don't get into conflicts about it. But he's so different!"

She ended up marrying him. This is somebody I saw over twenty years ago. They've been together since. They're old now, but it worked. Because we were able to completely change the map. There's the wish, there's the internal expectations, or what you expect the other person's going to do instead. We call that the reactions of others. It's the negative belief system you have in your head about how people react. And then there's the characteristic way you've learned how to react to that, which never worked out very well—maladaptive coping. You can change all of that. And the research on that is fairly sophisticated.

Usually if somebody comes in with relational problems, from a Western point of view, you work from the bottom up developmentally. So, if they come in with attachment issues, you don't focus on CCRT issues, you focus on the attachment issues. If they don't have attachment issues, that doesn't mean they're free of disturbance. If they don't have attachment issues, the likelihood is that most people have CCRT issues, and you can fix them. So, then we work on the CCRT issues.

Just to streamline, because there's a lot of information to collect and get it right when you're doing CCRT issues, we made a questionnaire. So, when I see somebody, I have people fill it out ahead of time. It takes about an hour to fill out. Then I have eight, ten, fifteen relationships, and it takes me an hour or two to read all the material, but then we can do a much more rich and detailed formulation and get it right. I've collected hundreds of those now, and at some point, if I ever get time to go back to my clinical work, I'd like to write up some of that stuff like we did in our attachment book. It's the other half of the relational map.

You see, when you said that what you expect is some variation on the theme of rejection or abandonment, and the characteristic reaction is to acquiesce, you told me a lot. It's not the complete formulation, but we got a lot right there. You see, we operate out of these maps, and the whole idea is you can change the map. But you have to bring it into your awareness, and like anything else, you have to practice it.

I'm of a different persuasion about this because of my interest in Buddhism. In *Abhidharma*, the theory of mind, mental events, in Buddhism, it's said that the techniques that you use to work with negative states of mind, the techniques you use to work with positive states of mind, are complementary to each other but not replaceable [by] each other. That's something in the West we don't know enough about. What it means is if you work with negative states, and your techniques are effective, what you can reasonably expect is a relative reduction in those negative states or maybe their absence. But the absence of a negative is not a positive. It's just the absence of a negative.

The problem with the whole enterprise of Western psychotherapy, until recently, is it's all geared towards negative states. The psychodynamic tradition deals with intrapsychic conflict, cognitive behaviors, and deals with maladaptive behaviors, and limiting beliefs, negative self-talk. Developmentally informed treatment deals with developmental deficits. Where's the positive? And we get into this problem around attachment issues and around CCRT issues, because the traditional treatment for attachment issues comes from the psychoanalytic tradition. You interpret the resistances through attachment. You can do that 'til the cows come home, but that's not going to work. Because showing people where they fail at attaching doesn't necessarily develop a positive internal map for attachment.

So, what we did is develop a whole method based on visualizations of ideal parents who did all the things right, where the family of origin parents didn't do it. If you do those visualizations over and over again, imagination creates new possibilities and you can flexibly change the imagery until it feels right. You can actually shape a whole new different map, and then the old maps that are negative or fragmented or inconsistent become irrelevant because you're operating out of a map that works. But that's not a dominant position in Western psychology. The same with the CCRT maps. You can interpret how people are dysfunctional in their relationships and how they expect to get abandoned like in what you just now told me. But a far more important thing to do would be to develop a new positive map in which you kept visualizing not getting abandoned but [were being] with people who are carefully attuned to you and who are consistently available.

You change the negative map into a positive map; and if you keep doing that, after a while you start operating out of that positive map. You shift your basis of operation. You start operating out of that positive map because it works better. And the negative one just gets irrelevant. You don't have to interpret it. You don't have to show how it comes up in the transfers and plays out with you. All that becomes completely unnecessary stuff. Working on developing the positive is much quicker anyway.

Ultimately, it comes down to the theory of mind that you hold in terms of how you view people and what you do with them. In that sense, I think developing new positive maps for relationships is more of a Buddhist point of view than a Western point of view, even though our great tradition is relational behavior in therapy. But, from a Buddhist point of view, they would say that all that stuff is just stories. You'd learn to see that they're just empty stories, just constructions of mind, so you distance yourself from them; and you're not operating out of the story. You can operate out of the same old story about you're going to be rejected. And to prevent that you necessarily have to give away too much of yourself and accommodate too much in your relationships. But however many times that you repeat that same story, it's not a good story. You can change it. It's better to develop a positive story and operate out of that story.

You see, the view that you have to work through the negativity presumes that the negativity is always going to be there. And that, I think, is undermining the human nature. And it's very much dominant in Western psychotherapy, where the view that, "wait a minute, this is just a map, we can change the map," is empowering, because you can. And that's the message I'd rather give.

This is very important, because if you develop a positive map and you start operating out of that and it's starting to work and you're starting to see that people are responsive to you in the ways that you need, the positive feedback that it actually works is so [much] more compelling than the negative stuff that you just don't go in the negative again. In the negative we keep repeating because we don't know any better. We do it because it's familiar.

I once had a dear friend who, years ago, told me a story about when she was younger. She did some work in the Peace Corps in Sub-Saharan Africa. This is somebody who grew up in the city. This is really a very remote area. And once a month, there was an old dump truck that came into town with the mail and supplies. When the villagers heard the dump truck coming into town, they would get so excited that everybody, starting with the kids, would go run out to greet the dump truck. And all the villagers would jump up and down behind the dump truck as it was coming into town. And she found herself getting caught up in this whole thing. She was running behind the dump truck one day, when they're sort of slowly rolling in town. She was going [Dan breathes in as if it's really pleasant], and she noticed that she was breathing in all the exhaust fumes, and they were so wonderful to her because it was familiar to her from the city.

It's a good metaphor. Why do we breathe in the exhaust fumes? Not because they're healthy for us, it's because they're familiar to us. We keep playing out the same old same old negative patterns because it's all we know. But in my experience, if you develop a positive internal map, either an attachment map or a CCRT map, depending on what's necessary, then it changes. The positive things that happen in your life, the direct feedback from that, are so compelling, you're just not interested in that negative stuff anymore and you stop going there. It works. That's a very different view of therapy: "You've gotta work through all your stuff." But you have to ask yourself the fundamental question, East and West: what's the theory of mind behind the method? One [that's] behind working through all the negative stuff is a relatively negative and somewhat depressing theory of mind, and not necessarily accurate. You have to examine the assumptions of what you're doing. It's important.

So, there's another way of looking at this. What you've described, and what we've talked about, is the dysfunction that comes up in our relational behavior, either problems with relationship, attachment disturbances, or problems within relationships and how we select for the same old same old negative patterns, which are core conflict relational or CCRT themes. But from a spiritual perspective, there's a whole other thing, and that is how you use relationships as path, as the path. And that's something that really matters, and probably is going to be unique to it what means, as Buddhism comes to the West, because in our great tradition in Western psychotherapy, relationships are certainly a much bigger concern in Western behavior than they are in Buddhism. Because in Buddhism, relationship means you're trying to act compassionately to the different classes of beings. In the West, relationship means intimate relationships and working that out, because that's the source of happiness.

Maybe with the exception of rap music and hip hop, because that represents certain cultural issues, most popular music is about relationships. Almost all popular music is love songs of one sort or another, about what you want in relationships and what isn't working in relationships, right? They've made billions of dollars in the music industry off of people's dissatisfaction in relationships. So, it tells you clearly. All popular music is singing about relationships. It tells you clearly what our priorities are in the West. We're still trying to get it right. And not doing a very good job with it.

Given the fact that relationships are so much the stamp of this culture, it means that as all the great teachings from the East are coming into this culture, it will transform this culture, but this culture will also transform the *dharma*. And one of the ways that that's evolving is more relational-based dharma. Certainly, we've seen that in the pointing out style of teaching. All that we do are guided meditations with explicit explanations on what comes next. As one of our students said, this is like GPS for the mind. It's relational based. Hopefully, we do a better job than GPS will do. [Gentle laughter] Let's take a U-turn. [Dan chuckles]

But you know what I'm talking about. You see what that also means is that for us, the likelihood is that dharma takes footing in the West, and the *dharma* is reshaped by the West, that relationships are our path. And the best approach to what you're going to work out on the pillow is going to really happen in your relationships, not on the pillow.

My first teachers in Buddhism—I think I've talked about this before, but some of you weren't here—I was, what, nineteen years old. The first time Buddhism ever came to the West was in 1886, long time ago. And it was founded by a couple, Thomas and Caroline Rhys Davids out of the UK, who founded the Pali Text Society. They were the first people to translate the words of the Buddha and bring them to the West in beautiful bound texts. And their understudy was a woman by the name of Terry Havens who came to this country and married an American whose name was Joe Havens. Joe went to the University of Chicago in the Psychology of Religion program that I also went to. So, I followed in some ways in his footsteps.

And my first introduction to the *dharma* was with Terry, when I was nineteen years old. She had an interesting history. She was very smart. She was offered an endowed Chair in Buddhism in the mid-1930s at Yale University, and she declined. First of all, women didn't get endowed Chairs in 1936 for anything. And the fact that she declined, it was unheard of. And the reason why she declined it is she thought that the words of the Buddha couldn't be taught academically; they could only be taught lived. She lived it. It was a great message, and they lived it in their relationship. They were the first people to write about how relationship was the path for the West.

So, all the stories that you have to look at come up in your relationships with a certain intensity. If you're honest in relationships, you have a remarkable opportunity to work out everything you need to work out, because it all comes up. And I don't mean that just in intimate relationships. I mean that in meditation teacher relationships, student teacher relationships. I lived with my first Root Lama summers for nine years. And whatever my limitations were, he would throw them in my face. It was very difficult, but I learned after a while that that's where all the work was. It was all about the relationship with him and what he would stir up.

I remember one day him saying, "A great Lama is coming. You have to clean up the outside." And there was a driveway with pebbles, and there were all these weeds growing in it, so he said, "You have to clean out all that stuff with no gloves." So, I sat there, bleeding hands, picking out all the weeds in this driveway in the hot sun for two days. Of course, I wanted to please him. That was my fatal mistake. Because after two days of doing all this hard work and waiting for him to come by and say, "You did a good job," he came by and he said, "What a stupid thing to do." [Laughter] And I immediately got really angry. He pointed at me and he says, "I got you." And he did. That's what the lessons were like. Whatever your limitation was, he would point it out to you.

Menri pokes me all the time. He's always busting me. We do it with some bantering style. It's a different style but it's similar. It's only with Root Lamas, because that's about a relationship. And then, you know, I grew up in a family that wasn't very well off, so I didn't have any money to go to school so I had to go to the state school because that's all I could afford. And if I didn't get a scholarship to graduate school, I would have never gone. I got a Danforth that paid for four years of tuition and full living expenses at the University of Chicago. That was the ticket. I've always felt grateful for that.

But, not having money—I was always screwed up around money—when I first went to live with Geshe Wangyal, he said, "Well, you can't just come here. You have to pay for room and board." And I had to get a job weekends and was working on learning the Tibetan language and translating. And he said, "No, that's not enough money you're bringing. You gotta bring in more money." So, I started a second job on the side, translating. And then he said, "No, this is not good enough. You can do more." Whatever shame I had about money, he would just go right to it.

It was so painful for me. And I remember the last day of that first summer, he brought me to the bus. He didn't usually drive the car—he had somebody drive him—and he walked me to the bus, which was unusual. And as I got on the bus to go back to Chicago, he handed me this envelope. He said, "Here, you're gonna need this for school." It was all the money that he had taken from me that summer. He had no intention of keeping it. The lesson was to overcome all the stories about money.

I can have millions of examples like that. He would take whatever I struggled with and he put it in my face. It was hard, because I was young and defensive. But now, I look back on it, I feel enormously grateful for that kind of caring because it moved me along. But that's not just something that comes up in teacher-student relationships. You've got to be up for that one because it's intense. We call it *sentab*, intense means. But it happens in intimate relationships even more so. So, if you can use an intimate relationship as path, which is the shape of Western *dharma*, then everything that comes up in the relationship is stuff, it is path. You can use it.

Then, that's really profound. With all the stuff of ordinary relationships, all that stuff that would normally mire down the relationship, if you look at it honestly, it's your best teacher. I'm grateful to have a wife that I can do that with who's practicing along with me. She stirs up lots of stuff. She can stir up lots of stuff. We have lots of opportunities to work on it whether we like it or not. But mostly, we laugh together about it.

I remember once we were roofing. We were building this teaching building. And Geshe Wangyal, my first Root Lama, he was fierce. I was terrified of him. He would yell at us a lot of the time. It was always about safety and mindfulness issues. We were not very careful. If you misstep on the roof, you're dead, so he was yelling at us the way he typically would do. And all of us just started laughing. And he said, "Well, I guess I can't use this fierceness anymore, because it's not working." And he never did it again. But it was part of the play, the whole thing.

So, close relationships have this remarkable ability to stir up everything. And if you look at it squarely and it's right in your face, you can be free of that, really free of it. What we say is "mistakes become wisdom." The very things that hang you up the most, because there's so much energy in those things, if you look at it squarely for what it is, it's just a construction of mind. You're free. So, in those relationships, all your greatest moments for freedom. It's important.

Terry and Joe were a good model for that. They used their relationship every day as a path. She was ten years older than he was. She died before he did. He had an interesting death. He had advanced Parkinson's. And he got us all together as his friends and family and said, "I'm ready to go. Body's done now, so I'm going to stop eating." And he stopped eating and died that way, because there wasn't a legal way, any other way. But he came to completion and got together with everybody and completed his life. It was very special.

They went at it with themselves. But they always were committed to this larger view that their partner was their greatest teacher.

Buddha had a cousin, Devadatta, who also wanted to be a teacher, but Devadatta was enormously jealous of the Buddha and would get enraged at the Buddha's success at teaching. There were two occasions he was so jealous of the Buddha, he tried to poison him, kill him, so he could be the main teacher. And the Buddha's attitude was, "I finally found the right teacher. He's my greatest teacher." So, think of that. Donald Trump is your greatest teacher.

I have a story about that. The first time we went to Mustang, we were going up to these little villages, and this was the Kali Gandaki River valley; and it was a valley that all the great masters walked up. Padmasambhava has many retreat caves there and hermitage sites. And all the great masters, all the cave yogis used to be in that valley. That's where Atisha also walked up that same valley to go to Tibet for the first time. And in Kinay, the little village next to Ponling, where we built our irrigation project, there was an old man, a former lama, who was the keeper of this little very dilapidated, hermitage place. I went to him and talked with him, and he said there's a very special book inside that's nine hundred years old. So, I went inside, and of course, I could read the Tibetan. And it was amazing. It was half transcribed. It wasn't finished. It was a book on the Six Perfections written by Atisha. It was just sitting in this little place. He was obviously in the middle of translating it and didn't finish it and left it there. It's still there. And this little family, every generation, they guard the sacred text of Atisha. He didn't even know what it was. Amazing.

That was a good question.

July 19, 2017

Themes: Neurocircuits of Awakening; Sleep and Dream Yoga

Dan

Welcome everyone.

Somebody sent in an email question for tonight. The question is, "If somebody is trying to integrate the experience of awakening into everyday life and mix it into everyday life, how do they mix it into dreams in deep sleep?" That was the question. So, I'll try and address that.

Let's start with the question, "How does meditation practice affect sleep?" The answer really depends on the type of meditation practice you're doing. And a view that became very popular in the West starting in the early seventies with Herb Benson's work was that meditation was a kind of "relaxation response." And I don't think that's an accurate view. Since Benson's early work on meditation as a relaxation response, it became customary to view meditation in behavioral medicine as a kind of relaxation therapy and to classify it that way. But it's not a relaxation response, and here's why: If you think about the end of yoga class, and you relax, what happens to your mind when you're lying there? Usually, your mind wanders and you get drowsy and maybe even fall asleep.

So, that common sense experience, which most of you can relate to, will tell you that too much relaxation triggers mind-wandering mode, which means that you get drowsy and sleepy and your mind drifts into daydreams and self-referential thoughts. And the more the mind is filled with that extraneous distraction, distracting thought, it makes it harder to train meditation. That was a view that Herb Benson put out in 1975 in his book *The Relaxation Response*, but it's not accurate. In fact, when Benson put out that view, it related to relaxation, but he had never had any experience meditating. He just assumed that that's what it was.

Five years earlier than that, in Tokyo, [inaudible name] did a more scientifically sound study, and what he did was he took beginning and advanced Zen monks and wired up their bodies to look at the muscle responses of the large muscle groups in the body like latissimus dorsi and erector spinae, or psoas. And what he found was that when people were experienced meditators, meditation wasn't relaxing at all from the perspective of the striate musculature. It was best seen as an even output and distribution of muscle work.

And because they had to put the work into holding up the body posture and the upper trunk for twenty minutes, or half an hour, or an hour, or however long they sat, that constant output of muscle work did two things: One is, it activated the alerting center of the brain. It kept the mind alert so it didn't get dull or drowsy. And two is, it was associated significantly with less not more mind-wandering.

There was one study done with infants. Infants, when they first come into the world, they sleep all the time for the first days. And with each successive day, they get more and more alert. If you take an infant in the first days of life and you hold them prone, they fall asleep. If you put them on your shoulder or sit them upright, they immediately get alert. It's hardwired into the striate musculature that when you sit upright, you get alert. It activates the reticular activating system and the alertness function of the brain. But if you get too sloppy with the meditation and try and relax too much, it shuts that off and you get into mind-wandering mode.

So, for that reason, it's probably not a good idea or an accurate idea to view meditation as a kind of relaxation, because too much relaxation makes it harder to meditate. But if you're not meditating or doing some form of relaxation therapy, it would probably help you go to sleep better—that's the first point.

The second point is that if you look at the goal of meditation, the main goal of meditation is the experience of awakening—that always right here is an infinite, limitless ocean of awakened awareness-love, which is your true nature, but you don't recognize it. And if you do these practices, they're not just about relaxing. They're hard work. And if you do that work, eventually, if you do it correctly, it'll lead to the experience of awakening. Most of you know, but some of you don't, that in the last year what we did is we took a number of our students and did a study on the neurocircuitry of awakening with Judd Brewer's lab, the Mindfulness Neuroscience Lab at UMass Medical School.

And we convinced Judd, who took this course along with members of the Fetzer Foundation, who also took the course, that maybe it would be a good idea to not just study more mindfulness, but to study awakening. So, we gave Judd thirty subjects who had a taste of awakening, but didn't have it all the time, so we could look at brain activity while they were in the normal distracted state, ordinary mind state, and while they were in a stable awakened state.

And the main finding was that in certain brain areas, we had an unusual finding. When students were awakened, they were activating certain neurocircuits. One is in the anterior cingulate cortex, which has to do with concentration on one thing and tuning everything else out, in this case holding the view. And the other was in the parietal system, which has to do with taking a general orientation to the world out there, a global orientation rather than a partialized orientation. And in those two brain areas we found a very unusual finding on all thirty subjects, which was gamma activity.

Usually when we're awake and alert, the brain operates with a high frequency bandwidth, which is about 20 to 40 hertz. It's called beta activity. When we get relaxed, we get into alpha activity, which is slower wave activity. When we get deeply relaxed into mind-wandering and reverie states, we have even slower activity called theta activity. And when we get deeply asleep, we get into very slow [delta] activity.

This is the opposite direction. When people were shifting out of ordinary mind to awakened mind, they were having gamma activity, which is 45 to 60 hertz. That's best interpreted as in those brain areas, all of the cells were active, and they were all firing synchronistically.

Awake means awake. You're recruiting all the neurons and certain brain activity in certain brain areas and activating them all. That's what awake means. It's a very unusual finding. But that's not very conducive to ordinary sleep, because if the neurons are that active, it's going to interfere with sleep. And often times when people train awakening and they manifest it more frequently and for longer duration, and manifest it off the pillow in everyday activities, that awakening is going to naturally leak over into deep sleep and dreaming.

So, you're going to be awake during deep sleep and awake during dreaming, which means your overall level of sleep, the amount of time that you sleep, the total sleep time will be reduced, but without a sleep deficit. It likely means that you're going to be in lighter stages of sleep, because if the brain neurons remain active, you're not going to get that delta activity because the brain is too active. And you just don't need so much sleep.

So, that's a strong argument for how meditation, particularly the attainment of the heart of meditation, which is the experience of awakening, means a significant impact on deep sleep and dreaming.

So now we can get into the second part of the question, which is, how do you practice during sleep and dreaming? Before I answer that question in Eastern terms, I'll answer it in Western terms.

There's been, since the 1970s, a good deal of sleep lab research in the West. And we know a lot about the architecture of sleep. Normally most people get about seven or eight hours of sleep. And sleep goes through very predictable phases. The first phase is called "stage one, descending." And as the brain activity slows down, the ordinary involvement in the outside, seemingly outside, perceptual world stops as you close your eyes. And then you go through a period when all the head gets quiet. And then suddenly fragmented imagery comes up about twenty minutes to a half an hour after closing your eyes, sometimes quicker. And that fragmented imagery is called the hypnagogic state. So, as you go, you transition into deeper sleep, which is called stage one descending, descending into deeper sleep, you go through a period where you get this kind of spontaneously emerging, somewhat fragmented imagery. Then all the imagery subsides, and the mind gets quiet.

Then you go into stage two descending, stage three and stage four descending. There's no content in stage two to four. So, if you were to be alert or aware, you would notice a field experience. Normally we're unconscious during deep sleep, which is stage two, three, and four. But you could actually train yourself to be aware during deep sleep, or awakened aware, even better.

[Inaudible question.] If you wake people up, and ask them what's going on, they can't tell you anything. There's no content. We distinguish these stages in terms of the bandwidth, the frequency range. So, the mind is getting progressively slowed down in terms of frequency range. In each one of those stages, in addition to frequency range changing, there are certain functions that are occurring. Like in stage two, three, and four, in each one of those stages, there are distinct hormones that are secreted. Some of them are cell-regulating and cell-repairing hormones. Some of them are growth-regulating hormones.

So, most of the repair work on the body system happens during deep sleep. There's no activity of the mind during deep sleep, but the body could still be somewhat restless. So, when you toss and turn at night, you toss and turn at night during deep sleep, not during dreaming. After you finish the deepest of those four levels of descending deep sleep, it's called stage four, then you have rapid eye movements, and concurrently that rapid eye movement is a higher frequency band, which is concurrent with dreaming.

So, you go stage one, hypnogogic stage; two, three, four, no content; dreaming, rapid eye movement; two, three, and four, rapid eye movements; two, three, and four, rapid eye movements; two, three, and four, rapid eye movements. You experience about four cycles at night. And then after the last cycle of dreaming, you wake up. And that transition is called the hypnopompic state. The average time is about seven hours.

If you look at The Academy of Behavioral Sleep Medicine, they have very clear criteria for what's called sleep efficiency, where the cut-off point is 85 percent. So, what you do to measure sleep efficiency is you look at the total time that you actually put aside to sleep. So, let's say you put aside ten hours … and you sleep seven out of those ten hours, and the other three hours are trying to get to sleep, waking up frequently in the night, and then the time it took to go back to sleep. So, let's say that you were in bed for ten hours, and you only slept seven of those ten hours. The rest of the time you were struggling to get back to sleep. Then your sleep efficiency would be 70 percent. See how that works? Healthy sleep is defined as a sleep efficiency of 85 percent or above.

There are three types of disturbances in sleep according to Western psychology. The first of the disturbances is initiating sleep, sometimes called insomnia. That's defined in terms of sleep onset latency, the total amount of minutes it takes you to go to sleep. And anything above thirty minutes is considered significant insomnia. If you lie down to go to sleep and you toss and turn for an hour or two, you've got significant insomnia.

The second is frequent night awakenings with or without dreams. People will wake up two, or three, or four times. It takes them half an hour, an hour, two hours, or never to get back to sleep. And the third are early-morning awakenings, waking up at 5:00 a.m. and not being able to go back to sleep. Each one of those types of problems is completely different. The most common is insomnia. And the frequent cause for insomnia is thinking too much, usually about anticipating the next couple of days or reviewing what you just did that day. So, people who are vulnerable to insomnia have what we call cognitive hyperactivity or they're thinking too much at night. Why? Because they're too stressed out, and they never process things during the day, and the only time they get a chance to review what happened during the day is when they go to sleep, which isn't a good idea. So, if you take people who have that kind of insomnia and you get them to have a review and worry period a minimum of two hours before they go to sleep, and they take all that activity out of the mind, out of the bedroom, usually they can sleep pretty well.

Frequent night awakenings are usually associated with trauma, particularly if they wake up with frequent nightmares, or there are people who have trauma backgrounds who will wake up at night with playing out the trauma. And early morning awakeners are usually associated with depression. So, for each one of those three types of sleep problems, there's completely different treatments. But generally, what we say is that, in Western terms, deep sleep: mind still, body active. Dreaming: mind active, body still.

When people are dreaming, they can't move. Their musculature just doesn't work. So sometimes when people are lucid during their dreaming and they're aware that they're dreaming, they get panicked by the fact that they can't move their body intentionally when they try to. Deep sleep: mind still, body active. Dreaming: mind active, body still. There's a simple principle there. However, sometime those boundaries aren't so clear cut. There's a small group of people who have night terrors, and what happens for them is that when they have dreaming and the body should be still, they get physically active; and they can sleepwalk.

And when they're having deep sleep and the mind should be quiet, they have night terrors. So, the deep sleep where the mind is quiet, content leaks into it, which is terrifying. And when they're in deep sleep and dreaming, then the body becomes more active than it should be, so that mixing of these two usually discreet phases is genetic. It's a genetic vulnerability that causes that, and it's a deep problem. So, what you have to do to treat that is you have to wake them up when they get into the phase mixing and shift them out of it, shake them out of it and have them go back and reboot. It's a very rare problem, but it's a difficult problem.

Now, to continue in Western terms, the function of dreaming is to review the day. A dream is like an abstract, like if you read a journal article that's an abstract before you read the actual full-length article. It's an abstract. It's a shorthand for the main experiences of the day. It's a way of integrating ongoing experiences into our memory database by picking out the essential features of the main things that happened during the day and see what they activate from our memory database.

So that's what I would say about Western literature on dreaming. There is very little research on deep sleep except in terms of hormone secretion. So, for example, if you look up about people who have fibromyalgia, fibromyalgia is a muscle inflammation where throughout the body there are pervasive trigger points as a consequence of muscle inflammation. It turns out that there is in stage two descending sleep, there's a set of hormones that cause muscle repairs. So, if we stretch, and move muscles, and make minor tears, and stress the muscle too much during the day, and that causes local autonomic discharge of stress response hormones that build up in the muscle tissue, these hormones will repair and clean out those and metabolize those stress hormones at night and repair the muscle tissue.

There's some studies that show that not all but a number of people who are vulnerable to fibromyalgia have sleep deficits in that second stage; so their hormones that normally are used to repair the muscle stress are not functioning efficiently. So, it makes them have a kind of biological vulnerability to fibromyalgia. This is one example of sleep disruption. Of course, then when you get the chronic pain, that causes more sleep disruption, and you get into a vicious cycle you can't get out of. So, the pain is exacerbated by it and you get into a cycle.

But if they had normal secretion of those hormones and slept with good stage two sleep, it would never come up in the first place. So, the inefficiency of the hormone production in stage two causes the problem, and then the sleep which comes from being in pain compounds the problem, so they can't get out of the cycle. That's just one of many examples of how deep sleep is about hormone production and maintenance of the body, growth regulating, and repair.

The other thing I would say from a Western point of view is that there is a rather popular literature on lucid dreaming, and people who have their workshops on how you train people to be aware during dreaming. That certainly occurs, and you can teach people to be aware, but that's not the same as Tibetan dream yoga. And to put it simply, the main difference is that Tibetan dream yoga isn't teaching people to be aware during dreams, it's teaching them to be specifically awakened-aware during dreams. It's mixing awakened awareness into the dream, not ordinary awareness, whereas most of the literature on lucid dreams in the West has to do with just being aware, ordinary awareness. It's different. See the difference? Is it clear enough?

For any Tibetan who worked with dream yoga would say that being aware during a dream is not good enough: it has to be awakened awareness.

So, now let's switch to the other half of the equation, which is the Indo-Tibetan view of dreams and sleep. The function of dreaming is the activation and ripening of karmic memory traces. So, to understand this, you have to understand karma theory. Every action, and that doesn't mean simply behavior, it means mental actions, too; every action that you engage in causes a karmic memory trace, a *bakchak* in Tibetan.

So, you have millions of karmic memory traces that fill the reservoir, which is called *kunzhi namshe*, or storehouse consciousness. It's like a massive reservoir for all the karmic memory traces, not just for this life, but for all your previous lives, billions of karmic memory traces. And under certain conditions, some of those karmic memory traces will become activated. And when they become activated, they go through a process called *minwa*, which means to ripen.

And when a karmic memory trace ripens, it has wang, it has influence. And depending on the chuk, the strength of that karmic memory trace, it has influence in various ways. The first is, it influences the unfolding events in your stream of consciousness. So, all of the stuff that goes through your stream of consciousness, when you're observing that stuff, you're observing the ripening of karmic memory traces. Okay? So, all the ordinary content of the mind is the result of ripening of karmic memory traces, *minwa*, ripening.

When karmic memory traces are activated and they ripen, they first manifest as spontaneous emergent states of mind—content, mental content. When they ripen and have greater strength, they manifest as indirect influences on our behavior. We don't really know how they're influencing us. When they ripen and have even greater strength, they directly influence our behavior. When they ripen and have the greatest strength, they influence the events that we have in our life.

All events, positive and negative, are the results of karmic activation and ripening—first, states of mind; second, behavior (direct and indirect influences); and third, events. So, the fact that you're here listening to teachings is the result of karmic memory ripening. You have good experiences with spirituality in your past that would make you what are called *kaldens*, fortunate ones, in Tibetan, so that you get to hear these teachings. All that's a result of karmic memory ripening.

Now, in the Tibetan theory of mind, the time of your diurnal rhythms where you activate and ripen karmic memory traces most directly is during dreaming. Dreaming is the activation and ripening of karmic memory traces. All those bizarre states of mind that come up in dreaming are karmic memory traces being activated and ripened. When you wake up in the morning after just dreaming, because the last thing you do before you wake up is dream, you're on your fourth or fifth cycle of dreams a night, there's usually a little bit of drift or carry-over to your day. That heaviness of mind is a result of the influence of the karmic memory traces whether you know it or not.

So, we enter the day with that influence and that kind of heaviness that clouds over us, and we don't even know it. So, what gets activated? There are several things that explain—of all the millions of karmic memory traces in your storehouse consciousness—why is it that some get activated more than others? Part of it has to do with what's called *chuk*, the strength of the influence. So, if you engage in certain actions, some activities have more weight than others. If you think about getting angry at someone but you hold it back, that has less weight. If you think about getting angry at somebody and let it rip, that has more weight. If you think about getting angry at somebody and let it rip and you kill them, that has much greater weight.

So, the strength of the action is in part what determines what karmic memory traces get activated. The stronger the trace, the greater the probability that that will get activated. But the second factor is, what gets activated depends on what kind of experiences we have during the day. In other words, you have billions of karmic memory traces in your reservoir, your storehouse consciousness. And which of those from the past get activated has to do with your daily experiences. It's very similar to what Freud called "day residue." In the dream at night, some of the content comes from the day. You can see the residue, because there is something about that experience in that day that reminded you of something in the past that stirred up that karmic memory trace. And that's why that one as opposed to a different one got activated. Is that clear enough?

Okay. So, it's a complex interaction between the strength of the action and incidental learning, which means that whatever gets activated stirs you up. And the outcome of that is the ripening of this content in dreams. So, the phases of dreaming, in deep sleep and dreaming, are a little bit different in Indo-Tibetan psychology than they are in Western psychology. In Western psychology, if you remember, we talked about stage one, two, three, four descending, REM sleep, which is dreaming (REM for rapid eye movement sleep). Stage two, three, four, rapid eye movement—stages like that—three to five cycles like that a night.

The process of the unfolding of dreams is a little bit different. It starts with the seeming appearing world out there. That's called *nangwa*, appearance. Then, the second is gathering it all in, *duwa*. As you start to prepare to go to sleep tonight, you gather in, *duwa*, you don't look out there with a kind of out-thereness anymore. You start to gather in your senses. The physical act that culminates with that, you close your eyes; you shut down your eyes and your senses; you keep the body inactive as you prepare to go to sleep. And as you're doing that, all the sense impressions gather in, *duwa*.

The third phase is called [inaudible Tibetan word], subsiding. All the residual content after you gather in the senses, the residual content will subside like the setting of the sun, and then there's no content left. Then the next stage is called [inaudible Tibetan word], nothing, no content. Then the next stage is called *nangwa*, appearance. That's when you have either a dream or hypnagogic imagery. And then after you have the hypnagogic imagery, which appears ... Oh, I left out one stage. Before no appearance, there's a stage called blocking. When the mind is quiet and there's no content to come, there's an active setting up a stimulus barrier, so you're blocking out taking any content into the mind. That protects deep sleep. And then there's nothing left. There's no content left. Then you go through the appearance stage, then the gather and the subsiding, the blocking, the no content, and then it appears again.

Those stages are not terribly different from Western sleep research. The main difference is that in the Tibetan system, they don't make a distinction between the hypnagogic state and the dream state. They just call the whole thing dream state because it all has to do with content, where in the West that stage one descending, when you get content, the content tends to be fragmented imagery; it makes no sense. Whereas in dream work, there's a structure to the dream—it makes sense. In Western terms we see dreaming as a problem-solving activity. For each there's an underlying conflict, and there are attempted solutions to it. So, the mind keeps trying on different solutions until you come up with the right solution.

So, Tibetans don't make a distinction between the hypnagogic state and the dreaming; they see it as all, it's content-related, so we'll call it a dream. I think that distinction is really important myself in terms of training dream yoga because it's easier to train dream yoga in the hypnagogic state before you train it with real dreams.

So now let's talk a little bit about what you actually do with dream yoga and sleep yoga. The Tibetans make a distinction between two different processes: how you work with deep sleep, and how you work with dreaming. And they see those as separate processes. The superior practice is working with deep sleep, not dreaming, where in the West with lucid dreaming we get a fascination with dreams and dream content.

So, the reason why deep sleep is important: If you go through the process of appearance, gathering in the senses, the subsiding of mental content, no content, the act of blocking of all content, and then appearance of dreams, or hypnogogic imagery, if you go through that process, when you get to the stage of no appearance, deep sleep, and all content is gone, normally when you enter deep sleep, you are unconscious. Right? We don't stay aware during deep sleep. But, if you have a good taste of awakened awareness and you've worked to stabilize that awakened awareness so you have it more frequently, for longer duration, and more immediately on the pillow, and the *tak*, the sign that you're looking for is that just the intention of looking and setting up your view will shift your basis to awakening, so it takes you no more than a millisecond to shift your basis out of ordinary mind to awakened mind. If you can do that on a regular basis, then you have the basic eligibility for looking at the deep sleep yoga.

How you do deep sleep yoga, you set up the body posture. And the posture is called "sleeping lion posture." You lie on your right side with the legs slightly bent so you look a little like this: [Dan lies down on his right side]; I'll put a pillow under me here [arranges his zafu supporting his upper body with his right arm over the zafu, elbow on the floor]; I put my head like this [bends his right arm up so that his head is resting on his palm]; I'm going to rest where my legs are bent and rest the [left] arm on my thigh. And that's called "sleeping lion posture." Is that clear enough?

Okay, now, if I'm doing sleeping lion posture, there are, in terms of the energy currents in the body, there are three main channels. There's the central channel, which is about an inch in front of the spinal column. It's about the thickness of an index finger. There's the juncture, which is four fingers below the navel to the navel. And that juncture looks like a fennel bulb, like a celery stalk, like a fennel bulb.

At the top of the fennel bulb, there are three shoots coming out of it like this [Dan holds up his right hand, folds the thumb and the little finger into the palm, and, with palm facing out, holds up the three fingers—index, middle, and ring as representing the "three shoots"]. This is the central channel [indicating the middle finger]. This is the right white channel [the ring finger]. The central channel is blue. And the left is the red channel [the index finger]. The right white channel is called the channel of *samsāra*. All the negative states of the body are cycled through the winds of that channel. The left red channel is called the channel of nirvana. All the positive states, the *yonten*, the positive qualities of mind, are cycled through that channel.

The size of the right channel and the left channel is about the size of a pencil or a drinking straw, smaller than the central channel. Because it's smaller, if you lie in lion's posture on your right side, the pressure of the weight of the body is going to flatten that channel so the winds of the negative energy forces in the body that run through that channel will be partially obstructed. So where are they going to flow more freely? Left side.

So, if you do no more than take that posture and go train yourself to go to sleep in that posture, you're training yourself to manifest more positive states during dreams, and the karmic memory traces that are ripening are going to be biased towards positive ones. So, the dreams are not so scary, and the influence is more positive than negative.

You've got to train yourself to do it. So that's your setup. That's your posture. Then before you set up the posture, you enter awakened awareness. You shift out of ordinary mind to the infinite limitlessness of awakened awareness mind. And you lay down in that awakened awareness, [the] vast expanse of limitless awareness, awake, brilliant awareness.

The practice is essentially the King of Samādhi practice, which means the difference between that and ordinary concentration, when you're concentrating in ordinary mind, it's the ordinary mind that's doing the concentration. In King of Samādhi, you shifted your basis out of ordinary mind to awakened mind, so where you're coming from makes all the difference in the world. You're operating out of being that vast expanse, and you're looking at the body from that vast expanse. See the difference? So, that's called King of Samādhi. You're operating out of and your basis is awakened awareness and the limitlessness of that awakened awareness. That's where you're coming from as you're concentrating.

So, you have pinpointed focus on something against the backdrop of the vast expanse. So that's how you set it up. And you concentrate on the body; and you concentrate on the throat chakra. And in the throat chakra you imagine the lotus, a four-petalled red lotus. The throat chakra is sometimes referred to as the chakra of emanation, *trulku korlo*. And the reason why it's called the chakra of emanation is because it emanates speech. It also emanates the content of dreams.

So, if you concentrate on the throat chakra, you're concentrating on the site within the subtle body, the yogic body, where dreams are generated. The process of gathering in, subsiding, no appearance, blocking, appearance again, all those activities come from the throat chakra. So, you enter awakened awareness. You concentrate without distraction on the throat chakra. And you go to sleep. And as you get progressively closer to going to sleep, there's a window there. There's a barrier there, we'll call a boundary, and you learn to cross that boundary and hold the awareness and like threading a needle, you hold the awakened awareness into the deep sleep.

So now you have awakened awareness during deep sleep. Normally we're unconscious during deep sleep, but you can train yourself to have awakened awareness in deep sleep. And the level of skill is measured by the brightness of the field. When you first do it, the big accomplishment is that you have some awareness that you're actually in deep sleep. But you're awakened aware. As you get better, the field of awareness, there's no content, but it gets lighter. And when you get really good at it, the field is like a bright field of light, but you're fast asleep. And that's called recognizing the clear light of deep sleep.

Now the reason why deep sleep yoga is considered superior to dream yoga is because if you recognize the clear light of deep sleep, it's very similar to the clear light of dying. So, if you train yourself in the mastery of the yoga of deep sleep, when you get asleep, you stay awakened aware during all phases of deep sleep—stage two, three, four descending. You're still asleep. You're probably going to sleep lighter. You're probably going to sleep less hours. But there's a field of bright awareness during that deep sleep, even though there's no content. And if you can recognize that and you've trained yourself to do that on a regular basis, in the dying process when the body and the mind crash and burn, and all action plans stop, and all the sense systems stop, and all conceptual thought stops, what's left after all that—the systematic shutting down of all the systems in the body and the absorption of the elements—is what's called the clear light of dying. The experience of that is identical to the clear light of deep sleep.

So, when you're dying, if you recognize it, you say, "I know this. This is familiar to me." All it takes is that instant of recognition and you get fully enlightened during the dying process. So, dying becomes an opportunity for enlightenment because conceptual thoughts and the sense systems that get in the way of that realization crash and burn, and finally you're free of all that stuff. You have an opportunity there, but you have to recognize it. And if you recognize the deep sleep clear light, then you know, "I know how to do this. This is very familiar to me." You become a buddha.

So that's why, because the clear light of dying is similar to the clear light of deep sleep, deep sleep yoga is considered the superior practice. Is that clear so far? Are you okay with this?

Dream yoga is you have to train yourself to be awakened aware during the actual dreaming as it's occurring. And since we dream on the average of four or five times a night, that means [doing] that each cycle of those dreams. Many people find it hard to train themselves to wake up during dreaming. I personally, when I did this practice, I found that deep sleep yoga was really easy, and I found the dreaming really difficult because as soon as I would wake up—not wake up, but I was asleep, but I would notice that I was aware during the dream or awakened aware during the dream—I'd get, "oooh," I would get excited. I'd get reactive to it, and then it would wake me up out of the dream. So, I kept waking up out of the dream; so it was hard to do.

So, in talking about it with a couple of lamas that I translate with, they said, "Well, we have a special trick that we do." I said, "What's that?" He said, "We have a buddy system." So, when the lamas are trying to train themselves to be aware of their dreams, which is difficult to do, they have their roommate wake them up every two hours, suddenly wake them up and say, "What's your basis of operation right now?" "Uhhhhh, awakening!" [Dan chuckles] "What's your basis of operation right now?" "Uhhhh, awakening!"

So, you learn, because some of those times you're going to wake up, you're going to be in a dream. If you keep waking them up frequently every two hours, what's going to happen is they're starting to look, they automatically look at what the basis of operation is, and they find out that they are awake during the dream. So, they use that as a little trick to sort of help them train themselves to automatically carry awakened awareness into the dream, without disturbing the dream content or without disturbing sleeping.

So now they're awakened aware during the dream, and that's very different from all this Western stuff on lucid dreaming, because any Tibetan would say being aware, ordinary aware, during the dream isn't good enough. It has to be awakened aware. And if you can't do awakened awareness in the dream, you're just playing with things; you're not doing anything real. So, with all the fascination for lucid dreaming, at least we know in the West with lucid dreaming that you can train yourself to be aware during the dream. But what the Tibetans offer is a very different and more radical possibility. You can train yourself to be awakened aware during the dream.

Now, there are four levels of dream yoga practice. What you do is you start with the same sleeping lion's posture, and you go to sleep, and you focus on the throat chakra, one-pointedly, in an awakened aware state. And you thread that needle, and you go into deep sleep with awakened awareness, and at some point, while you're in deep sleep, content will start appearing again, and that's the hypnagogic state. It's easier to train dream yoga in the hypnagogic state, although the Tibetans don't make this distinction because they don't have a word for that. They clearly do it from what I've seen from the text that I've translated about this.

We once, in the West, this is many years ago, when we were looking at the hypnagogic state, and people have very vivid imagery in the hypnagogic state, so we were taking people who in their ordinary life claimed they couldn't imagine anything—they had no imagery—and what we did is we had them relax, lie down, and enter the hypnagogic stage, and train their awareness to pick up all that fragmented imagery.

And after three or four sessions of doing that, then they could carry it over, learning, to the waking state, and they could report having much more vivid imagery. So, we were doing that with athletes, we were training them to use visualizations. If they were poor visualizations, we did what we called hypnagogic training. So, the hypnagogic state is a state where it's easy to carry awareness into the transition into that stage of sleep more easily than it is to the dreaming state. So that's the one modification we've done, a Western modification of traditional Tibetan dream yoga. Do it in the hypnagogic state first. If the imagery is fragmented, so what? You can still be awakened aware during the fragmented imagery as it arises. Once you do that, you can go on to dreaming.

So, the first level of dream yoga is to train yourself to be awakened aware during every cycle of the dream at night, without waking up. And if you're doing both of these together, you're basically aware all night, awakened aware all night. You transition into sleep with awakened awareness. You get into the stillness of all the content of the mind during deep sleep, and you're awakened aware, and it's a bright, bright contentless field. And then the content starts to arise, and the dream comes up, and you're aware of all the dream content. And then the dream content subsides, it gathers in, subsides. And then you get into a stage where there's no content and all content is blocked out, and then the content appears again, and you go through the second dream cycle, etcetera. And you can basically, if you perfect this, you carry on a continuous awakened awareness through all the stages of your diurnal rhythms: deep sleep, dreaming, awakened during the day.

So, the first level of practice is mastery over carrying awakened awareness into the deep sleep and then also into dreaming. So, you're awakened aware during all the cycles of dreaming and hypnagogic state. Is that clear?

Now, the second stage in Tibetan dream yoga is not found in anything in the Western literature on lucid dreaming. It's called voluntary control over the content. And what they want you to see is not only can you be awakened aware during the dream, but you can actually change the content while it's happening. But they don't let you do that and open it in [any] way—it's very specific. They make you do impossible things in the dream because all of the literature on what are called *gunshes*, or supernormal abilities like flying through the air, or walking through walls, or materializing things, flying, all those things are done, all those are done by breaking down the beliefs about external reality.

And what the Tibetans say is the easiest way of breaking down those negative limiting beliefs is by changing dreams around, because those same beliefs occur in dreams because they're deeply entrenched in our mind. So, what they'll do in the second stage, which is called voluntary control over the dream content, is while you're awake and aware during the dream, you change the content around. You intentionally jump over a mountain in a single leap. You intentionally walk through walls or material things. You intentionally materialize things. You do special feats. You materialize. You have a dream about a horse, you change it into a *garuda*, and then you ride on the back of the *garuda* any way you want to ride.

You make all the dream content up, and you make it as fantastic as possible because it breaks down the limiting beliefs about how we live in this world. That's the second phase. It's called voluntary control over the content of the dream.

The third phase is more interesting. It's a little more fantastic. I remember when I was first translating it with Geshe Sonam, and the word was *pelwa*. So, I translated it as "increasing," which is not an incorrect translation. And I thought it meant that you were increasing the experience with the dreams. He said, "No, that's not what it means." And I said, "What does it mean?" And he said, "It means multiplying." I said, "Well, what's the difference between increasing and multiplying?" because, he said, "It means something very specific. It means making many copies of yourself."

So, in the third level of mastery, you make thousands of copies of yourself doing different things and helping beings, and that's how you train for buddhahood: make hundreds of thousands of copies of yourself simultaneously working at different planes of reality and helping beings. And you do that by multiplying many copies of yourself intentionally in the dream state from a vantage point of awakened awareness.

Now, that pretty much covers the domain of what sleep and dream yoga is about. It's very different from Western literature on lucid dreaming, and it's very different from other traditions on dreaming. So, I'll mention one other tradition just to give you a contrast here.

Many years ago—this was, oh, it has to be back in the maybe early 1970s—I met a Western woman, a Canadian woman, who was a curator at the British Columbia Museum. And she was a very unusual person. As a woman, she lived with a North Pacific First Nations tribe called the Athabaskans.

She was an anthropologist, and she lived with them for twelve years. And what she was concerned about is that they had no written language and no way to codify their great tradition other than to tie knots in different ways, and that's how they communicated. So, she actually developed a language so they could preserve the great oral tradition and write it down. She spent twelve years doing that. And as a woman, there are lots of taboos in that culture about how women had to live. And she observed all the taboos.

And as a result of living with them for twelve years, she developed their trust in a way that they had given no Westerner, let alone a woman, and they trained her to be a master shamaness. And one day she took a group of us out to the forest and lit a big bonfire, and she started doing all the traditional, the longhouse dances, which they do all winter. And what they would do is they'd dance a certain animal. And when you dance the animal, you get possessed by the animal's spirit, you become that animal. And that's how you learn the ways of that animal.

So, if you want to hunt the bear, you have to become a bear. Somebody in the tribe has to become a bear, and the bear will dance out all of the ways of the bear. So, you can hunt the bear and do it with respect for the ways of the bear. If you want to fish salmon, you don't just put your line in the water or your nets in the water, you have to dance out the ways of the salmon and treat them with respect as you catch them, and you can only catch so many because you have to respect their ways.

Everything is done with ecological harmony, but in their dream yoga, they use dream yoga combined with trance dancing so you become the animal in question. So, you know, it's vital if you're in a hunting and gathering society that you know the ways of all the animals. They used the content in very specific ways. It's very different from either the Western material or the Indo-Tibetan material. It's a different kind of shamanic dream yoga. It's very powerful. I did that with her in Canada, and I also did a field study in Haiti with the *manbos*, [female priestesses in the Haitian Vodou religion], learning how they do their trance dancing and how they access their *lwa*, their spirits.

So, there are three types of dream yoga here. There's Western dream yoga, which means being aware during the dream, which is not much of a big deal. There's the dream yoga that accesses you to spirit world so you can live in harmony with the spirits and do that with respect. And there's the dream yoga that leads to awakening and using that awakening as refined conduct and inexhaustibly help other beings. That's the overall domain of sleep and dream yoga.

Myself, I don't sleep that much anymore. I get about four hours of sleep. And my sleep is very light. I'm not usually tired the next day. You just don't need it. My current teacher, His Holiness Menri Trizin, he sleeps about four hours. With my first Root Lama that I lived with for nine years in the 1970s, he slept two hours. Awake means awake. You don't need it. You still go through deep sleep, it's just lighter. And the hormonal, phase-specific hormonal secretions happen anyway. But if you're doing something else, you're training the awakened awareness of the clear light of deep sleep with all the body still doing its repair process. But the dream stuff is just a ripening of karmic memory traces, which is mostly useless. So, you're releasing them.

When you get advanced with your practice, you do what's called *thun* practice, session-based practice according to diurnal rhythms. Cave and hermitage yogis do a lot with this. They'll do certain practices at a certain time of the day to take advantage of diurnal rhythms. So, the first thing you'll want to do in the morning, because you wake up from a dream, is self-arising/self-liberating. You let the dream content come up in the vast expanse as lively awakened awareness and don't engage it at all. Just let it run through and pass through. That way you're releasing all those karmic memory traces that have been activated until there's nothing left. It takes about twenty minutes to do that.

Then you do the same thing at night before you go to sleep so all the new karmic memory traces that are happening during the day that are now actively ripening, you're free of all that. So, you can accelerate the process of *dharmadhātu* exhaustion, releasing all karmic memory traces by doing it in the morning and doing it at night. Best time to do it. If you do that, you'll begin the day with a kind of freshness or not all that heaviness from the ripening of dream content. You'll tell the difference right away. That's a good practice to do.

The dreams are not interesting anymore. Every now and then you'll have a zinger dream that's different from anything else, but mostly it's not terribly interesting anymore. I remember when I was at Menri's, the first time I went there for the first retreat for the first month. He had previously built what's called a yogi temple. They put a lot of money into this building, and it's where they do all the tantric rituals. And right after they built it, during monsoon season, there was a mudslide and the building went "ehh," and it looked like it would slide off the mountain. So, the first day I got there, I had this weird dream—I don't have dreams like this. It was a giant serpent, a gigantic serpent about twelve feet long, a big black snake. It was really angry and lived in the mountain. And it was wreaking havoc on all the local villages.

So, since I don't have dreams like that and since I just arrived with this teacher, I told him the dream, and he was really interested, and he said, "Oh, I see what happened." He said, "There's a *naga* who lives in the mountain, and we didn't appease the *naga* before we built this project, and the *naga* is pissed off." So, he said, "We'll take care of it." So, they did a ritual to appease the *naga*, and then they didn't have any trouble with a mudslide after that ever again.

Nagas—it's a world of beings who are sort of half human, half snake. And they have very special powers. And you don't want to mess with them. There's a number of sutras which are held and teachings, tantric teachings, that are held only by the *nagas*. And you have to negotiate with them to get these teachings—they're not given easily. But if they're respected, they tend to be quite respectful back and cooperative.

*Naga*land is probably Assam, Eastern India. That's where the highest density of mostly cobras, poisonous snakes live anywhere in India. That's why it was originally called Nagaland. But these are mythical creatures that are half-human, half-serpent. They live underground. And they have very, very important abilities, and you want to get the *nagas* on your side. There are a number, in Bon, there are a number of rituals to appease the *nagas* and get them to be collaborative. Don't want to piss off a *naga*.

But that was not a usual dream, and he was quite interested in it. And they fixed it. So, in our new building project in Jomsom that we're trying to build, a spiritual campus and a school for the kids, we had six lamas come for three days to do ritual and appeasing the *nagas* and all local spirits. It was part of our architectural plans, building plans. We built the rituals into the proposal. Different world.

Student 2

[A student asks an inaudible question about having to get up during the night to go to the bathroom].

Dan

If you get up to go to the bathroom, then go back to sleep. The art of it is to not have that be the difficulty of getting back to sleep. Just go right back to sleep. If you go back to sleep, there's not a problem. You measure sleep inefficiency in terms of the difficulty of going back to sleep after frequent night awakening. And you can't stop that, but you can control it by cutting down the amount of liquids you have at night. That'll help.

August 16, 2017

Themes: Gene Smith; Conduct as a Sign; Spiritual Pride

Dan

Welcome everyone. You have a question?

Student 1

This is something I've been thinking a lot about, and it has to do with what it means to live a life of service. I see it, a lot of my coworkers who I feel are living their lives that way without even realizing it, and it's really beautiful to see. Then I also see, sometimes, patients who are taking care of each other, and one in mind who speaks Spanish, and she's trying to take care of a little ninety-year-old woman who speaks Italian, and she sits with her every day and helps feed her even though they can't really communicate. So, what I've been doing is wondering how this idea of being in service to all beings could be realized at every stage of the practice.

Dan

Okay, a very important question, but my answer is probably going to surprise you because living a life of service towards all beings isn't the same at every level of practice. But, the great American psychologist, William James, over a hundred years ago, when he wrote his classic, *The Varieties of Religious Experience*, in that book he describes a whole number of different types of mystical experiences. He was asked the question, "How do you tell the authenticity of a spiritual experience?" And his answer was, "By their fruits, ye shall know them,"[4] that the only true measure of authenticity is conduct, how you live your life.

So, if you take the practice to be not about meditation, meditation is just a means, but it's a means to developing realizations. Meditation leads to meditation experiences, *nyampa*. Meditation experiences lead to realizations, spiritual realizations, *tokpa*, in Tibetan. But how do you judge the nature of those realizations? The main purpose of the path is to develop the realization of awakened awareness, that always right here is an infinitely boundless, timeless, ocean of awakened awareness-love.

But you don't recognize it because your mind is clouded over by too many structures of mind, like all the mass of conceptual thought clouds over recognizing that awakening. Your sense of self clouds over recognizing of awakening. The sense of things coming and going in conventional time clouds over that timeless awakening. Your localization of an individual consciousness clouds over the boundless, non-localized nature of awakening. So, the path leads to that direct experience of awakening where you shift your basis of operation—where you're coming from—out of getting caught up and lost in thought mode; you shift out of being lost in sense of self mode. You shift out of being caught up in conventional time. You shift out of the localization of your information processing system. And what you find yourself, if you shift out of all those things that we get caught up in, what's left is, you find yourself being that unbounded wholeness love. You recognize awakened awareness as your true nature, like recognizing that the sun always shines even if you can't see it because it's clouded over by whatever.

But how do we know that people authentically experience that awakening? How do we know that they're not just thinking about it, making it up even because they want it so much? And we say that if you have the experience of awakening, it's more likely to be authentic if it's accompanied by opening the heart. If it's accompanied by spontaneous gratitude, by spontaneous compassion, by spontaneous devotion, then you're probably on the right track. But

4 Bible: Matthew 7: 16-20.

if you describe it as some abstract way, this nature of spacious mind, then it's probably likely be conceptual and not really truly awakening. So, part of the measure of that is whether it opens up compassion.

Rahob Tulku has a specific way of judging authenticity. He says, "If you find yourself in the most difficult of life circumstances, and your awakening falls apart, it was probably mostly conceptual. But if it's authentic, then when you find yourself in the most difficult of life circumstances, the realization of awakening deepens in the worst of life circumstances." So, that's a pretty good test.

We have several students who were followers of a very charismatic Western *dharma* teacher who was self-realized. He had a lot of good things to say when he taught. Only trouble was that when he got older and had cancer and was dying of the cancer, he panicked and seemed to lose his realization and turned on his best students and got mean. When he found himself in the most difficult of life circumstances, like facing death, realizations went down the tubes. On the other hand, if you have faced medical issues, and you take that as an opportunity to deepen your realization, then it's probably more genuine.

The third answer is that the best and most true measure of authenticity of realization is conduct—how you live your life. So, the most authentic manifestation of realization is not necessarily how you describe what your realizations are, because that doesn't mean much. It is how you live your life. So, genuine spiritual masters leave behind themselves a wake of positive influence, and you can tell by what they do in their lives, the nature of their realizations. But they rarely talk about their realizations unless it's useful for teaching purposes.

One of my oldest friends who got me started in this whole field was Gene Smith. Gene was a student of Dudjom Rinpoche, the great Nyingma lineage holder. And when Gene was young, he lived with Dudjom for twelve years. He became a great practitioner of Dzogchen meditation. And because of the nature of his realizations, he felt that these practices were very precious, and they were on the verge of being eliminated, because when the Chinese took over Tibet, in the first week of the invasion, they spent an entire week, day and night, burning all the sacred texts in Tibet, a hundred thousand volumes on states of mind. It's Chinese Kristallnacht. It destroyed an entire textual tradition, a spiritual tradition of a hundred thousand volumes in one week that had been collected over eight thousand years. Remarkable. And Gene, being a librarian, working for the Library of Congress, realized the importance of saving this tradition. So, he spent his entire life working for the Library of Congress, where they had a budget where they could get sherpas to sneak into Old Tibet and sneak out with block prints. And he built a whole series of cheap publishing houses in Old Delhi and reprinted everything.

So, in his lifetime, he reconstructed about eighty thousand volumes of what had been lost. One person did that. But if you asked Gene about his spiritual practice, he would growl and change the topic right away. He would never ever talk about his spiritual practice. But obviously, he lived it. But he would never talk about his realizations or even the nature of his practice.

Tulku Thondup is a Tibetan lama who's lived in Cambridge here in this area for years, and no one's ever heard of him because he doesn't teach. He doesn't like to teach. He wrote one book on Dzogchen, which is very good. And the only reason why he wrote it, because the previous translation was so bad, he said, "I had to retranslate it accurately." And not because he wanted to. He doesn't like to teach. The only student he ever had in the last forty years was Gene Smith. I suppose that says something. Gene died in 2010. And in the 1990s, when all of the books that he had republished and all the manuscripts he had reconstructed on cheap Indian paper started to rot, he decided that was a bad idea, so he started scanning everything on the internet.

So, the irony is that the Tibetans may never have their own country again, but their entire library which was once destroyed has been reconstructed and survives for all, can be accessed by everybody on the internet, in hyperspace. Future Tibet is hyperspace. And all that was left behind by one man. "By their fruits, ye shall know them." That's what one person did with his life.

So, the only real answer to your question is what you leave behind and your conduct. And people who have realizations leave behind the positivity. They're sensitive to others. They're concerned about others' welfare, and they act single-mindedly to help others along the path.

But, although that's the general answer to that question, it changes depending on the nature of your practice and the level of your practice. So, at the beginning, conduct doesn't make a lot of sense. What makes a lot of sense is that your duty to your practice is to give up all your busyness and give priority to your practice. If you're first starting on this practice, if you don't make the time for it, it gets lost rather quickly. We've had many students take the full week retreat, the level one retreat and get a taste of awakening, and then never practice after that. They lose it, waste it, because they're too caught up in the busyness of their everyday life. That's stupid.

If you have a genuine realization, you have certainly the capacity for that, and you throw it away because you're too caught up in everyday life? But it happens, more frequently than not. So, at the level of practice where you're going from the beginning of practice up to a taste of awakening, the nature of conduct means that you prioritize your daily life: you try and make it so that you make a time to do a daily practice on the pillow, and you practice off the pillow. So, it becomes a central reference point in your life. At the beginning of practice, if you can't manifest that as your conduct, the spiritual practice goes down the tubes. It's not going to go anywhere useful. Don't have any illusions. It's not going to go anywhere.

If you have a taste of awakening, your conduct isn't immediately to go out and serve the purpose of all sentient beings because that awakening is fresh and fragile. So, your duty at that point, in terms of your conduct, is really to develop it. The word in Tibetan is *chungwa*, which means to cultivate it. It also means to nurture it. It's very precious. You've got to nurture it like a newborn. You've got to give it care. You've got to bring it out more frequently. You've got to bring it out for a longer duration. You've got to bring it out immediately, and you've got to have it so that it's all the time on and off the pillow.

But, at that point, your conduct isn't so much to serve others as much as it is to develop the practice realization. The outcome of stabilizing that is that you'll experience the world as far more interconnected. And, if you see the world as more interconnected, the conduct spontaneously arises in terms of the aspiration to help others coming from that state. But really, the conduct at that level of practice is to stabilize awakening. And if you stabilize awakening, and you're on the third map of practice, which takes you from stable awakening up to enlightenment, full buddhahood, what do you do with conduct then?

Your conduct is to purify the mind. If you've gone that far with the practice, you can spend too much time helping other people in such a way that it distracts you from really developing your own practice. That's not skillful. What's skillful about that? You have a shot at buddhahood. Develop the practice so that that shot at buddhahood becomes something that's quite real. Then, when you get far along that third map of practice, and you've purified the residuals of the ordinary mind, as we say, you begin to make a connection to the threefold embodiment of enlightenment, even though you haven't fully manifested that.

At that point in mind, the view, or the experience, becomes so vast it includes an ocean of beings. That's when service to other beings becomes legitimate. It naturally arises from the view. Then you can legitimately think about devoting your practice to the service of all beings. And all advanced practices are the same way. If you stabilize awakening and you have it all the time, you can have voluntary control over the dying process. You can voluntarily control how you come back if you so wish, and usually, what you'll do is the practices that will allow you to recognize the clear light of death and have control over that process so that you can recycle yourself and come back and help other beings.

But at that point in practice, you don't really need to develop your own practice anymore. It's pretty far along. But there are many stories of people who think that they should help sentient beings, and in the course of doing that, they get so caught up in helping sentient beings that they leave aside the heart of their own practice.

There are many stories in the Akhrid book that we translated recently. And we have a lineage of the Akhrid masters. There's one master who developed a good deal of realization but not full buddhahood. And then he thought what he needed to do is manifest that, but it was a thought. So, he spent a number of years becoming an abbot of a monastery and teaching people and doing all these things that got him away from his own realization. And the realizations went flat. Finally, his teacher said, "Look, this isn't going in a good direction. Go back to your meditations and devote full time for that. Then when you stabilize the realizations, you can come back to this."

So, this conduct, which means the duty to develop your own realizations, and there's the duty to, what you do to other people. Both of those are necessary. One's given more and less emphasis at various stages of the path; and it changes. So, there's no one answer to your question, you see. It depends on what level of realization you have.

But generally speaking, the principle is if you have some fresh realization that's authentic, you probably want to spend some time developing that, stabilizing it, nurturing it. Then, once it's stable, conduct towards others naturally arises from that realization. But if you leave the realization too quickly and go back to your everyday life or to the idea of your life of helping other people, it just distracts you from the realization, and you lose it. The realization then is just an idea, remote, a more and more remote idea. It's gone. But ultimately, when your realizations are stable, you inexhaustibly serve the purpose of all beings, and that becomes a single-minded realization. You just live the realization in terms of how you act towards other beings.

Yeah?

Student 2

I had a question or, not ... I wanted to share a few things that I learned, some breakthroughs and then to have you to comment about ... It's about getting the kind of teachings all the way in my body. I'm just going to mention very succinctly four things that have really helped me. One is I've come to realize, like my brain or the crown chakra it seems to operate at a different frequency maybe than my body. I've long been a heady person. And so, I've learned to slow down a lot, and slowing has really got me in touch with my body a lot better. That's really helped me at the practice, and just be in the moment instead of being in my head. So that was the first solution.

The second solution that's helped me is a couple of truths that I've learned. For example, I've learned just that I can be okay with whatever, which is another version of automatic emptiness, but I have been prostrating, getting down on the ground and surrendering to that truth. Sometimes, I'll sit on my cushion, and I'll just think about that and make a circle, like a yes to it, and it seems to settle my body.

And the other thing that I use that same technique with is understanding there's an immutable law in humanity that all humans can really only accept the level of truth that they can handle. When I was able to prostrate to that and surrender to it and say yes to it, I was kind of like, made me more compassionate because I realized everybody's just a composite of their past and their history, and I was able to forgive myself and other versions of myself and other people, which cleared up a lot of clouds and opened my heart. It just amazed me that it just helped me be in my body.

And lastly, I guess I've just kind of learned that we have a lot of trauma. It's not just psychological, but it's in our body, and I've used techniques like network spinal analysis, which is we have nervous systems in the spine, and they use light touches to get that out. That just helped me a lot, and also, cranial sacral therapy. And there's lots of somatic therapies that kind of deal with that. So anyways, I guess I give that to you. What are your thoughts on the teachings and getting in the body and the kind of things I've learned?

Dan

There's a lot to what you're saying. There's so many points it's hard to know how to focus it, but I'll try. The Buddhist logicians talk about two types of knowing. There's conceptual knowing, and there's knowing through direct awareness. In Western philosophy, we don't appreciate the fact that knowing can come through direct awareness and not through conceptual knowing; or we think that conceptual knowing is all there is. But you can't think your way into awakening or enlightenment.

So, one strategy for getting out of the over-identification with thought is to focus more on bodily experience. And what you're saying is in terms of you knowing yourself and your propensities for conceptualizing that's been helpful to you, because it is. It's the same reason why we focus in concentration on body-centered objects, like the felt sense of the breath or the felt sense of the body posture, because the more you take as an object the body, and get out of your head, the quicker you get out of thought mode or over-identification with thought mode.

So, as a pathway to minimize or to correct the over-identification with thought, the emphasis of the body is useful, as long as you don't reify the body. That becomes something that becomes a source of attachment in itself. Then it becomes its own problem. So, I agree with you that the focus on the body-centered approach is useful, but not as an end in itself. As a vehicle for getting you out of the over-identification with thought, it's useful. But you're raising another issue I'm going to answer probably a little different than what you expect.

You talked about prostrations. It's a concept that's fairly alien to Westerners. Why do Buddhists and Bon spend a lot of time doing a hundred thousand prostrations? The reason why the prostrations is so frequently used as a foundation for the practice is that right from the get-go, you are correcting for the danger of spiritual pride, because it means you're willing to humble yourself at any level of your practice, at any level of realization.

So, shifting gears to a Western approach, Johannes Cassian was commissioned by the church in Rome to go out and study the Desert Fathers, because they were afraid that the Desert Fathers … people were flocking to the desert to study with the cave yogis and leaving the Church. And since the Church was interested in building its constituency and power and money and enrollments, they were threatened, terribly threatened by the Desert Fathers. So, they commissioned two sets of investigations of the Desert Fathers.

The second was Johannes Cassian. Cassian wrote two works after living with the Desert Fathers for several years. One was suppressed by the Church because they didn't like Cassian's theology, because what Cassian said is if you went out and study with the Desert Fathers, and you practice what was called the prayer of quiet, and you practiced it and brought it to its endpoint, like St. Anthony and the yogis around the first generation of Desert Fathers that was around Anthony, he said you became Jesus. And everybody had Jesus nature.

If you did these practices, everybody here potentially became Jesus. The Church didn't like the theology of that at all because it implied that it was accessible to everyone. An institution like the Church wouldn't be required, because anybody could do it with the right set of experiential practices. So, you could see why the book was terribly threatening to the Church.

Then he wrote a second book about the so called seven deadly sins. And what he was writing about there wasn't about everyday sins. It was about the excesses of yogi practice in the desert—the extremes of practice, the extremes of sensory and social isolation.

So, [he was saying] if you go off and give up your everyday life and all the sensory stimuli and sensory overload, the first sin that comes up is gluttony. It's like going camping, and you give up all the sensory stimuli and business of everyday life, and you go out to the forest, and it's quiet. And you spend the rest of the time thinking about food, right? That's what you do when you go camping. You eat and clean up and eat again, because the mind isn't used to that sensory isolation. So, it strategically plays out everything around food.

And if you continue to isolate yourself on a long retreat, the next is lust. You start thinking about human contact, which you have deprived yourself of. We used to see that in the three-month retreatants who would go to mindfulness retreats for three months. We call it "the *vipassana* romance." You sit there in your third week into your silent retreat, and all of a sudden, you realize that the love of your life is sitting two pillows away. But you never met her. You spent most of the time fantasizing about this person. It's complete fiction, and you're making a hit. Why do we do this stuff? Because it's a natural reaction against the extreme of social isolation.

And the third was called avarice, hoarding behavior. If you keep depriving yourself over time, the little things in your life you cling onto because it's all you got. We used to see that in the mindfulness retreats and the three-month retreats where the people would start taking the bananas and the apples and oranges at tea break and hoarding them in their rooms. They're not going to eat them. They're going to go rotten. But you have to have them because it's all you've got left.

Then the fourth deadly sin was anger and dejection. At some point, because you keep depriving yourself, you get pissed off, saying, "What am I doing?"

And the fifth was sloth and torpor, and the sixth was acedia, which means agitation of mind and all the extremes of being over-aroused and under-aroused come up. If you get through all that, the seventh deadly sin was called pride. Who's doing the meditation? When you do the prayer of quiet, after a while you calm the mind so much that thought drops away, but sense of self drops away, and the problem of who the observer of the meditation is comes up. But then Cassian did something very interesting. You don't see it in Buddhism.

He said the [seventh] deadly sin is only for advanced practitioners. He called it spiritual pride, and what Cassian said about it is, "The more, not the less you practice, that becomes more of a problem." So, you see, anchored in your body and the deep imprint in the body, in every step of the practice, if you make prostrations, you're saying, "I'll never put myself above anybody else. I'll never get to the point of thinking my realizations are important," because when you get further along, the tendency to say, "My realization is important," becomes a big deal.

It becomes a big deal particularly in people who have legitimate realizations that are not part of a lineage tradition. There are people teaching in the West who have legitimate realizations, it looks like to me. When they teach, they never talk about how the other people can do it. They spend the time talking about themselves and their own realizations and how they came to it. How does that help you? See the problem there? But every step of the way, the problem, the spiritual pride becomes more, not less of a problem.

We see that all the time in our students. It's exhausting to me. If you have somebody that gets caught up in spiritual pride, and you try and point it out to them, what do you think happens? Do you think they take it in? No, they become indignant and righteous, and they reject their teachers. It happens all the time. There are many, many examples of that.

We make a clear statement. It's not subtle that to get the advanced teachings you can't just sign up for them because that's spiritual pride—you have to be followed by your teacher on a regular basis.

So recently, we offered for the first time the most advanced course we've ever done, the inner fire practice, which is a transmission teaching. It's never been taught to this depth in the West before. We taught it in Switzerland. Three weeks before the course, I asked the course organizer for the list of people who signed up. 70 percent of the people who signed up for the course, knowing that they need to be followed by a teacher, had not been followed in the last year. They just signed up anyway. That, my friends, is massive spiritual pride.

Do you really think you got to the point that you can get beyond following with your teacher anymore? Because if you are, you're delusional. So, it made a great inconvenience at the last minute. Well, I have a dilemma here. I can cancel the course and say, "Screw you guys. You're not following the rules," or I can offer the course, which would be a big disruption of everybody's practice and saying, "You got to do better than this."

The lama that I taught with was very angry about it. He said, "Here's what to do. You give them a year grace period, and if they don't follow through, don't nag them anymore. If they don't follow through in the year, you cut them off. They're done forever with any spiritual teachings. You're done." Because we can't teach people who are caught up in spiritual pride. So, it meant scrambling at the last minute. Do a lot of last-minute interviews to give people a chance to try and do it differently. Some of those people will do it differently, and some of those will no longer be students in another year.

We have course organizers that help us organize the course. That's convenient because we teach all over the world. We have a number of course organizers that haven't followed with a teacher for the last two or three years. They think that simply because they organized the courses they're entitled to take the advanced courses. That, my friends, is spiritual pride.

Spiritual practice doesn't come with entitlements. But what you're saying is something that's very precious. If you start with prostrations, which we don't require, right from the get-go you're humbling yourself. You're always reminding yourself through the repeated prostrations to humble yourself. It's a reminder not to let the pride take over because it gets in the way. Once you get filled with spiritual pride, you can't make a dent in it.

I had a student who wanted to come and visit His Holiness Menri Trizin. He had gone through some good changes in his life, so I thought, "Well, maybe it was a time where Menri would keep him on track." So, I brought him to Menri's. He loved His Holiness, but His Holiness at the time was sick with cancer, and I told him [something] explicitly because the next time I showed up there to visit His Holiness, he had brought a bunch of people. And I told him explicitly, "This isn't a tour place. You don't get to just bring anybody you want here because it's a cool thing to do to meet the teacher. You've got to protect his time. He's sick. You don't get to bring people here. You've got to promise me that you won't bring anybody here unless you clear it with me in his office." "Okay," he promised. Next time I went back, he was there, very friendly. Then I found out from the monks that the week after I was leaving, he was going to bring a whole tour of people, and they didn't want it because it was too much of a strain on His Holiness.

He lied about it because he thought that because he had made the connection, he had enough pride that he could do whatever he wanted. So, I wrote him a letter saying, "You're filled with spiritual pride, and you can't just do what you want with a great teacher like this." You know what his answer was? "I made the connection with His Holiness. Now, I don't need you anymore as a teacher. Fuck you. I'll do whatever I want." Yeah, pretty much, that was the answer. I wrote him back, "You're filled with spiritual pride. I can't make a dent in you. You don't listen to anything. We're done. You broke the connection with your teacher. Finished. Done for this lifetime."

I talked with His Holiness about it. He said, "You know, he's going to do whatever he wants. He's not going to get anywhere with this practice." I could give you a thousand stories of Western students like this, and everyone's as bad as the next, because most of you just don't get it.

You're raising something very important. Maybe we need to build into this some more reminders. It's not about self. The self is a habit of mind that's incessant. The emptiness of self-practice puts it in perspective. If you learn anything about spiritual practice, self-importance isn't terribly important. But the further you get with the practice the self-importance comes back in the form of this disguised way; you get caught up in it. It's so easy to get caught up in it and to not see it.

We just went through that last year. We were trying to raise money for the building of the monastery. We spent three years with His Holiness. The architect spent many, many hours at the monastery asking His Holiness what he wanted us to build. We spent five town meetings with the local people about what they wanted us to do in their community for them. We have all these people on the Foundation who think that they're there because they're business people; they have a much better idea of what needs to get done than these people say they want. That, my friends, is spiritual pride. Our mistake was to put people on the Board who essentially had business skills, and the worst of those business skills come out. It's all about corporate raiding. It's not about making money. It's not about doing things you want to do. It's about listening to what other people say they need in their community.

We actually had one of the people sit down with Asonam because we found out he wasn't helping us with the fundraising, which we asked him to do explicitly. He's a very well-to-do businessman. He could help us a lot. We found out he was discouraging people from the business from helping us with the fundraising. Why? He actually told in front of Asonam that all these Himalayan cultures are going to die out on their own. It's not worth funding them from a business point of view. How arrogant is that? Why? It's from a business point of view. It's not an investment, folks. It's about listening to what these people need and helping them and getting yourself out of the way.

So, all we can do is convey the teachings as clearly as we can to you and ask you to follow carefully with that. But if you get bitten by the pride, we can't make a dent in what you're doing from there, because once you get bitten by the pride, you're not going to listen to anything we say. Then your practice goes down the tubes. You sever the relationship, and the karmic loss of that goes down lifetimes.

I can't fix that for you. It's your own actions. All I can do is remind you of it, so you don't get caught up in it. And that's the value of being part of a lineage tradition. I remember once, because Menri openly reads minds, so he knows whatever you're thinking. I remember going there once, and the first thing out of his mouth, I didn't say a word, he said, "You're doing a lot of teaching. Watch for the pride." I said, "Busted. Thank you." I found that very helpful. He's always busting me. In fact, every time I go to him, he busts me in a very playful way. I like being busted. It keeps me on track. It keeps me honest. Being busted by Menri is my prostrations. Prostrations are self-bustings, and you're anchoring the realization in your body as you were saying.

Student 2

Yeah, I found that really freeing to do the prostration surrendering almost. There's prostrating in general and being humble, but I was also using it to surrender to certain truths I was learning, like about how the recognition, everybody's just doing the best they can. They're at the level of truth they can handle and just getting that in just helped me get certain things deep, deep within me, so it just wasn't a mental idea. It was like my whole body …

Dan

Yeah, but don't make the body into a whole thing now. You've got a whole story there.

Student 2

I'm just telling you it worked.

Dan

Yeah, for now. And now it's not working the other direction because you start making the body the goal. The goal is the nature of your realization. The body is just a device to that realization.

Student 2

Sure. I'm just saying, like sure, experiences connect to the whole thing. It just feels more …

Dan

And even the story that you do in your mind. That's got to go at some point too.

Student 2

What?

Dan

The story that you're too much caught up in your mind. At that point, you move beyond that story, too.

Student 2

Yeah, I mean …

Dan

Now, you can move beyond that story, too.

Student 2

I am moving beyond the story, yeah, now that I have new tools, and I've been learning to do that. Yes, I can move past that.

Dan

There you go.

Student 2

It's done. [Laughter] Did you have anything to say? I know I asked a lot of stuff. But the whole thing about the frequency. Is it the slowness? Or is that about how different chakras work at different frequencies?

Dan

Is that the whole story, too?

Student 2

I think it's the story too ... I don't know.

Dan

You're looking for stuff.

Student 2

I don't know, if it works.

Dan

Yeah, but if you look for stuff, you're going to miss the main heart of this, which is the realization of awakened awareness. We don't care about chakras. It's just stuff.

Student 2

Okay.

Dan

Don't get caught up in the stuff.

Student 2

I'm not. I don't feel like I'm caught up in any way, shape or form. I'm just saying they're tools that help with my awakening.

Dan

Yeah, but then you're replacing the tools of the mind with another set of body-related tools, and there's still the same pattern. I'm saying step out of the whole pattern, and then you're really free.

Student 2

Okay. I mean, the goal is to be awake and I agree with that.

Dan

Okay, we can agree upon that then.

Student 2

Yeah.

Dan

I'm going to keep pestering you about this. It's my duty. [Dan chuckles]

Student 2

Fair enough.

Dan

Yes?

Student 3

So, Dan, as I was listening to this, I got scared that how do I guard against spiritual pride? I don't even know what a prostration is. How does one, well, I understand that the physicality of it. But what's the devotion behind it?

Dan

That when you prostrate you are literally saying with your body posture that you're not putting yourself above anybody.

Student 3

It's just that simple?

Dan

Yeah.

Student 3

Okay.

Dan

It's like the example I gave of the guy who thought that he could bring anybody because he wanted to be the tour guide for all the people coming to the monastery, because it was a cool thing to meet the main Master, at the expense of the Master's physical health and his level of fatigue He was really ill. It was selfish. But his idea that he knew what was best, that's putting yourself above anybody else, including your two teachers, particularly when they said, "No." I had to talk with him, but he didn't listen, too. The lamas had to bring it up. Everybody brought it up.

No matter who brought it up, the entire spiritual community, all the people in the spiritual tradition, all the lamas brought it up to him. Nope, he knows better. Well, where's the humility in that? He's wrong.

Somebody sent me this wonderful Photoshop of Donald Trump in a Tibetan monk's robe, and it says, "I am the most spiritual person in the world." [Dan and students laugh] "I know more about spirituality than anybody else." So, it's like that because he thinks that. There's a kind of spiritual pride there. It's the same issue. So, you're on safer ground if you expect the likelihood that it will come up in one form or another.

Student 3

And hope that you'll bust me?

Dan

No, in yourself, with your metacognitive awareness. You look for it.

Student 3

Okay.

Dan

And you expect that your teachers will hold you in line with that. If you have good quality teachers, they'll do that. But you've got to listen to it at that point.

Student 3

How does one understand the distinction between developing confidence in my practice and acknowledging the progress maybe that I have made without developing a pride about it?

Dan

That's a great question. All you have to do is keep that questioning before you without an answer, and you're going to do just fine.

Student 3

One of those?

Dan

Yeah, just one of those. Do you understand what I'm saying?

Student 3

I do.

Dan

That's a great question. As long as you're concerned about that question, you're going to do just fine.

Student 3

Go to my grave without an answer.

Dan

You have the answer. The answer is in that tension that you want to develop confidence in the view, as we say, that comes from your direct experience and seeing the realizations working. But then you can't have that confidence go beyond that and shade off to another extreme. You know, maybe now it becomes self-importance, because the fundamental essence is that self-importance is not terribly important.

We found that—and it was really interesting to me—I wrote this with a number of other people, so we didn't put it in the paper in a way that I would have emphasized. But as you know, this last year, we did a study on the neurocircuitry of awakening. We did it in Judd Brewer's lab, the Mindfulness Neurocircuitry Lab at UMass Medical School. And Judd, of course, did all the original research on mindfulness, meditation and neurocircuitry of mindfulness. What he found in the findings that are consistent with mindfulness, what you see is the posterior cingulate cortex gets deactivated. And the posterior cingulate cortex is that part of the brain that judges and categorizes and classifies experience.

So, when you get into this non-judgmental awareness, that's because of PCC deactivation. What's called non-meditation meditation in the Tibetan system does that even more strongly. But what's interesting is, the main finding that we had was that when people shift to awakening, there's a part of the parietal system that gets activated, and it's the part of the parietal system that shifts from localized to global awareness—you get a larger perspective on everything. And that activation is in the gamma activity. It means very high frequency. All the cells are firing, and they're all firing in the same synchronous way.

So awake means awake. It's an unusual finding. But when we looked at the sense of self, which is the medial prefrontal cortex, Dan-ness, the sense of self representation, in mindfulness, which is the first turning of the wheel in Buddhism, the medial prefrontal cortex gets deactivated. It goes offline—*anatta*, no self, and one of the first realizations in older Buddhism. But that realization was considered not the best realization in Mahāyāna Buddhism, so they revised it in terms of the theory of emptiness.

We found that what happened in the Tibetan meditation is the sense of self doesn't go offline. It doesn't change. It just becomes irrelevant. You just shift your perspective to a more global perspective, and the self is part of that ocean of awareness. It's like a wave in the ocean, but it's not what you're operating out of. It just becomes irrelevant. So, there are clear differences between mindfulness and awakening in terms of what happens to the sense of self. In the older Buddhism, which is mindfulness, sense of self is deactivated, so you have no self, *anatta*. Whereas here, the self just becomes irrelevant, because it's not what you're operating out of anymore. You just leave it there. You're operating out of a much larger perspective where everybody and everything is interconnected, and you can operate out of that.

But what's clear is in either case, you're not operating out of self anymore. At any level of the tradition, the self becomes unimportant. The opposite of spiritual practice is when self becomes too important, and now it's tagged to spirituality just the way that the habit of self comes back and creeps back in, and you don't even know it comes back in. Now, you know better than anybody else about what's best in your practice and you don't listen to your teachers anymore.

Student 3

That's a useful distinction for me that it's irrelevant because …

Dan

It's simply not where you're operating out of. It's still there. It's just not what you're operating out of. It's irrelevant.

Student 3

The Western story that I am, is it took a long time for me to establish a sense of self.

Dan

In everyday relative reality, it's useful. It's a central organizing principle. I organize a lot of my everyday life around Dan-ness. But ultimately, it's just a story. The idea is not to get caught up in the story and to see beyond it and operate out of a much larger perspective in life. So, the story is just irrelevant. It's like a wave in the ocean while you're being the ocean. Better to be the ocean than the wave. And from that larger perspective, of course, everything and everyone is interconnected within that. So that's where your compassion comes from because you get that larger view where everybody is interconnected.

But it's the same when the question about conduct is raised. There's no place for the self in there. So, both of you are raising the same issue. But what you have to watch out for with conduct and spiritual pride, same thing, you do conduct, basically, based on some idea of what you think is going to be helpful to people rather than what they really need. It's based on your own ideas. It's like my best friend Stevie. When I was growing up, he was ten years old, and he was very proud that he bought a turtle for his mother for her birthday because he really knew that she wanted a turtle. [Dan chuckles] So he gave too many turtles rather than thinking about what his mother really might have wanted. He got what he wanted which is what he thought his mother wanted. So, you've got to stop giving turtles. True compassion is when you stop giving turtles and you give the people what they need.

Yes?

Student 4

Hi. I have some questions about setting up the practice, and I think maybe these questions are related. There seems to be three points. I find that it's difficult for me to empty to go to vastness, to go to boundless. I mean, time I can empty fairly well because all that feels inside. But when you start talking about emptying to realize vastness and boundlessness …

Dan

You're not getting it right.

Student 4

Yeah.

Dan

All emptiness practice is an affirming negation. You negate A in order to affirm B. You're getting the negation part, the negation of time, but not the affirming part of what's left, which is the ocean-like, changeless, boundless awareness.

Student 4

Yeah, I don't ... There's no shift there. I can't feel the shift.

Dan

Okay, we'll go through the instructions after. I won't answer that now. I'll answer it as a meditation. I'll give you the direct instructions for that, which is from Shri Singha.

Student 4

Then I have some follow-up, which is, then maybe a specific order of emptying that I'm not following, so I'm getting myself confused. What I mean is, so thinking about the exemplar, and taking on the qualities of an exemplar. It felt like, you know, in a felt sense, a metacognitive awareness to then go right into emptying of self. But then I got confused because I go, "Wait a minute. I just thought of ..."

Dan

That's the correct sequence.

Student 4

Yeah, but this happened once just this week, where it's like, "Well, wait a minute. I'm identifying now with my exemplars. So, if I empty the self, wouldn't that include the qualities of the exemplar?"

Dan

It still exists relatively; it's just not substantial. You're not going to get rid of relative reality through emptying. You're getting a nihilistic view of emptying. You're not getting rid of anything. You're going beyond it. You shift your basis of operation so that you're not operating out of it.

Student 4

Right. I do need help with that.

Dan

You shift beyond self. See, that's where this notion of other-emptiness comes in, *shantong*. All relative phenomena are empty of themselves, in and of themselves, but not empty of permanent reality. There are certain positive qualities that the more you try and practice emptiness, they shine forth more clearly. You don't get rid of them because those qualities represent ultimate reality. There are eighty positive qualities of a buddha mind. If you practice cultivating one of those, like patience or diligence or something like that through the exemplar method, you're not going to get rid of that quality. It's going to get stronger.

Still, there are a lot of stories and labels about it. If you see it as empty, I mean, if you clean it up with the stories and labels, you're not going to get rid of the quality, it's going to just shine forth, this quality, much more strongly.

Student 4

Yeah, that makes sense. It's clear.

Dan

Watch out that your emptiness practice doesn't shade off into nihilism or eternalism. You've got to find the middle path. You're not that far off. Just a little off. Just correct it. Do the affirming part of the affirming negation. What's left after you negate the emptiness of time. What's left is a level of awareness that's outside of time, so it's timeless and changeless on the one hand. Since time and space are related, it's boundless and vast. If you're not setting it up, you're not doing the exercise. You're only doing half of it. You've got to finish it. I'll give you the instructions on how to do that. I'll give them to the whole group.

Student 4

Thank you.

Dan

Sure.

Student 5

I had two questions.

Dan

Okay.

Student 5

One is, I heard you say, "My realizations aren't important," and what I heard in that is the realizations are important, but it's not important that they're mine.

Dan

You heard it correctly. It's a good distinction you're making, a really important distinction. Thank you.

Student 5

Thank you. My other question is that I thought that I was justified in having done this before I walked into this room. But I wanted to ask you if this would serve as an example of spiritual pride. I went to dinner with my aunt, and knowing full well that she has a difficult time not letting her anxieties become visible or vocalizing them.

Dan

Manifested. Spilling over, so to speak. Okay, got it.

Student 5

Yep. I said, "No parent should ever project their anxiety onto their child." And, while I believe that in principle that might be good advice, in retrospect it seems to me now that I thought that it was crucially important that everyone knew, in the room, knew that I had this realization, and now, I was going to instruct them.

Dan

That's a good example. [Laughter]

Student 5

Okay. [More laughter]

Dan

I appreciate your honesty.

Student 5

Thank you.

Dan

It's good. But if you're that honest with yourself, you're not going to get caught up in it. That's the whole point. It's when you get caught up in it, you're not aware of it, you lose the metacognitive awareness. You don't even know you're coming across like that.

Student 5

Well, I didn't until I'd just thought about it. [Laughter]

Dan

But you thought about it correctly and honestly. What more can we ask for? It's good practice.

Student 5

Thank you.

Dan

I appreciate your clarity. It's really, for somebody's who's been here for the first time, that's unusual. Thank you. That's very touching. You're getting it, and you're absolutely honest about it. That's a good model for others.

Student 5

Thank you.

Dan

You've got to do what he's doing. Now, he's going to get more proudful. [Laughter] You'll have to bust him on that.

Student 5

I'm going to go home now and tell everyone that I was complimented. [Laughter]

Dan

And then we'll have to bust you, you see? That's how it works. Let's take a break here, and then we'll do a practice. [In a hypnotic voice:] You are becoming more and more awake. [Laughter]

September 13, 2017

Themes: Unpacking Teacher Scandals; Conduct Is the Best Test of Authenticity

Dan

Welcome everyone. You have a question?

Student 1

I hope this is okay. So, as I think you know I work with a Nepali teacher, so I have a lot of contact with …

Dan

You brought him here at one point.

Student 1

Yes.

Dan

But I wasn't in town; I didn't get to see him.

Student 1

It was really nice, yes. It was great. So, I've had a lot of exposure to what we call traditional *vajrayāna*, and with a lot of benefit. I've gained a lot from that. And as I think you may be aware, and most people are aware, there's been a lot of scandal come out recently with certain Rinpoches, Sogyal Rinpoche, etc., coming out into the open.

And it was real shocking for me being part of this more traditional *sangha*, Asian, Nepali. There was a tremendous amount of defense for those actions which, for me was traumatizing to go through. And under the guise of it is the ideal of pure perception, and for those of you who are not familiar with it, I probably won't do a good job with it, but pure perception is to see all actions of one's teacher, and then it can expand beyond that to everything, as good, with no room in between. And there were some active defenses by some Rinpoches that I have admired and feel connected to.

Dan

What was the content of the defense?

Student 1

That basically if you'd received *abisheka* ["empowerment"] from a Rinpoche, if you had made that connection, then you had an obligation to see everything that they had done as pure perception, and that therefore those actions could not have been wrong. Which meant I almost hit the roof, and somebody I admired quite a lot and I basically told my own Rinpoche I think this is basically crap, which is pretty much heresy within that, but I said I don't care.

[Here we're not talking about Dzigar Rinpoche, but rather the defense published by Dzongsar Rinpoche.] And I think he's getting a lot of flack for it. And my own mentor and teacher has emphasized pure perception, one out of the traditional, but also his point has always been to me and others if you see your teacher as an ordinary person, you will get the blessing of an ordinary person. If you see them as a buddha, you are open to receiving the blessing of a buddha. And so, the benefit is really for you, not so much as to give over something to the individual. So, I've used this over time to help me in my own shall we say skepticism, etc., over my own being burned over the years.

And it's helped in terms of my own relationship to faith, but I just ... something just split and just broke in me when this happened, and I said absolutely I am not ever going back to this. You know if it smells like a duck, if it quacks like a duck, it is a duck. You call a duck a duck, and you don't play mental gymnastics to get yourself out of doubt about the most straight-forward actions that are not looking so good.

And so, at the same time I wondered about pure perception. What value? What place? What is a way we could hold it? Is there a new way we could hold it and retain its value? His Holiness the Dalai Lama has said this isn't necessarily the way we should relate because we shouldn't coddle the teacher. We shouldn't spoil them, and things like this happen. And so, I'm at this place of wondering, and I've had my own thoughts about it, but I was wondering from you, is there a way that we can benefit from what the original intention of what pure perception is in this day and age, and still hold on to the type of discernment that will allow us to see and speak out and not stand for actions that are harmful to others and that harm *sanghas* and harm individuals and ourselves?

Dan

It's a really great question. So, in terms of what you're calling pure perception, there's the sutra and the *tantra* versions of that. First of all, Tibet as a culture is strongly devotional. Lamas are revered like gods. So, the standard of expectation on the part of a lama for the students is that the students are devoted, they're faithful, they have unquestioning acceptance of the lama's teachings. That's not the case in the West.

I remember once talking with Rahob Tulku about how difficult it is to teach as a Western *dharma* teacher because of the level of disrespect that we get. And he had an interesting response. He said, "In our culture lamas are like gods. They're revered. But what's the model for a teacher in Western culture? College professor. Ha ha ha ha ha!" And he couldn't stop laughing, because no one really respects college professors. So, he said, "Look, don't expect to get any respect, because you won't, because it's not built into this culture. Where there's uncritical acceptance of the lama's role, particularly if they have notoriety and fame in that culture."

Rahob was my roommate in 1979 and 1980. We meditated together. We lived together. He was my buddy. But when we went for the first time to old Tibet with him it was quite an eye opener because on the way, everybody knew his route and fifty thousand Tibetans came out to revere him, and I'd never seen anything like it before. So as a culture we are iconoclastic, whereas uncritical acceptance is the norm in Tibetan culture.

Look at our own religious tradition. I remember once teaching a course and I invited some outside authorities in trauma to come up and teach, and they taught. This was back in the early '90s, so they were so popular that I invited them both up to teach the next year and they were at that point embattled. They had like four or five different lawsuits against them for planting false memories. And one of the young woman psychiatrists in the course said, "This is such a wonderful course. You are our role models. You are our idols. You're our teachers. How can you be getting sued?" And one of the senior teachers said, "In this culture we have a long tradition of killing off our leaders. From Jesus Christ to John Kennedy to Martin Luther King to Bobby Kennedy." And I was always struck by that comment. If somebody achieves a certain respect, we kill them off. So, the cultures are very different in terms of how we approach respect of teachers that have some renown. So, that's in the normal *sutra* traditions.

Secondly, in the *tantra* traditions, what you're calling pure perception has a very specific aim. If you open to the infinite vast expanse of limitless, awakened awareness-love which is always right here, and you hold the view or it opens up *dharmakāya*, the embodiment of all the teachings, the limitless vast expansive of an awakened mind, then you have to purify the residuals of the ordinary mind to open up *sambhogakāya* or the realms of the pure lands.

And if you practice either purifying karmic memory traces or practice purifying perception with Great Completion Dzogchen bypassing visions, or purifying the body with, say, inner fire practice, whatever of those tracks you take, they all result in purification; and the idea is to open you up to the realization that at some point if the residuals of the ordinary mind and body are purified enough, then suddenly it dawns on you that you're not looking at this ordinary deluded world anymore. You're looking at an organized sacred world of the mandala. And that you are a deity body, a very specific identification within that mandala. So, the world is not seen as an ordinary relative reality anymore. You see your pure realm. Okay? And when you open up *sambhogakāya*, you keep opening it up until everything is a pure realm. It's all one big, organized mandala, and there's nothing but that. And the ordinary realms of *samsāra* simply cease existing the way you would normally perceive them at that point. Then you open up the urge to have everybody else have the same realization, and that opens up the *nirmāṇakāyas*, the emanation bodies that guide sentient beings still dwelling in *samsāra* from their perspective out along the path. Then you achieve buddhahood.

So, you see, the whole point of what you're calling pure perception is a device. It's a way of saying, "if you perceive the lama who you have a close attachment to as sacred, then that can become a vehicle by which you can come to see everything in the world as sacred, as a pure realm of the mandala. And your lama is just one of the members among that mandala cast." So, it's meant to be a view, *dawa*, a point of view or perspective that you take that will help enhance the direct realization of *sambhogakāya*. That's why you take it.

But as was said earlier, even if you hold that view unwaveringly, you still exist in the world of two truths, ultimate and relative reality. That doesn't exempt the teacher from his behavior in relative reality. That's a misunderstanding of this. And we could say that the most authentic expression of realization is conduct. So that makes you more, not less responsible in your conduct, the more evolved you are spiritually. You don't have the freedom to act out! It's not possible.

So how do we explain all this misbehavior? We can explain it in various ways. For some people, the motivation for spiritual practice is wrong. And they may appear to be spiritual, but that wasn't the original motivation for getting into it in the first place.

There are lots of people who enter the spiritual path because it's the path of exploitation. They can get famous. They can get powerful. They can exploit others, sexually, financially. Basically, they're sociopathic. And every tradition is vulnerable to that. East and West alike. We've all seen stories in the last twenty years of priest abuse. Many examples of priest abuse. Well, the bottom line is that some people who are pedophiles go into the priesthood because that's the way they can get access to young kids and unquestioned acceptance. Duh! Where would they go? They have to be around kids. If you want a cover to be around kids ...

I worked on the Shanley case. I worked on the grand jury. I helped prepare the cross-examination for the trial. And I helped write the rebuttal to the appeals to the Massachusetts Supreme Court. He was not a nice guy! He was "The Runaway Priest." He dealt with all these runaway hippies in the 1960s. Everybody loved him! Well, the fact of the matter is he was one of the co-founders of NAMBLA, an international organization of sexual trafficking, one of the first international sexual trafficking of kids' organizations. And he was using the Church as a cover for that. That's not a nice thing to do. He found a great niche for himself. I thought we put him away for life, but recently he was released on parole. They didn't ask me to consult on the parole. Had they done that I would have made sure he stayed in jail. I was pissed about that.

There's no difference with lamas or Indian gurus that come over here. Some of them do it because they're sociopathic. The worst example of that probably in terms of modern Western culture was Osho … or he had a different name when he came into this country. He didn't have a single day of spiritual practice ever. He ran a spiritual bookstore and he memorized the lines and people would go, "Wow!" Sort of like Peter Sellers in *Being There*. He got his great spiritual proofs from watching TV, and people would go, "Wow!" He did the same thing! But he did it intentionally. And he had a big following and people couldn't see anything wrong with that. But maybe when you've got five hundred people in the audience and people are bouncing around on the floor doing yogic exercises and all the women are topless, maybe somebody raised the question there's something wrong with this picture.

But then it went really wrong when he moved to Oregon and decided he wanted to take over a town and be the mayor. But he didn't have enough votes. But in that state, people from out of town can register to vote. So out of this great move of compassion he brings in all these homeless people from all around the country and gets them to vote. But he doesn't bring them back and bus them back to their original homeless communities; he leaves them alone with no place to go—thousands of homeless people panhandling off the street. At least in their own habitat, their own niche, they can get some money because they know how to do that, but now you get them all competing against each other with no food and no money. How compassionate is that my friends? It's absolutely cruel! But he got them to vote.

And when he was still threatened that he wasn't going to get the election, he poisoned the water supply with salmonella so all the townspeople would get food poisoning that day and wouldn't show up at the polls. But everybody loved him! All the students were deeply devoted to him, because that's "tantra practice." That, my friends, is bullshit! And if you can't judge that, there's something wrong with your judgment! He left the country with seventeen million dollars in unpaid taxes, in tax evasion. Went East, retooled himself as Osho, and did the same thing all over again. That's the worst of it.

So, one motivation that people get [is] this is a good hype to coming to the West! People are naive enough; just let's exploit it as much as we can. That's one explanation for the most severe things that we've seen.

The second explanation is a little different. You can trace its roots to the great French anthropologist Claude Levi-Strauss in an essay he wrote called "The Making of a Shaman." It was about a Native American, a contemporary Native American who didn't believe in all the witchcraft and shamanistic powers and healing powers and trance dancing and all this kind of stuff. He thought it was all crap. So, he decided to debunk it. So, in debunking it he takes on the role and fakes it and goes to another village and becomes a great shaman healer.

Only as the story goes on, he gets caught up in the role and he actually develops some powers, or at least he believes he has some powers. And the truth is that he never really had any formal training, but he develops some things along the way by taking the role, and he's pretty good at it. Not great at it, but pretty good at it. And that's another explanation for some of the people that have come over here. They think that this … they get caught up in the role. And sometimes they act successfully and sometimes they act in useful ways. But they get caught up in the role because it's beyond the role that they had in their own culture. And they just do it! Sometimes it works out well and sometimes it's a disaster, and sometimes it's somewhere in between. Usually, it's in between.

The third explanation is probably the most frequent one, but we don't consider that enough. The third explanation has to do with that these are largely monastic traditions. So, what does it mean to go into a monastery as a novitiate, as a kid, and then at the age of usually eighteen and nineteen you become a monk, and you become celibate, you take your vows of celibacy; and you're celibate at the age of nineteen, a critical period in adolescence when identity and sexual identity develops, but now you're celibate. And you do that for fourteen years of your monk training and then three or four years of meditation training; so that's about anywhere from sixteen to eighteen years of training. And then you're a full monk. And you've learned a lot about the practices, and you learned about meditation and all the scriptural tradition, and you have responsibilities as a monk doing the prayers and the rituals in the local communities, and then suddenly there's an interest in having you teach in the West.

So, you come over to a culture where there's open sexuality and we deal a lot with intimacy. They don't have any intimate relationships. They hadn't had any sexual experience, and they get put up as great teachers. And a lot of them bite the dust, because they're simply unprepared for the role change. They're seen not as beginning monks in their twenties and thirties. They're seen as great lamas beyond the fact that they never had that capacity, because we idolize.

They get lots of women as students who idealize them. They have to deal with attraction that they never had to deal with before. They have to deal with intimacy in a way that they never had to do before. And a lot of them simply lose it because they're not prepared for that. No one's prepared them to deal with Western culture, sexuality, intimacy. And they lose it! Because they go from one extreme to the other. They go from celibacy to sexually acting out. But they have to keep it secret because they have to put on this front. And this scenario gets worse and worse and worse because they keep covering their bases. And it doesn't work out very well, does it? We've all seen many examples of that.

Kripalu, with the teacher there, there are many accounts of sexual misconduct. Seungsahn, the Korean monk who came, I gave a talk at his Zen center. And while I was giving a talk in front of him at his Zen center, which was hosted by the abbot of the Zen center, he was sleeping with the abbot's wife! Go figure! It was a mess.

So, part of the explanation, the most common and frequent explanation, is that people within a monastic tradition are simply not prepared to deal with sex and intimacy in an open society like Western culture. They have no tools to deal with it, and they come over here and they bite the dust. We can understand how that happens, but it doesn't excuse their behavior. They have a duty as teachers to be impeccable with their conduct. Any way you rationalize, that is bullshit. They owe you a duty as a student to have impeccable conduct.

So how do we get into this mess? Both sides are at fault. Both sides contribute to it. In the West, we don't have evolved spiritual traditions. So, we're craving, we're looking for something about authentic spirituality. We have belief systems. You can take Jesus into your heart, and if you only take Jesus into your heart you're saved. That's not about practice. That's about unquestioning faith. And in some sectors, that's fine. But it doesn't involve experience, spiritual experience. There's no method, other than adopting a belief system. And that's what's missing in this culture, which is why the grandfather of modern psychology, who was here in Boston, William James, in his great classic, *The Varieties of Religious Experience*, which is a catalog of all kinds of legitimate spiritual experiences says, "The biggest impediment to spiritual experience is religious institutions." We have lots of religious institutions but over the years they become sort of empty.

There was a great tradition of Desert Fathers, yogis in the Syriac, Egyptian, and Ethiopian deserts in the mountains. It lasted about two hundred years. It stopped with Saint Augustine. Saint Augustine was a great yogi, but his mother

Monica had designs for him to be the biggest and most and famous bishop of the day. And she forced him, because she was so over-intrusive in his life, to give up his mystical practice to become the bishop for the entire Church of Rome.

He never wanted the job. And after he accepted and gave up his mystical practice, he became somewhat embittered and became somewhat condemning of mystical practice because he couldn't do it himself; he wasn't allowed to do it by his mother. That's a personal experience that changed history, because after that there's no live spiritual tradition anymore of practice, of the prayer required. You get pockets, like the Spanish mystics and the German mystics, who come up fifty or a hundred years at a time, and that's it, but there's no lineage anymore. So, the Church becomes what? A set of beliefs you can adopt, but it becomes an institution, as William James talked about, that's mostly interested in power and money.

I know that first hand. I worked on seventy priest abuse cases against the Church. The Church has unlimited funds to take me out. I take great pride in the fact that I pissed off the Church that much. They have unlimited funds. Do you think they care about protecting the victims of abuse? They only care about protecting the institution. I was involved in a case in Arizona. It goes back to the 1950s. A priest gets involved with an altar boy, sexually abuses him four times. The last time he does it in the boy's home, on the second floor of the boy's home, and he's anally raping the boy and the father walks in. The father's in the military. The father goes berserk and wants to kill the priest, but the neighbors call the police before he can shoot the priest.

The priest goes to trial. He gets convicted. Six months later is the sentencing hearing. This is the 1950s. The bishop goes to the hearing and he pleads with the judge to have compassion on this one-time thing and besides the priest is so remorseful. So out of compassion they let him off. We've tracked that priest for thirty years. We have over a hundred identifiable victims in four states. He's a sexual predator. But then we find out there were two cases with the same priest before that—that the bishop knew about—and he covered it over, and perjured himself and lied directly to the judge. So, we finally catch the local bishop in a coverup. We've got a smoking gun.

So, what they do is they buy out of the case for seven million dollars to the victims in exchange for a gag law to cover it up. Then after that they claimed bankruptcy in the state of Arizona, so there's no further claims against them. That's evil! They got off. Do you know how much work that goes into doing one case? That's over a hundred victims for one pedophile. I don't have any illusions that the Church doesn't protect itself. It doesn't care anymore about its compassionate flock. That's complete crap. All it cares about is making more money and taking advantage of tax laws to make a more powerful institution for itself.

Everybody loves the current Pope. Wonderful man, right? Look at when all the children went missing in Argentina. It was mostly a sex-ring operation of stealing kids and selling them to the wealthy, run by a group of judges and bishops out of Argentina. And guess who was one of the main bishops at that era? He never talks about that. Such a wonderful compassionate Pope. But nobody seems to read the news. Six months ago, the Chief Financial Officer got picked up and arrested in Zurich with twenty-six million dollars in laundered money in his suitcase. But the Vatican says that really wasn't their money; it was his own money. I found that to be mostly lying bullshit.

It's an institution that covers its own bases and there's no compassion there anymore. Look at the tax holdings of the church. They only claim poverty if people sue them. I've been involved in this for too long. I have nothing good to say about it. But that's just *samsāra* in Buddhist terms; the way the world appears isn't the way it really is. It's all bullshit.

So, part of the problem is that we as a culture missed authentic spiritual experience, not belief systems. So that makes us very vulnerable to other traditions that offer us methods. And because our need is so great to get a plan, a method—if you practice this and watch your mind and you meditate this way and that way, these are the results you'll get—we so much crave that that it makes us vulnerable to suspending our metacognitive judgment. When you sit with a spiritual teacher you don't park your metacognitive intelligence outside the door. You take it with you. Is it any different from finding a good doctor or a good therapist? Some people just uncritically accept whoever comes along. Somebody gives them a name, and they say, "Okay!" But the best consumers, they interview several therapists or several doctors and they do research into their backgrounds, and after a while they get a sense of who they're talking to. And they're comfortable that they've made a good choice, because they check it out.

And as was said earlier, that's built into the Indo-Tibetan tradition. There are many texts that talk in great detail about qualities of a qualified teacher versus a bad teacher. You read the checklists; you check it out. My teacher wasn't Tibetan. My first Root Lama was Mongolian. He was a horse trader. And he would say, "Look, you don't buy any horse. You check out the hooves. You check out the teeth. You don't just buy any horse. That's stupid!" You don't just buy any spiritual practice because the guy gives you Peter Seller's *Being There* statements and you say, "Wow! Far out!" Your duty is to bring your metacognitive intelligence and judgment to this, and to make an informed and good choice.

In the therapy traditions there are certain duties owed, they're ethical duties. You have to keep up with the field and at least know as much as the standard peer in the field. Your practice has to be as good as general people who practice in the field. You don't get to just do weird things because you want to be a therapist and hang out your shingle. There are certain duties owed. It's called reasonable prudence. There are lots of people who call themselves therapists but there's a license and regulation board, and the whole purpose of that is to make sure that people have certain qualifications and certain minimal training. Now there's wonderful ways of going around that. You can call yourself a "coach." You can bypass all the regulations and years of training. Everybody can be a self-important coach these days.

But the whole point is that if you're reasonably prudent as a consumer, you check out the qualifications and research the therapist or the doctor that you're getting involved with. It's no different with spiritual teachers. You don't uncritically accept them. You check them out. And in the Buddhist tradition, there are long checklists of what you look for that's a good teacher. What are some of the things on that list? That the teacher lives the realizations. That the conduct never shows you any evidence of departing from those realizations.

That they always put the welfare and growth of their students above their own needs. They're humble as opposed to self-important. They don't have much concern for material goods or possessions. They don't show much concern for self-importance. They don't accumulate power and wealth. And their behavior, in the smallest ways, they're always being helpful to people. Those are some of the bottom-line things. And on the same lists—I'm not going to go through all the details of those lists—are the things that you avoid. If your teacher is getting involved with students intimately or sexually, that's a red flag. It doesn't happen in these traditions.

Now there are exceptions to that. I have the deepest respect for my first Root Lama who I lived with summers for nine years before he died. And in his eighties, all of us that lived there, we had about, in the retreat house there were about maybe a dozen Westerners, and we all had all of these complicated intimate relationships. And so, in his eighties he had a girlfriend. He was in his mid-eighties. She was in her late seventies. She was a yoga teacher, ran the first East-West bookstore in New York City. And she would come and spend the weekend with him, and they were the cutest couple, and while he was in his eighties. And we asked him, I mean, "Why are you doing this? You're a monk."

He says, "I don't understand this intimacy thing, the sexuality thing and why it's such a big deal for you. So how can I teach you about this stuff? I don't know anything about it!" So, I always respected the fact that he said, "If I teach in the Western world, I have to learn about this stuff." He intentionally gave up his monastic vows, which is a big deal for him, out of compassion for his students so he could learn about this sex and intimacy thing because it mattered to him. So, he could say, "I know something about this by looking into it myself, so I can teach something about it." Go figure! Have you ever heard that one before? Why not?

So instead, we put up a front, and commit sexual misconduct with many students, and we keep hiding it as if it's not really happened but all the people in the community know that. How many times have we heard that story before?

So, you see, part of the thing that's a red flag is if a teacher is accumulating wealth, if they're accumulating fame, if they're accumulating sexual misconduct, if they're exploiting their students in any way, those things should serve to us as a great warning sign of misconduct. I'm not saying error of judgment. So, I'm not saying as some people rationalize it, "I made a mistake." That's bullshit! They knew what they were doing! It's easy to say you made a mistake once you get caught, but you don't say that before you get caught, right? So, it's really bullshit.

Sogyal is a good example of that. I didn't know anything about what happened with Sogyal until I went to a conference, a week-long conference, years ago with the Dalai Lama, back in the early 2000s. It was a conference on Tsong-kha-pa's *Lam rim chen mo: The Great Treatise*. And it was a week-long conference. And the Dalai Lama said, if anybody ever translated this main book of Tsong-kha-pa, the founder of the Gelugpa, that he would give a week-long teaching, and he did, after fifty people worked for ten years translating that treatise. In the middle of the conference, he sticks his tongue out in this standard Tibetan very rejecting way about Sogyal, and he was angry. I've never seen him like that before. So, during the break I went up to Thupten Jinpa who's his translator, who I know pretty well, and I said, "Thupten Jinpa, what's going on here?" And he said, "Well, he's sort of disgusted after his collection of twelve

Lamborghinis and other fast cars and fifty counts of sexual misconduct, he's sort of had it with Sogyal."

How do we explain that? Monk. Highly regarded. Comes over to the West in a monastic tradition. Writes a best seller, on the New York Times Best Selling list for two years—The Tibetan Book of Living and Dying. And after getting that rich and famous—he got rich from it; he got famous from it—it changed his whole view of the world, which he was unprepared for as a monk. He thought he could do anything he wanted. He could accumulate power and money. Any relationships he wanted. Ordered his women students to do whatever he wanted sexually. That's not very good. And what did he do? He split apart the entire community. And every time there's an allegation of sexual misconduct, what happens? The community splits right down the middle. Half are fiercely defending in this stupid way and the other half are damaged, seriously. The same way that sexual abuse causes damage of kids. And once they get damaged, they get disillusioned.

I make a distinction between disappointment and disillusionment. Disappointment is a strong negative feeling. But disillusionment is a strong negative feeling of disappointment plus seeing the relationship differently. Once you get disillusioned, you can't go back because you can't conjure up anything positive about that person or that tradition anymore. The teacher is responsible karmically for that disillusionment being caused because it means that the student has lost any basic faith or trust, and they will not practice again with any teacher after that. That is the karmic debt of the behavior of the teacher. Any way you want to rationalize it, go ahead and rationalize it. It's bullshit. If you harm a student like that, the karmic debt of that goes down the generations and lifetimes.

One of my best friends was one of the two attendants of Sasaki Roshi, the Zen master in Los Angeles in the seventies and eighties. The other attendant was Leonard Cohen, the musician. They were deeply devoted to the practice. They were very excited by the practice. My friend Rich was a very good practitioner until it came out that his close attendants knew all of the sexual misconduct allegations against Sasaki Roshi. He was so disillusioned he never practiced again for the rest of his lifetime. He will not talk about it. He's too embittered. He never worked it out. That's Sasaki Roshi's debt. Now Leonard Cohen felt that even though his teacher was flawed maybe he could still study with him. Eventually he got a lot out of that practice. Even a taste of awakening.

So, you see, there's two sides to this issue. One is that as a Western society, because our need is so great for genuine spiritual experience, and we're such seekers and we lap that up so much, that we're vulnerable to suspending our critical judgment. And we get into the disease of idealization. And the stuff that we rationalize away is truly amazing! But it's okay because it's a spiritual teacher.

Is it any different from what we're doing with our current president? It's not about spirituality. We can rationalize it away as misogynism. We can rationalize it away in the way that he's an oligarch because he cares nothing about the common people. And his profound disrespect for anybody of difference. But it's really all okay, even though he's a white supremacist. That's really okay because he's leading the country because he talks tough. It's all bullshit friends. We're doing the same thing again outside of spirituality in a way that's really on a dangerous slope. A rigid nationalism that never goes in a good direction. But it's not just happening in this country. It's happening everywhere. It's happening in London. It's happening in Europe. And the more we go back to the rigid nationalism, the more that gets into conflict and global war again unless we turn it around.

So, on our side, our duty is to have good intelligence about who we get involved with, and not suspend our critical judgment at the doorway when we walk into a meditation hall. Because if we do, then we're vulnerable to the disease of idealism and the negative effects of that. That's your duty. The teacher's duty is to never exploit that. So, if you have a teacher that seems to be filled with his own self-importance, I would worry about that. Because if you learn one thing in the spiritual traditions it's that self-importance isn't terribly important.

But if you get a teacher who's calling attention to himself, then I would worry about that. And then we have a lot of people who don't represent lineages in the West who have self-realizations, and those realizations may be very valid, but where that leads to, once you set out and get a community of people, is you start making those realizations more important than they are. And that leads to the disease of spiritual pride. So, students have the disease of narcissism as their main risk. The teachers have the disease of spiritual pride as their main risk.

And in the Desert Father tradition, Cassian said, "The further along you go, the more, not the less, spiritual pride becomes a problem." Or as the great Dzogchen master, Longchen Rabjam once said, "Even to say, 'this is it' is to miss the mark." As soon as you label it, you have to watch out for the pride. I like the fact that in the Tibetan tradition there's an unspoken rule, and you never talk about spiritual attainments because if you talk about your own spiritual attainments it leads to pride. So, it's not allowed. When we were doing work with our tachistoscope—a high-speed electronic board that measures events in thousandths of a second—and we lugged all of the equipment over to Dharmsala, and the Dalai Lama gave us his best meditators, he said, "You tell them what state you want. It's implied that they can do that, but don't ask them about it," because they can't talk about it. They're not allowed. So, they build certain checks and balances into the tradition, and I think that's good.

We had a dialogue with His Holiness, the Dalai Lama, a long time ago—I think it would have to back to the mid-1980s—and he was asking us about what to do about this issue of sexual misconduct. And I said to him that the way that we handle it in psychotherapy in the West is we have licensing boards. And at least people can file formal complaints against their therapist or doctor for misconduct. And there's an evidentiary hearing, and there are reviews, and if the evidence turns out, the findings are positive, then there are sanctions. It means that they get suspended or they get under supervision or sometimes they outright lose their license. And there are procedures in the West to handle these issues. And he said he liked that. So, he's the only person in the Tibetan tradition who set up a review board. So, if lamas come to the West and there are complaints written to Dharamsala about those lamas, he takes that very seriously and there's a review board under him that reviews those complaints, the fact-finding complaints, and acts on them, which is what they did with Sogyal and others.

But I think that we've seen enough evidence of gurus who bit the dust in the West in the last thirty years that it's no longer viable to sort of rationalize this stuff and say, "Well this is just how they're taking on the karma of their students." That's just garbage. It's a serious cognitive distortion. And there's no place for it even within the tradition.

It's a Western misunderstanding of this tradition. And the people who espouse that view that it's pure perception, and that there's a teacher, and whatever they're doing you just unquestionably accept that, that leads to ignorance. It undermines using your own intelligence, which is one of the factors of enlightenment, using your own meta-cognitive intelligence; and it's just self-serving. It's used to rationalize extreme behaviors of lamas by devoted people who can simply not accept the fact that the lama bit the dust. That's their own rationalizations. It's all it comes down to, as I see it.

Student 2

Do you think perhaps if we had a little more confidence that there's a teaching here that leads step by step to awakening, and in our capacities, that we wouldn't need to give authority to or worship some other person?

Dan

Well, it's a very good point that you're raising. It's the whole frame about how we approach teaching. In the psychotherapy field, which I've been in for forty-six years now, I have the view that every patient has within them the resources to get better. And my duty to them is to supply the right ambiance of relationship so they can discover those resources and use them to get better. So, if the patient leaves treatment and feels like I didn't do very much, and they know how to get better and they're confident about what they know, I feel like I've done a good job. Because I don't need to get in the way.

And it's the same thing I would say about spiritual practice. If you want a good marker in Western terms, but it's not in the traditional Eastern lists, the best teachers are the ones that empower the students to use their own internal resources and intelligence to figure things out along the way. So, the student becomes confident about their own capacity to recognize the progress along the path. That's what you're talking about and it's a very important point—the importance of your metacognitive intelligence. But conversely, if a teacher is talking about their own self-importance, their own realizations, then I would worry about that.

I told this story once before but I'll tell it again because it fits here. I taught for a number of years at Kripalu, which I don't do anymore. And it's a nice setting in the Berkshires. And as you know when we teach it's a lot of work. I teach morning. I teach afternoon. And I teach evening. Three classes for eight days. And in the breaks, I'm usually seeing students. So, it's full-time work for at least eight days. So, we did that for four or five years at Kripalu and we went there to teach again, as we usually do. And they have a nice teacher's quarters on the side of the mountain overlooking the Berkshires which is very nice. And what I like about it, there's an open space, so for other teachers who are teaching there that weekend, during the breaks you can get to talk with the teachers and schmooze with them and learn what they're doing. So, we show up about an hour before the course and they say the teacher's residence is full, you're being put in an ordinary room. They didn't tell us that ahead of time. So, we walked in the ordinary room, and it was not clean in there. There was a broken glass on the floor. You have to take your shoes off so we cut our feet walking into the door. And I wasn't happy with that.

Then I said, "Who's staying in the teacher residence?" And as I researched it there was a Western woman who was staying there with all of her attendants. They had moved me out, and a Zen master of forty years, for her attendants. So, I looked into her background. She was a Western psychotherapist with no formal training in psychotherapy. And her entire spiritual practice consisted of a pilgrimage to the Ganges River and looking a *sadhu* in the face and saying, "This is it."

Now, during the weekend we don't have silent retreats. They imposed a silent retreat on us for the week, even though we'd never requested that. And I'm teaching morning and afternoon and evening. Her teaching consisted of showing videotapes of herself talking about her own realization during the day and evening, and one class at night when she would show up self-importantly to answer questions. And never during the week did she ever talk about showing people a method, which is what you're emphasizing, to develop their practice. It was all about the self-importance of her state. And that, my friends, is the danger of Western self-realized people because they never work through the issue of self.

And what you end up with is an enormous amount of spiritual pride, rationalized as realizations because they don't function in lineage traditions, where there's some checks and balances as to who gets to teach what. I love my relationship with His Holiness Menri Trizin because he's always busting me. I remember going there once and he says, "You're teaching a lot. Watch out for the spiritual pride." I said, "Busted. Thank you." That's useful to me. Because it's not hard to get filled with yourself in this role. You constantly have to monitor that. And as soon as I think I have something to say, I got caught.

So, beware of teachers who talk a lot about their own realizations and not talk about their method that shows you how to get there, because real teachers will get out of the way and just show you what to do in your own mind and leave you with that realization to develop, with a confidence that you can develop it. And they give you pointers along the way that will help you to develop it further. Because ultimately, they put aside their own needs. And it's all about your welfare and your spiritual development. If you're not getting that, you're not getting something that's authentic. This is a time in history, there are going to be a lot of false teachers out there. So, it requires you all the more, not less, to not suspend your metacognitive intelligence. Don't park it at the door when you walk into a meditation retreat center.

My second teacher was in the Patanjali Yoga Sutras. His name was Dr. Vasavada. He was an Indian psychologist and master of the Yoga Sutras. And he told me how he got interested in the Yoga Sutras. He lived in a small village in India and he was in high school, and he finished high school and he had some minor interest in spiritual practice, but he was mostly then going to college and trying to develop a profession as a psychologist. And he delayed the finishing of his training because one day he got a knock on his door in his little village and this man came in called Anatma. And he said, "I'm your spiritual teacher, I'm here to help you. I'm moving in with you." *Anatma* means Mr. Nobody.

And Mr. Nobody says, "I'm here to serve you and teach you all this practice, all the path." He stayed with him for five years and then he said, "Okay, you've mastered the practice now. You'll never see me again." And Anatma disappeared. He said, "Now go out and teach it." And he came to Chicago and I was one of his students. He was very generous and he was not filled with himself. Like myself, he had a dual role. He was a psychologist and meditation master. And he was authentic. You'd never know anything about his spiritual practice unless you worked with him, because he never tried to show it to anybody. He just lived his life fully. And if you asked him, it was his duty to show you.

As [the Sufi poet] once said in one of his poems, "Great masters roam through the marketplace every day, and no one ever recognizes them." Great masters don't have a need to call attention to themselves. No one ever recognizes them. But the ones who have the eyes that are bright enough to recognize, they get something useful. Lots of false prophets these days. Trust your gut and hold out for the real thing. Stop the rationalization of all the bullshit. Then you might get somewhere useful.

In my other hat, I'm mostly a trauma and abuse expert. I work in the courts with child abuse cases, rape cases most of the time. Right now, I have, well, it's stopped now because it's in Florida, but I have a series of cases in the Special Victims Unit in Southern Florida with all the worst child abuse cases. That's what I do for a living, so I'm not very tolerant of people's exploitation of others. I hear too many stories. So, it's a topic that makes me impatient. There's no place for exploitation of others. We live in a culture that's structured on exploiting others. That has to stop.

Student 3

Something that's very much in my mind is, and I think you said something quite a while ago that always stuck with me about studies, certain studies that showed that people get even more harmed in large groups, their capacity for harm and the dynamics.

Dan

Yeah.

Student 3

And I'm looking at it in terms of *sanghas*.

Dan

There were detailed studies of the first thirty years of group therapy with the National Training Institute and there were a lot of detailed studies of the harm that comes particularly from casualties in group settings, as opposed to individual settings, and it's pretty severe. Yeah.

Student 2

And having lived through a situation like that, and it's been, oh, it's been twenty years now. It's been just an ongoing learning experience, and so much has been learned and I think what I observe is that the capacity for what I would call cultic thinking, it's just rife in so many places. In other words, the people a have willingness to, like you say, they don't have a strong center, think someone has got some experience for me, and I'm willing to give over all manner of ethical boundaries and overlook so many things that happen to other people on behalf of that experience or whatever hole that seems to fill. And I think what's concerned me is …

Dan

Well, cult method is such that you don't even have to be vulnerable. Cult methods are pretty sophisticated these days. If you look at the history of coercive persuasion, there are three generations.

The first generation of coercive persuasion was mostly the Soviets in the 1930s and '40s with the Moscow Show Trials. And what they would do is in the middle of the night they would capture somebody, imprison them, subject them to sensory isolation, physiological manipulative ordeals like staying up all night, standing in a corner on one foot for hours and hours on end. And through the infliction of mostly physical discomfort and pain, they would eventually form a relationship with you. The most famous case of that was Cardinal Mindszenty, who came out after being brainwashed and publicly denounced western Christianity and his role in the Church and talked about how communism was his saving grace. It's purely a result of brainwashing.

The second generation was what happened in the Korean War with the Chinese communists. And they found that a more effective technique was small group behavior. So, they would have twelve people in the cell and one or two of them would be informants, but you never knew which one was the informant. And they would use the group process as a way of changing ideology. And small groups were more effective than all the ordeals that the Soviets used.

And then the third generation of research on coercive persuasion was the research that came out in terms of cult behavior. And you didn't have to use ordeals. You didn't have to use group persuasion. You had to do one thing. You systematically attack the core self of the person and you can get them to do anything. And people who are more vulnerable around their sense of self are the ones that are more vulnerable to cult behavior. And cults are very sophisticated now. We know how to do this. Look at all of you here tonight, see? This works. [Laughter]

So, the idea is that the vulnerable point is always our sense of self. And that's where the leverage is in these groups. People who don't have a strong sense of themselves are the ones that are most likely to park their metacognitive intelligence at the door, and easily be persuaded particularly by people who are sophisticated and know how to exploit that. Some people are very good at that. Some groups are very good at that. So that's where the vulnerability is enhanced.

October 25, 2017

Themes: Processing Simple and Complicated Grief; Motivation to Heal vs. Dying

Dan

Welcome everyone. You have a question?

Student 1

I know there are a lot of important teachings about dealing with our own death and dying. Over the last five or six years, a lot of people I know have died, people very close to me or even just cohorts from my generation dying, like Tom Petty, for instance. So, I'm wondering about …

Dan

Start reading the obituaries and see all your friends—then you know you're getting old. [Laughter]

Student 1

Yeah, so I'm wondering if there are teachings and practices about how we deal with the death of others, either recent deaths or long-ago deaths.

Student 2

This is the teaching you gave last time you were here.

Dan

Yeah, I don't remember back that far. [Laughter] The last one was more specific and that was really a memorial to His Holiness's death, but it was about teachings on dying, yes.

Student 1

So, the question is on how to help serve people who are passing away, have passed away?

Dan

So, there's a Western and Eastern answer to that question. In the Buddhist tradition, the Eastern answer is that grief is a form of suffering. So, the best practice is to see the emptiness of all states of suffering. So, you would look into the nature of the grief, and the more you try to find the substantiality of that grief, the more the thing you're looking for would slip away as unfindable. And there would be something remaining. In other words, you handle it the same way you do with any emotional state. When you work with emptiness of emotions, you start with the emotion, either spontaneously emerging, or evoked. So, if you were in a state of acute grief, then the grief would be spontaneously present. Or if you didn't experience the grief, you could remember that the person recently died and then it would generate the grief.

So, you can either work with something that's already present, or you can generate it by remembering it, something recent, that caused you to feel that way. That's target selection. Then as with any emptiness practice, you search through it. So, find grief. So, you search through areas of the body. Where in your body do you hold the grief? Can you find the grief substantially existing, or independently existing anywhere in the body? So, look where you think you find it the most. Is it in your gut? Is it in your jaws? Wherever you roam around, in that awareness, the target that you're looking for as independently existing or a substantial thing keeps slipping away as unfindable.

As His Holiness, the Dali Lama says, the essence of emptiness practice is *nyerme*, unfindability, in Tibetan. The more you look for it, you can't find it. That's the first part; that's the negation part of the affirming negation. Then you look into the field of awareness that's remaining after you roam around and look for the grief. And, the grief, all emotions, become lively awareness, expressed as what we call the pure energy of manifestation of that grief. So, if you clean the grief up of the stories that go with it, the memories that go with it, the grab that goes with it, and you do an emptiness practice on grief, what's left is that grief is awareness expressing itself. And it has a certain pure energy of manifestation. And the manifestation of grief is pure energy; the manifestation of grief is connection. It's human connection. So as long as you don't make that connection into a thing, that's what you're left with. It's awareness expressed as human connection. It's a good thing. But, the loss, the stories of the loss, the memories of the loss, the self that lost, all that stuff goes. It's just pure energy.

So, you first evoke the grief, roam around in areas of the body, and roam around in the physiological systems. Can you find the grief in the nervous system? Can you find it in the gastrointestinal system? Can you find it in the muscle, the striated muscular system? Can you find it in the skin? Then, you affirm what's left after you get that experience, the shift of unfindability; and what's left is the pure energy of lively awareness expressed as the pure energy of manifestation of grief, which is a kind of connection. That won't go away no matter how much you search for it. The connection gets stronger.

Then you evoke the grief a second time—with emotions, you do it twice. And now you look for the self that experiences the grief. So, find the grieving self, find the grieving Larry. Where's the Larry that experiences the grief? And the more you look for the Larry that's experiencing the grief, in your field of experience, it slips away, it's unfindable. Then when you get that experience, the shift of it slipping away, look into what's left. Lively awareness expressed as a pure energy of manifestation of grief, which is connection.

Then if you want to make it thorough, search for the searcher who just did the search. That slips away too. Then the grief isn't grief anymore. It's transformed fundamentally through its pure nature, its original, what we call the *kadak*, the original purity of the grief, which is the basis of human connection. It's a good thing.

Student 1

Thank you.

Dan

Okay, the second answer is how we would answer that in Western psychology. And in Western psychology the first work on grief that was worth anything came out in the 1940s with George Engel's work. And he talked about grief as a natural process. When we experience the loss of somebody significant to us, there are a natural set of reactions that people go through that are somewhat predictable. And that was the first work on the stages of grief.

So, grief is a natural process, and we go through predictable stages. But not everybody goes through the stages the same way. What makes grief resolvable is you go through the stages and it reaches resolution. But sometimes people don't reach resolution. So, there's what we call simple grief, and complicated bereavement.

Complicated bereavement doesn't resolve itself within a reasonable time. And the person who wrote the most about that, the first early studies of complicated grief was good old Sigmund Freud, and his contemporary Karl Abraham. And what they said was that grief looks very much like chronic depression or melancholia, in a classic article called, "Mourning and Melancholia."

So, that's the similarity. But the difference between complicated grief and simple grief—that is, grief that doesn't resolve itself within a reasonable time—the difference is about conflict. When grief doesn't resolve itself, it's because there's an underlying conflict about the nature of the relationship that we had. So, if you lose somebody that you love, that you're close to, actually the grief is easier to deal with because the relationship was uncomplicated by conflict. But where grief gets more complicated is if the person you lost, you had an ambivalent relationship with. And there were good parts of the relationship and bad parts of the relationship. And that makes the grieving more complicated. Because it's hard to find a way when the person is dead, and you lost them, to deal with the complications that are unfinished business in the relationship.

So, melancholia was like a chronic state of depression. And Freud noticed that there was a certain similarity between that chronic depression that doesn't resolve itself and chronic bereavement. They were the same state, phenomenologically. They look very similar. And the difference between that and the kind of grief that you deal with and then resolve it, has to do with, there was some fundamental conflict in the relationship that never really got worked out. So, for example, if you have a loving parent, and you lose a loving parent, you go through the stages of grief, and it resolves itself. But if you have a parent who's chronically alcoholic and abusive, that's much more difficult to resolve. Because you didn't get what you needed from that parent. So, the grief tends to linger for long periods of time because how do you resolve it? Because there's so much unfinished business in the relationship.

So that was the fundamental distinction that was made, first by Freud in the 1920s and Karl Abraham. And then again by George Engel's work on the stages of grief in the 1940s. And then what emerged in the '50s and '60s was the idea that grief is something that needs to be processed. And depending on the recovery environment, if you provide the right conditions, that people have a chance to make sense out of it, then they process it, and it resolves itself. But if they don't get that environment to process it, it doesn't resolve itself, it tends to get delayed and prolonged.

And the famous case in the West for that was here in Boston. It was the beginning of the trauma field, in the 1940s—the famous Coconut Grove fire. Coconut Grove was a restaurant, a hotel restaurant downtown, which is now the Howard Johnson's hotel on Stewart Street, or actually the theater district. There's a plaque on the wall of the HoJo's, about it, which is the original site of the Coconut Grove fire.

And in the 1940s, it was a night club. It was a dinner night club where they had singing. And they had revolving doors, you know those revolving doors. And they had a fire that broke out in the hotel in the night club where there was singing going on and the restaurant going on, at night. There were three hundred people in the club. And there were no exit doors. The only exit door was the main door which was a revolving swinging door. And when the smoke—the wallpaper was plastic, and it burned rather quickly, and because it was plastic the room was billowing with all this thick smoke, and nobody could see anything. Everybody panicked and tried to push each other out of the way to get out of the doors, and they jammed each other in the doors. And all the doors got jammed with dead bodies. So, nobody got out of the hotel, or the restaurant. Three hundred people died. That was the beginning of the modern trauma field. It started here in Boston.

So, they got together all the family impact victims and tried to do grief counseling for them, the people who had family members that were lost in the tragic fire. That was the beginning of the trauma field. And what they discovered was, early response matters. Helping them make sense out of, meaning making, getting the surviving family members to talk it out, and make sense out of it, made sense. And then if they did early intervention and people got a chance to make sense out of the loss, then six months later, they were not symptomatic. Whereas, if they didn't do anything to process it... and that became part of the modern trauma processing theory, or grief processing theory. If you provide the right conditions of a recovery environment, the process, and make sense out of the loss, it goes away. And that was popular in the '50s and '60s.

But then in the 1970s, there was a famous book written by Mardi Horowitz called Stress Response Syndromes, which is a beginning of the modern trauma field. And what Mardi said was, in his book, that we're forgetting something here. It's not about providing the conditions of the recovery environment and then making sense out of it, because even if you provide that, all that, some people make sense out of it and they get better, but some people don't. They still have complicated bereavement. And what was lost was the original thread that Freud had picked up on, and Karl Abraham had picked up on: for some people it's complicated because there's conflict in the relationship that was never resolved, there's unfinished business. And you have to deal with the conflict. If you don't deal with the conflict, the loss goes unresolved.

I'll give you an example of that. Anybody ever remember the Iowa? It was a battleship. And it was out, very far out at sea, and they had an explosion. And fifty people were killed. And they were too far out to sea to get planes and helicopters in, and no boats around. So, the ship was sinking. I saw somebody who was a senior officer on the Iowa ten years later, and he was still traumatized. He still had unresolved grief about being on that ship. And it took three sessions to resolve the grief. And what he told me was that he was playing cards with three or four guys, one of the guys he didn't know very well, but the guy talked about his family and showed him pictures of his kids. And then there was an explosion shortly thereafter. As a senior officer, he had to assess the damage, and pick up the parts of the bodies. There was a magazine explosion in one of the big guns, and fifty people were either killed or blown to pieces. And it blew a gaping hole in the side of the ship.

And the reason why the grief didn't resolve was there were two levels of conflict. The first level of conflict was that he was a body bagger. He remembered picking up this guy's head, the guy he had just shown his pictures of his kids, and having to stuff the head in a plastic bag. And the discrepancy between seeing this guy's real life, and his family and his kids, and pictures of his wife, and then stuffing the guy's head in the bag was just overwhelming to him.

But that wasn't the real conflict. It took about three sessions to find the underlying conflict. And the conflict was that two senior officers and the captain got together and they said, look, we're too far out to sea, there're no helicopters that are going to come, there are no ships around, this battleship is going to sink, and then six hundred people are going to be dead. So, they made the decision, the three of them, to wall off that area of the ship. Fifty soldiers were inside that—fifty sailors were inside that ship that they walled off. And they knew they were going to put those fifty sailors to death, to save the rest of the ship, to save four hundred and fifty more people. That was a conscious decision. He couldn't live with that; he put it completely out of his mind. That's conflict. And we could identify the conflict and see that he made the right choice and that he could say it, "I made the right choice, under the circumstances." Then he resolved the grief.

So, you see how important conflict is in resolving grief? It's terribly important. If grief lasts a long time, you can assume that there's some kind of conflict there that needs to be resolved.

But all of this comes down to a processing model. You have to process the relationship, and you have to process it in such a way that you identify the underlying conflict that's involved in grief.

So, the best work I found on this really came out of Australia, and not in America. And it was an obscure paper in one of the hypnosis journals in 1989, by a guy named Manthorpe. And he reported the study of sixty-three cases of unresolved, long-term grief, all of which were resolved with a maximum of three sessions. Now that raised my eyebrows. But as was common in papers of those days, he didn't tell exactly what he did, he gave the general outlines, but never the wording of it. So, we took the protocol and we used it for about two hundred subjects, and fiddled with the wording of it, in terms of how to get it to work. And like Manthorpe, we never found anybody that went over two or three sessions to resolve their grief, no matter how long, twenty, thirty years later. It works, it's a profound protocol.

I was just teaching a course on the West coast, and one of my students had just lost both parents. It took one session to shift that with this protocol. So, it's very profound. After the break, I'll introduce it to you, so you can see how it works.

So, the difference, East and West, is that the West is kind of a processing model. If you provide the right conditions to resolve the underlying conflict, then the grief stops. And you're done with it. In Eastern terms, if you look into the emptiness of grief, or any emotional state, you're left with the pure energy of manifestation. So, they do it in very different ways, but they end up in a similar place.

If you resolve the grief, the last part of this Western protocol, or Australian protocol, is you resolve the conflict, and the third part of the protocol is called leave-taking. You keep the memories, but you have to say good-bye to the relationship. You make a difference between keeping the good parts of what you remember, but you have to say good-bye. So, it forces the resolution of the grief. You still get to keep the memories. And it's not so different in the emptiness protocol. You get to keep the pure energy of manifestation which is connection. So, in both East and West, you end up in the same place, from very different methods. You keep the sense of the human connection, which is the most important part of relationship, in a good way, in a positive way. And if you end up with that, you end up with something valuable.

Good question. It comes up a lot. I'm appalled with how little this protocol is known and how little it's used in the clinical field, as you know. And every time I do a retreat for a week, there's always one or two people who come up with some grief reaction, that on the side we have to deal with this protocol, and it works, just about every time. Doesn't take long to do it.

There's another question, you had your hand up.

Student 2

So, my question is, grief is an energy manifestation, you say the root being some connection, and this past year I've been really focused on mind and body, and I've got mind and body, but a lot of energy stuff has happened along the way, and I see looming thoughts and emotion rolling through my presence and awareness, and they come and they go. And I guess just as one aspect of energy and as manifestation, and the emotion of grief, all kinds of other things are presenting themselves, and maybe everything, quite honestly obviously everything is presenting itself in some fashion as energy.

Dan

It manifests itself. Okay. All emotions come from lively awareness having the potential to manifest themselves in a certain way. And the potential for the emotion of grief is to manifest itself as connection. It doesn't mean you look at it as energy. You look at it as an awareness. If you make it as energy, it's just making it into another thing. So, it's not energy that way. The energy of manifestation means the potential to manifest itself and express itself in a certain way. Does that make it clearer?

All emotions … look, the whole show here is awareness. Thought is awareness, emotions are awareness. Visual forms, as much as they seem solid to us, are awareness, like a holograph. Sounds are awareness, smells are awareness, tastes are awareness, the body, body-sensations are awareness. The whole show is awareness. And awareness manifests itself as light. The whole show is light. But you have to make sure that you see it as insubstantial. It's still vividly occurring. It's like a holographic image. If you see a three-dimensional image in a science museum, you know you can put your hand right through it. It's very vivid, but you don't take it to be real. This whole show is a holograph. It's a very vivid holograph, but we take it to be real, that's the problem. But, if you see it as empty, it means you see it as just a construction of mind; it doesn't mean it stops existing. It means you see it for what it really is, which is a construction.

Because the ordinary mind, its function is to represent. That's what it does. But the whole point of going through the process of searching into its nature is so you stop representing it as something solid, or independently existing. But you don't want to make it into something else like energy. Even light. And you're making it into a thing again. It's vividly occurring yet insubstantial.

So how you see it though, the view, matters. If you see it as energy, you make it into another thing. Just as seeing it as solid in space. If you see it as light, you make it into a thing. If you see it as awareness, you don't make it into a thing because awareness is insubstantial.

So, to say something is empty is really a synonym for saying it's merely a construction, or merely a representation of mind. It still exists, but it's not independently existing out there. It's just a construction. Because the ordinary mind constructs, represents, that's what it does. But if you look at everything as a construction, you see beyond the constructive nature, and what you see is the deeper nature of this is all about awareness.

The thing is, if you're looking at it in terms of the constructive process, the thing is to see beyond the constructions of the mind, not to replace them with another set of constructions. You're replacing them with another set of constructions; you're just doing the same process over again. You're not going beyond it. The whole point is if you see everything as awareness and see everything as empty or merely a construction, that defines the way out. Otherwise, you're just making more of the same old, same old. You can replace the world with seemingly solid forms out here with the world of energy and light, and that's just replacing one form of construction for another. That's not going to get you off the wheel. But if you see them all as empty constructions, there's a way of looking at that that defines the way back to true nature, which is the experience of awakened awareness.

Student 2

I think I'm with you.

Dan

[Consider the awareness of sound.] What you do is plug up your ears for three days, and then you go beyond the "rrr rrrrr rrrrrr" sounds, the constant sounds, and then you get very specific sounds, and they're all internally generated. They don't come from "out there" anymore. And they're completely nonsensical. And it's a remarkable cacophony, a symphony of sounds that make absolutely no sense because they have no meaning, and it's remarkably fresh. And it's all internally generated. And you see that sounds don't come from "out there" anymore. But as soon as you make it into a thing you've gone off track and back to ordinary mind again. Watch out for looking at it as an energy. You've got to get out of this habit of seeing it as energy. You're not going to get anywhere. You're going to keep reinforcing it; it's going to be a reinforced view. It's not energy, it's just awareness.

Every time you see it in terms of energy, view that energy as awareness—as lively awareness. All thought is lively awareness, all emotion is lively awareness, all sight is lively awareness, all sound is lively awareness, all taste, all smells, all the body, body sensations is lively awareness. Every moment is a continuous uninterrupted flow of lively awareness. Then see what happens. The view is the meditation. Not energy. If you want to see everything in terms of energy, you're going to end up with a contemporary view of Western physics.

Student 2

It's not a constructing it into energy, it's not …

Dan

But you have to watch out that you don't deviate with that.

Student 2

Yeah. They're different.

Dan

It's a subtle reification of the energy, and as soon as you do that, you're back in ordinary mind again. Make the correction, and see the difference. The ordinary mind wants to hold onto the structured reality. And it's not going to get you anywhere. You've got to let go of it.

And if you keep coming back to it, and you say, "but, but, but …" it shows you there's a grab there. Your ordinary mind wants to hold on to this structured reality, and it's not going to get you anywhere. You've got to let go of it.

Student 2

It's gone. [Laughter]

Dan

Then in that moment you understood it. Alright, better.

Another question?

Student 3

Thank you. Hello.

Dan

Hello.

Student 3

Hello. I wanted to ask you for a long time, how to fully heal oneself, including metaphysically, to fully heal oneself, including all severe structural injuries, deformities, scars, malformations, wounds, and missing, or non-functioning organs? And how can one do so by effective means when structures are non-functional, or no longer exist? Including removing surgical implants of metal and plastic which obstruct the healing of those physiological structures? How do you turn oneself into a healthy organism from a Frankenstein—a walking, mechanically mutilated, and mechanically sutured, or crudely reconstructed organism?

Dan

Let me address the healing of the body part. And the answer is what's possible versus what is generally done. So, within the spiritual traditions of Indo-Tibetan Buddhism, you could use the mind to heal the body. It's possible, but it's generally not done. Because it raises the question of motivation. Motivation.

So let's say that you had been afflicted by some physical illness, and you wanted to heal the body, and you did all these advanced meditation practices to heal the body. Technically, you could do that, but you wouldn't. The reason why you wouldn't do it is because it would usually be self-related. The motivation is to do something for the self. So, you wouldn't interfere with the bodily processes of your karmic ripening simply because, for selfish reasons, you wanted to get better. It's not the right motivation. So that's why great masters generally don't do that. That's why great masters, when they get illnesses, they succumb to the illness. Do they have to do that? No.

I'll give you some examples of that. My first Root Lama died when he was eighty-seven of liver cancer back in the 1970s. My current Root Lama just died in September with a combination of liver and stomach cancer at the age of eighty-nine. Could he have continued to live and heal that? Yes. But you don't do it. You don't do it because it's not part of the etiquette of what you do. The body is limited, and you don't try and change it around, unless there are special circumstances that would merit that.

For example, I once studied with an old Mahāmudrā master called Konchog Lama, and Konchog had been in this long retreat. He was an old cave and hermitage yogi. He was a practitioner. He practiced for [twenty-five] years uninterruptedly in the same cave because he was trying to perfect these practices to get them right. At the age of eighty-nine, he came out of his cave, because he had advanced cancer, and he was dying. So, he went to the Dalai Lama and said, "I've been practicing for [twenty-five] years to perfect these practices, but I now have cancer so I'm not going to be able to continue. What do you want me to do?" And the Dalai Lama said, "You can't die. After [twenty-five] years nobody has this kind of level of experience before. I need you to live to a hundred, and teach these all around the world." He said, "Okay." And then two months later, he didn't have cancer anymore, because the Dalai Lama asked him not to. And he used his special, extraordinary abilities to heal his cancer, and he lived for another ten years of teaching. He died at ninety-seven; he didn't make it to a hundred. But he did it because he was asked to do it, because of the value of that level of teaching.

So, he transcended the physical structure of the body in order to teach because he was asked to do it by the Dalai Lama. If he were to say, "Well, I've done this for a long time, I'm getting sick, I think I'll heal myself," you just don't do that. It's not part of the etiquette of this, because it's selfish.

And there's a practice that was called dead-entering, where you can actually, it's a secret practice of the cave yogis, where you can actually, if you're old and you've taught a lot and your body's worn out, rather than healing the body, you can enter a fresh body at the burial ground, and go to pick up a dead body. You go to the burial ground, you find a body, typically one that's died of acute intestinal distress, which in those days was coming in a lot of bodies like that, the body's intact otherwise, and you project your consciousness into that body and take it over. You walk out of the burial ground with a new body and the same mind as before.

There's a famous teacher named Patrul Rinpoche who wrote the famous commentary on Garab Dorje's main teachings in Dzogchen, the Nyingma system. And his nickname was The Great Zombie—Ro-langs, Ro-langschenpa, the Great Zombie. And the reason why he was called that is because he had three thousand students, which is a lot in Tibet, and he was a very popular, charismatic teacher. And his body was worn out and he was dying, so he went and found a fresh body and he came back in a new body and said, "I'm back." And he taught for another thirty years. Now those are secret practices; they exist. I've translated them; I know something about how they work. I'm not doing them, obviously. [Laughter]

But I have a funny story about that because I was staying at the monastery and I was practicing this and Rich was with us and we had a little small space in the monastery, so Rich was my roommate, and I was translating this text and I was reading some of what I was translating and he said, "I was up all night, I was worried you were going to take over my body," and I said "Rich, you have bad ankles I don't want your body." [Laughter]

But these are practices that they sometimes do, but you can't do that. I couldn't say, "Well, I've taught for a long time, I'll go out and get a new body because my body is getting worn out." But if the students petitioned me, and said, you must do this, then that's a different story, because the motivation doesn't come from me. So, we're going to pass out a petition later in the evening … [Laughter]

They actually do these things. But you can't do them because you want to do them. There's an etiquette to it. And there're some practices that reverse the aging process. There's a not very common practice, it's rare, it's in the Mother Tantras, and it's called, "Youthful Vase Body." And what it does is you do these practices, reverse the aging process. Wrinkles go away, the hair turns to its original color again. Obviously, I haven't done these practices. But there's an actual text and teachings on the details of the youthful vase body practice. It is known within the tradition that if you got a significant medical illness, you could reverse the process, but generally you don't. Because you don't interfere with the karmic forces of dying, unless they're extraordinary circumstances that make you want to do that. It's better to let the body drop than to have control over the dying process. You can voluntarily recycle yourself in any form you want. You just come back in a new form.

But some people would say (and that's the controversy in the tradition), well, that takes a long time, because it takes you ten or twenty years to remember what you used to want to be able to do again. So, it's better to just take a fresh body at the burial ground, the charnel ground, and come back and keep teaching while you're still in this body. Then you don't have that twenty-year hiatus before you remember what you used to do. So that's the controversy within the field. Do they know how to do this stuff? Yeah, they know how to do it, but they never talk about it, because it's generally secret. They don't put the zombie practices out there, but they know how to do them.

In fact, in the Six Yogas of Naropa, the dead entering was one of the six yogas. It was passed onto Marpa's son. And Marpa's son officially had a horse accident and died. He was the only one who remembered the practices; he's the only lineage holder. So, officially it died out. But it didn't really die out, everybody knows it didn't die out. They just stopped talking about it. They used that as a cover for the fact they didn't have to talk about it anymore, so it wouldn't be discovered by people and misused. And there's a version of that that you'll enter another body and take it over for the sake of continuing to teach. You can also take a dead body and raise it to life again. There's a whole set of teachings on how you do that, one of the teachings that Jesus discovered, but he wasn't the only one who knew how to do that. There's actually a text on how you do that. That stuff is extraordinary.

So, the answer to your question is, could you possibly do that? And heal yourself? Yeah. But generally, you don't do it, unless it's some extraordinary circumstances that would militate that. And usually what it means is that somebody else asked you to do it, for the sake of compassion and helping others. But never for your own benefit. It's just not done.

The sixteenth Karmapa died of cancer. All the great teachers die of one thing or another. And rarely they'll intervene in that process. You just don't do it.

November 29, 2017

Themes: Steps in Practice; Neurocircuitry of Awake Awareness; Processing Trauma

Dan

Welcome everyone.

When I was going to graduate school in Chicago, I loved blues music. So, I used to go to this all-Black bar in Cicero. I was the only White person who ever went there. So, when I first walked in it was like a version of that scene in "Easy Rider," when they walk into the red neck bar, except it was all Blacks, because they'd never seen a White walk into the bar before in this area, Cicero. So, there was an awkward silence. I went there to see the Howling Wolf Band. So, I shot pool with them for a while and then they became more comfortable.

We bantered around for a while, and then the band started playing and everything was cool, and I danced with a girlfriend I was having, and let everybody else dance with her and everything was cool. And the bar tender said, "This is a weird thing you did. I think I appreciate your courage, but when you come back, call us ahead of time. Here's my private number. When you come back, we'll take care of your car for you, otherwise it's going to get trashed and stolen."

So, every time I'd go, they'd take my car and park it for me and escort me into the building. And we became like a family. And we watched this music that was not played for an audience. They would just play for each other, jamming for each other. And every now and then, somebody would get up in the middle of a set, and just leave to get a beer, and then go back to playing again. And every now and then, they would find something in the music together, because they played for the love of the music and what they were discovering in the music. That's real improv.

So sometimes we find something like that here, too. Whatever comes up in the discussion takes us to places that we would never otherwise conceptualize about, and that's why it works. It's like going to a good improv blues bar. Here's my Russian *samādhi*. [Dan holds up what looks like a bottle of clear liquor.] It's not vodka. It's really water, but it looks like it. So, let's open for discussion. Yeah.

Student 1

I'm loath to speak after such a glorious introduction to improv because I'm feeling very much frustrated with my practice.

Dan

It's the holidays. What can you expect? [Laughter]

Student 1

I wish it were that simple.

Dan

Okay, what's the frustration with your practice?

Student 1

Well, since doing Level 1 ... I mean before that, I thought I knew something, and then I did Level 1 (student laughs).

Dan

Well now you're getting somewhere if you think you know nothing. [Laughter] Then the next step is you realize everything you do is wrong. Then the next step is actually lightheartedness about it. Then you start moving on from there.

Student 1

Well, I'm insisting on enthusiastic perseverance. Let's put it that way. I don't know if it's that I'm looking for some kind of states, because I experienced something in August that was extraordinary to me.

Dan

Like?

Student 1

Like ...

Dan

Describe.

Student 1

I disappeared.

Dan

Yeah.

Student 1

I disappeared and there was a connectedness that even speaking of it, it's ... What did I tell you? I don't know how to describe it. I could hardly speak when I came home from there, about it, because... Let's put it this way, at the end ...

Dan

Okay, so you disappeared.

Student 1

I disappeared, and there was a sense …

Dan

Was there a place that you were looking from, observing this?

Student 1

Was ...?

Dan

Was there a place that you were looking from, while you were observing this shift?

Student 1

I don't know how to answer that. I felt connected to everything. It was the last ...

Dan

Where was the looking coming from at that connection?

Student 1

[Long pause.] I don't know that I was looking. It was more like seeing, without looking.

Dan

Where was the seeing coming from?

Student 1

Ahhh. [Long pause]

Dan

If you can remember … [Long pause] Here's what I'm asking. You can have the sense of self drop away and operate out of awareness free of self. Self doesn't disappear; it becomes part of a larger field, but your basis of operation is that larger field, which could be changeless, timeless awareness. On the other hand, you could be dropping into a field where there's no localization, and you are the total field.

Student 1

That sounds more like what I experienced.

Dan

Then you had a taste of awakened awareness, which is why it felt so familiar and so distinctive. Everything within that field is interconnected and you are that field.

Student 1

Exactly.

Dan

It's not just the self dropping away; it's the localization of consciousness dropping away.

Student 1

Okay.

Dan

Okay? And it's such a memorable experience that it rocks your foundation.

Student 1

Yes.

Dan

Okay.

Student 1

And I can't restore that sense.

Dan

Because, the trouble is, if you have something compelling like that, the good news is you've developed a learned pathway, so you know it exists and you can find your way back to it.

Student 1

Okay.

Dan

The bad news is, you're trying to remember your way back to it. That's conceptual, and it gets you further and further away from it.

Student 1

[Chuckles]

Dan

That's what you've been doing, that's why your practice went off track.

Student 1

Hmmm.

Dan

We call that the flaw of representing a memory.

So, what you have to do is set up the same exact conditions that got you there: emptiness of self; emptiness of time; set up Ocean and Waves as your basis of operation; look more quickly so you catch everything at the head, so you get automatic emptiness by sealing through immediacy. Then you refine that to the natural state, which is five things: nondual awareness, a single nondual field without inside and outside. Everything that arises within that vast nondual field is immediately and automatically empty upon arising.

All doing is empty upon arising; all conceptualization is empty upon arising, and therefore, without conceptualization, the field is bright and lucid because it's not clouded over by concepts. You set up the natural state; then you set up your view of Lion's Gaze. You set up all those steps correctly, step-by-step, methodically, without trying to take the shortcut of remembering your way back to something where you're going to get further away from it.

The thing about the natural state is it's a clearing agent for all conceptualization because any conceptualization, including memory that occurs, is immediately empty upon arising, so it can't get in the way. So, if you set up the right foundation, and you set up your view of Lion's Gaze, then the awakening, it will shift you back to that awakening again. In fact, it will be easier to shift back to the awakening from the natural state in the Lion's Gaze view because you've opened up that pathway already. As soon as you try and remember your way back into it and think about it, conceptualize about it, you get miles apart from it and that's frustrating.

Student 1

I also realize I tried to back myself up to just concentrate, "Just take your breath and concentrate." I'm so lousy at it.

Dan

Open up the basis of awakening more and more. Your task is to set up the right conditions so you can take the view and open it up more frequently, for longer duration, and more immediately. Frequency, duration, and immediacy. You never take the Lion's Gaze view unless you have the natural state, because that clears conceptualizations. Like a clearing agent for all conceptualization. If you try and think or remember your way into it, it hardens the mind. It makes it harder to awaken. You close off that pathway.

Student 1

Now I'm scared. I probably have done that.

Dan

Just do it right.

Student 1

Okay.

Dan

And check in.

Student 1

I know …

Dan

I'll follow it with you.

Student 1

When I came …

Dan

The trouble is that if you start losing it in the practice, that's when you call less rather than more. Most people don't contact me when they're having problems. They contact me when it's going nicely. We don't need that. I don't need to pat you on the head. I need you to go over it when you're having difficulties. Hmm?

Student 1

Thank you.

Dan

Clear enough?

Student 1

It is. I have a piece of information. I don't know if it's useful, is that I did the day long, with Robert, and I realized that it was easy in a room with so much other energy in his voice, but not at home by myself. Same answer?

Dan

Same answer.

Student 1

Got it. Thank you.

Dan

It's not about the conditions. It's about setting the mind right. You don't need the recordings; you don't need the class. You just need to set the mind right. The view is the meditation, the view is the meditation. The view starts with Ocean and Waves, natural state, Lion's Gaze. The view is the meditation.

Student 1

Could you do me the favor of making those distinctions again?

Dan

Ocean and Waves …

Student 1

That I understand.

Dan

… is beyond time, and it's limitless. It's beyond ordinary constraints of space. But it's still cast within duality and it's still localized in consciousness.

The refinement of the natural state is nondual, so it's timeless, it's limitless, and it's nondual—no inside, no outside, but it's still cast within individual consciousness in this localization. Awakened awareness is being the unbounded wholeness, the limitlessness of that field. There's no location, there's no reference point, because you are the entire field. The localization of consciousness drops away. And the infinite individual consciousness that is localized we say merges with the ocean-like mother consciousness of awakened *dharmakāya* space.

And the field of awareness is lucid. It's distinctly different from ordinary awareness. It has *dangpa*, brightness. It has *gnar* intensity. It has *hrige*, awakeness.

It's very awake. It has *bole*, softness. It has *trule*, sparkling immediacy. It has *danpa*, sacredness. Everything has a sacred hue to it. If you don't make those into qualities and take them as guidelines of recognition, you recognize the distinction of that state. Most people, when they first shift to awakening, use their non-localization pathway. That's what you were doing, but you didn't know you were doing that. After a while, you start seeing more the lucidity of awakened awareness. When you learn to look for that, all it takes is the intention to look and it shifts to awakening and you don't have to keep opening all the state upon state and foundation upon foundation. It just opens up because you've opened up a learned pathway. It will come more frequently, for longer duration, and more immediately that way.

The sign of progress is just the intention to set up shifts your basis to awakening, almost immediately and frequently. Then you're getting somewhere. That's when you start taking it off the pillow and mixing it into every day experiences.

I should say that our paper on identifying the neurocircuitry of awakened awareness has been accepted. It's coming out in two months. It will be in a journal called *Consciousness and Cognition* and we got good results. We scanned people in normal ordinary waking distracted state, in Ocean and Waves, and the natural state, in Lion's Gaze, and in stable awakening.

In the three meditation conditions they had strongly activated the anterior cingulate cortex, which is the concentration center of the brain. But what was unusual about the finding was gamma activity in all twenty-nine subjects, which meant that they were ... Gamma activity is high frequency. It's higher than normal waking fast activity. It's very fast brainwave activity. It means that all the neurons in the region are all activated and all are acting synchronistically. So, we interpret that as during these three meditation conditions, people were holding the view intensely. But what was interesting is only during awakening, and not the other three conditions, they shifted toward an area of the parietal system. They activated an area of the parietal system that's associated with shifting from local to globalized awareness.

They're shifting out of localized individual consciousness to being the entire unbounded, limitless field of awakened awareness. And again, the activity was gamma activity, high frequency activity, which is a very rare and unusual finding. So, what it suggests is that awakening is awake, but not the whole brain, only in the regions of importance of this practice. It's a very rare finding and it's a very unique finding and we actually identified the neurocircuitry of awakening. So, it's going to be a big deal in science. We now validated the existence of [an] awakened state.

Student 2

You said it was well received and accepted. Who ...

Dan

The Fetzer Foundation funded the research. It was done in collaboration with Judd Brewer who runs the Mindfulness Neuroimaging Lab at UMASS Medical School.

And when we reviewed the results, they had an independent consultant from the National Science Foundation who said, "What are these people doing?" He's never seen anything precise in terms of precision of the mind before. He was very excited by it, somebody who's never meditated before. He thought they were great findings. So, they funded us to do a replication of it with a more fine resolution with functional MRI, with the same subjects.

They also funded us for the future to do a study on *sangyé*. There's the results of self-arising, self-liberating, which is the purification of all negative states within the mind—*dharmadhātu* exhaustion—and the flourishing of all positive states of the mind. We have enough subjects now who can do that. So, we're going to look at the neurocircuitry of purified, flourishing states, which is the next big change in your pathway. It's the penultimate state before enlightenment. So maybe we'll get the neurocircuitry of buddhahood, enlightenment, some day. We have enough students to get that far along. But we're going to take the next step with it now. They funded the research for that. We're going to ask [those who participated before] to participate again. We're going to do a replication with functional MRI.

Student 2

I knew I moved back to Boston for a reason. [Chuckles]

Dan

There you go. Yeah, the results were terrific.

Student 2

My question is around trauma and it has a little bit to do with the *dharma-dhātu* exhaustion stuff. I've been working a lot on going into the deep, deep—going into the closet, not just keeping the floor clean—and wondering about really digging into the stuff that is hard to accept, the stuff that you know sticks with you. It's your favorite piece of trash that might float through your brain.

I'm wondering if there are techniques beyond the basics that would really help you dig into that kind of scary place that really cuts to the root when you go down three or four levels. That's the lens I'm using is trauma and then also justice, in terms of things that happen in daily life where you know that that's not okay but you give it spaciousness. And you ask yourself, "At what point is it okay to not be okay with that?" So, I'm struggling with those two poles for some harder stuff I've been working on.

Dan

Well, that's an interesting question. They're really two very different questions here. The first question about how you deal with trauma, I'll answer. The second one will be for Trump to answer. And I'll answer that.

From the Western point of view, the trouble with trauma is that we don't process it. We put it out of our mind. And there are two reasons to put it out of our mind. People who process the trauma and deal with it, the residual effects go away and they're not symptomatic anymore. The people who don't process it, the symptomatic effects last for decades.

And there are two types of individuals who don't process it: those who have extremely high fear arousal or anxious arousal during the trauma, so they get overwhelmed so much by the disorganizing effects or the anxiety that they simply can't process it. When they try and revisit it, they get overwhelmed by too high a fear arousal. In neurocircuitry terms the amygdala doesn't shut off, which is the fear arousal center of the brain. So, they can't process it because the anxiety is too high.

On the other extreme of the continuum are people who can't process it because their fear arousal is too low. Those are the high dissociative people. They put the trauma out of their mind, they disassociate from it so they can't process it. Those two extremes of too much arousal or too little arousal predict the people who don't process the trauma. And those are the ones that tend to linger with delayed symptoms for decades.

There's a study that was done on coping styles in child sexual and physical abuse. What they found was that kids who have an externalizing coping style, who were sexually abused, they showed nightmares, phobias and fears, and behavioral problems at school. The sexual abuse that was happening either in or outside the home was easy to detect by the behavioral changes and the psychiatric symptoms. Therefore, they usually got treatment and they processed it, and they got disorganized around the time of the trauma because they remembered it. By processing it, they eventually got better.

Then there were the people who had high dissociative, and they didn't process it at all. They had higher grades in school, showed no signs of disorganization, and they had more friends. But twenty, thirty years later, something reminded them of their trauma, and they recovered the memories and then they got disorganized, and at that point became symptomatic, disorganized.

So, the difference between who remembered and who didn't remember was an issue of coping style. The high dissociaters tended not to remember. So, when they remembered, they got disorganized and then they had to deal with it. So, you're going to deal with it one way or the other. The question is whether you deal with it at the time of the trauma or years later on the layaway plan. You're going to pay for it one way or the other. You can pay for it now or you can pay on the layaway plan. You're still going to pay for it. But the underlying issue is you have to process, and the people who don't process the trauma are the ones who show residual and enduring symptoms.

Almost all the cognitive behavioral treatments like exposure-based treatments of trauma are based on that model. The greater the avoidance, the more the exposure-based treatments work. The more you put it out of your mind and put it out of your behavior by avoiding situations, the greater the likelihood that exposure-based treatments will work. And the heart of exposure-based treatments are [to] bring it to mind, keep bringing it to mind with all the thoughts and feelings and memories about it, and keep processing it until it settles down. If you notice yourself wanting to avoid it, bring it to mind even more. Simple procedure, then it's done.

So, what exposure-based treatments do is they provide you with the supportive conditions to allow a recovery environment by people for processing the trauma and then it settles down.

Now there's a shorter version of that, which was done by Jim Pennebaker called the Confession Studies. It wasn't intended to be about trauma. What he did is he said to people the following, "Bring to mind whatever in your life is most emotionally unfinished. It may be a relationship, a breakup of a relationship or a loss that you never fully processed. It may be something that happened to you that was traumatic. It may be something you did and you feel really ashamed about or guilty about. Whatever it is that you feel most emotionally unfinished in your life, bring it to mind now and continue to reflect for it, with all the memories and all the feelings about it without avoiding it. And keep doing that until it shifts."

He found it took people on the average about four sessions to do that. Then it shifted by providing a context to process it. He tried three different conditions. One condition was talking to a live person who was a confederate for the research, not a therapist, just talking it out. The second was writing in a journal everything about it, and the third was talking into a tape recorder. It didn't make any difference in the three conditions. It all worked.

The issue was the underlying factor that was common to all three, was processing, and setting up the environment that allowed the person to process what they didn't deal with, and giving it permission to go for right what's most emotionally unfinished. That's how the instructions are set up. He found that it contributed to reducing of any symptoms, residual symptoms, increased sense of well-being. But what was a surprising effect is it contributed to healthy immune systems. People showed enhancement of most immuno-surveillance functions.

The following year they replicated the study, found the same thing, and they had people keep journals related to colds and flus and things like that during the year. And the people who were confessing were healthier and not getting sick. So, confession is not only good for the soul, it's good for the body, in terms of health maintenance. Those became known as the Confession Studies. When they analyzed the data more specifically and they found out who it was most effective for, they found that the main contributing factor was processing what was emotionally unfinished. But the people who did that most effectively, while they were processing it, shifted perspectives. They got a new perspective on it, so after a while they began to build that into the instructions. "Keep processing this until you get a new perspective on what happened to you." That's the best of the Western models.

And what we know is that the more you fail to process it, the symptoms persist. Or you get delayed and prolonged reactions. Or as I like to say, resistance guarantees persistence. It's a good little acronym to remember it by. On the other hand, the more you process, the symptoms settle down. Whatever is unfinished, you have to process it. The more there is avoidance, cognitive or behavioral avoidance, the greater the likelihood that the exposure-based treatments work. That's what they're designed for.

They don't work for people who have complex trauma. They work for single incident trauma or simple cumulative trauma. Complex trauma is not just trauma, it's disorganized early childhood attachment, later aggravated by later subsequent childhood abuse, sexual or physical abuse. And people who just process who have complex trauma, they get more dissociated and more disorganized in life. They need to treat the attachment issues before they can do this kind of stuff. So, that's not somebody we would use it for. And they don't work very well for victims of sadistic sexual abuse because processing openly, in front of other people, is useful in, say, in somebody who has a sexual abuse by a pedophile or an incest survivor. But, with sadistic sexual abuse, it's not about sexual addiction, [where] they minimize the involvement of the subject. They just don't care about the subject's mind-state; so, validating the abuse helps. Sadistic sexual abusers are very smart. They know that they need to read the mind and behavior of their victims because they get off on having power. It's not about sex, it's about power, and exerting dominance and control. That's why sadistic abuse is often accompanied by verbal abuse and physical punishment, and inflicting pain. The dilemma there is if you process the trauma and you have somebody know it, in the transference, the more you know and the more vulnerable you're going to be in having somebody take control of your mind. You can't do that. So, processing trauma doesn't work for victims of sadistic sexual abuse. You have to work with the psychodynamic way with processing the transference. You have to interpret straightforwardly, "Look, if I get to know you, the dilemma is that you think I'm going to take over your mind and then take advantage of that and abuse you, so you can't let me know. On the other hand, you want to let me know." So, you just hold the dilemma before you and work through it and work it through in the transference.

So, there are two exceptions to trauma processing. One is people who have disorganized attachment, complicated by trauma. The other is people who are victims of sadistic abuse that need special treatments. Other than that, the trauma model works for most trauma survivors who are victims of trauma and abuse.

Now in the Buddhist path, you don't process content at all. You want to get to that point where, beyond awakening, you take the Lion's Gaze, which is the vast expanse, and orient awareness towards the totality of awareness and open up awakening as your basis. Once you establish awakening as the basis, holding the view of the vast expanse is redundant. So, the view naturally shifts from what we call the basis aspect of awakening to the appearance aspect of awakening. The view becomes uninterrupted liveliness of awakened awareness. All thoughts, all emotions, all sights, all sounds of the body, body sensation, it's all lively, awakened awareness. You train yourself to see everything moment-by-moment as the dance of lively awakened awareness.

Then the view of the vast expanse, which is the context of that, will drop away by the salience of looking at the liveliness of everything. Then the next step after you get that nice and stable is you do what we call the inseparable pair. You take both views simultaneously, so there's no contradiction—the vast expanse and the uninterrupted liveliness of whatever arises within that. Out of that, that's the third view. The fourth view becomes self-arising, self-liberating. Out of that view, not as a strategy, everything that comes up, you let it run its own course within that vast expanse without engaging it—engaging it by going towards it to process it more or going towards it to stop it from processing and then go onto the next thing.

Any kind of strategy of engagement forms karmic memory traces. That's what forms karmic memory traces. All those karmic memory traces are put in the storehouse mind. You have millions of karmic memory traces over lifetimes. They get activated and they ripen, *minwa*, in Tibetan. And what gets activated is dependent on two things. One is the strength of the karmic memory traces. If you get irritated with somebody, that's lesser than getting really angry at them or raging at them. If you hit them, that's even a stronger memory trace. If you kill them, that's even a stronger memory trace. The stronger the memory trace, the more likely it gets activated.

But the other thing is day residues, that things during the day that you encounter in your current life will trigger karmic memory traces from years ago because there's an affinity. They're similar. So, it's an interaction of things that are encountered during the day, and the strength of the karmic memory trace is going to ripen anyway, even if you didn't encounter it or experience this during the day. That causes karmic memory traces to get activated and ripen. Dreams, as they ripen, are karmic memory states. When we're dreaming four or five times a night, that is the expression of ripening karmic memory traces. That's why when you wake up in the morning and the last thing you do is dream, that's why there's a heaviness to everything, because the karmic memory traces have a not so subtle influence on everything you're going to do during the day.

They influence your outlook, they influence your behavior. But, if you set up the view right, what we call everything without mental engagement, in that vast expanse everything that arises is the liveliness. It just runs its own course without any engagement. You just let it pass through, and it immediately liberates itself because you're not forming any karmic impressions. It rises, runs its own course with no mental engagement, and immediately liberates itself. It becomes an automatic process. And because you're not forming any new karmic memory traces, it forces the mind to release all the storehouse of karmic memory traces at a rapidly accelerated rate.

We call that the process of *dharmadhātu* exhaustion. You're exhausting the bin of all the karmic ripening. The average time it takes six or seven years, if you do it 24/7. It becomes an automatic process if you do it all the time. The outcome of that is there are no negative states left or any karmic memory traces to produce negative states ever again. Because the negative states mask the positive states, you get a flourishing all at once of all the eighty positive states of a buddha mind. That's called [a] completely purified, flourishing state. That's what we want to look at the neurocircuitry of next.

I have the strong impression that *sangyé* is good for mental health. We need to explore that as Western psychologists—the implications of purified mind and flourishing positive states for mental health. So that's what we're going to look at next. Some years ago, we had a small number of subjects who could do *sangyé* and we gave them the Rorschach. We gave Rorschachs to people at different stages of practice. They had no negative states left, only positive states, so we're going to do that now. We're going to look at the neurocircuitry of that, which I suspect would be the complete deactivation of the amygdala, which is negative emotional states, and complete activation of the medial prefrontal cortex, which is all the positive states of the mind and social connection and compassion and all that wonderful stuff. These people are retraining the neurocircuitry of the brain is what I think. So, that's what we're going to look at next.

If you get *sangyé*, that would be a superior practice over processing trauma because you don't look at the content. At some point, there's a natural progression to this. The things that are most difficult for you, there's a natural wisdom to this unfolding of what … First you get random states related to current memory traces. Then you get bursts of memories from the past and they just automatically release themselves. Then finally, you go through a phase where the most difficult things from this lifetime come up right in your face. And if you don't engage them, they just release themselves and you're done with them once and for all.

Then you start to get stuff from previous lifetimes that come up and you just let the process run itself out until it exhausts itself. This would be the superior practice but it takes … a stable awakening is the foundation for this, before you can do that practice. Self-arising, self-liberating, *rangnang rangdröl*, is the key that opens the third map to buddhahood. It opens what we call "the path of liberation," liberating from all negative states. That is the foundation for enlightenment. If you liberate from all negative states and you purify the mind, then you can perceive not only the *dharmakāya*, the vast spaciousness, but you can perceive the *sambhogakāya*, which is all the pure realms.

This world here is not the ordinary world. This is deluded perception. If you purify perception, you start to see this very world as an organized mandala and everybody in this room is a deity in the mandala, including yourself. The world becomes sanctified. You open up the *sambhogakāya* that way. So, this is the path that opens up the *sambhogakāya*. When you finish the *sambhogakāya*, and it's absolutely stable, the aspiration will naturally develop to bring these teachings to all of the beings of *samsāra* that don't have this realization. It will break your heart. And that will cause a shift in perspective that will open up the *nirmāṇakāyas*, the urge to emanate in various planes of reality to help beings and guide them along the path.

When you open up the *nirmāṇakāyas* and start opening it up strong on many levels of reality, then you get all three buddha bodies at once in a stable way. We call that fruition enlightenment. So, it goes from awakening to stabilization to awakening, so you have it all the time, on and off the pillow, to self-arising/self-liberating which opens up the path of liberation, to the perception of the *sambhogakāya*, then the *nirmāṇakāyas* and then full buddhahood. Then it's expressed as enlightened activity towards all beings. Game over.

That's the path. So, you got a good start. Don't mess it up. Go back and set up the stages carefully. And then you keep opening up the awakening. Don't strive for anything. Automatic emptiness clears all the striving, clears all the conceptualization, purifies what you need to do to keep the view straight and fresh. That's all you need to remember. Simple.

We've got enough time for another question. Yes?

Student 3

This is the other end of the spectrum of those of us who …

Dan

The reluctant elephant?

Student 3

Say again.

Dan

The reluctant elephant?

Student 3

Yes, back at the bottom of the Chutes and Ladders game. [Laughter]

Dan

You like those chutes, don't you? [Laughter]

Student 3

Yeah.

Dan

Perhaps there's a limiting belief there.

Student 3

Say again.

Dan

Perhaps there's a limiting belief there.

Student 3

Well, I'm sure there is, but those of us who dwell in the very coarse level of mind, that's …

Dan

Well, you made it into an identity.

Student 3

Probably. I guess the point is that when I've heard you talk and I've been through the practices a number of times, but awakened awareness to me still is, to be candid about it, a concept that I believe exists because you are credible and other people are credible witnesses, and now we've got fMRIs to prove it. But what do you do for the folks, the rest of the world who are like me, who are still trying to master concentration?

Dan

We have compassion on you.

Student 3

Sorry, I just couldn't understand.

Dan

We have compassion on you.

Student 3

Oh, okay.

Dan

And we're stubbornly persistent with moving you along the path. Look, you've come a long way with the elephant path. You just have to adjust your criteria to see where your progress is so you actually see it. We've gone over that a lot. You're much better than you were a year ago with it. Accept the criteria in terms of completeness and continuity of concentration, not in terms of whether you get the subtle level of mind. It's not necessary.

You're much better with the tools, you're much better with directing attention. You're much better with intensifying, you're much better with metacognitive detection more immediately when you get distracted. And your continuity of the completeness of staying is better. Certainly, the continuity of staying is better over time. You're getting there.

Student 3

All right, that's fine. I just, it's nice to know there's a progress point for those of us on the lower leg.

Dan

Anybody else? Yeah.

Student 4

Well, this is sort of in a different area. It's about Myanmar and the treatment of the Rohingya. Being aware of it, hearing about it, it's pretty heartbreaking. Then sort of the next level, hearing the particular Buddhist monks justifying it is, again, sort of heartbreaking, although I understand every … you know, Christianity certainly has done horrible things in the name of Christianity. So, in some ways, I don't know, it's just hard for me. I guess I'm used to, most of the people I've seen, just people I've been personally in contact with, who have been Buddhist monks have been such wonderful, sweet people, it's hard for me to accept that.

Dan

That's a nice stereotype. A lot of people enter the Buddhist monkhood because they escape dealing with the external world. It's a cushy lifestyle and they're fragile people so they enter the ... Mel Shapiro, an anthropologist, did studies in Burma. He did his fieldwork there. And what he found was a lot of people who entered the Buddhist monastic community were very fragile people, and it worked for them. It provided them with a rigid belief system that they could latch onto. They weren't really very good practitioners but they were fragile people and it made them safe. And it held them together.

Don't have the illusions that people who practice in the monastery are very good yogis because most of them aren't doing it for that reason. They're doing it for the cushy lifestyle. We think that because they're nice smiley people, then they're really evolved people. That's not the case at all. Most of them are going there for the wrong reasons. It's true in Christianity, and it's true in Buddhism.

Student 4

Yeah, well the next level I think that thinking about it, that, "Okay, that is true," but then comes the reaction of the rest of the Buddhist community towards these people who are, I would say, using what, their brand of Buddhism for evil purposes. And, maybe I'm missing it, but it seems like there's an awful silence about that. I know I heard the Dalai Lama said something in September about Buddha would ...

Dan

It's a good test of who authentic practitioners are. Any authentic practitioner would say, "No, this is wrong." Any less of a reaction than that is rationalized bullshit.

Student 4

Okay, but I don't hear it. I mean why aren't, you know, there are a lot of good Buddhists. Why aren't people shouting from the rooftops and I guess being a product …

Dan

Because it's a monastic tradition, they're not good practitioners, most of them. They do rituals, they do prayers; they're not yogis. Monastic tradition is the worst place for being a good yogi.

Student 4

Well, what about our good guys, the guys that we know, who we know are genuine? I don't hear them shouting from the rooftops like, "Hey, these..." I mean, the Dalai Lama did say, in I think September, something like, "Buddha would be nice to the Rohingya." But I haven't heard people really, you know, calling these people out for ...

Dan

The really realized yogis within that tradition should be calling the people out.

Student 4

Why don't we hear it?

Dan

It's wrong. They should be calling it out.

Student 4

Yeah, that's what ... Okay.

Dan

Look, when I worked for the War Crimes Tribunal in the 1990s in The Hague, the prosecutors ... my first case was an important case. It was a woman who … she and her husband were well-to-do. They were Serbian Muslims. They lived in a town, half Serbian, half Croatians. Her husband had a number of factories. He gave many people jobs. He was a philanthropist. They donated a lot of money for schools, for hospitals, to the local community, to support the community. But some of the people were jealous of them and the war broke out. It was a civil war. So, the Croatians in the same villages were against the Serbians in the same villages. She was picked out because of her husband's wealth by the very people they supported, the Croatians.

The Croatians wanted to take her three boys and recruit them for the Croatian Army. She had boys in their teenage and early adult years. She wouldn't let them know where the boys were. So, out of resentment, they kidnapped her and they used her as a plaything for the troops. She was raped on the average of ten times a day for six months. Her nipples were bit off. She had bite marks all over her body. These were the very people that she helped in the village. The case was that she came forth, six months later, she was free on the part of a prisoner exchange program with the UN and she then came to the War Crimes Tribunal to testify.

The guy that kidnapped her and raped her and set her up with the rape every day was killed in the secure … he was trying to be captured by UN Security Forces, but the trial was not against him. It was against the head of the Croatian troops, who forced themselves after SSF Officers. And what we wanted to get on the law books is that the tradition that started with the Iliad, when the victors of a war, who roll into the village and take the women as spoils of war and rape them, that tradition we wanted to stop. So, I worked very hard on that case. And the defense actually helped me. They brought in [Elizabeth] Loftus as an expert to try and say that victims of severe war atrocities should not be allowed to testify because they have unreliable memories because they were traumatized too much.

That violated my sensitivities so I destroyed her in the world Court so much that the defense actually pulled her testimony after she testified and brought a new set of experts. The new expert they brought in was a guy from Yale who tried to say that trauma causes hippocampal damage and therefore, they have brain damage. It affects memory structures of the brain. I said, "Bullshit." That violated my sensitivities. So, after they presented all this neuroscience stuff, the chief prosecutor, it was his last case, he was retiring, he was a Nazi hunter, he said, "Dan, I don't know about this neuroscience. What do you want me to do with it?" I said, "Take a risk here. I want you to waive the cross examination and give me five minutes on redirect, because this Tribunal is not going to, they're impatient with the defense. Just give me five minutes, that's all I need." He said, "That's risky." And I said, "Just do it. Trust me."

So, he said, "Okay. Dr. Brown, what's wrong with the study?"

"It was done in the VA. They didn't control for alcoholism, which is rampant in the VA, and we know that alcoholism causes hippocampal damage, so you can't say that trauma does it. Second of all, the statistics of the study were invalid. Here's the retraction letter for the *American Journal of Psychiatry*. I'd like to enter it as an exhibit in the evidence. I wonder why the good doctor failed to mention that?"

The Tribunal turned angrily to the defense and said, "You just wasted four hours of the Tribunal's time. The case is done. You're done. No more testimony. Case over."

Then they turned to me and said, "Doctor, what would be a fair standard of evidence?" I said, this, this, this and this. "It's been the standard of evidence for twenty-five years. It's been challenged on five appeals, never successfully. I'm happy to say we have a 93 percent conviction rate of international war criminals based on that standard. But, the most important thing is we got a new law on the law books, that who's ever in charge of the rape, not who commits rape, not the troop who commits rape, the soldier. Who's ever in charge of those troops is now, that's a thirty-year non-parolable international war crime." So, we thought we finally ended the tradition starting with the Iliad.

Unfortunately, I was deeply humbled right after that because right after that Rwanda started. And the wars are so crazy there; they did it anyway, as in Rohingya are and all these other places. It didn't serve one bit as a deterrent because wars are too crazy. After the war is over, all those people in Rohingya who raped women will be prosecuted by the War Crimes Tribunal. It gives them a lot of ongoing work, but it doesn't serve as a deterrent. I failed at that. I tried. But I failed at it because wars are crazy. But will they be held accountable for that, in the World Court? Absolutely. But if the people in the Buddhist community are just preserving the cushy lifestyle and the monasticism and don't speak out about it, they're not good practitioners. It's wrong. That's my belief strongly.

Student 4

Yeah, I guess mine too, and I just wonder why the silence is there. Because, you know, yeah, there's a lot of cushy people but there's a lot of ...

Dan

People protect themselves.

Student 4

I guess. It's almost sort of like, I guess being a product of Vietnam War resistance is ...

Dan

Most of the practitioners in Burma came from Mahāsī Sayādaw, the same practices that are popular in this country. He took the Visuddhimagga, the path of purification, which is the main stage-by-stage practice, and dumbed it down and made it actual popular meditations for Westerners about a hundred years ago. But look what he cut out. We're working with aggregate practice to work with the issue of self. He cut that out of the practice. There's no procedure in Burmese mindfulness that deals with the issue of self, unlike all the work we do on emptiness of self. The only thing is the *anatta*, no self. If you concentrate enough the self goes away. That's different from having the self be there in the background and just not what you're operating out of, which is emptiness of self practice.

So, what does it mean? There's no procedure within Burmese mindfulness in this country or in Burma that deals with the issue of self. So, you get a lot of teachers in the West that are filled with themselves as mindfulness teachers. And they're filled with self-importance, spiritual pride, because there's no technique in that system that has you deal with it. In Burma, you get a lot of the monks protecting their self-interest as a monastic monk, so they won't speak out against anything because they're filled with self. They can't muster their compassion for the most obvious situations that are awful, just to protect themselves. And we found that no-self versus emptiness of self was true in the neuroscience study that we did.

There's six studies that show that the medial prefrontal cortex—which is sense of self, Dan-ness in my case—that gets deactivated in mindfulness practice. But that's not what we found in the Indo-Tibetan practice with our subjects: the sense that the medial prefrontal cortex was just as active in a normal way but that's not where they're operating out of. They were shifting to the parietal system of global awareness and operating out of that. So, the sense of self is still there in the background; it's just irrelevant because you've shifted your basis of operation to a larger picture where compassion is included within the interconnectedness of everything.

It's a much more mature practice. The issue of self in older Buddhism, which Theravadan and mindfulness represent, including Burma, is very different from the revisions that came five hundred years after that in emptiness practice. And it makes a huge difference in terms of how you act. That's what I think is going on. They don't have the tools in that culture.

Student 4

So, why aren't the enlightened Burmese speaking out publicly? I mean, I think in ways, what's going on is giving Buddhism a bad name. I don't think that's the main reason we should speak out. People should speak out because it's wrong.

Dan

People protect self-interests. Genuine practitioners have no concern with that. They just say what's right no matter what. Then you deal with the consequences of that. You've got to speak the truth. So, it's a good litmus test of who has genuine realization, who's just speaking the talk and not walking the talk, I think. It tells you right there.

Student 5

Just briefly, as a Christian leader in the world, I would say my experience is that I and my colleagues are extremely careful about speaking out about such things. There are many horrific things that Christians are doing all around the world that I do not speak out against. Not because I don't think they're wrong but because my sphere of influence and the things that I'm choosing to focus my attention on are very strategic and efficacious, you know, in terms of they're just very targeted within a particular circle.

I'm guessing, I don't know which leaders you're talking about, but I'm guessing if you went to any of our friends who have taught here and asked them what they thought, they would have an opinion. And I'm also guessing that speaking out publicly in an international platform is not their primary locus of their energies and their focus. Anyway, so that's just a thought.

Dan

Yeah, that's a good point. Mandela and Desmond Tutu, when they joined together, there's a lot of atrocities they didn't speak out against because the priority was to build a coalition so that Black factions didn't break down into a civil war amongst Blacks. That was more important. You choose your priorities.

December 6, 2017

Themes: Implicit Memory; Awareness During Amnesia, Dreams; Most Precise Teaching to Buddhahood

Dan

Welcome everyone. You have a question?

Student 1

So, I was wondering about awakening and the awakened state in anesthesia. I've just had someone in the family going through surgery, and I was thinking, "Okay, awaken in the day, awake in sleep, awake in death." What about during surgery? That doesn't sound like a good time, right? I was wondering about that and how that might affect being awake.

Dan

Wow ... Yeah ... [Long pause]

Student 2

They're using it as a treatment now.

Dan

For what?

Student 2

For depression.

Dan

What's the treatment?

Student 2

Giving them like this kind of anesthesia, and they do several rounds of it. But I don't remember …

Dan

I don't know anything about that.

Student 2

I know. It's strange. But the person who did it said it was like she was sort of semi awake, kind of a dream state, and she was working through all these issues, and her therapist sat there and guided her through it. It sounded like they were using it kind of like hypnosis.

Dan

I don't know what it was. We'd have to find out what it was.

Student 2

Yeah, it was done … The person is at McLean who's doing this.

Dan

Okay.

Student 2

They are using it.

Dan

There's no study on the effect of drugs on awakening. We just did the first study on the neurocircuitry of awakening. So given the fact that no one studies awakening, certainly the mindfulness people don't, we're not going to see very much about the nature of awakening until we open it up for inquiry. There are studies on whether people retain awareness during anesthesia, and the prevailing view up until the 1960s was that when people took a general anesthesia, they were largely unconscious, and they were completely oblivious to what was going on around them.

But then there was a famous lawsuit called the Beached Whale lawsuit, and Beached Whale won the lawsuit. It was a woman who had some sort of surgery, and she weighed over three hundred pounds. They put her under general anesthesia, and they assumed that she would not remember anything that they said. And under the anesthesia, after it took effect, she seemed to be completely out of it. The surgeons being somewhat sarcastic were making fun of her weight, and called her a "beached whale," and made a lot of other derogatory comments. When she allegedly woke up from the anesthesia, she remembered everything, and she sued the surgeons, and the surgeons lost. She won her case for several million dollars.

And that rocked the anesthesiology world because it was no longer the case that we could assume that people are knocked out by the anesthesia, that some people are not necessarily unconscious. So, then that began a series of scientific studies about whether or not people could remember things under general anesthesia, where they were really out of it. And the studies focused on the issues of what was called implicit versus explicit memory.

Explicit memory is when you can say, "This is an event that happened me when I was under anesthesia and this, this, this, and this had happened," in an explicit narrative. An implicit memory is when you can't remember any narrative details of the event, but you still remember the event, and you express it behaviorally.

So, under the conditions of anesthesia, whether it is caused psychologically or emotionally, or by drugs, people don't have a general narrative memory, but that doesn't necessarily mean they don't have an implicit behavioral memory of the event.

I made a film once for 20/20. They contacted me about a kid who seemed to have dissociative fugue. He was a twenty-one-year-old who had just gotten married, and immediately after the wedding they went to the airport to go to their honeymoon for a week. And he said he left something in the car, and went back to get it and never came back. He went missing for over a week. He was on an all-points bulletin all over the country. And they found him a week later, wandering on a golf course disheveled and a bit out of it, about a mile from the airport parking lot where he left his car. And he had no memory for any of the events of his life and he had no memory of his identity. We call that dissociative fugue. Where the person has dissociative amnesia, they don't remember certain traumatic events in their past; when they have dissociative fugue, they don't remember who they are, and they have no memory or access to their previous life.

So, I tested him with the SCID-D for dissociative amnesia and established that he had dissociative fugue. He had no sense of his identity up until the point that he went to the parking lot and after that he remembered nothing about who he was. But I was able to show on camera that he had implicit memory for certain things. Like, for example, he had a cat, and even though he didn't claim to remember the name of the cat, if I handed him the cat, he would show immediate recognition and pet the cat, and the cat would show immediate recognition to him. So, he was acting like it was his cat even though he doesn't remember having the cat, or the name of the cat. That's implicit memory.

He was also a very good soccer star, so we put him on a soccer field and we had him kick the ball around. And he explained all of these moves that he made, but he had no memory of ever playing soccer. He couldn't remember why he was playing so well and why he was making all these somewhat professional moves with the soccer ball. So, we were able to show that even though he had no personal identity, he still had an implicit behavioral memory for the events in his life. He got his memory back 364 days after the original loss of the memory, almost exactly a year later.

It came back, in his case, all at once. And with all the testing that I did with him we were able to come up with some explanation for why he had a fugue state. Normally what causes people to lose their memory, or lose their memory of their identity, is trauma. But it's not always a traumatic event; it can be caused by internal conflict. And we were able to find out in his case what was going on that caused him to not remember the events.

There were two things that were going on. We know that people tend to have more assault and narrative memory if they're on drugs. And, for about six months up to the time of his wedding, he did ecstasy a lot. And ecstasy causes depletion of vitamin B12, which affects the hippocampus and contextual memory. So, if you take vitamin B12 or B-complex supplements after you do ecstasy there's no effect. But none of the kids on the street know how to do that. Given the amount of ecstasy that he took, that would be a reasonable explanation for why his memory retrieval cues would be faulty.

But the main thing was conflict. It turns out that when he was sixteen, from a small town, Texas Christian fundamentalist family, he got a girl in high school pregnant—unwanted. And, since they're all Christian fundamentalists, that means abortion was not a question mark. So, he had a kid when he was sixteen, unwanted. He never had any involvement with the woman or the kid, and never paid any alimony. The other family decided they would keep the kid, raise the kid, but he was under court order to pay alimony, and he'd just skipped town and never paid it. And it turns out that a week before his wedding to another woman, he got a notice in the mail. He had to pay all this back alimony as a deadbeat dad. So as the case of conflict, he didn't know what to do so he put it out of his mind. But what he did was literally put his mind out of his mind.

We came up with a reasonable explanation for what would account for the conflicts that would allow him to put his identity out of his mind. He simply erased it. Not that he had control over that; it just happened. And a year later when he recovered his memory for his identity, he also recovered his memory for the conflict. At which point he told his then wife about it, who stuck by him for a year even though he had no memory of who she was, and she stuck by him anyway. He ended up in a good stable marriage. And he even paid back the debts of his past.

When we did a national airing of this on 20/20, he did not want us to put in the explanation about the deadbeat dad stuff; he didn't allow us to tell the story. So, 20/20 rewrote the story as a love story; and rewrote it as why his woman stuck by him with all those difficulties, and romanticized it. So, we never got a chance to tell on film the explanation for how this weird thing called dissociative fugue could actually happen. He's somebody who put his identity out of his memory.

It's a well-documented case for which we actually came up with an explanation for why it happened. But in his case, what was left was implicit memory. He never lost the implicit memory for important events in his life like playing soccer and playing with his cat. Even though he could not speak, those parts of his memory were well preserved. And we see that in survivors of priest abuse. I worked on all the cases in *Spotlight*.[5] I worked on the grand jury and helped the prosecutors to prepare their cross-examinations for most of those cases.

On the Shanley case I worked on the appeal before the Supreme Court, and we got a 7-0 unanimous decision to keep Shanley in jail. Unfortunately, they recently let him out, which I had no say over. But, had they asked me I would have given the testimony that would allow him to stay in jail, but they didn't ask me. But in all those cases, it is often the case with the children who grow up and repress their memory, and don't remember for twenty or thirty years and recover the memory, they still have an implicit memory. I remember a case of a guy who met the priest ten years after he was abused in earlier adolescence, puberty years. He didn't remember any of the abuse, but when the father came up to him and he was very friendly with him and wanted to shake his hand, he pulled his hand back, and he couldn't explain why he pulled his hand back out of fear. He had no memory, but he had implicit memory. And that's common.

On the Fells Acres daycare case, which was a case of ritual abuse, all the kids had behavioral memory of things they did—they enacted the abuse even though they had no narrative memory of the abuse. So, in defending the Fells Acres perpetrators, the defense came in and brought in a false memory person to say that the interviews were highly suggestive. They said this is suggestive, this is suggestive, this is suggestive. So, I took all the interviews and broke them down into what I call high and low magnitude suggestion effects. There were almost no high magnitude suggestion effects. The fact that if somebody was asked a question, they called it a suggestion and made it look ridiculous to them, that they were snowing the court with all this stuff about suggestion that wasn't really suggestion. But in a cross-examination, I told the prosecutors

---

5 The 2015 film about *The Boston Globe*'s investigation into priest abuse.

to ask the expert Maggie Brooke, from Canada. I said, ask her are there any laboratory studies that show you can give suggestions to kids and make them put, repeatedly, and insert hot-dogs into their vaginas? Is there any laboratory study that shows you can produce behaviors like that?

So, we asked her a whole series of [questions about] behaviors like that that the kids were actually doing. And she had to say, "No, no, no, no", and then we won the case. The "science" was bullshit. And all these kids had preserved implicit behavioral memories of the abuse, the things they were enacting on themselves and their own bodies. That case failed under appeals, and the perpetrators are still in jail.

So now that applies to the whole thing of anesthesia again. Because after the Beached Whale case there's a question that maybe people wouldn't have a narrative memory of the things that the surgeon said during the actual or general anesthesia, but would they retain the behavioral memory? Or would they retain some degree of that narrative memory?

So, there were four studies that were done in the 1970s and '80s of mock crises during surgery; these were real surgeries. And during the real surgery, which is hard to get through IRB, if used these days, but in those days, deception was used in research much more than now. In all four studies, during the surgeries, even though it wasn't happening, the surgeon turned to the anesthesiologist and said, "The patient is breathing heavily and is turning blue," or some other crisis in the course of the surgery that was unexpected. They announced it clearly in words. And the idea was to see, even though it was not a real crisis—it was a fake crisis, like fake news, the person under anesthesia was not told that it was a fake crisis—the idea was, would they remember the mock crisis verbally as an explicit memory, or would they do it implicitly? And they were told to recall, freely recall anything they could about the events after the anesthesia took hold, and they were not cued, but given prompts. "Was there anything happening that was unexpected?" That's pretty general; they weren't told what it was.

Then they were given using the method that Cory Hammond developed in "Hypnosis and Ideomotor Questioning Technique." Now, although the conscious mind doesn't know, the unconscious mind might know these things. So, if I ask a question to the unconscious mind that knows the answer, the index finger will float up if the answer is yes. If the unconscious mind knows the answer, and the answer is no, the middle finger will float up. If the answer is, "I don't know the answer," another finger will float up.

So, in these four studies they had a genuine mock crisis, and most of the people didn't remember anything, but some of the people remembered the words that were said: "Something has changed"; "this person's turning blue"; "this person's not breathing." Some people actually remembered the explicit words, so that some people—a small percentage of people—preserve an explicit narrative memory while being under general anesthesia.

And more people preserve an implicit memory. Was there a situation that occurred, "yes," with the index finger. Did the surgeon seem worried, "yes." Even though they couldn't say anything narratively, the index fingers responded correctly to the target. And since another person was doing the inquiry who didn't know what the target questions were, the target crisis was ... so the target questions were done blind, so they couldn't be cued. Which is a good way of doing it.

So, there's no research on whether or not one can be awakened aware during drug induced states, anesthesia or not. But what we're talking about is ordinary awareness during anesthesia. The answer to that is some people can be aware, and explicitly describe that memory, and some people can be aware implicitly, but not explicitly aware.

There was a time when Ram Dass told a story. Remember Ram Dass was one of the three researchers with Timothy Leary who got kicked out of Harvard for giving the graduate students too many psychedelics. So, it was always an obsession of Ram Dass's to see whether LSD would affect his master. And at one point he gave his master LSD, 400 micrograms which is a hefty dose. That's about a thousand times more powerful than on the street. And he waited, and he waited, and after about an hour, his master starts screaming and writhing on the floor, and shouting incoherently. And Ram Dass's mind was spinning a mile a minute saying, "Oh, I just destroyed my masters mind, what have I done?" This went on for about ten or fifteen minutes and the master shot up and smiled, and said, "Is this what's supposed to happen?" [Laughter]

He was playing with him. It had absolutely no effect on him. I had done hallucinogens in my teens, and worked with them legally in the last human subjects project in 1970 and 1971 in the Maryland Psychiatric Research Center. We were giving it to terminal cancer patients. I was part of a team, working four days a week, sixteen hours a day giving trips to cancer patients to prepare them to die.

So, in those days I ingested a fair amount of psychedelics, but I haven't done anything since, since those days. And about five years ago somebody gave me a hit of ecstasy for New Year's, so I said, "Well, maybe I should try it." I was curious because I hadn't done it in years and years and years. Other than the fact that I had a lot of energy to dance it had no effect on my mind whatsoever, none. Very boring. It was a very energetic plant. Other than having more energy for dancing, more like kelp. [Laughter] I rolled back and forth. But I can't say that it had much effect.

And the idea is to sustain awakening at all times in all situations, and that means at all times and all situations. Including drug induced states. So, it shouldn't have any effect if you have awakening; it doesn't make any effect. But it is harder to sustain awakening in altered states of consciousness; that's why it's not so easy to bring awakening into deep sleep. It's not so easy to bring awakening into dreaming, but there's a whole practice designed to do that. And, I suppose if you can bring it into deep sleep on a regular basis, and bring it into dreaming on a regular basis, then bringing it into general anesthesia would be something that would be not so different from that. Because typically we get unconscious during deep sleep and we get unconscious during dreaming, the same way we do during anesthesia, so I don't think it's very different.

So, indirectly we have evidence from deep sleep and dreaming that people can bring it into states that we wouldn't normally bring it into, and you can train to do that. Personally, I found it to be easier to bring it into deep sleep than dreaming. You take a sleeping lion's posture. You lie on your right side, because the white right channel is the channel of *samsāra*, and the red left side channel is the channel of nirvana. So, if you sleep on your right side, the body weight will slow the winds in the right channel, which is where most of the negative stuff comes out to, so you have more positive dreams, just by sleeping on that side.

And the way that you train it is to focus on the chakra of emanation, which is the throat chakra, because dreams come from the throat chakra—the winds in the throat chakra is what generates dreams. So, you take awakened awareness as your backdrop, or ordinary awareness if you can't, but it's supposed to be awakened awareness. And then you focus on the four petaled red lotus at the throat. So, it's King of Samādhi practice. You're practicing from the vast expanse of awakening with pinpointed focus on the lotus and the throat chakra, and you wait. And you wait till the world subsides, disappears, and then imagery comes back. We call that the hypnagogic state, the state of transitioning into deep sleep. It's a state where you get fragmented imagery. You watch all the imagery come back from [the perspective of] the awakened mind. You learn to hold all that, ride that threshold just before you fall asleep, and cross that threshold while you have awakened awareness.

And when all the hypnagogic imagery comes back, you are letting it arise within the expanse of awakened mind. Then the imagery will disappear completely. And the idea is to hold awakening during deep sleep, so you're not unconscious during deep sleep, you're at least aware during deep sleep. And you measure the degree of success in terms of the brightness of the field. So, the more [you] practice it, you're not deep asleep but you're awakened-awake during deep sleep even though you're still sleeping.

The body gets restless during deep sleep, but the mind is quite quiet, so there's no content during deep sleep. Then at some point, you enter the dream state, and the content will get very active within that field. And the idea is to sustain awakened awareness while the dream content comes. During dreaming the mind is very active and the body is completely still. In sleep research in the West it says, "Deep sleep: mind still, body active. Dreaming: body still, mind active"—the opposite.

Many people find it's hard to determine that point of recognizing when you're dreaming. So, one of the things that they do in Tibet is they have a buddy system. You have your roommate wake you up every two hours and say to you, "What's your basis of operation right now?" And, of course, if you wake up every two hours, some of those times—we dream about four or five times a night—some of those times are going to be during the dreaming process. And if someone suddenly wakes you up in the middle of a dream and says, "What's your basis of operation right now?" you might correctly be able to put your metacognition online and recognize that you have awakened awareness during the dream, and just take it from there. If you get woken up a number of times, then you train yourself to wake up on your own, not to wake up but to recognize the awakened awareness during deep sleep.

There is a good literature on Western lucid dreaming, but it's not the same, because all the literature on Western lucid dreaming is about having awareness, ordinary awareness, during dreaming. This is very specific. It has to be awakened awareness during dreaming. That's a big difference. So, that's the difference. You train yourself to have awakened awareness during all the deep sleep we should normally be unconscious in, and during dreaming, when we should normally be unconscious. Then when you can do that, you have awakened awareness 24/7, because you applied it to the deepest levels of your mind that you'd normally be unconscious in. That's an analogy that fits your question, I think. If you can do awakened aware during deep sleep when you're normally unconscious, and during deep dreaming when you're normally unconscious, it's very similar to do doing it with drug-induced unconscious states.

Student 3

You're able to do lucid dreaming. And if you're practiced in lucid dreaming then you know you're dreaming, and then you can choose how you act, so that, or can you at that point practice, and then say, go through practice and bring yourself into awakened awareness from a lucid dream?

Dan

I think it's harder.

Student 3

Really?

Dan

I think if you train yourself to operate out of ordinary awareness in dreaming, then it's hard, and you get attached to that. It's hard to shift to awakened awareness.

Student 3

You mean to get attached to the lucid, being awake and …

Dan

Being ordinary aware during dreaming. I think it actually makes it harder. So, I'm not sure it's a good practice to do. It's the same thing that we find with all the people with mindfulness who think that being mindful is enough. But, if they train themselves into being mindful all the time, it's actually harder to awaken because they are looking for the wrong thing all the time. It's a different neurocircuitry operating out of mindfulness and operating out of awakened awareness. If you learn to put that circuitry online, it keeps opening up. How are you going to put the neurocircuitry of awakening online if you train yourself to open up the wrong circuit, because you train yourself to open up the wrong circuit?

I think these things that we do in the West make it more difficult. But people aren't looking for awakening, they are looking for a fascination with states. I can control my dreams; I can be aware of my dreams. So what? What does that do for anybody? There's another way of calling attention to yourself, become self-important. That's mostly what it's about. Ask yourself the question, if you study lucid dreaming, why are you studying it? What are you getting out of it? How is it helpful? Mostly it represents attachment to the states.

Go ahead.

Student 1

Awakened awareness in a dream, how do I say this? When things come to you that are inexplicable, it's like a clarity dream, I would call it. It's like a dream you've never had before, and so clear, so ringingly clear. Does the awakened awareness put you in some kind of field, you're beyond yourself? Then are you accessing other consciousness, or is other consciousness accessing you?

Dan

Well, if you're opening up awakened awareness, you're opening up a limitless field of everything that's contained within that field. That's if you open up awakened awareness. But if you're not opening up awakened awareness, but ordinary awareness, during the dream it's true that on the more refined level of conciseness everything is interconnected. But one could argue since because it's not awakened awareness you have a partial view of things. I mean you can have big dreams; that's true. But you have to be aware of the source of the big dreams, because, in the Tibetan system, in certain states of mind, particularly in altered states, different from awakened state, you're more vulnerable to negative demonic influences. That's why, for those of you who've done the inner fire practice, there's a whole series of protections that you do with the *ḍākinīs* before you do the inner fire practice. Because when you do the intensive fire practice you are more vulnerable to demonic forces. So, you let the *ḍākinīs* take care of the demons for you. They do a good job with it, because of their fierceness.

The same thing in dream states, and in deep sleep—you are more vulnerable in those states to outside forces. So, you can get lots of messages in dreams and the messages may be negative messages disguised as positive messages. So, the trouble with reading dreams as important is what's the source? If it comes from awakened *dharmakāya* space, you can rely on that, if it's true. But if it comes from the dream itself, it could come from any source. That's the trouble with channeling, because sometimes you get small level demonic figures who give negative messages just for the sake of being tricksters, or for the sake of having a laugh at other peoples' expense.

Student 1

The trick is being aware …

Dan

Yeah, so you have to be aware of the source of where you're coming from. So, you get enamored by the self-importance of it, if it's a big dream. You see that with people that get into the psychic world; they get lots of messages, but there's no discrimination for where they get their messages from. They develop a kind of spiritual pride that since they're channeling, their messages necessarily must be true. That's garbage. So, when the messages are actually harmful, if you don't know what your source is, in other words if you are going to channel, if you are going to use dreams, do it from reliable sources. But, how do you know that? That depends on your state of mind.

A good example of that, which is a painful controversy, is the people who protested the Dalai Lama. They're students of a great tantric master, Kelsang Gyatso. There aren't a lot of tantric masters of that caliber anymore, of that age. He's one of the last of the greats. But somewhere like twenty years ago some of his students militantly began aggressively protesting the Dalai Lama, and harassing him everywhere he goes.

I remember going to a conference about ten, fifteen years ago at Lehigh University for a week on Tsongkhapa's Great Treatise. And Kelsang Gyatso's students were outside, and they were very aggressive, I thought. They were like a cult. So, somebody asked the Dalai Lama at the conference about the protestors. He gave, what I thought was a very reasonable answer, he said, "Look, this came up during the time of the 5th Dalai Lama," one of his previous incarnations. And he said that when Padmasambhava walked along the Kali Gandaki River Valley, [he] tamed a lot of the demonic forces and made them become protectors of the *dharma*. This deity, Shugden, was one of them. But it may not have been an effective taming. He may be acting as a *dharma* protector, but not really a *dharma* protector, sort of like a spiritual double agent.

And the Dalai Lama said that the 5th Dalai Lama wrote extensively about this. He said, "I'm not telling people not to do it, I'm just warning them because I did my due diligence on this, and I think there's some reason to be concerned. So, I'm not telling them not to do it, which is what they're protesting, in violation of their religious freedoms." He said, "Just be careful. This may not be what you think it is." Which I thought was very reasonable to say.

And I talked to the protestors outside and they were pretty much mindless. They couldn't… they were so aggressive. It's like the cult, they couldn't hear anybody else's opinion. I had no vested interest in one way or another just to find out what this whole thing was about. I thought that probably the Dalai Lama's position on it was correct, that this was a demonic force.

So, I asked another Tibetan lama who was of the same ilk, who was a great *tantra* master, who I know pretty well, who does a lot of the visualizations in the same way that Kelsang Gyatso does. And I said, "Look, the two of you are peers, so what is your take on this?" And he said, "Well, off the record," he said, "we've done a lot of the same visualizations; we think that there is a deity that's disguising itself as a protector, and is really demonic. And we think that he's done it so long, for twenty years now, and it's taken over his mind, and he's just lost it." And I thought this came from a reliable source. So, two people that I respected … a lot came down with a reasonable explanation for why one should watch out for these things. And I tended to think that they were right, and this whole thing was unfortunate.

Kelsang Gyatso had written—if you look at his books, they're lucidly clear. But he is responsible for the behavior of his students, and he lets these things go on. So, there's something off about this, really off. It's wrong to allow his students to be that unleashed in their aggression towards the Dalai Lama, repeatedly, relentlessly. It's wrong. It's not behavior becoming of *dharma* students, which is wrong. So, I think that there was probably something to all this. So, watch your sources, and use reliable sources. And, if you don't know the sources, don't put a lot of stock in it.

I had one of those big dreams once, and I don't usually have dreams like that. But because I had it, it was unusual. And it was the first time I went to Menri

Monastery for a month. And it was the first night I got there. At night I had this dream of a giant, a monstrous, huge monstrous black serpent, a snake that was much bigger than the size of this room. And it was really, really angry, and it was wreaking havoc on the land. It would come out of the ground. And it was so unusual that I told His Holiness about it.

And he was very interested in the content of it because they had done a yogi temple, which is where they do all their *tantra* rituals. It cost a couple of hundred thousand dollars to build this thing. And as soon as they built it, a mudslide came and it went, yihh, a little bit over the side of the mountain, and it looks like they could lose the whole thing they just built.

So, they did things to shore up the wall, and build drainage systems and all that kind of stuff. But he wasn't interested in that, he was interested in the dream. He said, "It sounds like a *naga* spirit, sounds like there was a *naga* spirit living in the mountains." He wanted to know where this snake came from, and I didn't know. In the dream I didn't pay attention enough. He said, "There's probably a *naga* spirit living in the mountains and we didn't know that; we didn't do the proper rituals." So, then they did the proper rituals, and since then, the temple's been fine, no more mudslides. And it's back, it's righted itself again. So, go figure, the dream meant something. But I didn't know; it wasn't a thing that I would normally have. I had it in that context. So, he found it useful. But, the motivation behind the dream was to be protective of the lineage. And that, of course, he was quite interested in.

Student 3

You mentioned earlier that in awakened awareness during sleep that, hmm, there was an opportunity. I'm not sure if you said this, but an opportunity to do it the right way, or for your motivations to be right. Did you say something like that?

Dan

No. I was saying that if you want to take messages from dreams or channeling then the motivation has to be right, otherwise you open yourself up for negative demonic influences. And you read messages, and they're fake messages, but we take it and give it too much power, because power comes out of pride, and self-importance.

Student 3

So, what should your motivation be when you are doing that practice?

Dan

Your motivation should be helping people.

Student 3

Same motivation as the whole path.

Dan

And sincere exploration.

Student 3

Sincere exploration.

Dan

Ram Dass tells a story of a time that he got involved with some Western spiritual channeler in New York. Everybody's running to this woman, and they did it for four or five years, and he was really taken by all the messages. Then they found out that her seances were fake. She was getting stuff on peoples' backgrounds, and then feeding this story that somebody was killing them. But the whole thing was staged.

He came out publicly and said, "This is spiritual greed. I got so caught up in wanting it to be true." He made himself vulnerable. When you have people channeling messages, what's the motivation? It's about self-importance, and I would stay away from it.

Student 4

Dan, when you mentioned this watching the source, and you don't get into trouble, are you talking about the motivation, or are you talking about …

Dan

It's about motivation. Why are we doing this?

Student 4

So, it's the motivation?

Dan

Yeah, the motivation should always be to help other people. I remember once when I was with my first Root Lama, Geshe Wangyal, and what I liked about him was he never played the guru game. He had about a dozen and a half students over thirty years in the US, and no one ever heard of him. He just lived this life. He gave one public talk. In the mid 1970s there was the Himalayan Institute doing the first Western international conference on yoga and meditation.

About five thousand people came to this conference. And they invited him to come, and he accepted it, which was unusual because he doesn't ever do things like that. He gave the last talk, after three days of workshops on meditation and yoga. And he got up there and he said, "I'm not going to talk to you about methods for meditating, there's lots of people who showed you things about that. I have only one thing to say. When you sit down to meditate, the first thing that should go through your mind is: 'Why am I doing this?' Then answer the question to yourself. If you're doing it because it would be helpful to other people, and you're doing it because it moves your heart, then you're on the right track. If you can't answer it that way, don't bother to waste your time." And he walked off the stage. That was the end of his talk. He made the point, because it was so brief. Because no one had ever said at the talk, "Why are we meditating, why are we doing this?" So, he made the point eminently clear: why are we doing this?

And you have to answer it in the way that comes from your heart. If you can't, don't waste your time. It's just another mundane thing that you're doing in life calling it spirituality.

So, do you have a question?

Student 4

Yeah, but it might be a long, I mean, depending on how much time that we have.

Dan

On the subject that we're now doing?

Student 4

I think it is.

Dan

Okay.

Student 4

Because I really like the story about motivation and intention, because ultimately, it's always about the intention.

Dan

Yeah, it's always about intention.

Student 4

Now on the same line when you speak about different visualization practices as far as I can tell, you mostly draw it from the tradition from the Mahāmudrā and Dzogchen, and you just bring in here and there a little bit of a Western kind of practices?

Dan

Something like that.

Student 4

But for the most part you really kind of stick with it, even though when you give examples from your background, you've done a lot of mindfulness, you studied various kind of shamanic things, you've done psychedelics, it sounds like you've tried and seen a lot. So, in that sense it, that's kind of impressive. It sounds like you've seen and done a lot and it …

Dan

And there's still a few neurons left. [Dan chuckles; Students laugh]

Student 4

So my question is then, you really stick with the Dzogchen/Mahāmudrā, and then the little bit of Western stuff, but mostly with the tradition. My guess is because it's the most direct path.

Dan

There's nothing else like it.

Student 4

And it's kind of in line with the question. If the ultimate goal is awakening, you're reason is because it's the most direct …

Dan

The ultimate goal is to be a buddha; awakening is just a step along the way. So, I'm not going to use Western teachings to be a buddha, but if the Western stuff helps you understand some of the experiences, then it's useful. What's the question?

Student 4

The question is whether the reason you so closely, obviously with practices into philosophy and practices of Mahāmudrā and Dzogchen is it because everything you see, you're basically saying this is it, this is the most direct, you don't need anything else—it's good to know, but don't bother?

Dan

These teachings are far more profound than anything I've ever found before. They're much more detailed and explicit. And you can see that they're explicit. You won't get that kind of detail most other places, because it doesn't exist.

Student 4

Thank you.

Dan

I remember, and some of you know this story, but going to the last course that His Holiness Menri Trizin did in America, last spring in New Jersey, it was on the Akhrid system, which is typically fourteen sessions to awakening: There are five preliminary sessions on impermanence, and bodhicitta, and refuge, and confession, and Mandala offering to develop positive qualities, and a guru yoga. And after those five sessions there are two concentration sessions on the [Tibetan] letter A—the first on the target itself, and then without the target, the subtle level of concentration. Then right from the stillness of concentration you open up awakening. Then once you open up awakening, you're doing inner fire practice to brighten the mind so you recognize awakening more frequently; and then how to develop awakening so that you have it automatically; how to mix it into dream and sleep, and daily practices. And the last three sessions are on the limitlessness of the mind leading up to the connection of the enlightened buddha bodies. So, the whole thing is done in fourteen sessions. That's pretty amazing.

But what he did in that course that he had never done before is that he broke the whole thing down into one session. You focus on the A and concentrate. And as you get more concentrated you realize that you're not really focusing on, you're not seeing the A; you're seeing the mind. And when you start to see the mind rather than the concentration object, you're asked a series of questions, and the emptiness is implied. Then you open up, with opening instructions, the limitlessness of the mind. And from that vast and limitless scope of the mind, you open up the buddha bodies, all the way to buddhahood in one session. It's rather profound.

No one has ever given an instruction like that before. So, he asked me to unpack it, which I did for the group. But what he was saying is that, with his last teaching, he wanted people to have the instructions all the way up to buddhahood, because some of you will become buddhas. So, before he died and left his form body, he wanted you to have the complete transmission of the instructions up to buddhahood. So, he gave them. What's not profound about that? There's nothing else like it anywhere. And there's an enormous, if you will, generosity, to give that kind of explicit detail that you won't find anywhere else—in a Tibetan tradition, or any other tradition. That's why.

December 17, 2017

Themes: Losing Loved Ones; Full-catastrophe Living; Common Humanity

Dan

Welcome everyone. You have a question?

Student 1

So, Dan, I have a curiosity about my emotionality, I guess is the category. My brother was here to visit last week, and I adore my brother. We're best friends. It took a long time. We were not friends as children, and as adults we became friends, so he's really a chosen friend as opposed to just a sibling, and I see him once a year when he comes to visit from Texas. His leaving, I found myself really emotional, like even talking about it brings it to me again, the sadness of how far away he is, and how much we just have telephone with each other, and that I miss him, and it surprises me. I don't know quite what to make of that, and the other side of that is this contrast of being with other people, friends who I also love, and adore, but I don't understand the emotionality behind it, and that he's going to be seventy tomorrow, and I feel this panic of, "Oh my God, our lives are coming to an end, and will I see him again, and again, and again because I want to." So, I don't know how to make that into a question, but ...

Dan

Well, it's a good question, but I suppose the immediate question back is what's wrong with the emotionality?

Student 1

Nothing, but it's a surprise I guess, the tearfulness, and the longing to be closer to him.

Dan

From a Western attachment point of view, we would say that's a good thing. It shows that in that longing you value attachment, and that's healthy. There's nothing wrong with it. What the real issue is isn't really about the attachment, or even the discomfort with that; the real issue is that it's finite. You're not getting any younger, he's not getting any younger, and now that you've in some ways earned closeness, something you didn't have originally with your brother, and now you have, you want to keep it, and there's no guarantees at this age.

Student 1

No.

Dan

Somebody once said, "You know you're getting old when you start reading the obituaries, and you see your friends in it." You, me, we're at an age that is finite, so there's no guarantees anymore when you'll die. How you'll die. How quickly that will be. How slowly that will be. And, the more precious that relationship has become for you, the more you don't want to lose it, but the fact that you see it as precious, and don't want to lose it, that's a good thing, because in whatever the uncertain time it is you have left, you can nurture that. You can make time to be with each other more if you both so wish. What's the worst that's going to happen if you become more attached, and one of you dies? It will be painful. You'd be enriched for what you had together, so what's the matter with that?

Student 1

I guess I just don't like sitting here having tears come out of my eyes about all of that. There's nothing wrong with it.

Dan

No, there's nothing wrong with it. In a different tradition, the Spanish Christian mystic, Saint Teresa of Avila called it the gift of tears. You have the gift of tears. The practice and the realizations have opened your heart up. That doesn't stop, because now you feel more deeply. That's a good thing.

There's a famous passage in one of the poems, [by a great Sufi] mystic saying, "I don't know what's happened to me. God took away my books, and filled me with poetry, and song." If you do the practice, the realizations open up your heart. You live more clearly out of that heart, so the worst that happens here is that, at the time that it comes from one or the other, you will feel enriched for what you had together, and that will hurt. So what?

Student 1

It's a better hurt than some others I've had in my life.

Dan

Right. You see, we have this misconception about spiritual practice that it should mean that we become less attached.

Student 1

That's the surprise.

Dan

That's sometimes an inaccurate construction of mind. We say that "the near enemy of compassion is indifference." "The near enemy"—something that appears like something, but it's not really that thing. So, some people practice spirituality and they think that they should be equanimous, and not react to anything, not have any feelings anymore, and that becomes an illusion of indifference. You think you're not being reactive, but what you're actually being is indifferent, and stoic. There's no caring in that. It's not even genuine spiritual practice. It's an idea. You still get the feelings. The issue is not to get the grab of the feelings, but you don't try and do away with the feelings. In that sense, you live life more fully.

Many years ago, when the mindfulness tradition was starting in this country, one of its proponents, Jon Kabat-Zinn, wrote his first book, and he titled it Full Catastrophe Living. He took the title from the film *Zorba the Greek* with Anthony Quinn. What he was trying to convey is that the best way of leading a spiritual life is to embrace the full catastrophe of everyday life, and live it fully without reactivity. That doesn't mean without feeling. See the difference?

Student 1

Now I do, I guess I was …

Dan

Otherwise, it's just an empty construction you have in your mind that, "I should not have these feelings, and that means I'm progressing spiritually," when you may be a spiritual robot.

Student 1

When you say it that way, it seems ridiculous.

Dan

What's lost is the grab to the feeling. You feel it cleanly, and it's done.

Student 1

Well, this has been going on for a day and a half now.

Dan

Because, you're fighting against it. Whereas someone said, "Resistance guarantees persistence." Allow it, make space for the feeling, it will come, it will reach its peak intensity, it will subside, done, clean. The worst that's going to happen here is it shows you that the longing and the relationship matters. It's real, and it's not some fake version of spirituality like fake news when you try and act a certain way—you have no feelings because you think that's what spirituality means.

I would say personally, the nature of the realizations opens the heart more. It's hard for me to sit through a movie without crying most of the time these days. I was flying back from London, and I just put on the films that were on, and I watched this film *Collateral Beauty*, the Will Smith film where he's a high-powered advertising agent who loses his daughter, and he's completely out of it, and he can't accept the loss. I spent two hours sobbing through the whole thing. But I can't help it these days, nor can I see anything wrong with it. But it's not just the tears; it's also the joys, and the laughter. All of it, the full catastrophe, embrace it, and live it. There's no guarantee how long it will last. You've got a precious opportunity.

Personally, when my parents were old, I took care of them. My mother had four heart operations, and she stayed with me, and I did the rehab, and those were the best moments I had with her. I took care of her the way I know I needed to be taken care of growing up, and didn't get taken care of, and it fixed it down the generations for both of us. And I won't miss any of those times, because we got really close from ages eighty-eight to ninety-two, while we could still do it. And when she died, I had no regrets whatsoever, because the relationship was complete. Do that with your brother. If you have been seeing him, or talking on the phone more, pump off everything you can get. Live the relationship fully so when one of you dies, there's no regret, and you can say, "I did this to the fullest."

Student 1

I will. Thank you.

Dan

It's a good question.

Student 2

I had a similar experience this week kind of. I've been friends with someone for forty-three years. We've gone through like so many things together, like boyfriends, kids, divorces, illnesses, and she ended up having a brain tumor, and so she just had surgery on Monday, and she was so scared, and I just kind of was thinking about how much I really loved her, and how much we had gone through, and how we had this really, really, really special friendship, and it also made me realize too that I could very well lose her. I mean, it's just the whole part of life, yeah. I mean, it's just, that's where we're going to end up eventually, but throughout all these years we've had all these experiences together, and it was just … Reflecting on that, and like really appreciating what we did have, and also coming to the realization that, that is how we'll part one way, or another, you know?

Dan

What's her brain condition like?

Student 2

She actually … I have excellent news. She had a ten-hour surgery with the team of doctors at the Brigham, and she just got sent home today, so that's amazing, and so, and I guess she's, so far like her functioning seems really good, but …

Dan

Do you know what area of the brain was affected?

Student 2

Yeah, it was … She had a meningioma, and it was near her optic nerve, but the symptoms she was having were … She felt really woozy, and also really shaky, so, but her eye is fine. I mean, she's responded to all the tests really well, and so, I guess so far so good, but I'm just so thankful.

Dan

Left sided?

Student 2

What?

Dan

Left sided?

Student 2

Yes.

Dan

Frontal?

Student 2

Frontal. What does that mean?

Dan

Executive functioning. Metacognitive awareness.

Student 2

They think it's intact.

Student 3

It wasn't in the brain; it was on the surface cover of the brain.

Student 2

Is that what it is?

Dan

We don't know how far it extended?

Student 2

I think it did go deeper into the carotid artery almost, like couldn't get it all, but you know that better. I don't … But, I'm just so thankful. I mean, I realized like, God, that is what's going to happen, you know, we've had birth, we've had life, we've had …

Dan

While you have a chance, express your appreciation for all that you've had over these decades.

Student 2

Definitely, yeah.

Dan

While you can still do it.

Student 2

Yes, absolutely. That's what … Yeah, and I was so happy too, because I went to walk her dog for yesterday, and her husband was home, and I'm like, "Oh my goodness, I'm so glad to see you." Because, he was, I didn't want to … there's a fine point of infringing, and also, but I was just so happy to see him, to hear she was doing so well, and talked to him today as well, but I'm thankful. Really thankful to have a friend like that.

Dan

Express it.

Student 2

Yeah.

Dan

So, in Western terms, in the positive psychology field, in the last two decades there's been a lot of work on gratitude and appreciation, and how important it is to express our gratitude and appreciations, because gratitude expresses the sense of being gifted. You have a special relationship that's gone over what, four decades now?

Student 2

Yes, and like I'll do anything for her, like if she wants me to sleep in the hospital, I'll sleep in the hospital …

Dan

It's useful to express what that means to us.

Student 2

What's funny is she doesn't always, she has a hard time accepting things from other people. She likes to be the person to be the giver, and I did say to her, "Hey look, you know, like this isn't a one-way street, and I'm helping you, and you're going to let me help you."

Dan

Do it anyway.

Student 2

Yeah, that's what I do. Like, I'm bringing you ice cream, like how about lunch? And, "It's not necessary." I'm like, "I know, it's not necessary."

Dan

Do it anyway.

Student 2

Right, but it's our friendship. I want to do this.

Dan

But, it's not about the ice cream or the …

Student 2

Oh, no.

Dan

The instrumental things that we do.

Student 2

No, no, no.

Dan

It comes from the heart.

Student 2

It's an excuse to be with her. It's a way to be with her, and to kind of distract her a little from what she's worrying about, or I'm worrying about.

Dan

There's an old French proverb that says, "Gratitude is the memory of the heart." So, the more you express what you appreciate about her, the more it consolidates the sense of the gift of the relationship.

Student 2

I know, and I'm feeling it.

Dan

While you can still do it?

Student 2

Exactly.

Dan

Do it. That applies to friendships; that applies to all relationships.

If you look at couples in Western research, John Gottman took films of couples fighting, and he developed a ratio for, showing you can empirically calculate how much trashing goes into communication, all the negative things that couples say to each other. And what he found is that when the trashing, the mutual trashing, reaches a certain critical tipping point, the odds of staying together are almost zilch.

The contrast to that is the work that Harville Hendrix did in his Imago therapy with couples, and one of the things he builds into his exercises is what he calls The Three Appreciations. When he works with couples, one of the homework assignments is at the end of the day, the spouses have to get together, and they have to say three things, however little or not so little, that they appreciate about the spouse, about that day, and they practice that on a regular basis, because what he found was that if you cultivate intentionally the positive, it offsets all that negative stuff.

It builds goodwill, and trust, and love in the relationship, but that doesn't apply just to intimate relationships, it applies to all relationships. How rarely is it that we have somebody that we appreciate, and we never tell them that until it's too late. So, if you have the opportunity, express it. It works for both of you. The worst is, she's uncomfortable with it. She'll tolerate it just fine.

Student 2

Her husband said, "She way underestimates how much she means to people."

Dan

Yes, and if she says, "No, no, I'm uncomfortable with this …"

Student 2

I say, it's all right, okay, I'm coming.

Dan

Remember the famous Shakespeare line, "Me thinks thou doth protest too much." [Laughter]

Student 2

Right. No, I actually was really lucky, because she had, she didn't know what was wrong with her, and that was a day I said, "I'm bringing you lunch." And she's, "No, no, no." I'm like, "I'm coming, like tell me what you want." And, when I got there, thank heavens she said like, "You're not going to believe this, but I just found out I have a brain tumor." Like, thank heavens I was there. I mean, can you imagine being all by yourself with that?

Dan

Well, she's lucky to have you.

Student 2

I'm lucky to have her.

Dan

That's good. Thank you for sharing that.

Student 2

Thank you for listening, too.

Dan

Similar questions.

Student 2

Yeah, and that's why ….

Dan

The theme is the explicit and intentional appreciation for the closeness that we have with others, and while you can do that, make it matter. Anybody else?

Student 1

The contrast to that feeling of connectedness, and intimacy with a person, to the other folks with whom I feel so unacceptable, both on my part about them, and vice versa, particularly that I'm the unacceptable one. It puzzles me to understand how to bridge that, when we're all swimming in the same ocean. I don't understand how to, without changing who I am for somebody else, to become acceptable, or to find the other that I find unacceptable, acceptable to me, and is that just more of the same? More of this grab, but of a different color?

Dan

I think some people are much more difficult than others.

The work on that, both East and West is very similar. So, in the West, the best work on that was, really, if you look at the Harvard Negotiation Project, Roger Fisher's work, in his early book which is called *Getting To Yes*, which is a remarkably simplistic title, but the book has some depth. They began to look at what constituted effective negotiation, and the first thing is you have to see where the common interests are; and then the second thing is you have to make a list of things that people are closer to agreeing upon, and further apart on, make a hierarchy, and then get them to practice negotiations with the things that they're likely to agree upon, so they can get some practice with agreements; and then when you get to the ones that are most difficult, and nearly always unmet emotional needs, then you handle those accordingly.

So, the best effective example of that negotiation project was that Roger and his team negotiated the end of apartheid in South Africa. That was an effective scripted negotiation, and using the categories that they developed. The first thing they tried to do is look for common interests, and the common interest between the Afrikaners, the white Afrikaners, and the Blacks was, nobody wanted the country to be absorbed in the civil war, and that actually gave them a lot of leverage, because neither side wanted that, because it would destroy the country. Then they negotiated things that, they made a list of things that are easy to negotiate, and the hardest negotiate.

And, the easier things were, where do we have the meeting? Is the table going to be round or square? Who sits where at the table? And all of those things become symbolic of practicing negotiating things that people are likely to get agreement on. They're necessary, and after they got all that stuff worked out, they started to look at the things that each side was different, most far apart upon, and those are always unfulfilled emotional needs. So, the Afrikaners, if they gave up apartheid would lose face. They would be ashamed. And the trouble with the Black side was that there were too many different warring Black factions for power. This was when Mandela was just getting out of jail, and he didn't feel, after being in jail for so many years, that he had any power base.

So, the solution was actually scripted. The team called up Oslo, and asked the Nobel committee to give a Nobel prize to both Mandela, and de Klerk, and by giving the Nobel prize to de Klerk, the Afrikaners saved face, because their man was now a hero. He had won a Nobel Peace Prize. And by giving Mandela the Nobel Peace Prize, he would have chance to consolidate international power, and then that would mean he would get power at least for some period of time with most of the Black groups who were vying for power, and give him a chance to consolidate his power, and it worked.

De Klerk agreed, because it allowed them to save face, and met his emotional need, and the need for the Afrikaners; and it gave Mandela a chance to consolidate his power, Black power, in the country. It was entirely scripted according to the guidelines of what works in a healthy negotiation, and it worked very successfully. It all starts with getting the undergoing common interest that both sides can agree upon. And, the common interest is neither side won the civil war. Then they negotiated what was easy. They came to what was difficult, and found out what the underlying unmet emotional needs were, and addressed them accordingly, systematically.

They tried to do the same thing with the first Iraq war. The same team negotiated that, and it failed; and three times they came up with agreements amongst the people doing negotiation, which were the chiefs of staff, both in the U.S. and Iraq. Before the war broke out, there were three agreements, and each time there was an agreement that either Bush or Hussein negated. And the conclusion of the committee after three failures was that the personalities were such that they wouldn't allow it. They couldn't get out of their own way. Otherwise, we wouldn't have had the disaster in the Middle East that's happened since. But they tried. So the whole starting point of negotiation with people who are different from us, or difficult, is to find that there's always some undergoing common interest, and get them to agree upon that.

Since then, Roger Fisher and his group have come up with a book dealing with difficult people, using the same principles, and applying them to difficult negotiations, and there's a series of guidelines that one can use to work with difficult people. And if you look at Buddhism, and the work on compassion, there are two kinds of compassion. One kind of compassion is compassion for the suffering of human beings. So, if you imagine the deity Avalokiteshvara, or Chenrezig in Tibetan, he's the embodiment of compassion. So, what you would do is you imagine Chenrezig or Avalokiteshvara manifesting compassion towards all suffering beings in the world. Then you imagine yourself as Avalokiteshvara, and if you do that visualization every day, you become more like Avalokiteshvara. You find yourself spontaneously acting more compassionate to the suffering around you.

The Dalai Lama is Avalokiteshvara. He is the emanation of Avalokiteshvara for this generation, and if you look at his life, he lives it, he embodies it. He is Avalokiteshvara, just the way that Rahob Tulku is the emanation of Padmasambhava. These non-ordinary beings recycle themselves.

Or you could do tonglen, taking it in and giving out. You can imagine breathing in all the suffering from all the six realms of existence, and then when you breathe out, you imagine giving loving-kindness to all those beings; or you could imagine each of the specific sufferings of the hell realm beings, and the hungry ghosts, and the animal beings, and the demigods, and the gods, and the humans, and then imagine the compassionate response as if you were Kuntuzangpo guiding all of them out of the realms of *samsāra*. There are many types of compassion meditations, and all of those have variations on the theme of responding sensitively to the sufferings of humans and other beings.

Then the second category of compassion meditation is compassion with respect to common humanity, and that's very similar to what we just talked about with Getting to Yes, and the Harvard Negotiation Project, because what it starts with is the sense that all humans deserve the same dignity and respect despite our differences, because we all share the same common concerns about life. Even people that we have remarkable differences with, even people who are enemies, all deserve dignity and respect because they have the same concerns in life.

Everybody wants to be healthy; everybody wants their family to be healthy; everybody wants to be prosperous and successful in life. They want that for their family members. Nobody is different in that regard. However, you may disagree with their terrible tactics, even members of ISIS want betterment for their people. They want to get out of the culture of poverty. They want recognition, they want to be taken seriously, they want health and prosperity, they want recognition as a people, and the recognition for their family. How is that different from what we want? The means are remarkably different, but there's always a common set of underlying common concerns, and that's where you bridge the gap between people.

You always start with what both sides want no matter our differences, no matter what the magnitude of the differences may be. As long as you have that, you've got some leverage there to work with. Get just a little tidbit is all you need. That's enough motivation.

I've done a lot of work in the hypnosis field over the years, and I remember once Milton Erickson, who was one of the greatest of the masters in hypnosis, somebody came up to him once and said, "You can't hypnotize me." Milton immediately put him into trance. When he was asked about it later someone said, "How could you do that? The guy was defiant to you, and he said that you couldn't hypnotize me." And, Milton said, "But he came up on stage, and there was a part of him that allowed him to come up on stage showing that he was curious that maybe I could. That's all I needed."

See what I'm saying? So, no matter what the magnitude of the differences are, there is always a little tidbit of common humanity in there where you could identify a common interest. That's all you need. It's enough. It goes pretty far. Then you can find compassion for the people who you have most differences with. It's important.

There was a book that Bob Thurman wrote about why the Dalai Lama is politically important in this generation as the embodiment of compassion. And when he wrote that book about four or five years ago, he was interviewed by Debbie Solomon when she was part of the New York Times book review interviews. She's no longer there. Bob's got a good sense of humor, and she said to him, this was during the Bush administration. She said to him, "And, when you practice compassion, how do you practice compassion?" He said, "I imagine myself as a young mother, and I have an infant Dick Cheney suckling on my breast." And, he meant that seriously.

We tend to demonize our enemies, but as someone once said, "The only real enemies are those within our own hearts." It's the construction of that other person as an enemy that's our real enemy. And you can think in your own life, of people that you've had remarkable differences with. Maybe you're friends with them now. Or people that you were really close to who now you are enemies with. You know, it all changes.

I don't condone what dictators like Saddam Hussein did, but when I heard the story of when they found him living underground in a hole for six months, a broken man, and the indignity of that, and the suffering that he must've endured, it just broke my heart. All human beings deserve dignity, and respect, no matter what they've done. It's a good question.

Student 1

What you're saying reminds me of the … to, just to recall, no matter who I'm in front of, that each of us has that being that is way beyond what we've done, or what we've said, or who we've been in the world in terms of our doing, that no matter what that has been, that being inside is pure and whole.

Dan

And, you try and see beyond their limitations to that deeper layer of their basic humanity, which is, there's a central core of goodness there.

Student 1

Right.

Dan

I mean, sometimes it's hard to access that, but you can, most of the time, and if you don't, it's a block that is within you.

Student 1

Right.

Dan

Right?

Student 5

Always. Thank you.

Dan

But it's hard sometimes.

Student 1

I know.

Dan

Sometimes the evil is just remarkable, and the ignorance that is behind that. It's hard to fathom. But as best we can, we try and see the underlying basic good. No matter how thoroughly that's been clouded over in some people, you're still going to try and see it. Well, maybe if you see that, you can have a role in bringing that forth more. You're going to have a role in bringing that forth more, but it's not easy. Some people get pretty hardened.

When I started working in the trauma field in 1979, my first introduction was harsh, because my first assignment was with kids from Operation Phoenix. Maybe you don't remember what Operation Phoenix was, but during The Tet Offensive in the Vietnam War, we were concerned with a numbers game. We had to make sure we killed as many bodies as possible to offset the fact that we were losing, because the North Vietnamese were sending troops into the South at a remarkable rate. That was The Tet buildup. So, we were losing the tipping point, and Westmoreland tried to tell Johnson that, and every time he tried to tell him, which was on a daily basis in the meetings, Johnson would have a rage fit, and trash Westmoreland, and after getting trashed too many times, Westmoreland said, "Fuck you, I'll take care of it myself."

So, along with the CIA, he developed this brilliant plan called Operation Phoenix. It took eighteen, and nineteen-year-old kids, and trained them to be killing machines. And they would go out at night, and do an entire village up by hand with a knife—women, children, everybody. They would slaughter an entire village by hand. Then we would count the bodies the next day. We had the bodies we needed. We didn't care what the bodies were, so after doing that for five or six years, you can imagine what it was like trying to treat these kids. That was my first introduction to the trauma field.

How could I find compassion for somebody who had become a machine, a professional killer? And, the person who supervised my work—and we worked for ten years with one kid—after ten years the best we could get was a statement, "I feel a little sad." That's how blocked they were. But I developed a kind of compassion for how robotized these kids had been trained to become. They had lost so much of their basic humanness that we could not feel anything but compassion for them. But it took a lot to get there.

Sometimes, it's hard to develop compassion, because the forces are so strong it's almost incomprehensible. In the late '70s, when I left sitting in Burma at Mahāsī Sayādaw's place, I immediately went to the camps at the Thai border, Khao I Dang [a Cambodian refugee camp], and saw the refugees from the Killing Fields. And every day I would watch kids die [for lack of food], while three hundred yards away all the food is piled up, stuck in bureaucratic red tape while the kids were starving to death. I found that hard to find compassion for, and the worst was this crazy woman with a necklace of live dripping blood livers from the kids who died that day. She would rip them out with a knife, and make a necklace for herself. Now, I must say I had a hard time understanding that, and finding compassion for it. Preying on the death of young infants, it's hard not to see that as evil. Until this day, I still don't understand it. I'm still trying to find compassion for it. How deranged can a person get? Then I can find some compassion for it, if I look at it that way, but it's hard.

I do a lot of work on child sexual abuse and, as you know, one case that I worked on was with three kids who were in a halfway house, and they all came from broken homes, and the head of the halfway house was a thirty-year-old guy. He'd physically restrained one of the kids too harshly so that there was a complaint, and while they were investigating the complaint about undue force, they made him move out of the halfway house.

So, he got pissed off and stomped out, and threw all of his stuff in plastic bags, and put them in the garbage, and left early the next morning, [and] when the cleaning lady went into one of the bags he had opened up, and there were all these Polaroid pictures of what he had done to the kids sexually. None of the kids remembered any of the sexual abuse, but he took detailed Polaroids, and then videos of all the kids, and what he did to them. "There's no such thing as repressed memories," [say some,] but none of these kids remembered any of this stuff. And it's all documented.

One of the most haunting memories I have is—you can't watch this stuff, because it's illegal—but as an expert witness, I had to be apprised of what I was giving my opinions about, so I had to go to the judge's chamber privately, in front of the judge, and watch all these videotapes. It was really difficult. It's still difficult. It's hard for me to find compassion for the perpetrator. It's an ugly game.

So, there are limits here. It's hard, and I suppose that's the nature of being in the trauma field. It's good training in the sense that I see all the worst of what people do to each other. If I can't find grounds of compassion in that, I have nothing to teach, but it's not easy, so it's been very humbling. Those are the images that stick the most with me. That's where my fierceness … fierce protectiveness comes from.

December 20, 2017

Themes: Sirhan Didn't Kill RFK; Forgiveness

Dan

Welcome everyone.

I was going to suggest the topic tonight, because it's on my mind from events that happened yesterday. The topic is forgiveness, and the spiritual importance of forgiveness.

You can't hear me? I'm sorry I don't have much of a voice. I have a tumor on my vocal cords, so it interferes with speaking and sometimes my voice goes out. I have to get it surgically removed, but the good news is it's benign and it's minor, it's like getting your tonsils out. But I get to eat ice cream popsicles. I remembered that from being a kid. [Dan chuckles] That was a good deal. I also remember feeling betrayed because they told me I'm going to get all the ice cream I could eat, but they didn't tell me I was in so much pain I wouldn't want to eat it. They sort of left that part of the story out.

So, as many of you know, for the last twelve years, I worked on the Bobby Kennedy assassination. And the reason that the case got opened up is because in 2006 a CNN reporter was going through the surviving evidence in the Sacramento archives and found a videotape that a Canadian film[maker] had dropped his camera when Sirhan started shooting at the Ambassador Hotel the night of the assassination, and the camera kept running. And it was collected by the feds but never entered into evidence. And then when you listen to the recordings with a naked ear, it sounds like there are thirteen shots. With the current generation of acoustic software, which is much better than forty-eight years ago, if you analyze it, you can show with almost 100 percent accuracy that there are thirteen shots fired, five simultaneously.

Since Sirhan's gun only had eight bullets and probably only six shells in it, he couldn't have been the main shooter. So, that opened the case wide open, along with the other conclusion that the pathologist who wasn't testifying at the trial said it couldn't have been Sirhan because the fatal bullet was a hollow point. There's no identifying markings on a hollow point because it blows up into two million pieces in the brain. And it was point blank, because of the powder burn. So, Sirhan was never more than four feet away and it was the wrong angle. It sort of opened the case wide open again and as an expert in non-suggestive interviewing, I got to spend over two hundred hours in the federal penitentiary with Sirhan over the last twelve years trying to get him to remember what happened. And technically, we are trying to expose the coverup of what really happened.

It went to the federal court under the matter of innocence and they squashed it. It went to the Supreme Court and we caught the Supreme Court in a lie because they denied our appeal, but they can't explain why the denial was written two months before we sent it in to them. It's not just a clerical error or mistake, they actually denied it before we sent it in. So, go figure. Obviously, some people don't want to open this thing up.

But, Sirhan is the most hypnotizable person I've ever met. You can get him to do anything under hypnosis. He doesn't remember anything. So, technically, he was a Manchurian candidate. He was suggested to go there as a distracter and shoot wildly on command, and then while he was doing that, they would pick him up, and he would be the main shooter, and the real assassin would just pop Kennedy point blank and then walk away while all the chaos was breaking out, which is basically what happened.

But all the evidence was submitted to the court, so it's now part of the public record and I'm happy to say that we're making a documentary. It was first picked up by Robert Redford and Sundance,[6] and then they added it on Showtime and Netflix. If you've ever seen the documentary *Making of a Murderer* or the other one on the four series of OJ, it's going to be the same group putting

6 We reached out to Sundance but they did not respond. As far as we can tell, this project was not completed.

this together. It's a four-hour series. Whether they edit stuff out, I don't know, but we filmed it. We've been trying to tell the story.

The side story, and why it's present on my mind, it brought tears to my eyes, because when Kennedy came, he was accepting the nomination; he won the California primary and that gave him enough votes to get the nomination for president. That's when, at the last minute, when he gave his acceptance speech, he was supposed to go to the press room, but somebody changed the route at the last minute and he went to the kitchen. So how would an assassin know where to go if the route was changed at the last minute? But Sirhan told me that he remembered a man with a badge and a clipboard coming up to him and saying to the woman who was his handler, the woman with the polka dot dress, "Take him to the kitchen." And she walked him to the kitchen.

And I showed a film that was made ten minutes before the assassination in the same route, and Sirhan says, "There's the guy right there." So, he actually identified the guy. We identified the government coverup of the DA's office and the pathologist not allowing to testify. We got a lot of stuff out of this case. So, whether it gets told or edited out, I don't know that. But, as a result, I got punished. I got four tax audits. I have a tag on my account to harass me as much as possible in the boundaries of the law for the rest of my life in the IRS. For two years, every time I got on a plane, my bags were stolen for three days and rerouted to the military base in San Diego and searched.

This is stuff that was witnessed by other people, so I'm not paranoid here. What kind of person has the power in this country to make a phone call and violate a citizen's search and seizure rights, put a tag on their IRS account forever, and get the federal court and Supreme Court to violate its own laws? That's sick scary stuff if you think about it. I happen to think that we had a precious democracy in this country and we're pissing it away and it's worth fighting for.

But the issue of forgiveness came up because of two reasons. One, when Sirhan shot wildly, he shot four people. One was seriously shot in the head, and his name was Paul Schrade, who was Kennedy's best friend. At the time he was the young president of the United Auto Workers. Paul has done his own investigation. He's working with us now, and he's also convinced that Sirhan wasn't the shooter. He was the one who exposed a lot of the government coverup. And, when I did hours and hours of psychological testing, I found out there's nothing wrong with Sirhan. He was supposedly diagnosed as being a schizophrenic, but there was nothing wrong with him, except that he's too hypnotizable. But there's actually nothing psychologically wrong with him.

Since the prison had no control over my testing, they brought in their own independent person to do testing and she did a lot of the same testing and also found out there was nothing wrong with him. They didn't like her results very much. I was not allowed to testify at his last parole hearing. They wouldn't let me go and they kept all the press out, but Paul Schrade, who is now convinced that Sirhan wasn't the shooter, and he's in jail for forty-eight years for something he didn't do, went to the parole hearing. He's ninety-four years old. And he went to Sirhan with tears in his eyes and said, "I forgive you for shooting me. And I'm sorry you're in jail for something you didn't do." It was very moving. He went to hug Sirhan and the security guard tackled him and pushed him out of the way—a ninety-four-year-old man.

And three weeks ago, the lawyer that I worked with on this case got a call from Bobby Kennedy, Jr. out of the blue saying, "I'm familiar with your work. I want you to set up a meeting with Sirhan." And after, she says, "For years he believed that this man was the killer of his father and now he understands that it's not true." So, we didn't know whether we could do this because the prison has been so difficult to us over the years. But Laurie, the attorney that I worked with, did the usual thing that we do to contact the prison. They couldn't refuse him because he's technically an attorney and he was saying he's writing a book on the case and he's working with us as a consultant, so they had no legal basis to refuse him from seeing Sirhan, and that was our in. They don't want the publicity on it, and neither does Bobby.

So, yesterday, the attorney that I worked with for twelve years, met with Sirhan and with Bobby at the prison, and I couldn't go because he wanted to do it this week. It wasn't a week I could go because I've had the lama I'm translating with staying with me all week. I wanted to do it next week. But he wanted to do it before the holidays. June is the fiftieth anniversary. So, it was very heartfelt. He went to Sirhan and said, "I thought for years you killed my father and now I understand you didn't do that and you're in jail for something you never did. I forgive you." It was very moving.

If that's what I got out of twelve years of working, and all the harassment, it's worth it. That's the way I look at it. I never got paid for the case either. But if that's what came out of this case, to facilitate a meeting with two remarkable men, the whole thing was worth it. It's something right, you know what I mean. It set something right.

That's what I wanted to share. And my own feeling is the American public has a right to know. So, we'll see where this goes. But those kinds of extraordinary moments are rare in life, so I wanted to share it with you.

The social philosopher, Simmel, once said, "Forgiveness is the moral memory of the heart." When you hold on to something and you can't forgive, the danger of that is that you become more hateful and resentful. And it clouds your true nature. But, in the studies on forgiveness, it doesn't mean you have to condone the person's behavior. But you have to come to see that the steps that you take in forgiveness are necessary because it frees you from whatever you hold on to, and unprocessed.

Most people who can't forgive can't forgive because they are obsessed about going over the same old same old process again the same way, which usually means they keep reviewing in their mind the way that they were wronged, and it becomes a kind of righteous indignation after a while. And that never goes anywhere useful. It just leads to more either preoccupation with what happened to you that you can never metabolize, or it leads to more hatred and bitterness, cynicism. So, how do you free yourself of all that?

In the domain of positive psychology, there's been some good research on forgiveness in the last four, five years. We actually have a pretty good understanding of the process by which forgiveness works when it's done correctly. There are two major components to processing things. One is you have to process whatever's emotionally unfinished. You have to metabolize whatever you keep going over in this obsessive preoccupied way until it shifts. And the second is perspective taking. You have to get a wider perspective on it. It goes beyond what happened just to you in one narrow perspective. Those are the necessary ingredients.

That larger perspective is often spiritual. You have to reflect on the benefits of being forgiving, even when bad things were done to you; sometimes awful things were done to you. Because if you don't, the risk is that you hold on to it as a fixation point so you stop developing and growing. A worse risk is you become like the perpetrators, and you do to others what was done to you.

I remember two years ago, you probably remember that, I was glued to the TV. There was a mass shooting in South Carolina, a young white boy shot up a Black church. A number of, most of the adults were killed. And there was a Black couple who had lost three family members in one day, at the same church. And they had this extraordinary event. The couple went on national TV and they did a split screen. On one half of the TV was the couple, obviously deeply in shock and grief for their recent loss of three family members, and the other side of the screen was the assailant, in his orange prison suit with shackles on his arms and legs, standing there. You got to see both parties.

And they were making a passionate plea on the news to the nation to not hate, that they were personally forgiving this boy for killing three of their family members because they thought that if they hated the boy, it just generates more of the same. That was profound. Deeply profound, I thought. So, from a spiritual perspective, holding on to the hatred and whatever's unfinished about the thing, not being able to forgive, is more and more restricting and damages any spiritual development, whereas forgiveness opens the heart wide open. The more difficult it is to forgive, the more the heart opens.

And none of that means condoning the behavior, because you don't.

The other reason for forgiveness is that not only does it narrow the [hurt] person in terms of being stuck with negative emotions that are unprocessed, [but also] that runs the risk of the person becoming like the offender, the victim becoming the offender, but there's a third risk that is also something to consider, which is how that runs down the generations. That was the great spiritual vision of Mandela after his years of imprisonment. When he developed the Truth and Reconciliation Committee, he had the vision that what we've seen throughout history is cultures that are traumatized pass it down two generations—three, four, five, six generations. Everybody's affected by it. And the reason why they're affected by it is because nobody on either side—whether the perpetrators or the offenders, the offenders or the victims—ever talks about it. They just put it out of their mind. But they don't really put it out of their mind, because it comes back on them.

You've got to deal with it. And most of what we know about trauma is you have to process it. There are studies of children who were sexually abused and their coping style, and kids who were externalizing in their coping style, when they're abused, they show signs of it immediately in their behavior. And they show symptoms, mostly anxiety and fears, and nightmares, and behavioral problems, and conduct problems. So, they're easy to detect in the school system that there's something wrong. And then if they get treatment, they deal with it, and they're done.

But people who are internalizers, mostly those who dissociate, they put it out of their mind and the studies show that they have more friends in school, higher grades. It doesn't affect them. Because they dissociate the trauma and never deal with it until twenty, thirty years when something triggers it and it comes back upon them, and then they deal with it then, and then they start showing a decline in their functioning.

So, the only difference between the ones who deal with it immediately and the ones who deal with it after twenty or thirty years when their memory gets triggered is coping style. You can pay for it now or you can pay for it on the layaway plan. But one way or the other, you have to pay for it.

The significant difference is coping style. That's one of the reasons why I've done a lot of cases around recovered memories in the courts, because if you say that the ones who recover, who never forget, can have rights in the courts, but the ones who forget it because of their coping style and then come back twenty, thirty years later when something triggers it, they don't have rights, that violates the fundamental principle of equal rights under the law. You're punishing the people who have a dissociative coping style by virtue of their coping style. That violates any principle of equity, and justice, and fairness. That's why it's worth fighting for. Most of the [film] *Spotlight* (if you saw the *Spotlight* movie), all those cases were cases I worked on.

I worked on their grand jury, I testified with the grand jury for the Shanley case. I did the preparations, the cross examinations for the Shanley case, but not the expert witnessing of that. I helped prepare the argument before the Massachusetts Supreme Court for the appeal. I worked on many of those cases. Sort of timely, isn't it, that Cardinal Law finally died. Not a nice man. Nor was Shanley. Shanley everybody loved because he was "the hippie priest" who took in all the runaway kids and he was so compassionate. Well, he was one of the founders of NAMBLA, an international organization for sexual predators of young boys.[7] He was using the Catholic Church as a front for that. Wasn't a nice man.

They put him in jail for life, he appealed, and the Massachusetts Supreme Court denied the appeal unanimously seven to nothing. I'm very proud of that. I worked hard on that appeal. And recently they let him out of jail. They have a new prosecutor, some new joker expert that said he's okay. That's because we don't have a sense of history anymore in this country. If they asked me to testify, they would have kept him in jail. But even he has to be forgiven, right?

---

7 The North American Man/Boy Love Association (NAMBLA) is a pedophilia and pederasty advocacy organization in the United States.

The consequences are it narrows you because you can't process things and it eats away at you. The risk of becoming more like an offender in your own actions and not knowing that you're acting something out is then you pass it down the generations. That's the brilliance of what Mandela came to in his vision after spending years and years in solitude in jail. He wanted to stop the process down the generations, and he did something extraordinary in history. He got the offenders, the perpetrators of the violence and deaths, and the victims, the family victim impact witnesses together in the same room. The surviving family members who had lost family members through torture and murder had to sit in the same room with the torturers and the murderers and talk it out together. That's never happened before in history. And it worked. Everybody got a chance to revisit it and not pass it down the generations.

After that, it worked so successfully there was some attempt to do that with children of Nazis and children of the Holocaust survivors, and do something similar. I visited Berlin for the first time this year. I do a course on performance excellence, and all you have to do is just walk the streets of Berlin and you can see the effects of the war. They've never overcome it. It's a lost city. They've never dealt with their history. And there are aimless people looking for meaning in life. It's sad to see. But they've never dealt with their history honestly.

But Mandela had a vision, that dealing with it squarely and honestly, in the heartfelt pain of death [Dan's voice breaks up with emotion briefly], and getting people in the same room matters. Sorry about that. I realized recently that one thing that spiritual practice has done to me after forty-six years is I laugh a lot and I cry a lot. I can't do much about that.

So, what are the steps?

The first step is selection. You have to decide in yourself where the areas of forgiveness have the most need. Who is it that's hardest to forgive in your life? And if you ask the question in terms of who is it that's hardest to forgive, that's the part that's most unfinished emotionally. You have to go right to the source of what's most emotionally unfinished. So, who is it that's hardest to forgive?

The second step is you have to honestly and openly reflect on the transgressions that were done against you. Forgiveness is about acts of transgression. So, you have to think about actually what was done, behaviors. So, that means if you were sexually abused, you would think about the details of what was actually done to you. If you were physically abused, you'd focus on what was actually done. Whatever the form of the trauma is. You're a prisoner of war, victim of torture, you'd think about what was actually done to you, in detail. If we learned anything in the trauma field in the last thirty years, it's that whatever is not processed, you have to set up the right conditions for the person to feel safe that they could actually process it, empower them to process whatever they most avoid.

As I like to say, "resistance guarantees persistence." The more you're avoiding it, either behaviorally or cognitively, the more exposure-based treatment works, that is dealing with it squarely, processing it. That probably sounds crazy to you. The bigger the avoidance, the likelihood, if you stop avoiding it, the likelihood is the best gain, is the highest. Stop avoiding it. All that stuff you do in mind that we call cognitive avoidance. All the stuff that you do behaviorally to stay away from certain situations or interactions with people, or certain people—the victim of priest abuse who doesn't go to church anymore, or avoids the rectory, or avoids the priest or anything to do with the church. You have to put yourself in the situations that will evoke the feelings and memories of the trauma.

And if you notice yourself having a tendency to turn away from it, you note that. Make sure to make space for it. And you start not with the feelings, you start with the behaviors. What was actually done. All of it. All of it. Or, what was not done. Because in the field of transgressions, there are two broad categories. One is what we call "hurts of commission," what other people commit, what they do to you that are bad things that they do to you. The other, which sometimes are worse, are the "hurts of omission." The things that should have been done that weren't done.

For example, we think of sexual and physical abuse as acts of commission. But neglect, failed attunement, failure to provide the right attachment conditions, those are hurts of omission. Sometimes the hurts of omission are more damaging, right? You have to keep bringing to mind and processing over and over again whatever was most unfinished. And if you do that, what's going to happen? You're going to stir up the feelings.

And there are two levels of feelings that come up. The easiest feelings to access if you've been transgressed against, the first things that will come up if you review the behaviors, actually look squarely at what was done to you, is anger, indignation. Those are the main feelings, some sort of aggression related state. Mostly anger. But anger is never the main feeling. I call anger a secondary emotion. It's the easiest thing to come up. But always behind the anger, there's another set of feelings. So, you have to go deeper than the anger. See, most people who process things that really are unfinished, it hurts and they can't forgive somebody. When they keep going over and over in their mind, they get angry.

But then you have to go to the next level of processing, which is processing the unexpressed feelings, the deeper level of feelings.

What are the deeper level of feelings?—hurt, fear, abandonment, betrayal, shame, guilt. Those are the main ones. Because if you just process the anger, because it's a surface level and more accessible feeling, does it ever get anywhere? I see that if I'm dealing with couples, like couples are fighting with each other and somebody, one of the spouses, says to the other spouse, "You're angry." Does that ever go anywhere useful? You acknowledge how angry they are? Not very much. They just go around and they get more and more angry and it escalates. But as soon as you say, "You know, you're angry and you're hurt," [Dan sighs] it shifts. Or, "You're angry and you feel afraid, vulnerable," or "You're angry and you feel betrayed." Or. "You're so ashamed. You feel so guilty and so bad about this." What happens at that point?

Everybody knows what I'm talking about. It shifts to a deeper level of processing. Right? It shifts to a deeper level of processing. So then, what you're processing is not the more manifest emotion, you're processing the deeper, latent feelings, which are harder to access. It's much easier to be angry, particularly when you have righteous anger, because it feels right: "I'm justified to feel angry," right? Or as we say in the meditation, "attachment to clarity leads to anger." "I'm right, dammit." Is that ever useful? Doesn't go anywhere useful, usually. Just more of the same.

But when you drop it to that deeper level, "You're hurt. You're ashamed. You're afraid of being abandoned," then it starts to shift, and couples get quieter or individuals get quieter when you bring it to that level. Right? You all know what I'm talking about. You follow it in your own process right now.

Now, if you really want to settle the processing of trauma or things transgressed against you, the next level and the hardest level to get at is what I call the unmet need. Behind everything that's not processed, or everything that the process is perseverating so it doesn't go anywhere, behind every one of those incidents, there's some unmet need. And that explains the reason why you keep going over it and over it endlessly and exhaustively either to yourself or to your people around you, till they get sick of it. And the reason why you can't stop and get off that water wheel is because you're not getting to the deeper level, which is whatever the unmet need is.

So, the way you get at the unmet need in childhood with attachment issues—since we wrote a whole textbook on how to treat attachment issues with ideal parent figures—is whatever you didn't get in childhood, you imagine ideal parents giving you exactly what you didn't get. Just the way they're needed. It doesn't make any difference if it's fictional because what it brings forth is the acknowledgment of the unmet need, because you imagine parents who are responsive to you, ideal parents, fictional parents who are responsive to you in just the right ways, all the ways. They're emotionally responsive in just the way you needed.

And you can do something like that in this forgiveness exercise, because what you can do, even though you'll never get it, think of all the times you keep obsessing about this thing about whatever was done against you by whomever. You really want to settle with that. Imagine that that person, even though they'll never do it in reality, you can imagine. Imagination by definition creates new possibilities, right? So, you imagine that that person is actually responding to you and just what you most need. What would they be doing if they could do that, as a hypothetical?

Suppose the perpetrator said, "I finally get it. I finally see the effect on you." What would they acknowledge? They would acknowledge one of several things. They would acknowledge something about that they see the things that they did and how awful they were from your perspective. They would validate that. Or they would see the effects of that on you in the short term and, more importantly, the long run. They would be able to see the damage. And thirdly, whatever that unmet need was, they would be able to acknowledge that. You'd imagine them actually responding to it, even if you never get it in reality.

Because what it does, as a mental exercise, is it makes you acknowledge and access in yourself what that unmet need is that you're still going around and around the water wheel around. The reason why you keep going back to it is because there's something that you want that you're not getting. So, it's simple. You imagine yourself getting it. And that brings the need more into the awareness, the consciousness.

And even if you will never get it from the perpetrator, the fact that you can imagine it being spoken to, and met, and addressed is enough. Because at that point, there will be an experiential shift. All that obsessive processing and unfinished stuff settles down. You have to look for that experiential shift, because that's a sign that you're doing it right. Follow me so far?

That's the processing piece. That's the first half of this equation. Questions about that so far? Anybody? Following what I'm doing or I'm talking out of left field here? Yeah.

Student 1

You mentioned three things that ideal parents would do and I missed the first one. The second one, they would acknowledge the damage and the third one, they would ...

Dan

They would respond to the unmet need.

Student 1

Right. What was the first one?

Dan

I have no idea. [Laughter]

Student 1

Is there a third one?

Dan

They would see the things … they would acknowledge the severity of what they did in terms of the acts themselves. They would acknowledge the impact on you. That's the second one. Okay? The short-term and the long-term impact on you. And third, they would be able to see what the unmet need is and respond to it in just the right way. Those are the three things.

Student 1

Thank you.

Dan

Is that clear now? Anything else before we go on to part two of this? It's important to get it right. You have to do this right. You can't leave any pieces out. Yeah?

Student 2

Can this be done with self as well?

Dan

Yes.

Student 2

Because it seems, I'm listening to you and it feels convoluted.

Dan

No, you can do the same thing with yourself.

Student 2

Okay.

Dan

If you beat up on yourself mentally or you do things that are abusive to yourself, you can use the same thing.

Student 2

It's the piece of, there can be forgiveness and not necessarily condoning, but to be personal, I also don't condone. I mean, I also don't forgive. I don't do either with self.

Dan

Yeah. It's hard. You don't have to condone the behavior. It took me a long time to understand that.

Student 2

I can get it with another, to forgive, but not necessarily condone.

Dan

But you have to see from a larger spiritual perspective that if you don't forgive, then you're narrowing yourself in some ways. In one way or another.

I'll tell you a story about that. For years I ran the Harvard Trauma Conference. It was a flagship conference. We'd have somewhere between six hundred and a thousand people for three days, and I'd bring in the best people in the trauma field. I did that for over a decade. One time I was running that conference and we had a lot of really good people, experts from around the world talking. And during the break, this woman came up to me. She said, "You'll never understand victims fully, because you and your conference are biased towards only working with treaters of victims. Until you work with perpetrators, you'll never fully understand the whole story."

And I took that, I said, "You're right." I took that very seriously. The next year, I invited a person who was an expert on working with sex offenders to come in, Anna Salter, who was then at Dartmouth. She's in Wisconsin now. And I was so impressed with her work that I invited her back to do a private workshop, more extensive than a two-hour talk. She did a several-day workshop. She showed us all these films of sexual offenders. My counter transference is so strong that the next day I spent $5000 on a security system for my house that I never used. [Dan and students laugh]

These stories are so horrible to listen to all the time, and how easy it is to get access to kids. It was just, it overwhelmed me, the professional offenders and what they're capable of doing. But I saw her point. And then I began working with offenders. It was much more easy for me to see how victims internalize the offenders after working with offenders. And she was right, I only had part of the picture, it was too narrow. And then I could find some compassion for offenders. That doesn't mean condoning their behavior.

For years I thought I had a counter transference, I couldn't work with rapists. Just thought what they did was so vile. But then I found that I could do that after that, but not condone their behavior. But some people I still have a hard time with. There's a smaller group of sex offenders, about eight or nine percent who are sadistic sexual offenders, and they're different animals. It's hard to fathom that and find forgiveness. I'm still working on that one. They cause a lot of damage. It's a different profile.

Student 2

Here's the piece that feels convoluted. If I'm both the victim and the perpetrator, which do you treat?

Dan

You can do the same process with both, but you don't do them both at once. Do them separately.

Student 2

Okay.

Student 3

This is kind of an answer to her thing, but I have a lot of experience with forgiveness, and it's extremely powerful and helpful. The thing that, the perspective that really helped unlock things for me was taking the perspective that whoever's the perpetrator, whether it's yourself or someone else, is doing the best they can that moment.

Dan

We're going to get to that.

Student 3

Oh, okay.

Dan

That's part two.

Student 3

I'm jumping ahead. Sorry.

Dan

That's okay. But what you're saying is quite accurate and it's consistent with most of the research on this.

Student 3

Yeah. So, how can you be mad at someone who's just doing their best self? And I'll just finish saying that, actually, if you first do it in yourself and you find it in yourself, and you're able to forgive yourself, it's a lot easier to forgive other people.

Dan

That's true. That's true.

Student 3

It's powerful.

Dan

Thank you for saying that.

So, the first part is the emotional processing part, and you do that until it's finished. You take what's most emotionally unfinished and that's where you work. You keep bringing it to mind with all the feelings and thoughts about it and all the memories about what actually were the acts that were done. It seems so violating and transgressing. That will stir up the immediate present feelings, which are variations on the theme of anger. And that will get to the deeper feelings, the underlying vulnerabilities.

And that will lead you naturally to the next step, which is acknowledging the unmet need. If you do all that correctly, there will be an experiential shift that will seem like something settling down. That's the first half of the work.

The second half of the work is perspective taking. Don't do the second half until you get that experiential shift, otherwise it's just conceptual. It won't work on an emotional level.

So, the second part starts with what we call contextualizing. You take a larger perspective in terms of what might've been going on for that person that made them act like that. Not that you're justifying it or rationalizing it, and not that you're condoning the behavior. But you might look at their underlying vulnerabilities. Like in the field of research on sexual offending, there are people who are, there are two types of people. There are people who do it situationally. There's always something going on for them that they're reenacting. And there are people who have an addiction. They're going to do it many times. That's why they have multiple victims that they try and cover up.

And they're both different situations. If you're looking at the context, for situationally based people, you might want to see what was going on for them that caused them to be like that. I remember seeing somebody who was in the field once, who was in twenty years of two different therapies, never got better. And he came in and worked with me for about a year. He was really emotionally frozen. And what he told me was that when he was training as a therapist, he had a sexual encounter with a patient, one patient and then another patient. And he never forgave himself. He was like Raskolnikov[8], with this kind of chronic guilt for things that had happened almost twenty years earlier, and was early in his training.

But when I looked into it, it was really interesting. On both occasions, when he was sexually attracted to the patients that he was with, and this is going back to the 1950s, he disclosed it to each of his supervisors at the time. And both of his supervisors eventually lost their licenses for sexual misconduct on multiple occasions. He didn't know that. They were very interested in his behavior, but not for the right reason. And he had this enormous guilt for years

---

8 Raskolnikov is the fictional protagonist of the 1866 novel *Crime and Punishment* by Fyodor Dostoyevsky.

for something that, when he was just talking about sexual attraction, there was a kind of covert permission to sort of act it out, which was not uncommon in the '50s. Very authoritative men. We're seeing an epidemic of that again this time, aren't we, recently?

This stuff about all the disclosures are about the one thing that's been useful that Trump's done since he's been in office, because he's like that himself and it's causing everybody to sort of disclose everything that's happened over the years that no one ever talks about, which is wonderful to see. Painful to hear, the epidemic proportions of this. But necessary.

The stats in this country, or in North America, or in Europe or Western culture in general are one out of three women have unwanted sexual contact before the age of eighteen. That's remarkable. It's an epidemic. That's not okay. It's out of control. So, to look at the social structure that allows for that, and to talk about that openly and honestly, maybe this is moving towards our own Truth and Reconciliation committee, so we don't pass it down the generations. But what really needs to happen is women not just disclosing, but sitting in the same room with the offenders, letting them hear the impact. That's what really should be happening in this country. We need a vision of a Mandela to arrange for that. Then maybe we don't pass it down the generations and keep playing out the same cycle over and over again.

One out of five. One out of five, yeah. They don't talk about it. Anyway, the first step in perspective taking is contextualizing, allowing yourself to reflect on what was the context under which this behavior, this transgression occurred. Not to explain it away, but to understand it, what might've been going on. But you don't explain it away. Sometimes the offending is sadistic. And sadistic offending is not about sex. It's about power. That's why sadistic offending is often accompanied by verbal and physical abuse, and asserting dominance, because what they get off on is not sex. They get off on having power and asserting power over their victims. It's a much more serious offense.

I worked on a case over the last two years of hypnotic seduction, a case in Ohio. Some people say that you can't get people to do things against their moral standards under hypnosis. That's bullshit. This is a case where a divorce lawyer was seducing women under hypnosis. And it came forth because there was a woman who went to his office for the first time because she was getting divorced, and all she remembered was he told her to relax. She remembered nothing after that, but her bra was on backwards and panties had cum stains in it. So, she went to the DA and said, "I think I was raped." And the DA said,

"That's not enough evidence." So, she had the courage to go back and put her bag on the desk with her iPhone recorder on and let herself submit to an entire documented hypnotic seduction. Perfectly detailed record of everything that happened to her.

So, if anybody wants to argue that this is not theoretically possible, this sort of puts that argument to rest. There were forty-six victims that came forward. That's as many as we know about. Not all were hypnotizable, so he didn't do everything to everybody. But then they did a sting operation. They filmed him to the point that he was actually about to do something and then they went in and arrested him. Nobody's condoning his behavior, because he's in jail now. Lost his license. He was very good at hypnosis. But the thing that got him going was that he had prostate issues. He couldn't get it up. So, he would seduce them and get them to cum in front of him. He would get off on that.

So, we could understand the context, but that doesn't condone his behavior. He's still a perpetrator and what he did was evil. And the consequences are he's in jail now, he lost his license. And the victim had the courage to develop a really detailed documented record for future cases. But I'm saying that you can explain the context, we can understand why this guy might've got started. It doesn't condone the behavior.

Yeah?

Student 4

I can understand why it's important to forgive, because that reconciliation eliminates a lot of the suffering from the victim. But it seems to take so much energy to bring consequences and justice in the real world so often. In that way, the concept of turning the other cheek seems like there's another half of it missing. So, I wonder what is the role of justice? Can justice actually be brought by the victims or is it the responsibility of the people who are not the victims to carry out justice?

Dan

We don't have a perfect justice system, but we try. It's not very perfect. But, you know, there are good changes in that. Women are taken much more seriously for allegations of rape these days, and with rape kits and things like that and DNA testing, people are held for the consequences for what they did much more. We've improved a great deal on that. Where we don't improve is certain situations. Like I'm a memory expert, so the case that I don't do a good job with is if somebody comes to me, a DA comes to me and says, "This woman was a victim of roofies[9]—date rape. Can you help her remember things?" Not much. The roofies work in that sense. The woman's not going to remember very much, or sometimes the man isn't going to remember very much about what happened. There's not much we can do about that.

Student 4

Feels like a *ḍākinī* would help here.

Dan

Yeah, but there aren't many people like that working in the law enforcement agency. There are some. So, it's not perfect, but we're getting better at it. We've improved statute of limitations. But the courts aren't fair in the sense that the sentencing is not very fair. I think we need better sentencing that's more equitable in this country. Like if you look at women who in domestic violence contexts murder their husbands, they are nine times more likely to get convicted than the men are for doing the same thing to their wives.

And the racial things are more obvious. Blacks and other minorities and women don't get the same rights as men do, white men, in courts. If you look at sentencing issues, there's a lot of documentation about that. It's not so much in the justice system itself, it's the sentencing. We need a more fair system. But I want to go on with the other parts of what we were talking about.

The first thing is to get the perspective on the context. What might've been going on that would let this person do this kind of thing? Not to condone the behavior, but to understand it, at least. The second step is what you're saying; we should look at common humanity, that we're all vulnerable in some ways. We all share the same strengths and weaknesses, the same fallacies. And if you look at that, you might sort of see that that person is vulnerable. Not that you

9 "Roofies"—Rohypnol is a central nervous system depressant that impairs mental functioning and can cause amnesia, confusion and impaired judgment. It's often referred to as the "date rape" drug.

explain away their behavior, what was done to you, but you can look at their underlying vulnerabilities and insecurities. That will soften things a bit. Not get rid of it, it will soften things a bit.

I remember that we were all socialized into thinking in the 2000s that [Muammar Gaddafi][10] was the most evil man in the world, the worst dictator ever outside of Hitler. We all were socialized into believing that. But I remember the description of when they found him and he was wounded and hiding in a drain pipe by rebel forces who dragged him out, tortured him and killed him. What a way to die. I wouldn't wish that on the worst enemies. And my heart broke, even though what I had been socialized into believing. He's still human.

The next point, which you can sometimes do, though it's more difficult, is if you're looking at the common humanity perspective, you might want to reflect on things that you've done that you don't feel comfortable with. Maybe they're not quite as serious, as the level of what was done against you and why it was so hard to forgive, but you can think about things that you've done that you don't feel good about in your life. If you're really honest with yourself, it's important to look at that, too.

I remember dealing with a therapy patient who was a victim of sexual abuse, and the hardest thing with dealing with abuse victims is not only the working through the memories of what they went through, the transgressions, but what's harder is the tendency to become like the perpetrator. Nobody wants to deal with that. The worst thing for a victim is to think that they could actually become like the offender, but it's the most abhorrent thing, so therefore it's unconscious.

But if bad things happen to you, you internalize that. We don't look at that internalization piece. How do you train a torturer? Torture them. The best torturers are people who were tortured as part of their training. They become great torturers, bizarre as that seems. And a lot of victims who are of a repeated offense will end up to be perpetrators, more men than women. So, dealing with the potentially internalized potential to become like the perpetrator has to be done at some point. So, a part of taking the perspective is to take a perspective on yourself and look at the things that you've done.

---

10 On the recording of this talk, Dan says "Sadam Hussein" in the story, but it was actually about Gaddafi.

Like that woman, the thing that really changed her the most is that she came in one time and she talked about, in her job, things that she did that she covered over, that were wrong. And she said, "Look, I'm not so different." And her famous line to me was, "The real enemies are those within our own hearts. The real enemies are those within our own hearts," looking squarely at the things that you've done that you don't feel good about. Then we all share the common humanity. We have strengths. We have weaknesses. We have limitations. We have good things that we've done. We have bad things that we've done. And still, you don't condone anything about the other person's behavior against you. But you look at the flawed humanity that we all share.

And then finally, the last step is to take a wider perspective, a spiritual perspective. And you reflect on the benefits of forgiveness, not for the perpetrator, but for you. What if you really let go of all this and moved on?

I'll tell you a very personal story about that. I have two brothers, an older brother and a younger brother. And we had a summer cottage, not a very expensive place, but it was on a pond; and I come from generations with my father and my grandfather on both sides fishing. I grew up fishing in that pond and when my kids were young, my plan was to take them to the pond and take them fishing as the fourth generation. And one day when my oldest kid was four years old, my father and mother came up to the birthday party. My father pulls me aside at my four-year-old's birthday party and says, "I hope you don't mind. I just gave the cottage away to your younger brother. But he can't sell it. But it's his."

I said, "Yeah, I mind a lot. It's totally inappropriate to tell me this at my son's birthday party out of the blue." And I said, "If you do that, you're going to alienate me and my older brother, Dave." Then I wrote him a heartfelt letter and I said, "Look, we have a good Irish family. We have a history of cutoffs down the generations. You have control over that. You don't have to do that. If you do this, you're going to split the three brothers apart. You're going to create a rift that's not necessary. It's more important than the property not to create the rift. You have control over whether you go ahead with this decision or not."

Next day, he was hospitalized. He told everybody that I caused him to have a heart attack. Good Oedipal thing, right? "You're killing your father." Turns out he didn't have a heart attack; he had a panic attack because he didn't want to hear what I was saying. There was cutoff, good Irish, Irish knew how to cut off, right? I had no contact, my older brother and myself had no contact with my younger brother for six years. Or with my father. Then my father got old and he was getting vulnerable and frail. And I said, "There's enough of this silence," so I reached out to him and took care of him, he got old. And then when my mother got sick, and she had four heart attacks, I took care of her.

She came to my house and I did the post op stuff for her four times, a couple months each time. And I treated her like the attachment figure that I wanted. I was the good mother to her. And that solved it for both of us. But the thing about forgiveness that was most amazing was that, and my wife convinced me to do this, she says, "It's not your mother's fault. She wouldn't go against your father. She never felt right about this stuff and she's going to take that to her grave. You have to change that. So, even if you don't agree with her, reach out to your younger brother." So, I grumbled and said, "Rrr, Rrr," but then I thought she was right. So, I called up my older brother, the one who was also estranged from the younger brother, because, whoa, I forgot to tell you the other part of the story.

Right after my father died, he sold it, so my kids never got a chance to use the place. Didn't tell anybody in the family. Did exactly what, against my father's wishes. So, it stopped the property down the generations. So, I called up my older brother and I said, "This is a weird suggestion. What if we got together with our younger brother around our mother one more time before she dies, so she would see us all together? Because it wasn't her fault. She faults herself for this because she wouldn't go against our father. And you don't have to like it. You don't have to agree with it. But if we did that, it would allow her to be at peace."

So, there was total silence on the other end of the phone and then about three minutes later he sort of squeaked out, "Okay." It really amazed me. So, we met with my, my mother was in the hospital at the time, so we met with my younger brother for an hour and we worked out what we could work out. And the three of us showed up at her bedside. My younger brother bought an old Polaroid camera and took a picture of us, all of us together and put it right by her bed. That's what she died with. She died with a sense that we had forgiven each other and moved on.

But I wasn't prepared for the response. I thought I was just helping my mom. But when I walked out of that room, I was free. There was something that shifted inside that was profound for me. So, I thank my wife for seeing that. It was a necessary thing to do. I don't belong to it at all anymore.

So, final step in the process is it frees you, from a spiritual perspective. And that's what that couple was saying in South Carolina. If you hold onto the hatred, you're bound. If you let go by forgiving, and you find this essence of your loving core, you live out of that. There's nothing to forgive, no one to forgive at that point. There's no hatred, nothing you're holding on to.

Those are the steps of the process. It's very powerful. So, since it was fresh in my mind today because it was an historic day yesterday—the press doesn't know about it because we did it privately—but I thought since it's a holiday time, this is a good time to do this.

January 10, 2018

Themes: Four Immeasurables; Religious Institutions; Ethics Training in Law Schools

Dan

Welcome everyone. You have a question?

Student 1

I've had a kind of emotional last couple of days with you on retreat, and I'd love to talk about equanimity and non-reactivity, and ways to cultivate that.

Dan

Okay, that's a good question. What's been your experience on the retreat? What's the reactivity about?

Student 1

Everything from extreme frustration when I felt like I wasn't keeping up or not understanding a concept.

Dan

You're the last kid on the block to figure this out, right?

Student 1

That kind of thing. I couldn't find the field. All the way to getting back on the bus, so to speak, and having more rapid advancement in my practice than I ever have in the last couple of days, and really just having amazing states while simultaneously not feeling attached to those states.

Dan

So, you're on a rollercoaster.

Student 1

Yeah.

Dan

That's the way it is. [Laughter] But it sounds like when it's not happening you get frustrated easily.

So, equanimity. There's a difference East and West here. And the teachings on reactivity were really the very first teachings that Buddha Shakyamuni gave. So, when Buddha reached enlightenment under the *bodhi* tree, he walked to the next town, which was called Sarnath, and he gave his first teaching. And the first teaching was on the Four Noble Truths. And the first of the Four Noble Truths was the truth of *dukkha*, which unfortunately many people have translated from the Pali as meaning suffering.

So, it's been passed down over the years as the truth of suffering, but that's not an actual translation of the term *dukkha*. What Buddha was trying to say is, if you look at your mind, carefully, every moment a new experience comes into your mind. The mind moves towards it if it likes it to make more of it. And if it doesn't like it, it moves away from it to make less of it. So, there's a built-in reactivity of trying to make more of what we like and less of what we don't like, and that's become so much of a habit that it's actually built into our information processing system moment by moment.

And because of that constant changing of things around and reacting to what we're doing, the result is suffering. But the trouble with translating *dukkha* as suffering is you miss the method. What Buddha was trying to say is that you can actually look at your mind and see how it moves towards what it likes to make more of it, and what it dislikes to make less of it. And, if you see how it does that, you can change it and find your way beyond the bias in your information processing system that's constantly creating suffering. And we do that in meditation practices as well as we do it in everyday experience. If we like what we're experiencing and it's a good state, we can try and make more of it. If we don't like what we ... then we get frustrated.

Now there's a difference East and West here, in that what Buddha was describing is an inherent property of our dysfunctional ordinary information processing system. So, we're always moving towards what we like to make more of it, and what we dislike to make less of it, away from it.

There are similar concepts in Western psychology, but they're somewhat obscure and they never really caught on. In the sixties, there was this concept of "leveling and sharpening," that if we like an experience, we sharpen it, we intensify it, and if we don't like an experience, we level it, we distance ourselves from it. It's a very similar concept, but it didn't quite catch on with the universality that the notion of *dukkha* has in Buddhism, the truth of reactivity that's built into everyday ordinary information processing moment by moment.

But there's an interesting difference East and West because in the West there's a good deal of research on individual differences in reactivity. It's not incompatible with the Buddhist studies, it's just different because it's clear that certain personality traits are heritable; they run in families. And you can calculate the probability that if one person in the family has a certain trait, then what's the likelihood that there's somebody in the next generation that will have the same trait? That's called a heritability index. And most traits come into the 0.4 range, which means that they're moderately heritable, which means that traits tend to mildly run in families.

And there are some studies that show that reactivity to the stimulus is inheritable. So, some infants come into the world and they're very reactive to the immediate sensory stimuli; they cry and fuss when they experience colors and light is too bright or sounds are too loud. They're just reactive to the sensory experience in a way that other kids aren't. And that's well-documented in the West, that there are individual differences in the degree to which individuals are reactive. And kids who grow up to be reactive tend to be more unhappy, and they tend to be more impulsive.

But not all kids have the same degree of reactivity, some are much more reactive and some are less reactive. So, we can still put these things together East and West, and we could say generally most of us are reactive because it's built into our information processing system. But even though that's the case, some people are much more reactive than others, but we all have some degree of that and that would be a fair integration of East and West views on reactivity.

So, what's the positive opposite of reactivity? The positive opposite of reactivity is equanimity. It means that you don't show positive reactivity to make more of something that's a positive experience, or you don't show negative reactivity and try and make less of what you don't like. And in meditation, of course, that reactivity plays itself out because it destabilizes your meditation experience. You have a hard time doing your meditation; you get frustrated, and the frustration then makes the meditation deteriorate even more. Or where you have a good experience and it was a good experience because you were staying on track, and then the good experience is something you react to, and then the reaction gets you off track, so it's not a good experience anymore. Experienced meditators don't do that anymore, they allow what there is to be there without undue reactivity.

But how you handle the reactivity, from a Buddhist point of view, it really depends on the level of practice that you're at. So, at the beginning level of practice, the best way of handling reactivity is to practice equanimity. And the way you do that is with an exemplar method. So, you think about who's the best exemplar of non-reactivity—nothing phases him or her. So, you can think of a figure in history, you can think of a figure in film, you can think of a spiritual figure that you know or know of. You can think of a figure in a good novel. You can use an acquaintance who's not very reactive, or you can simply use your active imagination and make up a fictional person.

It doesn't make any difference what the sources are, but you come up with somebody who's the embodiment of equanimity. And then you imagine a series of scenes where that person is being equanimous and non-reactive to various things, including the things that you're very reactive to. Then you bring the person into the room as a live presence, and you dissolve the form body into a shimmering bubble of light, and you let this descend down into the space of your body until it settles into your heart. You know the visualization. And then you let light rays burst forth from your heart. And the more the light rays emanate from your heart, the more that quality grows, is strengthened in your own heart.

And when you finish doing the visualization, you take the view that that quality is no longer your deficiency but your best strength. And if you practice that every day, after a while you get more equanimous. You don't react to the experiences that come up during the meditation, you just let them be there without reactivity. So, you're training yourself to develop the positive quality of equanimity. Then you don't get destabilized in your meditation so much.

Now there are two explanations within Buddhism about why this exemplar visualization works. One comes from the Sutra tradition, and the Dalai Lama describes it in terms of "successive approximation." You become more and more like the exemplar through practicing having equanimity and by acting as if you have it. It's like learning theory.

The other view is more interesting, it comes from the Essence traditions, Dzogchen and the Tantras. And there it's said that all of these positive qualities—patience, equanimity, lightheartedness, trust—all the array of positive qualities are there as part of our original buddha nature. But we've deactivated them, we've taken them offline. So, when you do the visualization, you're putting them back online. It's not like you're developing it from scratch; you already know it. And that would explain why sometimes people very quickly develop these skills with little training. So, I think it's a better explanation, a better fit to why it works.

Equanimity was included into the Four Immeasurables. The Four Immeasurables developed in Theravāda Buddhism. The first immeasurable was loving-kindness. So, you practice offering loving-kindness, random acts of kindness to all beings in your interpersonal field. [Holding up the bottle from which he's drinking.] It's really water. [Laughter] It's not Russian *samādhi*. Okay.

And the second was compassion for the suffering of beings. The third was called sympathetic joy, which is the positive opposite of competition and jealousy. You practice cultivating a genuine joy for others' gains, even if they gain things that you don't have; rather than being jealous about them or competitive with them, you are happy for their fortune and gains. And the last was equanimity. After you do the three—loving-kindness, compassion, and sympathetic joy—you do equanimity so that you don't have preferences about who you direct it to.

That was the original order of the Four Immeasurables in Theravādin Buddhism. In Mahāyāna Buddhism, they used the Four Immeasurables, but they changed the order around. So, equanimity is the first. And the reason why they changed the order around is so that when you develop loving-kindness, you don't get reactive to who you're delivering it to. When you visualize the sufferings of all the beings in the world, you don't get reactive to the suffering when you practice compassion. And when you practice sympathetic joy, you don't get reactive to the people who you're competitive with or jealous about. So, the better order was to do the equanimity upfront because it helps you to be more stable in your approach to the other three Immeasurables.

So, if you don't cultivate equanimity, then there's a constant reactivity to the experiences you're having during the development of meditation. So, you're constantly destabilizing it. So, you have to keep practicing the equanimity. And that's what you recognized in the last couple of days, which has been quite a whirlwind. The problem isn't the meditation experiences you're having, the problem is the reactions to them.

So, how you handle the reactivity depends on the level of practice. At the beginning level of practice, you handle it with exemplar method. You come up with the exemplar of non-reactivity. You take it into your heart and you view yourself as if you are non-reactive, and that [reactivity] will diminish if you practice that on a regular basis, every time you meditate, the beginning of the meditation, as part of the premeditation routine, you'll diminish the reactivity, or at least the severity of the reactivity during the meditation. And after a while it just doesn't come up so much anymore.

However, since you've done emptiness practice now, a superior practice would be to take the practice of Ocean and Waves, practicing from the vast perspective of ocean-like, changeless, boundless awareness, and whatever comes up comes up in that field of ocean-like awareness without any grab to it whatsoever. So, if you hold that view of the vast expanse, the view itself is the meditation; the view is the meditation. And just by holding that view, there's no reactivity left. So, that would be a more profound practice of non-reactivity. It's impossible for reactivity to come up if you're holding that spaciousness.

So, those are the usual practices, and you've been introduced to both of them. So, at this point I would do the Ocean and Waves practice for reactivity. And another practice you can do in terms of emptiness of self is that when you get reactive, search for the agent who's reactive. Who is it that's being reactive? Roam around and search for it, your standard emptiness practice.

All are things of which you now know. But make sure you look into the nature of the reactivity. Are you telling a story to yourself, "I'm going to be too reactive"? Is that going to be a story, a limiting belief? Don't get hung up in the stories. It's limiting you. You've done this for how many days now? Saturday, Sunday, Monday, Tuesday, Wednesday, five days.

Student 1

I missed the first evening session.

Dan

Okay. But we don't count Friday because we didn't meditate Friday. You've done five days of meditation. Look how far you've come. So don't set the bar so high, you're doing just fine.

Yes?

Student 2

This is a bit of a similar kind of maybe ... Anyway, I'm just going to ask the question. So, we've been hanging out a lot with Jack who's been sitting behind me, and he's a professional golfer, and we've talked about competition and how it seems like competition seems so juxtaposed to what we've been practicing in all of the positive traits. And that's something that's kind of stumped me. And then the extension of that is the ultimate competitions like violence and killing. And I'm wondering what your perspective is on whether it's ever justified and where competition falls on …

Dan

It depends on whether the competition is part of play or whether it's destructive.

Student 2

Where's the boundary?

Dan

Whether it's constructive or destructive. The lamas in the monastery, they debate all the time, and that's competition, they like to win. So, when they debate, they like to beat their opponent with clever arguments, but it's all done in the spirit of play, and it's done with goodwill. So, they're not going to destroy their opponents. They think their opponents are part of the interdependence of this. There's no one to play with without opponents. So, it's done with goodwill, for the most part.

There are exceptions to that, there are lamas who are power-oriented and they're devious, the same way you see in the Catholic Church. So, just because it's from another culture that doesn't mean they don't have their problems. There's just as much intrigue about power and self-importance and things like that in Tibetan monasteries as there is in the Catholic Church.

But in the best sense, the debate does two things. It's a kind of sport. They obviously have competitions, there's a national championship. And it's a kind of divine play, if you will. And they sharpen their understanding of the *dharma* through debating. At Menri Monastery, there's two debate schools. There's the Sutra debate school, and then there's the Dzogchen debate school, and you debate different things depending on the level of practice you're doing. And I watched them debate a lot. I don't understand the structure of the syllogism enough to do it myself, except I had a funny debate once with one of the lamas about a translation thing that we were doing, and I actually won my first debate. But we were playing with it. So, it's okay to do that.

It's all about intention and motivation. When the motivation is self-motivated and rather than being helpful ... See, the lamas debate because they help each other along with it because they become sharper in their conceptual understanding of key terms in the *dharma*. It's a way of deepening their intellectual understanding of the *dharma*, not meditation practice, but deepening their conceptual crispness of how they come across with their ideas. And I have to say as somebody who's translated Tibetan for forty-six years now, and I haven't done it for a number of years, but I've been dusting it off the last eight years because His Holiness wants me to translate a lot of things.

And it certainly helped my meditation teaching because the wording is very precise, I think, because of all the translations I've had to do. And that's pretty much the spirit of the debates that they debate each other every morning. If I go to Menri Monastery and stay there, I get up at 6:00 in the morning and there's a morning blessing for all the monks, including myself and the other Westerners who are there. And then right after breakfast, they start debating for a couple of hours. And they do it in the service of improving their precision in terms of understanding of this stuff. So, it's done in the spirit of they all help each other along to be better students. So, the motivation is to help, it's not to win, it's not about self.

Student 2

That makes sense when you're debating, but how do you justify that wars of religion are on the basis of, "We're saving the rest of the people because our belief is better anyone else's," and then killing? Because isn't that just an extension of a really pure intention that is carried too far?

Dan

It was the great American psychologist, William James, who said that the biggest impediment to spirituality is religious institutions, and there's some truth to that. But that's a bastardization of spirituality. So, some people like Bob Emmons and his work on *The Psychology of Ultimate Concerns* showed, as a Western psychologist doing research on positive psychology, showed that people who develop a wider vision in life and operate out of that vision, which is often spiritual, have greater wellbeing; they're more resilient in the face of stress, and their life is more meaningful.

But, that's different from a rigid religious belief system. So, the danger there is that rather than developing a larger vision, which often is humanitarian and not serving the sense of self, people develop a vision which is really a rigid belief system and it's highly self-serving. That's what happens in fundamentalism. One of my friends has a good definition of fundamentalism: "fundamentalism, high on the mental and low on the fun." It's a good definition, isn't it? [Laughter]

Student 2

Yeah, it's pretty spot on.

Dan

It is spot on. But see, that's the trouble. Humans are the only people who will kill for an idea. We're the only species that actually do that. And we've destroyed entire cultures in terms of missionary behavior. How arrogant is that? That we actually think that our beliefs are better than somebody else's and we should destroy their beliefs and their cultural systems because we want to impose ...

But see, that's not really spirituality, it's the guise of spirituality, but it's really about power motivations.

People who do that are trying to push certain power motivations. They're trying to push their institution. They're trying to take over other people. Power motivations can pervert religion very easily because we think we're not doing that because we have remarkable ways of rationalizing to ourselves. That's all about power, it's not spirituality. If you learn anything about spiritual traditions that are genuine, the one thing you learn through spiritual practice is self-importance isn't terribly important. If it's feeding the needs of the self, then it's perverted spirituality. So, I understand what you're saying, and it's a big concern, but it's not anything to do with genuine spirituality, it's a perversion of spirituality.

Student 2

But then, can religions and different belief systems coexist and be equally as powerful? Because doesn't it diminish other religions if you ... like part of some religions, and what my friend and I were talking about the other night, was that it's impossible to believe both as valid. So then how ...

Dan

I don't know about that. The people who have some degree of spiritual realization are generally pretty tolerant. I told you a story earlier in the week about that, when the Catholic Church was developing from the year 50 AD to the year 250 AD, for 200 years, there was a strong movement of yogis, the Christian Desert Fathers, and they practiced in Syria and Egypt and Ethiopia, and they were very experienced yogis. They did a practice called the Prayer of Quiet. And lots of people were leaving the cities to go study with the cave yogis, the Desert Fathers.

The Church was threatened because they were losing their constituency and their power base. So, they sent out a person by the name of Palladius [of Antioch] to live with the Desert Fathers for the sole purpose of debunking them. And he lived with them for two years, and he wrote a fantastic treatise of miracles that he observed—people raising people from the dead, flying through the air, living for months without food while extracting vital essence from the universe. It's a remarkable, fantastic voyage of things that he claimed that he observed. And the church was so embarrassed they suppressed the publication of this book for almost 2,000 years.

And Palladius heard a rumor that there were yogis who did these similar practices far to the East. So, he hitched a ride on a camel train through Petra, and went to what we now call Rishikesh, and he wrote a second book about yogis in a very different part of the world who were doing similar practices. So, he was clearly taken by this stuff. But the Church, it failed in its mission to debunk this stuff. So, they hired somebody else. His name was Johannes Cassianus, a great scholar and respected bishop, to go and live with the Desert Fathers, and he did.

And he wrote two books. One of them was suppressed. It was terribly threatening, and they actually rewrote part of it for him. They redacted it, redacted as a way, it means you cross things out and rewrite it for the author. And what he said is [if] you go back to the early Desert Fathers like St. Anthony and you do these prayers or quiet practices, you became Jesus. And everybody has Jesus nature, sort of like buddha nature. And that was terribly threatening because that theological position meant that Jesus was not the son of God, that anybody could become the son of God if they did these practices.

So, they rewrote it that you didn't really become Jesus, you became an archangel like Gabrielle or Ezekiel or Uriel or Raphael or something like that because the implications of that were too profound. You couldn't build a power-based institution around anybody but an historical figure that was calling himself the son of God. But what if anybody could do these practices?

So, it's always been the case that genuine spirituality is at risk of being masked by religious institutions. They behave in such a way to perpetuate themselves, both in terms of their power base and their money. And mysticism and genuine spirituality didn't really make it in the Roman Catholic Church. It lasted as far as Augustine. Augustine was a great yogi, but his mom, Monica, wanted him to be the bishop for the whole Roman church. She had ambitions for him, and he did what his mother wanted, and he gave a severe negative reaction to the previous years he spent as a good yogi because his mother didn't want him to do it. And after that, there was no place for mysticism within the Catholic Church.

So, there's always been a tension in religious institutions, which are power-based, and that's the large motivation. And religious institutions basically represent interest groups; and what interest groups do is they perpetuate themselves and they try and assert their dominance over other interest groups. So, that's why we have infidels: "If you're not part of my interest group, you're in the other guy's interest group, and that's a bad group because my group is better." And we start thinking like that and we destroy other groups that are competitive with us. That's not spirituality. That's power motivation, and there's no place for power in genuine spirituality.

But Bob Emmons coined the term "spiritual intelligence." He took the term from Danny Goleman's work on emotional intelligence and social intelligence. And he thought that we needed to have some kind of comparable term for spiritual intelligence, that people need to use their intelligence to see what they're getting, and not let their practice be delusion, be unintelligent, blind following spiritual beliefs like fundamentalism. But intelligent and informed spirituality is informed by direct experience. Fundamentalism is serious, it can destroy this planet. It may.

So, you're raising a very important point, but ultimately it all comes down to motivation. What's your intention? People who are genuinely spiritual are highly tolerant of people in other religions, they don't make the distinction. There are a lot of studies in psychology of religion that show that to be pretty much true in empirical studies. People who are genuinely spiritual tolerate other people who are also spiritual.

Student 2

Thanks.

Student 3

The subject of intention leads into my question.

Dan

Sure.

Student 3

Where I'm at, which is the role of spirituality and, let's say, motivation, what someone wants to do with one's life. This is real for me at this point in that I'm currently unemployed and deciding, "Okay, wait a minute, I'm not interested in another job, I want to create something of positive value in the world, tangible." I want to spend my time doing that. So, forming that intention, and how does that fuse with, or how can it fuse with spiritual practice? And it seems it must in being able to, for me personally, filter out the petty personal self-aggrandizement motivations and stuff like that.

But I really feel that the power of vision, what one wants to do in the world with one's life is critically important. And so, for me personally, I also feel the importance of being able to quiet the mind and center and go inside. And I'm looking for that balance of being able to develop a clear vision of action that's positive and wholesome to the world and spiritual practice. Does that make sense?

Dan

The best work on this in the West is by Bob Emmons, one of the researchers in positive psychology. And he wrote a book called *The Psychology of Ultimate Concerns*. He's a psychologist who studies motivations. And he says there are different types of motivations. We all have power motivations, we have achievement motivation, we have the motivation for affiliation, and we also have a spiritual motivation to define meaning in life.

And in his research, what he suggests is that people who articulate a larger vision of life that answers the question about why is life worth living, what the basic question of the meaning is in life, which is often a spiritual answer, are much more resilient. They have greater wellbeing, they tend to be more pro-social, they tend to think more in terms of what we want to pass on to future generations. So, getting people to articulate that larger vision, which is spiritual or humanitarian or both, is important.

I do a course on performance excellence at Harvard Medical School, which I've done for twenty-seven years now. I have a version of it for primary care docs and surgeons, and I have a version of it for judges, and I have a version of it for CEOs. And especially the judges, when we did that exercise about finding the larger vision, it spoke to them because when they could articulate why they were a judge in the larger vision, which is often a humanitarian civic vision of the world, they were happier, they could resist the stresses of work and be more resilient without getting unduly distressed. It just worked better when they renewed that larger vision. So, the research suggests that people who spend their time meditating on or reflecting on what that larger vision is and articulating it until they operate out of it in a conscious way, an informed way, have much more meaningful lives.

And that leads to what other research, Jeanne Nakamura's research, calls "vital engagement." If you have a larger vision in life, everything you do in life is meaningful around that vision. So, you live a life as fully as you can in the precious little time that we have. So, getting people to stop and reflect upon and shape that larger vision matters. There are all sorts of positive psychological consequences to that. But people have to take the time to shape that vision. And if they don't have that vision, then they tend to be unhappy in life.

I did a peak performance or performance excellence course recently for the brain trust of Silicon Valley. And I was appalled because these people are shaping the future. They're the investment people for all the startups in Silicon Valley and around the world. And when I did the usual thing about articulating the vision in life, none of them could come up with an answer. They couldn't do it. And I scolded them about their lack of conscious articulation of what their larger vision was. And I said, "Look, you all have a vision that you're influencing millions of people's lives through computers, sometimes billions of people's lives through the computer. And you have a sense that you're influencing that many people. You have no sense of why you want to influence them, or for what real purpose. It's not good enough."

And I actually had a guy write back honestly, and he said, "Look," he said, "all my motivation for being a main investor in this area has been for selfish reasons; it's been for making more money and for self-importance. And you're right, I feel very powerful in having influenced millions of people through computers, and I have no idea why I'm doing it. Can I study with you and work with you to articulate that?" So, it's a good start because at least he saw there was a problem there.

And I actually think I can help this group because if they start shaping it in the right direction and think about where they want to go rather than having it be a runaway train, maybe we can move this in a good direction. Otherwise, it's not going to go in a good direction. So, now the new thing is bitcoin and computer currency. It's not funny. If we develop a bitcoin currency, think of the implications of that. In the power group in the world, the power, the wealth of the world is owned by a small group of computer individuals. There are no countries anymore, countries don't have wealth. It wipes out nationality and countries, and there's only a small group of powerful people who own everything. We've got to think this through folks. That's not a good vision. That's why it's important to have some influence in the right direction, otherwise we're going to go in a bad direction.

So, you're right, that this is an occasion in your life, it's preciously short, to take the time and shape that vision. We'll do a visualization around that after the break. And it's important because people who have that larger vision, and if they have it in the background of their awareness and they're always operating out of it, they're happier, they're more resilient, they think about what we want to pass down to the future generations, they're more generative in that sense, and they're better people. So, that's an intervention that's worth doing with everybody, I think.

And sometimes that vision comes naturally from spiritual development. If you have certain realizations that are precious then you naturally start thinking more in terms of the larger vision of the world. If you have a taste of awakening and it opens your heart, then you start thinking beyond yourself. The one lesson that I've learned in working with these traditions for forty-six years now is that self-importance isn't terribly important. Or somebody sent me a wonderful cartoon and said, "I finally looked at the larger picture in life, I wasn't in it." It's like that.

But if you do genuine spiritual practice, not religious institution stuff, but genuine spiritual practice, the only measure of authenticity is conduct. The great American psychologist, William James, when he was asked, "How do you tell the authenticity of a spiritual experience?" his answer was, quote, "By their fruits, ye shall know them." They leave a wake of positive influence around them. You can see it everywhere, and they may never talk about their spiritual realizations.

Yes?

Student 5

This is actually a follow-up of that question. What happens when you're trying to implement that into systems, like what Larry and I had been working on, integrating some of those concepts into the legal education system? Are there are practices that ... You had mentioned something about inner fire to make sure that it's on track with that. Is there something that you can talk about in terms of changing systems like that, where it's not on a small scale? Do you know what I'm saying?

Dan

Yeah, I know what you're saying.

Student 4

Because it seems like it's an individual practice, but then you're trying to change something that's a system, so it's on a macro scale versus a …

Dan

As you know, Larry and I worked on teaching concentration training for attorneys and law students. We wrote a paper on that, and I would like to see that being done more programmatically. We had another project that I wanted to do and Larry wanted to do, but I don't think we're going to get it through the IRB.[11] And that is looking at virtues and character strengths. And there's a questionnaire for virtues and character strengths called the Values In Action, the VIA. Just google VIA, and you can take the questionnaire yourself. It has twenty-four virtues and character strengths.

And if you take the questionnaire online (it's from University of Penn) they'll give you a printout of all of your three or four best virtues and character strengths, and the three or four of your weakest. So, it takes you about twenty minutes to get a good assessment of this stuff. We reasoned that we were going to give this to all the judges in Massachusetts—Superior Court, the district court, and the family court judges—because we win either way. If it turns out that the judges are more virtuous than the lawyers, then we can argue that in terms of training leadership, we should put virtue training in the curriculum for law students.

Student 4

But that's what I'm saying, it's like enhancing that. So, are there individual practices that you can do to do that?

11 Institutional Review Board.

Dan

Yeah, I'll get there.

Student 4

Oh. Okay.

Dan

And then the second was that if it turns out that the judges are not more virtuous than law students, and they're low in the virtues, then we win anyway because then we can argue that needs to be trained in law schools in general. Either way, the data argues for why virtue training should be part of the law curriculum. And certainly, we have to go in a better direction with that because legal education isn't going in a good direction, at least in this country. There's no concept of virtues and there's no concept of ethics anymore.

When I wrote my book on the memory for trauma, I spent a lot of time in the Harvard Law Library looking at a lot of the law books. So, now if I go over the law library, it's remarkable, there are security guards everywhere in the law library. And the reason why they have security guards in the Harvard Law Library is because the students are so competitive with each other that what they'll do is they'll take a journal, rip the pages out of the journal, so they're the only ones that will have access to that journal so they get the best grade. That's how bad it's become. So, the culture is bad.

Or, my best friend teaches at a law school, and he teaches an ethics class, and he took out computers, and he banned computers from his class because he had a friend of his sit in the back of the class one day so he could see people's computer screens. Half the students were playing solitaire and the other half were on internet porn. This is the ethics class. This is our future generation of attorneys. Right? So, we've got to change the culture. It's not good enough. So, things like trying to get virtue training in the curriculum are important and we're still working on it.

So, it takes time to change institutions, but Larry's gotten a certain receptivity. And, I think the trouble we had with the virtues program was the judges ... the software, if you go online, for taking the questionnaire, you have to give identifying data, and the judges didn't want to do the identifying data. So, we had to find somebody from Penn who we knew who said they would put up a dedicated site for us, so there'd be no identifying data for the judges. It's taken a long time to work out these little bugs, but we'll get there, I think. Imagine attorneys learning character strength and virtues as part of a curriculum. It's just what's needed.

Student 4

And then in terms of integrating a spiritual practice …

Dan

Yeah, but then if you want to integrate a spiritual ... you've got to find out what kind of spiritual practice. We spend a lot of time arguing why in this current generation, which is so distractible, why concentration training should be the core. Mindfulness is a poor substitute for that. But mindfulness is everywhere because it's over-marketed. That's the problem, even in Silicon Valley. There's a meditation course at Google for all the executives. They sit on a regular basis, but they don't have a very clear sense of why they're sitting or what they're doing in the practice because it's not well taught.

So, just the fact that people are doing these things isn't good enough, in my opinion, because they've got to do it in a way that has some quality to it. Otherwise, it doesn't go in a good direction. People develop the illusion, "I'm meditating at work." So what? What are they really doing? Are they helping other people? Are they developing something that's going to be generally helpful to this culture, passed down the generations? If we're not thinking like that, we're not thinking in the right direction.

We made a mess. The thing that's destroying this planet is selfishness and self-interests. Right now, 95 percent of the wealth is owned by 1.5 percent of the population. That doesn't work, we made a world oligarchy. It doesn't work anymore. So, that's why I spend time doing work in performance excellence for influential people to try and make a little bit of a contribution to try and change them, so they think along the lines about what we pass down to the future generations. Otherwise, it's about taking more for themselves in this generation alone, we've got nothing left for the world.

I have two kids; they're grown up now. I can't imagine how they're going to buy houses. They can never afford them anymore. We had that benefit, but the future generations won't because there's not equitable distribution of wealth anymore. We sold this country. I went on vacation a couple of years ago and we were driving around Northern Italy, and all these farms, they all had the same product, and they were all proud of selling the same thing.

And I was driving around the Central Valley in San Francisco because I worked on a case in the federal prison there, and I drove there frequently, and you see acres and acres and acres with nobody working the land, all owned by people in other countries, one big farm, no local families anymore. We sold this country a long time ago, not even owned by people who live here; it's all investments. And I said, "What do we do? Where did we go wrong here?" So, unless we change the self-interest and greed, we're not going in a good direction, folks.

So, developing a larger vision that's meaningful, and including in that vision how we help other people to make a better world and contribute to the greatest social good, that matters. It's a message worth giving. As long as I'm alive to do it, I'll still do it.

So, I agree with you, I think we have to fundamentally change the curriculum for law students, in some fundamental ways that include the values, and the larger vision of what we're trying to do with it.

January 24, 2018

Themes: Neurocircuitry; Clean Mind; Three Turnings of the Wheel

Dan

Today, we finished putting together the full text of the *Elephant Path* book for children. That's Michelle's doing. She's the senior author and it's a great book. We have four different sets of methods for four different age groups divided by developmental age. So, the book is now in draft form. We're going to pass off on the changes that we made and it'll go out to the copy editor in another couple of weeks. Hopefully it will be out soon enough. You want to say anything about it? Michelle is our resident child teacher.

Student 1

I just wanted to thank you for your incredible patience and support and cracking the whip and keeping me going.

Dan

Yeah, you did it. It's going to be an important book for kids. And we included all the research on distracting web involvement, and internet involvement, and mobile devices, and all this other stuff that this generation is involved with, all the research on that. So, it's updated. It's all in one place. Anything you want to know about distracted attention, we're the authorities on it. Not good attention, just distracted attention. It's good. Thank you for all your work.

Student 1

I saw the paper that's published as very impressive and …

Dan

Oh, the one on the neurocircuitry for awakening?

Student 1

The one from the UMass study, yes. And I wonder if you could do some translating because it's very dense.

Dan

You have to understand your neuroscience. The context of this was that in the basic retreats, as you know, we give specific lineage teachings that are very explicit, and the goal is to use the course to shift your basis of operation from ordinary mind to awakened mind. We say the confluence of all the teachings, the heart-essence of all eighty-four thousand teachings, the common factor, is the experience of awakened mind as opposed to ordinary mind. So, if you have that realization, however short it may be, then you have the heart-essence of all these teachings.

I was increasingly dismayed by the fact that their meditation is becoming so popular in Western culture, but rarely do teachers of meditation of one sort or another ever mention awakening. Why are we doing it? That's the purpose of doing it.

We had a serendipitous occasion where one of my students was a postdoc in neuroscience in Berkeley, and he moved to MIT to do another postdoc in neuroscience. And one of the labs that he worked part-time in was Judd Brewer's lab, which is a neuroscience lab devoted entirely to research on mindfulness. And Judd has done a lot of studies on the neurocircuitry of mindfulness meditation. But his post-doc convinced him to take this course. And in the same course, one of the members of the Fetzer Foundation family took the course, Bruce Fetzer.

So about halfway through the course, I had lunch with both of them and said, "Why don't you stop studying mindfulness as a technique and study the heart of this, which is awakening. No one's ever talked about awakening anymore. And if you are open to that, then I'll deliver you subjects who have awakening part of the time, but not all of the time, so you can scan them in the ordinary mind, distracted waking mind, and you can scan them when they're awakened and see if you can get identification of specific neurocircuitry markers or regions of interest that mark awakening."

So, they were convinced and Fetzer Foundation put up the money for a project on that. And we started with forty subjects. We ran thirty. And the way we did this, first we did the subjects by teacher nomination. My assistant teacher and myself identified students that we thought, well, since there was a limited budget, we tried to take local students who had awakening and run them as subjects.

We decided that we would develop rating scales on a one to ten scale. So, we rated the clarity and the description of four states: (1) Ocean and Waves practice—timeless, boundless, ocean-like awareness. (2) Then second was the refinement of that as the natural state—(i) The natural state is a vast nondual field of awareness without inside and without outside, with (ii) automatic emptiness of whatever arises within that state, and (iii) everything, all instances of doing are immediately empty upon arising so it's simple and it's free of doing; (iv) all conceptualization tendencies are immediately empty upon arising, so it's fresh and free of conceptualization. And because it's free of conceptualization, it (v) has a kind of obvious or transparent lucidity of awareness. So those are the five conditions of the natural state, which is the platform state of the foundation for awakening. So that was the second state.

The third state was (3) Lion's Gaze, the crossing over instructions for awakening, where you take the view of the infinite, vast expanse of the field of limitless awareness space, you orient the awareness not towards anything specific in the field, but towards the entire field, like the gaze of the lion or the child viewing a temple, taking everything all at once. So, those were the three conditions, Ocean and Waves, natural state, and Lion's Gaze. And the fourth was (4) stable awakening. We had the subjects report when they were in stable awakening.

We contrasted those four meditation conditions to ordinary distracted state. And then we measured the students with a one hundred and twenty-eight channel EEG. We didn't use functional MRI because MRI doesn't give real time reporting. And we thought that we needed to be able to have the student report in real time, "Now I'm in awakening. I've shifted my basis to awakening and stable." And so, at that point we could start looking at what the neurocircuitry was, activated or deactivated.

So, we ended up running, of the forty subjects that we rated, we both rated the subjects independently on a one to ten scale for each of those. And the criterion was they had to score six or higher on the ten-point scale for all four of those meditation states, including awakening, by both teachers. And there were three students that we disagreed on, so we eliminated them because we couldn't tell whether the awakening was conceptual or not. But the other thirty-seven subjects were viable subjects that we had, I think, 80 percent accuracy—agreement between independently rating the subjects—we had eighty percent accuracy of knowing that the students were in that state. We both said the same thing.

Then some of the students we didn't run because either they couldn't do it with their schedule or because they were too far away. We ran thirty of the forty original subjects. Once, the EEG cap was defective that day—they couldn't get it to work right, so we had to eliminate one subject because the technology was defective, but we ran twenty-nine subjects.

We ran them for an hour, so that the first thing they did is ten minutes of a baseline in their ordinary thinking distracted state. Then there were ten minutes where [they did] Ocean & Waves, and it was a guided meditation—all they had to do is put the EEG cap on and listen to the instructions and follow the instructions, in pointing out style; and then five minutes of talking about that. Then [there were] ten minutes of natural state and five minutes of talking about that; then ten minutes of Lion's Gaze and five minutes of talking about that; and then a stable awakened awareness whenever they had it, and then talking about that.

There were three sets of findings:

The first finding was that relative to the ordinary waking state (ordinary distracted mind), not in that state, and not in the stable awakening, but in the other three meditation conditions (Ocean and Waves, natural state which is automatic emptiness—and Lion's Gaze), one of the striking findings was that the anterior cingulate cortex was heavily activated in all twenty-nine subjects. And ACC activation is the... The anterior cingulate cortex is the attention center of the brain. So, it's used when there are competing attention demands.

The way we study that in psychology is with something like a Stroop test. If I show you an index card and the text has the word "green," but the color of the text is in red, you do a double take. Do you focus on the text? Do you focus on the color? So, it takes effort to tune out the text and focus on the color, or to tune out the color to focus on the text. And when you give people tasks that involve standardized competing attention demands like that, you usually see an activation of the ACC. The ACC is that area of the brain that's underactive in children and adults who have attention deficit disorder.

In the three meditation states, not the awakened state, but in the three meditation states, the students all were activating intense concentration. But the unusual part of the finding, which is very rare, was if you look at the frequency or the amplitude of the activation, it was in the gamma range. Usually we think of fast, normal, alert brain activity as beta activity, and then when you get more resting and relaxed it's alpha activity, it's more slow activity. When you get into reverie and daydream states, that's more slow activity called theta activity. And when you're deep asleep, it's delta activity, which is the slowest of all. So, this is in the other direction, which is very rare.

So, what you're seeing is high frequency activation, and there are two gamma bands: gamma one and gamma two. This is gamma one, which was sixty-five to forty-five hertz. So, the only interpretation of that is that this region of interest, the anterior cingulate cortex, is not only becoming activated, but all the cells are activated and synchronized, which is a very rare finding. It's hardly ever found in anything. It usually means that all the cells are firing at the same time, coordinated in a synchronized way. It's a very rare finding.

We interpret that as that in all three of those meditation conditions holding the view of ocean-like, changeless, boundless awareness, holding the view of the natural state and holding the immense limitlessness of Lion's Gaze, which leads to awakening, those three views take a certain intensity of holding the view. The view is the meditation. The view is the meditation.

So, we interpreted those findings as meaning that it took a lot of work for the subjects in terms of certain regions of brain activity to tune everything else out and just hold the view, who had nothing else interfering with it, and who held it in a sustained way. That was the first major finding.

The second major finding was more important in some ways because we found that during the awakened condition, but not in the three meditation conditions and not in the waking distracted condition, the ordinary distracted condition, only in the stable awakening condition, we found activation in the parietal area. And it's a specific area of the parietal area that has to do with perspective taking and shifting from local to global awareness.

So, let's take the opposite of that. Let's say we have a trauma patient who has non-epileptic seizures and they're writhing all over the floor and they're completely out of it for three or four minutes and they don't even know that they're writhing. The EEG of that shows the deactivation of that area of the brain that changes from local to global awareness. They have no global awareness. They're not even aware of anything in their surroundings. They're just completely writhing and of course deactivation of motor control systems.

Here we're finding the opposite of something like that—the positive opposite of that—where you're shifting from normal localized awareness to something huge, which is the nature of awakened awareness. It's limitless, absolutely huge, limitless awareness, and it's very alert and awake. So, it's like what you'd expect. There's no surprises here. Awake means awake.

And third: the other important finding was that the activation of that parietal region as a region of interest also showed 45 to 65 hertz gamma activity for all twenty-nine subjects, which is a very rare finding. So, it means that what awakening means is that you're activating a shift to a system that changes from local awareness to global awareness, and you're doing that with all the cells firing; and awake means awake. That area of the brain wakes up to its limitlessness and it's perfectly lucidly awake, and that's the main finding.

So those are the main findings. There is also some activation in the beta activity range of the insula, which has to do with body felt sense. And since the views are all anchored in the body it makes a lot of sense, but it's not the main finding, but those are the main findings. Does that make it a little clearer?

So, we hit aces [so to speak] in that the Dalai Lama said we should take concepts of Buddhism and put them into a scientific test. I thought that we should study something like the main confluence of the teachings, which is the experience of awakening. We did. It passed the test. Awake means awake, and it means shifting out of localized ordinary mind to absolutely limitless, huge, brilliantly alert awakened awareness, and its vividness.

And that's the, if you think about, well, you set up the view of Lion's Gaze, which is looking at the limitlessness of awareness and turning the awareness back on itself, that in holding that view, there are two pathways of ... You have to use your metacognition to recognize the shift out of ordinary mind to awaken mind. And there are two pathways of recognition. One is non-localization. At some point you may notice that you're no longer operating on a localized individual consciousness, but operating out of being the unbounded wholeness, a place that is no place, has no location and no reference point.

So, we say that the infant of individual consciousness—localized individual consciousness—merges with the infinitely vast mother consciousness of awakened *dharmakāya* space. So, what is being described there is very precise. It's the dropping away of localization of consciousness, and you are the unbounded wholeness at that point. That's your basis of operation.

Or, the other [path] is that you shift out of ordinary dull awareness to awakened awareness, which is bright and awake and alert. We call that the pathway of recognition through lucidity. And there are certain descriptors of awakened awareness that make it distinct from ordinary awareness: awakened awareness has *dangpa*, brightness; it has *gnar*, intensity; it has *hrige*, awakeness; it has *danpa*, sacredness; it has *trule*, sparkling immediacy; it has *bole*, softness.

And as long as you don't make those qualities into specific things, so you're staying with the wholeness and don't make them into states that you're looking for, then they can become guidelines for recognizing the difference between ordinary awareness and awakened awareness. And the non-localization pathway is illustrated by the shift from local to global awareness in the parietal system. And the intensity of that is that lucidity pathway. It's not ordinary awareness. It's different.

So, we were very happy that the findings were very precise and they're highly consistent with what we expect from all the descriptions of awakened awareness and all the pith instructions to point out how to do it. And we have some scientific validation for the nature of awakened mind now.

The debate that we had following that, which I don't agree with, is some of the scientists want to now develop a biofeedback technology to teach people how to shift from local to global awareness. And I think that misses the whole point of the heart-essence of the pith instructions. Before we did this project, I volunteered myself as a subject and told them what regions of interest to look for, and it was spot on. I thought it was going to be the ACC and the parietal system.

But then, after I'd shifted from local to awakening, and had the shift in the localization part of the parietal system, and told them that that's what they would find, they wanted me to do biofeedback to see if they could activate that part of the parietal system. And I said, "I'll try it." So, I did it for fifteen minutes and it keeps getting you locked back into a particularizing mind. So, it actually was interfering with the awakening, which was easy to do, to establish without it.

I reminded Judd of a study that was done in the seventies—as if people read back that far to the beginnings of the biofeedback field. When new technology comes out, of course the excitement is to give it to everybody. But what people began to find is that biofeedback didn't work as well for everybody. And the fact that people who had talent for hypnosis—the "high hypnotizables," actually did worse with feedback. They could do it better by making natural mind-body connections without the feedback. And if you gave them the machines, they actually performed worse. If you took the machines away from them, they actually did it almost immediately to make the mind-body connections that were necessary.

And I said, it's probably going to be something like that again with neurofeedback. You're going to find that some people who have natural capacity, if you give them the feedback, it's going to interfere with what they can do on their own. So, don't undermine their natural trust and confidence in what they can do. But for those who can't do it, and particularly those who over-conceptualize, for those people maybe the feedback will work.

So, we agreed to disagree and we agreed that maybe for some individuals the biofeedback might be useful, but it's not going to be a panacea and work for everybody and actually might interfere and cause harm for some people.

But I said that [if] they wanted to try it, they could do it. We had some subjects who were more conceptual, and although we didn't rate them high enough, they still wanted to be subjects. So, we used them for the biofeedback part of it, and it [the biofeedback] helped. So, I think the outcome is likely to be, in the second phase of the research, that biofeedback will help people who can't quite get it in a natural way and maybe it will be a useful aid for those people, but it's not going to be a technology that's going to be going to be working for everybody.

However, if we think about testing the heart-essence of these traditions, one thing we'd want to test is awakened awareness, right? It's "the confluence of all the teachings." If we went further along the path, what do we want to test? What? Okay, yeah, we could test enlightenment, but we could test something a little short of enlightenment.

When Mahāyāna Buddhism was in India, the nature of the realization was called … the person who had that realization was called a buddha. And buddha means realized one. When those teachings were transferred to Tibet, they didn't use the word buddha, realized one. They translated with a compound term in Tibetan, which is called *sangye. Sangwa* means complete purification. *Gyewa* means flourishing of all positive states. So, just short of full enlightenment, which is the realization of ultimate reality, the threshold, the platform for enlightenment, not the enlightenment itself, but the platform of enlightenment—sort of like the platform for awakening is the natural state, the platform for enlightenment is *sangye*, the complete purification of all negative states and the flourishing of all positive states.

And the way you get there is through the practice of *rangnang rangdröl*, self-arising self-liberating. You hold the inseparable view of the vast, infinite, expanse of limitless awareness space and the liveliness of whatever arises within that as liveliness of awakened awareness. So, everything is the dance and show of awakened awareness arising within that expanse. You hold both views simultaneously: the expanse and the lively activity of awakened mind that expresses itself through that expanse. And whatever arises by holding that view, you don't engage.

"Mental engagement" is when the mind goes towards something to make more of it to process it further, or goes away from it to make less of it. And that process of mental engagement in Dzogchen or Great Completion teachings is what causes karmic impressions to form. As soon as you engage something that comes into the field of experience, you make a karmic memory trace. That gets stored in the storehouse mind. And over lifetimes, there are millions and millions of karmic traces.

So, if you set up the practice of *rangnang rangdröl*, self-arising self-liberating, you set up that view of the inseparable pair, you hold the view of the limitlessness, of the expanse of awakened awareness space and the liveliness of awakened awareness as everything: all thought is lively awakened awareness, all emotions, all sights, all sounds, all body sensations, it's all lively awakened awareness.

And you hold that simultaneous view and you don't engage anything. You just watch the show without a watcher. And whenever something arises it goes its own course and just disappears, leaving no trace. So, you set it up in just the right way. It takes a while to get the view just right. It's not a strategy. You can't engage the mind to not mentally engage. It has to be part of the view.

But if you understand that and you get it right, it becomes an automatic process: whatever arises within that limitless expanse immediately liberates itself, leaving no trace next moment. So, what happens is that if you set up the view with no mental engagement correctly, or what's called "leave-it-aloneness," you stop forming any new karmic memory traces and it forces the mind to rapidly release all previous storehouse karmic memory traces in a rapidly accelerated rate. If you do that practice automatically 24/7, in the average of six or seven years you've cleaned out the storehouse with lifetimes of karmic memory traces.

The experience over time is that your field of experience gets what's called *drime*, which is often translated as stainless, but I don't like that term—I like to translate it as clean. Your field of experience gets cleaner and cleaner because it's more and more absent of negative states; and since the negative states mask the positive states, what happens after a while is the flourishing of positive states, and no negative states left. We call that process *dharmadhātu* exhaustion. You exhaust all karmic memory traces, negative—so there's no negative states of mind anymore. It's all positive, only positive states, and there are eighty positive states of a buddha mind. Imagine the implications of this for mental health, no negative states left and for the rest of your life and only positive states; it's profound.

Well, we have people who are getting into that range now. We can study them. And that would be the platform for enlightenment. Why don't we study the neurocircuitry of that? So, in the follow-up to this study on awakening, because they were pleased with the results, I suggested that they study *rangnang rangdröl* and *sangye*, the complete eradication of negative states and the flourishing of all positive states.

We looked at that almost forty years ago now. We gave Rorschach inkblots to people at various stages of meditation. Jack Engler and I did that some back in the 1970s. And people who were not meditators when they looked at the Rorschach, they had content. They saw bats and butterflies and people. When they were deeply concentrated and they stopped thought elaboration, they saw ink, didn't make it into anything. They just saw the ink and they talked about the shading and the shapes and the color of the ink, but they didn't make it into anything, consistent with the winding down of thought elaboration.

When they were in the Ocean and Waves practice, we had to stop the Rorschach at ten hours because they had infinite content because it's the simultaneous mind where everything exists within that cosmic database simultaneously. And we gave it to them the next day; we got completely different content, which is unusual.

When we gave it to people who had a taste of awakening, but not very stable, the Rorschachs looked like ordinary Rorschachs again. The only difference was when we scored the Rorschachs for defense effectiveness and defense demand using the Holt system, which is a tedious scoring system, we found that whatever conflicts they had were right out there, there was no reactivity.

And that's consistent with what the tradition says, that what drops away is this reactivity of the mind going towards something it would like and going away from what it dislikes. It's just there. You don't do anything to it anymore. It's consistent with this dropping off of some degree of mental engagement. But we found quite a disturbing finding that some of the people who had realizations of awakening had, from clinical standards, would meet the Western personality disorder diagnosis standard.

So, they might be less reactive and suffer less, but their behavior would certainly make other people suffer. And that helped us understand the guru game. Teachers can come over here, they can have a legitimate sense of awakening, however unstable it may be, and they haven't changed the personality substrate of their mind at all. So, they still engage in power and greed and money and self-importance and sexual misconduct and all these other wonderful things that gurus tend to do when they come to the West to exploit Western students. And none of that changed the substrate of their personality.

But then we had a smaller group, of course, that had *sangye*—complete purification and the flourishing of all positive states. And those Rorschachs were like nothing we've ever seen before. They were absent of all negative states, especially aggression-related states, and everything was positive. And what was memorable wasn't the content in the Rorschach, but the people we gave them to—they were the great saints and masters of this tradition and they were the most present, loving people I've ever met.

Now we want to revisit this issue of *sangye*, complete purification and flourishing of positive states, in terms of its neurocircuitry. I have some hypothesis of what we're going to find. The positive emotion center of the brain is the medial prefrontal cortex. It's also the pro-social behavior center of the brain. There was a study, a single study subject study of Matthieu Ricard who was, in his twenties, was a French molecular biologist who left molecular biology to become a monk in the Gelug tradition under the Dalai Lama. And for the last thirty years, he's practiced mostly compassion meditations.

Richie Davidson brought him into his lab to test him before and after studying prior visualizing of compassion. And he showed very strong activation of the medial OFC, the medial orbital frontal cortex, which makes sense because it's the positive emotion center of the brain and it's the pro-social behavior center of the brain, which means compassion and sensitivity to others suffering in a positive way.

So, what we would expect is that if we had subjects who had achieved complete purification or something close to that, and flourishing of positive states, we'd expect to see strong gamma activity in the medial prefrontal cortex, the activation of the medial prefrontal cortex, and probably strong deactivation of the fear system, which is the amygdala and strong deactivation of the negative emotion center, which is the limbic system. That's the working hypothesis.

So, I suggested that to Bruce Fetzer and to Judd Brewer and to the National Science [Foundation] advisor for this project who's a straight scientist who was very excited by our results. He has no experience in meditation. He said, "This is amazing stuff." What he liked the most is the precision of the meditations. You can actually get the mind states that refined and it's not schlock. It's very precise what people are accomplishing.

So, we agreed as a group that I would see if we can identify enough students who are far enough along, nobody's got the complete mastery of *dharmadhātu* exhaustion yet, but we have enough people who've cleaned up their mind of negative states sufficiently that we can probably get a good measure on this, and they agreed to fund it. So, if we get the neurocircuitry of awakening, the neuro circuitry of *sangye*, and eventually the neurocircuitry of enlightenment, then I think I left behind something useful here to the Western science before I leave my form body. So, that's the goal.

We found some other interesting things that are worth mentioning because in Buddhism, as you know, there's a difference between what we call the First, the Second, and the Third Turnings of the Wheel. The First Turning of the Wheel is the teaching of the Buddha Shakyamuni. The second is Mahāyāna Buddhism, and the Third is the Essence traditions like Dzogchen (Great Completion), Mahāmudrā (Great Seal), and *tantra* practice.

And I like to see these Three Turnings of the Wheel as something analogous to the structure of scientific revolutions[12] in the West. When we have anomalies, after a while there's a whole paradigm shift that occurs in science to explain those anomalies and we consider that generally an improvement in science. So, for example, we used to think in the days of Ptolemy that the sun and the other

---

12 Dan is referring here to Thomas Kuhn's famous *The Structure of Scientific Revolutions*, 1962, U. Chicago.

planets revolved around the earth. And then when the technology of making telescopes developed enough, there were enough anomalies that it didn't seem to explain that accurately anymore. And what came about was the Copernican revolution. We began to see through an improved technology of telescopes that it is more likely that the other planets and the earth all revolved around the sun. That was a better explanatory model and that was considered an improvement over the inaccurate previous model.

I like to think about those Three Turnings of the Wheel as scientific revolutions. And the reason why I have to mention that is because mindfulness meditation is very popular in the West. As of 2010, there were 710 peer-reviewed articles on mindfulness-based therapy for one thing or another. It's remarkable. But the trouble with its popularity is the teachings get watered down and we lose the heart essence. It's not about mindfulness as a trick technique. It's about the heart essence. How many mindfulness teachers ever talk about awakening? We've lost the heart of this.

And secondly, mindfulness, Burmese mindfulness, represents the First Turning of the Wheel and it doesn't include any of what I would consider great improvements in discoveries within Buddhism. I have students of mine who were mindfulness teachers from thirty, forty years ago, and thirty or forty years later, they're still talking about everything is suffering. That's not what it's about, folks. It's not all about suffering. Later Buddhism moved way beyond that.

So here are the main things of the first Three Turnings of the Wheel:

The First Turning of the Wheel was the teachings of Buddha Shakyamuni; and when he got enlightened under the Bodhi Tree, he walked to the next town, Sarnath, and he gave his first teaching on the Four Noble Truths. And the First Noble Truth was the truth of *dukkha* in Pali, which has often been mistranslated as the truth of suffering. A correct translation for the term *dukkha* means reactivity. And what Buddha was trying to say is that if you observe your mind in every moment of experience, if you like something, the mind moves towards it to make more of it. If you don't like it, it moves away from it to make less of it. So, it's constantly, incessantly reactive to that experience. That's *dukkha*. If you translate it to suffering, which is the outcome of that reactivity, you miss the method. And that falls short of what Buddha intended because he was trying to say, look, you can observe your own mind to see this and change it. And if you just take it as suffering, you lose the method.

And in that First Turning of the Wheel, there are three things you observe. The first was reactivity, *dukkha*. The second was impermanence, everything changes, nothing stays the same. And the third was more problematic. It was called *anatta*, or no self. And what it meant was something very specific. If you get deeply concentrated, thought elaboration drops away. So, you have long periods of stillness, absence of thought, and after a while thought elaboration winds down and pretty much stops. So, you have long periods where there's no thought activity. So where are you operating out of? You're operating out of awareness, not operating out of thought.

But if you keep concentrating, sometimes not only thought elaboration winds down and stops, but sense of self temporarily gets deconstructed. So, you're sitting there meditating, and in my case, Dan's doing the meditation, and then Dan drops away. So, who's doing the meditation at that point? Awareness is doing it. Probably awareness is going to do a better job than Dan. And that experience of the temporary deconstruction of the self-representation, in my case Dan-ness, that is called anatta.

Now what ensued was a five-hundred-year debate. And in that debate some people began to say that to expect the self to drop away is nihilistic, like we're trying to get rid of the self. And that becomes a negative practice. Reminds me of the first Monty Python movie where the Catholic monks have wooden Bibles and they're taking three steps and chanting and then whacking themselves over the head with the Bibles and taking three more steps and chanting and whacking themselves over the head with the Bible. They keep whacking themselves over the head with the wooden Bibles punishing themselves. Because self-representation is a bad thing, we've got to get rid of it.

And a similar debate went on in Buddhism. And finally, what came out five hundred years later by Nagarjuna was something quite different. And what came out was we're not getting rid of the self, but you're seeing it as just the way it really is, as a mere representation. And what came out was the theory of emptiness, which is an unfortunate term. And what emptiness really means is merely a construction of mind. It's very similar to Western constructivist psychology: that everything the mind does (the ordinary mind) is to make representations, models of the world. Sense of self is a construction, out-there-ness is a construction, sight and sound are constructions. You're not hearing a sound out there; you're hearing your own representation of that sound. You're not seeing anything out there; you're seeing your own representations as if they're "out there." You're not thinking anything; you're thinking your own constructions. Everything is a construction of mind. Sense of self is a construction.

Western child development tells us that children aren't born with a psychological sense of self. I didn't come into the world with Dan-ness, although I think I did. The psychological sense of self develops between twelve and twenty months, peaking at about eighteen months. And it's concurrent with the capacity to develop representational thinking. So, out of that comes this sense of self, Dan-ness, and that's useful in everyday life. It serves as a central organizing principle. I organize my daily life around Dan-ness—unfortunately. [Dan chuckles] But it's useful. It's a central organizing principle in everyday life. There's nothing wrong with that.

But here's where Buddhism is different. What Buddhism says is, if it's merely a construction of mind, we make the epistemological mistake (after a while when we operate out of self), [with] a lot of thinking that it's independently existing. I actually think that Dan exists independently and I take him way too seriously. I forget that he's merely a construction of mind.

If I make that construction and then make a mistake, I make that self all too real. The Tibetan word is *nozhin*, grasping it as too real. It's very similar to the Western term reification. I reify it. I take it as independently self-existing. What I fail to see is that in relative reality it exists because of the causes and conditions, not the least of which is the mind's capacity to represent. That's why I make a sense of self. But I fail to see it as just a construction. That's where I make the mistake. And if I don't see it correctly, there are two problems.

One is grab, *dzin-pa*. The self has a lot of grab. And that's the difference in Mahāyāna Buddhism explaining suffering. In the First Turning of the Wheel, suffering is the mind moves towards what it likes to make more of; it moves away from what it doesn't like to make less of it. Now, in Mahāyāna Buddhism, they say that's all well and good, but what makes the mind move towards and make the mind move against is the sense of self. So, suffering is the suffering of self-grab.

And that's pretty much consistent with modern Western research on mind-wandering. Most people spend 47 percent of their day in mind-wandering mode. If you look at the content of mind during mind-wandering, it's about the self, making the self important in one way or another, or "maintaining this tiresome project of self" as Hafiz, the Sufi poet once said. And the more you spend time dwelling on the fantasies of self, the more negative it gets for most people in terms of the research on mind-wandering. So, it's not a good thing. But it serves as organizing principles in everyday reality and relative reality. But ultimately, it's just an empty construction.

And the second trouble is *mümpa*, we get caught up in it [the sense of self]. It clouds over our real nature. So, this field of awareness gets mixed up with self. I think that sense of self and the field of awareness are the same thing. And if I do emptiness meditation, I see into the fact, I go beyond that. It's just a construction of mind, and I see it as just an empty construction. And I shift my basis of operation so I'm not operating out of Dan-ness. I learn in emptiness practice to shift out of operating out of Dan-ness to operating out of the field of awareness. Then I can go back to the meditation. The awareness is going to do a better job than Dan's going to do. Dan doesn't teach. Awakened awareness teaches. I just get out of the way. But that doesn't mean Dan doesn't exist.

So, that's a considerable improvement because what it means is you go beyond the self. The word insight meditation in Tibetan Buddhism is *lhagthong*, tong means to see, *lak* means beyond. It doesn't mean "insight meditation"—it means seeing beyond the obvious structures of mind to the deeper nature of awareness and learning to operate out of that. That's a huge improvement over "no self," because you're not getting rid of anything. You're seeing beyond it. And that should be a reassurance that you're not going to get rid of the self because it's useful in everyday life in ordinary reality.

I remember my first clinical placement in 1972 at Michael Reese Hospital (it doesn't exist anymore) in Southside Chicago. And the head of my department was Roy Grinker. He was old enough to tell me a story of his personal analysis with Sigmund Freud. And Freud didn't do these twenty-year analyses like Woody Allen did. He mostly pushed people and he got them better in two or three months before he had his couch. And he was pushing Roy, and Roy was afraid of changing too rapidly. At one point, (Freud didn't have the couch yet) he leaned over the chair and he said, he whispered into Roy's ear; he said, "Roy, when you finish your analysis, your friends will probably still recognize you."

When you do emptiness of self, your friends will probably still recognize you. And most masters, accomplished and realized masters, have rather strong personalities because they don't get rid of the self. It's just not where they're operating out of. It's like a bubble in the ocean, but it's better to be the ocean.

That said, there's a huge difference between the First Turning of the Wheel, which is no self and all is suffering, and the Second Turning of the Wheel, which is not all suffering, there's not getting rid of the self, but relativizing the self and not operating out of it, seeing it as just a mere construction and going beyond it to the deeper level of awareness.

There's no concept of levels of awareness in mindfulness meditation. But in Mahāyāna practice, you learn to go up to different levels of awareness. And you know that (those of you who took the course) as illustrated in the Heart Sutra mantra, "*Gate gate pāragate pārasamgate bodhi svāhā.*" This literally means in Sanskrit, "gone, gone, gone beyond, gone way beyond, oooh, what a realization."

What does it mean? We mix up thought and awareness—we think it's the same thing. If you concentrate the mind down, thought elaboration stops, you get long periods of stillness. Well, where are you operating out of if there's no more thought? It begs the question and you see in your direct experience that you're operating out of the field of awareness rather than thought: awareness gone beyond thought—the first *gate*.

But still, that awareness is mixed up with self. If you do emptiness practice, you go beyond self to a field of awareness that is no longer mixed up with self. So, I'm not operating out of Dan-ness, I'm operating out of the field of awareness itself as my basis for the meditation. That's the second *gate*—awareness itself gone beyond self-representation.

Still, that awareness is caught up in coming and going in conventional time. If I go beyond conventional time, I go to ocean-like, changeless, boundless awareness. That's a much bigger shift. That's called going way beyond—*pāragate*—to ocean-like, changeless boundless awareness.

Still, that awareness is caught up in localization of my individual consciousness and my information processing system. And with the Lion's Gaze and other crossing over instructions, I learn how to shift the perspective to step out of localization into becoming the unbounded wholeness as my basis. That's a much bigger shift. That's *pārasamgate*—gone way beyond the localization of consciousness. [Finally, *bodhi svāhā*] ooh, what a realization—to capture the metacognitive recognition of that shift.

The reason why the Heart Sutra mantra is so popular [is] because the whole path is right there; and it all has to do with shifting from one level of awareness to the other. And emptiness is the pathway that allows you to clear away the clouds of the mind so there's no clouds anymore, so the radiance of awakened mind is always right here. Simple.

Now, we found that in the studies of the neurocircuitry of mindfulness [compared to] the studies we did of Mahāmudrā, in terms of the sense of self, it's quite different. So, for example, in mindfulness meditation, in Burmese mindfulness meditation, which represents the First Turning of the Wheel and the truth of *anatta*, no self, there are five studies on neurocircuitry that show a deactivation of the medial prefrontal cortex, which is [the] sense of self-representation, Dan-ness in my case. Like the teachings promulgate, you actually deactivate your sense of self. I'm not sure that's a good thing.

Jack Engler and I found in the '70s when three-month mindfulness (Burmese mindfulness) retreats were first getting popular at a center called IMS in Barre, Massachusetts, the first one hundred and twenty people would take a three-month course on a regular basis, and we did outcome studies on them for ten years. But we found a lot of kids who had significant self-pathology from a clinical perspective and were hearing the language of no self and saying "finally somebody understands me." They would take these silent retreats where they'd interacted with no one, get all sorts of shifting states, get disorganized psychologically, have lots of transference reactions and play out all sorts of things with the teachers, and it was a disaster. They were regressing too much and they needed to be pulled from the retreats and get into a good treatment that would allow them to develop a strong sense of self, not to weaken the self.

So, we actually recommended that the mindfulness teachers set up a referral service for people and pull them from the retreats, which they listened to. Where, as Jack Engler once said, "You have to be somebody before you can be nobody." You have to develop a sense of self in the relative sense before you can go beyond it. You certainly don't want to try and get rid of it.

I remember seeing a kid in his late ... he was twenty-nine at the time. He had done ten years of long "rounding"[13] with TM. He had a psychotic depression. He said, "I spent ten years avoiding developing a sense of myself through meditation. I used meditation in the service of defense, and now I have to go back and spend ten years rebuilding something I wasted all this time." And he was right.

The language of *anatta* is not something that I strongly support, although it's one of the languagings of the popularity of Burmese Buddhism, the First Turning of the Wheel. I think the emptiness practices are an improvement over how we deal with the issue of self. It was shown in the neurocircuitry study because the sense of self, the medial prefrontal cortex in our study with our Mahāmudrā subjects, did not get deactivated. The medial prefrontal cortex stayed activated

13 A sequence of simple asanas, breathwork, and meditation designed to release stress in a short period of time, derived from the Vedic tradition.

and stayed online, but that's not where they were operating out of. They were operating out of the parietal system on the global awareness. Sense of self was like a bubble within the ocean, but better to be the ocean.

So, the actual studies on what happens to psychological sense of self make a lot of sense to us. But to go back and say, as a lot of the people of mindfulness who don't know anything about the history of Buddhism try and say, that "this is the authoritative teachings of the Buddha, so therefore it's the only truth." That's like saying we should go back to Ptolemy because Copernicus was wrong—or that Ptolemy's idea that all the planets revolved around the earth was correct because it was the authoritative view because it was the first view. It's not logical folks!

We take things from other cultures and we say, "Okay, this is the truth because it was taught by the original Buddha." Well, what about the improvements that came after that? We're going to negate all that stuff? Doesn't make any sense from a scientific point of view.

I tend to think that the theory of emptiness and going beyond self, but not getting rid of it, was a significant improvement. And this idea that there are different levels of awareness that you shift to—*gate gate pāragate pārasamgate bodhi svāhā*—shift out of the thought to awareness, shift out of self to awareness itself, shift out of time to ocean-like, changeless, boundless awareness, shift out of that and the localization of that into the unbounded, being the unbounded wholeness, ooh, you got it—what a realization! [*bodhi svāhā*].

It's as simple as that, folks. It's not even hard to do with the right instructions. And what's exciting is to see that science validates exactly what we'd expect, knowing how the brain works, the regions of interest in the brain, and knowing how Buddhism works.

So, now we'll continue to see if we can get some neurocircuitry markers for sangye, for no negative states, all positive states, because in my point of view as a clinician, that has profound implications for mental health, and we're not even beginning to think about that, and we should.

The other thing which … is we are not quite finished yet. One more thing I'll say about this. We did another paper. Andrea Ruff was a postdoc in Judd's lab from Brazil, and did a paper on neurophenomenology. She took our twenty-nine subjects and had the computer do an analysis of the consistency of the language of how they describe these states because they had five minutes to describe Ocean and Waves, five minutes to describe natural state, five minutes to describe Lion's Gaze, and five minutes to describe stable awakening. And she had the computer analyze what they came up with. And what was really nice is the descriptions that the subjects came up with are not all over the place; they're highly consistent with what the texts say.

The only thing that was missing was that when in the Lion's Gaze, there are two conditions to recognize awakening. One is the pathway of non-localization and the other is the pathway of clarity or lucidity. But before you set up that, you have to set up the natural state as the foundation for that. And there are two features of the natural state that are very important because you can't shift from partialized mode to unbounded wholeness. You can't grasp the unbounded wholeness from a partialized stance. So, any kind of directed attention is partialized. So, you have to move beyond doing anything. You have to move from doing to non-doing. It takes a lot of work to get to the stage of non-doing. And automatic emptiness is what sets up this non-doing.

And the second was beyond all conceptualization. Conceptualization partializes. If it's about this concept, it's not about that concept. All conceptualization by definition is partialized. So, you can't think your way into awakening. You can only see all thought as automatically empty and it clears away. So, you move to what's called the fresh mind, clear of all conceptualization, and you move beyond all doing.

The only thing that didn't come out in the findings was that there wasn't enough data to signify... The non-conceptual piece came out, but the non-doing piece didn't come out clearly. So, I said, yeah, go back and look at this because it's really important. And she did and she found that they described it in different ways in our conventional language, but there's enough data there that when we reanalyzed that we found what we were looking for.

So, most of the concepts of why the languaging is so important turn out to work, and what our subjects demonstrated was pretty much close to what we expected to find based on what the authoritative texts, and the secret pith instructions say about how to do this. So, I'm happy with the findings, they're good findings, and that's what we found. Does that make it a little clearer?

It's profound. We struck aces with it.

Student 2

[Inaudible question]

Dan

Well, it depends on what audience we're looking at. The neurocircuitry argument will appeal more to our subjects and people in the *dharma* world; the neurocircuitry article will appeal less, but it gives a certain validation. But, from a scientific audience who knows nothing about this … at the Foundation meeting when we went over the results, we had an independent advisor in the National Science Foundation, and he was very impressed with the results. He was really excited about it, and he actually gave us a blessing to go ahead and do the *sangye* study now. Even though this is completely alien to him, he said, "You're doing something right."

I think what it does is it's going to open eyes in the scientific community about this gamma activity because it's just not seen [that often]. You can see it every now and then in a subject, but it means all the cells are being activated in a synchronized way. That's not something the brain normally does. So, it's a unique and very rare finding, and it's consistent with what we'd expect with awakened mind. It's not that the whole brain turns itself on; it's only certain regions, but those regions are very alert and awake. Awake means awake. So, that finding is worth the paper just the way it is because it's a unique finding. It's not something that's been seen before.

Any other questions about the study?

Student 3

As with other scientific papers, this is very scientific. Is it going to have to be replicated, and if so, is that in process or is there going to be a need to replicate the study?

Dan

Well, they're going to replicate it with a new, more efficient thirty-six channel EEG, which should do the same resolution as the 128. We thought of running the same subjects if we were willing to do it with some of the people here in this room again with a more efficient technology. So, the answer to that is yes.

There are three things that are planned. One is replicating it with more streamlined technology. The second is this biofeedback thing, which I'm skeptical of. And the third is the *sangye*, the self-arising self-liberating, and the complete purification of negative states and the flourishing of positive states. Those are the things that we're planning.

We thought we wanted to do a functional MRI because it's better resolution. We did the 128 channel EEG because you get real time. A person could say, "I just shifted my basis to awakening," and we could mark what the computer's picking up on in terms of the regions of interest of the neurocircuits of the brain at that point. But the subjects were so talented in being able to shift that state that we don't need it.

For example, in Buddhism, we have this notion called *shinchong*, or mental pliancy. It's a certain resultant skill. Whatever the mind does and intends to do, it does only that with nothing interfering with it. It just does it with lightning speed. That's an outcome of all this practice.

I found that when I played with it as a volunteer subject myself the first time, because when I shifted to the natural state with automatic emptiness, what came up was deactivation of the posterior cingulate cortex. Now in mindfulness, there are five studies that consistently show (mostly out of Judd's lab, but some other labs) that the main finding in mindfulness is the deactivation of the PCC, the other half of the cingulate system. And that's the part of the mind that categorizes and judges. So, when people are taught Buddhist Burmese mindfulness in saying non-judgmental awareness, that instruction is partially shutting down the categorizing and propensity to judge and provide labels to all experience.

Interesting enough, there are two studies on psilocybin use and both showed deactivation of the PCC. So, when you're sitting there and everything is equally as interesting and there's no preference and you're saying, "far out man" (not that I've ever done anything like that; you know what I'm talking about), it's the same state. You're deactivating the judgmental part of the mind and just having pure non-judgmental awareness, which is exactly how secular Burmese mindfulness is taught in the West since Jon Kabat-Zinn's book years ago.

But we found in non-meditation meditation (which is another name for the natural state) deactivation of the PCC also. The difference was the magnitude. It was stable and it lasted. So, when I shifted in myself, as a subject, to non-meditation meditation, I had one thought in ten minutes. It took me exactly two seconds in clock time to shift to that state, and it remained stable and there was a high magnitude of deactivation for ten minutes. It was completely stable.

That resolution of using certain neurocircuits is what's important with skilled subjects. It's like somebody who's working out on a machine and is a skilled exerciser so they're doing a new routine on the Pilates machine. They only isolate the muscles for that exercise because they're skilled, and somebody who's not experienced uses a lot of other muscle groups until they learn to isolate those out. The brain does the same thing. Very skilled meditators just isolate out what circuits they're going to use for that task at hand. They don't use all the other circuits. It's not a schlock.

We found that years ago when we brought a tachistoscope, a high-speed electronic board, to study the speed of the mind in meditators in Dharamsala with the Dalai Lama, who gave us his best concentrators. And we used to call out different meditation states, and the average time to shift into that the stable state was two seconds, like shifting gears in a car.

I experienced that when I was in Burma in the 1970s because the final exam when I was going through the stages of the practice where they'd call out the stages randomly and you had to produce them on the spot out of order. And they would tell by the skill and pliancy of how you did that whether you really got the realization, because you should be able to do anything at will. Just the mind intends, and that you got it.

So, that's what I found when I played with it myself in the lab. But then I said, "I'm not the only person who can do this. All my subjects who are really good can do this." And then they run in about five pilot subjects and they all did the same thing I did. So, there's no special skill here. They just were good meditators.

But the PCC deactivation is consistent in non-meditation meditation. But in my experience, non-meditation meditation does a better job with it from a neurocircuitry point of view than mindfulness. Mindfulness is a mixture of different techniques. It's not as precise. This precision is like nothing else, as you know. It works.

Student 3

During the study when the people were describing, making the descriptions in between, they still had the stuff on. Did the brain go back to just normal activity? I mean, obviously it didn't stay in those states.

Dan

I don't know how to answer that. I don't think I looked at that.

Student 3

Oh, okay. I'm curious if it went all the way back …

Dan

I'm sure the data is there. I don't think we looked at that. We had a massive dataset. You usually look in the regions of interest. That's why I pilot on myself first and I know enough neuroscience to say, "This is the areas we're going to look at because these are more likely to get a good yield." Otherwise, you're just doing thousands of correlations. And statistically the correlations, some of them are just not valid because you're doing too many correlations and you come up with stuff that isn't real.

Student 3

Yeah. I guess just my own curiosity as you were describing it.

Dan

Don't know. I'm sure the data is there. I just don't know how to answer it.

Student 4

I was wondering if you measured any other physiological variables or if you have a sense of what the effect on the total body is or the rest of the body?

Dan

Well, we had an effect on the insula. It activated the insula, which is body self-awareness. So, the realizations are very much anchored in the body. That's my interpretation of that.

Student 4

And when you were trying to describe awakened awareness to scientists that had never thought about it before, how did you describe that to people that would have no reason to think that that was an interesting thing to study?

Dan

I'd say, "It's the confluence of all the teachings. It's not about meditation techniques. It's about where the teachings bring you to. And there's an infinitely vast, brilliant field of lucid, awakened awareness. It's always right here, but we don't recognize it because the mind's too clouded over." I use the Essence traditions, which is the Third Turning of the Wheel as two things. One is the underlying metaphor of the sun and clouds. If it's raining outside and then the clouds clear after a while, "you say the sun just came out." Is that accurate? Of course not. The sun's always been out. But you can't see it from the perspective of the clouds.

And the awakened mind is always right here. It's part of our buddha nature, but we don't see it because it's clouded over by thought, clouded over by sense of self. It's clouded over by time. It's clouded over by the content of the mind. It's clouded over by the operations of our information processing system and localization of consciousness. And when you remove these clouds after a while, there's no clouds left; you see the awakened mind like the sun that's always here. You say, "Oh, it's always here."

So that's the analogy I use to describe it.

Student 3

And then quickly, if it's not a trade secret, and if I understood correctly, did you say that you were verifying the experimental subject states by observing them yourself?

Dan

No, no, no, no. By description.

Student 3

By their descriptions, not …

Dan

We interviewed them and we asked them to give us a description of their experience of Ocean and Waves, the description of the natural state. And we wrote it down and we rated it. We worked out rating scales and, as one does with coding, you see how consistent the coding is. We were about eighty percent consistent in our coding, but we had three subjects that we disagreed on. So, we eliminated the subjects we couldn't agree upon. And some of the subjects were below six—that was the cut-off score. They had to have more than not the experience of Ocean and Waves, more than not the experience of the natural state, but not all the features of it.

There are five characteristics of the natural state: nondual awareness; automatic emptiness of everything that arises moment by moment in that field; it's "fresh"—free of conceptualization; "simple"—without doing; and lucid. So, if they gave us three or four of those characteristics, but not all of five of them in the spontaneous report, then we'd score that about seven or eight. If they gave us almost all the characteristics and they pervaded the description, then we'd give it nine or ten. That's how it works.

So, we spent a lot of time developing these rating scales. And that was good because we found that we were looking at most of the subjects similarly, and there were a couple of subjects that we struggled about where we thought conceptualization was precluding the realization. They were just thinking their way through it and had the need to see it that way. And we both identified the same subjects we had doubts about. And pretty much like what we do when we talk about teaching. But we developed some rigorous coding scales for this. And it worked. And it helped us refine the teaching. So, now we know more what to look for in the descriptions of these states.

Student 4

So, when you were speaking about representations of mind and conceptualization, I was just wondering, because I am accustomed to thinking about what human beings as world-constructing in so far as that any particular thing we encounter is only possible within a world that we've constructed.

Dan

In relative reality that's true, but not ultimate reality.

Student 4

I guess that was my question. Is there the ...

Dan

The Buddhist logicians like Chandrakirti and Dignaga and others spent a lot of time laying an infrastructure to say that there are two modes of knowing. One is conceptual knowing, which is the heart of Buddhist logic. And there's direct experiential knowing through meditation practice, which comes from awareness, not thought.

And we don't really make room for both of those modes of knowing in the West. We think it's all conceptual. It's a problem. Even if you look at the studies on mature adult cognitive development in the West, stages beyond formal operational thinking, people like Commons and Richards, which are the Neo-Piagetians, will say, "Well, this is the idea of non-conceptual knowing," but they don't really take it seriously because they're locked in their paradigm. But you can move beyond all that, and you have to move beyond conceptual knowing.

That's why the crossing over instructions are kept secret. Because if you disseminate them and people try and think their way through them, and they're not having the natural state as the foundation, then that actually precludes awakening and makes ... it hardens the mind and actually makes it harder to experience awakening.

So, they're not given out until people have the foundation of pure awareness. So, they're not thinking enough, and all thinking that comes up is immediately released, is automatically empty. So, they don't sort of harden the mind because it makes it harder to awaken at that point. It's not like they're trying to keep them secret. They're trying to protect you from misusing them because invariably a number of people are going to misuse it because they get greedy. We live in a society of spiritual greed. People want stuff, they want attainments. But it doesn't work like that.

Student 4

So, I was thinking of the constructions of world as empty of any kind of independent reality. But my question …

Dan

Yeah, but useful in relative reality; they're still useful in relative reality. Enlightened masters still think. They just don't get caught up in the thought.

Student 4

So, world construction doesn't stop.

Dan

No.

If you refine the emptiness of thought and you take it as far as you can go, it becomes one of the five wisdom energies. It's Discriminating Wisdom. Buddha can look with lightning, laser-like speed with thought and know exactly what an individual needs because they see everything through that thought. It's like a smart target bomb. Every thought for a different individual. It picks out exactly what's needed by that individual. So that's called Discriminating Wisdom, which is the ultimate refinement of thought. It becomes the tool for how buddhas know how to use skillful means for different people and provide different teachings. You don't get rid of it. You just refine it until you use it in the right way.

But you're not operating out of that. You're still operating out of enlightened mind. So, you're not caught up in thought. It's the capacity of the thought to cloud over that is the real problem. So, it's not an enemy; just have to refine it and see it correctly the way it is. But they're operating on a pure awareness. They're not operating on thought. Thought just serves that purpose. Does that make it a little clearer?

Student 4

Yes.

January 31, 2018

Themes: Practice All the Time, On and Off the Pillow; Offer Everything Good

Dan

Welcome everyone. You have a question

Student 1

So, my question is off the pillow practice. Is it okay, for instance, if I notice that for instance that my sense of self is stronger than in the meditation, in other words that I'm not necessarily holding the view completely, is it okay to, out of sequence, do the emptiness of self on its own without these other components and then …

Dan

Of course. In your everyday life, the basic practice is following grab, reactivity. Grab to everyday experience is perceivable. And whenever you have the grab, you take your awareness and roam around in it. See if you can find anything substantial about the nature of that grab. So, you do an emptiness on-the-spot meditation. If you do that every day with the things that grab you the most, after a few weeks you'll see that there are patterns there. Not everything grabs you equally. What one of my students called "identifying my favorite clouds." Find your favorite clouds. What do you get caught up in the most? Do you get caught up in self? Do you get caught up in thought? Do you get caught up in out-there-ness. Do you get caught up in time? Do you get caught up in emotions in general? Is there a specific emotion you get caught up in? Do you get caught up in dualistic thinking? See for yourself and look at it with your metacognitive intelligence and identify the patterns. That's the second step.

And the third step is that after you identify the patterns, do a dedicated emptiness practice around that, whatever the major, your favorite clouds are, once or twice a week, not as a regular daily practice. So, if you get caught up in thought, you do emptiness of thought. When thought arises, is there anything substantial about where it comes from? When it stays for a while, is there anything substantial about what stays? When it goes away, is there anything substantial about where it goes? Does it have color? Does it have form? Does it have shape? Does it have any definable characteristics? And the more you search into it, as with any emptiness practice, the more the target you search for keeps slipping away as unfindable. Then you train yourself to see the thought as lively awareness expressing itself. It's not thought, and there's [not] a substantial thing that's out there. It's just the moment-by-moment expression of lively awareness. The whole show is awareness.

So, that's the basic practice you do off the pillow. And what makes that practice powerful is that thought and other things that grab you are perceivable. The more reactive you are, the more you are likely to be aware of that reactivity. And those are your best moments for practice because the very moments that make you reactive and grab you the most are the very moments that set you free. We call that "mistakes and problems arising as wisdom." Because all the stuff that's caught up in that grab, if you do emptiness practice, is the very stuff that sets you free.

So, that's the basic practice. If it's emptiness of self, if you get caught up in self, then do a more detailed version of emptiness of self. If you get caught up in out-there-ness, do mind only practice. If you get caught up in emotions, do emptiness of emotions. All the stuff that we do in the basic course.

But, the next level of practice off the pillow is if you can hold a strong view of ocean-like, changeless, boundless awareness from that vast expanse of timeless, limitless awareness, you let everything arise like a wave, like an ocean viewing its own waves. And whatever arises within that great spaciousness has no grab whatsoever. Then you walk around in your daily life in the realm of what's called spacious freedom. That's a much better practice. But don't do it when you're driving a car. Other than that, you can do it pretty much all day long.

If you have awakened awareness and it's relatively stable, you view everything as lively awakened awareness—thoughts are lively awakened awareness, emotions are lively awakened awareness. Sights, sounds, body, body sensations are lively awakened awareness. You train yourself to see everything in terms of it's all the dance of lively awakened awareness. If you're further along the practice and you're doing *dharmadhātu* exhaustion and everything arises within the expanse, arises without running its own course and with no mental engagement, it immediately liberates itself, leaving no trace.

So, the things that you do off the pillow change according to the level of mind you're operating out of, and whatever that skill level of your practice is. But there's a finite number of things that you do. Just it means working with your own metacognitive intelligence and with your teacher to determine what the best fit that the practice is to your level at that given time.

The idea is to get to the point to get there. The idea is to get to the point that there's no distinction between meditation, formal meditation sessions, and off the pillow practice. It's all one practice. You take your mind everywhere, so you never stop practicing with it. That would be the superior practice. Or as Milarepa says, "there's no distinction between sessions and breaks."

There are three levels of practice in Shardza Rinpoche's, the Bon lama's works, which I like. The first is *tunsang*, formal session meditation practice. You do it for a certain amount of time, say a half an hour, forty minutes. And most of your practice comes through the realizations that you get in the meditation session itself. It doesn't carry over a lot to everyday life. Then the second is *nangsang*, which means automatic meditation. If you're doing something like automatic emptiness, and it goes on all the time, whatever comes up next is automatically empty. So, it never stops. So, the idea that somehow if you ring the bell it's going to stop is ridiculous. You have the meditation all the time, it's completely automatic and it goes on, on and off the pillow. And that's when the distinctions between formal meditation and post-meditation sessions break down because it's all one practice. You do it 24/7. And the third is *longsang*, or mastery meditation. Whatever the mind does, it has full mastery over it with lightning speed. Then you're getting somewhere.

So, in this tradition, we try and move you, and in Dzogchen, in general, we try and move you beyond tying your meditation to being on the pillow to whatever you can do to continue the same insights off the pillow all the time.

Your mind's always with you. Either you're working on it or you're not. There's no formal or arbitrary period that this is, "I'm going to meditate now."

You're creating an artificial construction of mind that somehow that meditation is going to be something more beneficial than everything off the pillow; and you're going to get calmer or something—another construction of mind like that. It's just a state that you're constructing. It's a perfect delusion. If you're really honest with yourself, you practice all the time. And it's especially good to practice at times that are most difficult.

That's real practice, as Rahob Tulku says, "The only true test of your realization is when you find yourself in the most difficult of life circumstances. If your practice deteriorates, it was probably conceptual. Your realizations were conceptual. If they deepened, it's probably real." Bring on the stuff of everyday life. See where you are with it. Then you're really doing practice. If it doesn't serve you to soften the reactivity and grab to the things that are most likely to grab you the most, then your practice is an illusion, just a way of feeling good about yourself. It's not honest. Honest practice is you put yourself in the most, the thick of the worst of the *samsāra* situations and you come out a better practitioner as a result of it. That's good practice.

My favorite practice is working in the courts as a trauma and abuse expert with the worst situations of what people do to kids. I love being cross-examined. That's my best practice. It's my best moments of practice. Because otherwise I could be self-reactive or if I have a team of attorneys whose whole purpose is to discredit me, if I get shamed, shame-sensitive or reactive, I get nowhere. But if all that stuff dissolves into the expanse and all that's left is their full presence, all I need are three or four questions and I got all their arguments, then I'm going to have fun. And I'm going to do something useful for the sake of those kids.

So, you use whatever you've got in everyday life, the thick of it. All the stuff of *samsāra* becomes the vehicle for practice. You can't compartmentalize and say, "When I have a quiet time to meditate." All the stuff of everyday life is the time to meditate. There's no off the pillow practice, there's no on the pillow practice. It's just practice. The rest of it's an arbitrary distinction, an idea that you have in your mind. But the quality of how you use that practice and how you use that awareness to work with the stuff that's most difficult, that matters.

You had a question?

Student 2

Yes. We've been reading a certain section, well, your book, *Pointing Out the Great Way*. And there's one section in the preliminary practice I enjoyed very much being, incorporating into my preliminary practice. Do I pronounce it right? Vajrasattva visualization.

Dan

The confession.

Student 2

And the purification. Visualize the *bodhisattva* on top of the crown and the honey dripping down through your body.

Dan

Nectar. Yeah.

Student 2

So, here's the question. I've been practicing this for about three weeks just incorporating into the preliminary. But sometimes I wonder if I do it right. So, I feel like there's some comparison between this and what we've been doing the past, using lightning speed to search, roaming around your body to look for the self. I wonder if it's a similar thing or not.

And the second question is I tended to enjoy it very much. So, I visualized that, gave it quite a bit of time to imagine the honey from this *bodhisattva*'s body moving around on my body to transform it in the expanse of time. And I really enjoy that part. But because there's a roaming around your body to search for yourself, the unfindability, you said going to take the lightning speed. You can't spend ten minutes searching for it. But I did spend ten minutes to imagine the *bodhisattva*'s honey going through from my crown all the way to my toes. So, I worry if I do it wrong.

Dan

Now you have to practice sticky body. [Laughter]

Student 2

So, yeah. So, wonder if I'm reading it wrong.

Dan

Let's talk about what the aim of Vajrasattva practice is. It's part of the preliminaries. And in Western terms, if I randomly beeped you as psychologists have done during the day and ask you to fill out a mood questionnaire at various plot points during the day, say maybe twenty, forty times a day, and we assessed the emotions that you were having at that given point in time, most Westerners would find that they had somewhere on the ratio of four to five negative states to every positive state. So, the spontaneous emerging states of mind are predominantly negative. And since that's our ordinary experience and we rarely experience positivity, if I were to try and sit down on the pillow, at some point all that negativity is going to come up on the pillow and it's probably going to erode my meditation practice, and I wouldn't get anywhere.

So, as part, not all, but part of the aim of preliminary practices is to reduce the frequency of spontaneous emerging negative states and actively cultivate positive states. Those practices are done in a set. So, the way you practice working reducing negative states is Vajrasattva confession. And the way you cultivate positive states is Mandala offering. Those are the traditional parts of the preliminary practices.

So, how do you work with Vajrasattva practice? At first, it requires some honesty and metacognitive awareness of whatever your negative states are. So, you catalog your negative states. You have to acknowledge them to yourself, and you imagine that you acknowledge them in front of the Buddha Vajrasattva. So, you have to sort of publicly acknowledge all the negative states that you have. It's sort of like going to confession in Catholicism, because there's something about the acknowledgement of those that allows you to get some distance on it so you don't get caught up in them. So, the first is you have to acknowledge, and that's called the confession part of the exercise. You have to acknowledge the negative states and make a list of them. So, if you do this once a day, you do it whatever the main negative states are for that day. If you do it more than once a day, you do it frequently, for all the negative states you have.

The second part of the process is purification, having publicly acknowledged them in front of Kuntuzangpo, or in this case Vajrasattva. And then you imagine a visualization in which Vajrasattva is pouring down streams of light or nectar, or whatever you want to use, into your mindstream and purifying everywhere in your body, purifying all the negative states, so there's none left. So, they dissolve with this nectar or this honey or this light, whatever you use. There are different versions of this. So, you actually imagine, put the intention into imagining a purification process until it's gone. And then, if you do that on a regular practice basis, it's part of the hundred thousand preliminaries. If you do that a hundred thousand times, the likelihood after that repetition, you're not going to have a lot of negative states spontaneously emerging. So, it works more than it doesn't work.

And then having done the preliminaries, if you reduce the spontaneously emerging negative states, when you try to take a concentration practice on the pillow, all that negative state [stuff] doesn't spontaneously emerge and interfere with your practice anymore. So, you've increased the probability that you get some gain out of the practice.

Now, there are, in Western psychology, equivalents to confession, and that's the work of Jim Pennebaker, the so-called confession studies. And here's what he originally did. He took college students and he had them either write in a journal, talk with a live student who was a confederate to the research, or talk into a tape recorder.

And here's the instruction: "I want you to bring to mind whatever it is that feels most emotionally unfinished in your life. It may be a relationship that didn't end well, whether you didn't quite finish the grieving process for it, maybe something deeply traumatic that happened to you, maybe something that you did that you feel deeply guilty about or ashamed of, whatever feels most emotionally unfinished." And you word it in terms of emotionally unfinished. "And I want you to talk it out or write about it without avoiding it, everything that comes to mind about it. And keep writing about it until two things happen. One is you feel more settled about it, and second that you get a different perspective on it."

And what he found is it made no difference whether … and the control group just said whatever came to mind, free association, but it was never about processing unfinished emotional business. And he found that after four sessions, there were significant health differences, and there were differences in wellbeing that the students who were confessing unfinished emotional business and processing as opposed to those who are just saying whatever comes to mind and free-associating. They had significantly greater psychological wellbeing after four sessions.

And they looked at biological factors. They were looking at immune measures, like phagocytic index, t-cell enumeration, standard measures of the immune system's capacity to have immunosurveillance and to fight and resist disease. And they found that confession not only led to psychological wellbeing, but it was good for not just the heart, it was good for the body, so that the people had better, more robust immune surveillance, immunosurveillance.

Nobody believed the results. So, they replicated the stuff the following year, and they had the people who were in the control group versus the experimental group keep a journal for a year of vulnerability to flus and common colds and other illnesses. And they found that the ones who had confessed, they had greater psychological wellbeing, they had better immune markers of immunosurveillance, and they also were much more disease resistant. So, confession may be good for the soul, but it's also pretty good for the body, as well as the mind. And those are the Western studies.

When they looked at dis-aggregating the treatment, why it worked, there are two factors. One factor was processing unfinished emotional business. Whatever we don't process, we tend to hold onto, or I like to say resistance guarantees persistence. Whatever makes you uncomfortable because it's strongly emotional and you're conflicted about, if you don't process it it's going to come back to bite you. So, you make the conditions to process what's unprocessed, and simple wording of it is important, wording it in terms of what feels most emotionally unfinished. People were processing things they hadn't processed for years. It didn't take very long to do it. But the people who did the best in that study were in the process of processing it, they developed a wider perspective. They had some capacity for perspective taking, which is a metacognitive capacity. They got a distance on it, and they saw the value in not holding onto those states. Basically, they had a different understanding about themselves and whatever that event was. So, that's the confession studies or the Western equivalent of Vajrasattva visualization. They work the same way.

Now that's only half of the equation. The other half of the equation is the act of cultivation of positive states. And in the Buddhist *Abhidharma*, it says that the techniques used to work with negative states and the techniques used to work with positive states are not equivalent to each other, they're complimentary. So, if you have very good and effective methods to work with negative states and they're effective, we can reasonably expect a relative reduction or maybe even the absence of the negative states.

But the absence of a negative is not a positive. You have to use a whole other set of techniques to cultivate the positive. And that's something that Western psychology doesn't appreciate, until recently with positive psychology, that almost all of the enterprise of psychotherapy is about working with negative states as if the positive states have no implications for mental health, which is garbage. Sometimes the cultivation of positive states has much farther, far-reaching implications for mental health than focusing on the negative.

So, in the Tibetan system, they actually do a whole series of visualizations about positive states—all these Tibetan *thangkas* where buddhas are configurations of positive states. So, if you look at the blue buddha, the buddha of behavioral medicine, Menri, he manifests a positive state called "healing concern," *bākhyapa*. It means that, and that's a prerequisite to be a Tibetan doctor, if you want to be a Tibetan doctor, you have to have healing concern. So, what it means is that it's an active, cultivated presence. So, when you sit with somebody, you have a genuine focus on them. You're genuinely concerned for their welfare, and you exude a concern for their wellbeing. That's the prerequisite to be a Tibetan doctor. The opposite of that would be the kind of sarcastic distance of a Western surgeon. So, you do visualizations to cultivate the quality of healing concern or patience or trust or whatever else. And the more of those positive qualities you collect through the visualizations, the more it potentiates the best of your practice.

Now, rather than picking out certain qualities over time, this is something that Westerners don't relate to, what the Tibetans came to was this idea that the best way of developing positive qualities is to take everything good in the world and offer it up freely. The Tibetan version of a potlatch. So, you think of everything good, you think of all the treasures and jewels of the world, all the horses and all the cows and all the animals and everything good. And you just give it all away. And that generosity and giving everything good away cultivates a positive state of mind. But most Westerners can't relate to Mandala offering because it's too culturally specific.

So, you think about building the stacks of the Mandala together, and then there are four continents and eight subcontinents, and you stack up all the different jewels and the rice and the different stacks of the Mandala, and it's completely alien to Westerners and they have no idea why they're doing it. But the idea is, in Tibetan terms, to give away everything, offer up everything that's good, symbolically, as a way of reflecting on all the good qualities of mind and making a presence for those good qualities and then giving them freely.

We were once with His Holiness Menri Trizin, he was my Root Lama, and we were working on some of these preliminary practices with him, and my wife said to him, "I can't relate to the Mandala offering at all. It's so alien to me." And he says, "Oh, don't worry about it. Just offer up New York City." [Laughter] He was making a joke, but it wasn't entirely a joke though. He said, "Find a Western equivalent where you give everything away."

And you do these as a set. So, if every day you do Vajrasattva confession, and you're reducing the frequency of negative states, and every day you do Mandala offering or some other exemplar visualization where you're developing a series of positive qualities, over time, the balance, the ratio shifts. So, that you find that as if we were to randomly beep you during the day and ask you to describe what your emotional state or your mood state was at that time, you would find after you did these practices and laid a sufficient foundation with them, then essentially you would have a four to five one ratio of positive states.

There is a Western equivalent to the positive states, and it's important. There was the work of Barbara Fredrickson. She got the Templeton Award, which is sort of the Nobel Prize in positive psychology, for this work. And the basic question was to ask yourself, "What good are positive states from an evolutionary point of view? Why do we have positive emotions?" And she developed what we call the "broad and build model." If you evoke positive states, it builds internal coping resources and it broadens attention span and cognitive capacity and creativity. So, it makes the mind more spacious and gets a larger perspective, and you develop better coping resources to deal with life problems.

So, a good example of that is it's built into animals too, not just humans. So, the caribou, in the summer, lock horns with each other. They play at fighting and sometimes they play at fighting pretty hard, but they never hurt each other. Why do they play at fighting? Why are they expressing positive emotions like that, like play? Because in the winter when the food is scarce and they get surrounded by the pack of wolves, they want to know how to fight. So, in leisure time during the summer, they play at fighting as a way of building their coping resources and their survival skills.

Humans do the same thing. When we're not engaged in a task or preoccupied with some negative state, we experience positive emotions and that's how we build our resources. And there are many laboratory experiments to corroborate that model by having people listen to music that evokes positive states or visualize a memory or have a memory of positive times in their life, or watch a film that has some positivity to it. And then, before and after testing about creativity and cognitive capacity and attention span, as compared to the control group, the ones who have the induction of positive emotions usually have greater coping capacity and cognitive capacity and attention span and all those other good things.

So, in Fredrickson's work, she found some very important things that normally, as I said, the ratio of negative states to positive states is about four or five to one for most individuals. But some people over time learn to cultivate positive states. They can do that by doing these visualizations of positive states. They can listen to music that evokes positive states, they can watch films that evoke positive states and put positivity in the daily practice of, disciplined practice of trying to cultivate positive states.

And she found two interesting things. One was that what she called a tipping point, that when the usual individual is trained in positivity, cultivating positivity, when they get to—it's a mathematical formula—when they get to three to one or higher positive than negative states, over three times the number positive in their daily life, then they spontaneously grow and change in certain areas of life that were normally problematic without any further interventions.

So, all of a sudden, relationships start working, things are better at work or something like that. And when the individual gets to the point that they get eleven or more positive states than negative states, the ratio is that high, so they're mostly exuding positivity, everything in their life works without any interventions, without therapy, without twelve step programs, without anything else, without meditation, without yoga, it just works. And that has profound implications for mental health that the induction of positivity in one's life is more important for mental health than their working through negative states—the exact opposite message most psychotherapies try to do, as if working with negative states is the whole key to psychotherapy. It's not.

Now the epitome of that is what you find in Buddhism, because there's a certain point in the practice where if you hold in what we call the inseparable pair—the view of the vast expanse of awakened mind, *dharmakāya* space, and the liveliness of whatever arises within that, so all thoughts are lively awakened awareness, all sounds, all sights, all thoughts, all emotions, everything is lively, awakened awareness, and all you have to do is hold that view and not engage anything that comes up, just let it run its own course— things will arise and disappear. Arise and disappear, leaving no trace. It's that mental engagement of things that come up—the mind moves towards it to make more of it and likes it; mind moves away from it to make less of it if it doesn't like it—that built-in reactivity is what causes karmic memory traces.

So, at a certain advanced level of practice, if you hold that view just right, you're letting everything arise, run its own course without mental engagement and immediately it disappears. Now, if you do that all the time, 24/7, you are not forming any new karmic memory traces anymore. And it forces the mind to dip into the storehouse of karmic ripening memory traces and release them all, so there's none left. The average time is six or seven years if you do this practice all the time. We call that "the path of *dharmadhātu* exhaustion." You actually exhaust the bin, so there's no negative states left; and the negative states obscure the positive states, so they [positive states] all flourish. And that state is profound. It's a certain advanced level of practice where when Buddha got enlightened under the bodhi tree, he was called buddha, which literally means realized one.

But when those teachings in Mahāyāna Buddhism got transferred from India to Tibet, that's not how the Tibetans translated the word buddha. The Tibetan word is *sangye*, and it's a compound term. *Sangwa* means complete purification. *Gyewa* means flourishing. So, what they were saying is rather than just saying "realized one," which doesn't really say anything, the real change that occurs is there's no negative states left whatsoever. You've exhausted all negative states; they don't occur anymore. And because of that, there's a flourishing of the eighty positive states of mind in the buddha, in the Bon tradition it's eighty-five. But go figure, it's similar.

Imagine the implications of that for mental health in the West, that there are no negative states left and only a flourishing of all positive states. Those are the healthiest people in the world. And we have a number of people who are now working on self-arising, self-liberating and releasing all those things. And they're not that far along, but they're reasonably far along with the process, relatively speaking. And as a follow-up to our study on the neurocircuitry of awakening, we just got approved to do a study on *sangye*. So, my task is to identify thirty subjects who are far enough along that process that they've really changed the substrate of their mind. And then we'll look at the neuroscience of that and see if we can come up with specific markers for what it means. I think it's important to do that because this has profound implications for mental health.

Mental health and therapy in the West needs to rethink its aim. It's not all about talking about mommies and daddies and bad states of mind that you want to work through. The positive is much more important in some sense. But we have to retrain a generation of people to think about a larger perspective here. But we have the subjects enough probably to get a good test of this now.

So, if you evoke positivity more in your life, everything in your life starts to work, irrespective of whether you worked out all the negative stuff; all the negative stuff just becomes irrelevant because you're working on a positivity all of the time. So, it's a different mechanism of change. You don't have to work through anything. That was the original idea of the mandala offering. But most Westerners don't understand mandala offering at all. But the idea was to offer up everything positive. It's a way of cultivating positive states. You have to intentionally cultivate them.

From a neurocircuitry point of view, I think probably what was going on, the thing about *sangye* is—this is my working hypothesis—that people who have cultivated positive states activate their medial orbital prefrontal cortex. The medial OFC is three things: it assigns salience to emotions; it's the center for all the positive emotions in the brain; and it's the center for pro-social behavior. So, Richie Davidson did a study of Matthieu Ricard, who in his twenties was a molecular biologist in France and he became a Gelugpa monk under the Dalai Lama's tradition. And for thirty years he's practiced mostly compassion visualizations. And they did a pre-post study of his brain neurocircuitry during and after compassion meditation, and he strongly activated the medial OFC, which means that he activated positive emotions—and he's a very positive guy these days—and activated the pro-social behavior. So, it's about connection with people and being positive.

On the other hand, there are some studies out of Germany that show that certain classes of patients deactivate the medial OFC, particularly people who have major dissociative disorders. They get emotionally numb and they disconnect from other people so they lose positivity and they lose emotional salience and they lose the capacity to connect with others. So, it's the opposite of that, it's the extreme opposite of that. If you train positivity, you end up with getting more positivity and more connection with other people and that becomes the foundation of compassion and living a life where you concern yourself not with your own selfish preoccupations, but with the greater social good. So that's one of the things I think we'll find.

And the other is probably deactivating of the circuitry of negative emotions, which means the fear of the amygdala and the other negative emotions in the limbic system. I think it's pretty straightforward, what we're going to find. And I'll be surprised if we don't.

So, whether you look at the confession studies of Pennebaker or the positivity studies of Barbara Fredrickson, they're not far afield from the Buddhist explanations of confession and mandala offering because both share a common view that the task at hand is to eradicate negative states as much as possible and cultivate positive states so the balance shifts so that you're living out of positivity most of the time.

Now, whether you have negative or positive states, those states still are constructions of mind and they have grab to them. And that's where emptiness practice comes in because it removes the grab or the reactivity to both positive and negative states. But the foundation is to decrease the spontaneous emerging frequency of negative states and increase the spontaneous emergence of positive states in the frequency. That's what preliminary practice is about.

That make it a little bit more clear?

Student 2

I just had an observation because we're not just doing the practices as you've kind of laid out. It seems to be that negative states are expiring kind of on their own without ... This is a question that was coming up when you were talking about the emptiness. I'm just wondering if the emptiness practice has the side effect of actually doing what you're describing or if it's better to more directly ...

Dan

If you visualize the purification process at the coarse level of mind, then temporarily there's a relative reduction of negative states. But they don't get eradicated so that the karmic roots of those cause them to ripen again. So, you could do Vajrasattva for a hundred thousand times, which is what they recommended in preliminaries, a mandala offering a hundred thousand times. But the negative states will still emerge unless you completely cleaned up your behavior and conduct in everyday life; they're going to emerge anyway. But they don't tend to emerge as much if you do emptiness practice.

So, we come back to the story of the peacock, which you might've heard before. There was a story of an Indian family who found that there was a very poisonous tree that was growing in their garden and anybody who got close to the tree or touched it would die. So, they were very concerned about their safety. So, they brought in a gardener and the gardener cut down the tree except the roots were still there so it grew back. That's concentration practice. Or preliminary practice where you cut down the obvious negative states but they grow back because the roots are still intact.

Then they brought in a series of consultants and said, we can take the poison out and we can transform it into a medicine. It still grew back; it just took a lot longer. And that's the practice of the *tantras*. You take the negative states, you embrace them, and you transform them into something positive.

But then the best practice was somebody came along and said, "Look, just bring in a peacock." And they brought in the peacock and the peacock wasn't afraid of the poison and it ate it directly, and it didn't get harmed by it. And it kept eating it until there was no poison left and no plant left. Took everything completely, and the plant never grew back after that. And that's a metaphor for Dzogchen practice. It all depends on the view that you have. There are no negative states, there are no positive states, they're just all lively awareness. And you eat it directly. All the stuff of life, you just gobble up. All the negative stuff of life, you just gobble up. All the positive stuff, you gobble it up. If you view it correctly, it has no grab whatsoever left to it. So, that's the best practice. Eat the poison. It never comes back. Or, somebody's going to go home and try to eat poison and I'm going to get sued now. [Dan laughs]

If you do emptiness practices, like cutting not just the branches in the trunk of the tree but you're cutting the roots, it'll still grow back, but it'll take much longer. So, you can cut the tree, you can cut the roots, you can transform it into a medicine or you can eat it directly. And the superior practice is the Dzogchen practice because there's no negative states left. It depends on your view and you gobble it all up.

Student 2

But that's a form of emptiness practice, no?

Dan

No. Beyond emptiness practice. Yeah.

Student 2

Okay. So, you're saying just pure emptiness practice, the states come back.

Dan

Yes. It's a more subtle level of that practice.

Student 2

And so just could you just ...

Dan

It's liveliness practice.

Student 2

Okay.

Dan

You're viewing the poison as lively, awakened awareness. It can't possibly harm you. The awakened mind can't harm you.

Student 2

That's very cool. [Laughter]

Dan

You have to be a peacock.

APPENDIX 1

Biography of Dan Brown

Daniel P. Brown, PhD
September 11, 1948 - April 4, 2022

The following biography was published as an obituary in the *American Journal of Clinical Hypnosis* [65(1):79-82] by D. Corydon Hammond, PhD (University of Utah)

The beloved educator, researcher, author, translator, hypnotherapist, psychotherapist, and meditation teacher, Daniel P. Brown, PhD, died on Monday, April 4, 2022, at his home in San Francisco, CA. He was 73.

Author of over 15 books, Dr. Brown made significant contributions in many fields of knowledge and clinical practice. He was also well-respected for his courageous work as an expert witness or consultant on high-profile cases involving complex trauma and abuse.

Born on September 11, 1948, in New Bedford, MA, Dr. Brown was the first person in his family to attend college, at the University of Massachusetts, Amherst, where he received his undergraduate degree in molecular biology. He went on to receive his Ph.D. in Religion & Psychological Studies at the University of Chicago, where he also received a Danforth Fellowship, given for promise in teaching excellence, and received specialized training in how to teach.

His first clinical placement was at Michael Reese Hospital in Chicago, and he also commuted part time to The Menninger Foundation in Topeka Kansas to work on the treatment of substance abuse. In the late 1970s he moved back to his home state of Massachusetts where he did a clinical internship at McLean Hospital and a Postdoctoral Fellowship in Clinical Research at Harvard Medical School at The Cambridge Hospital. His research focused on the long-term effects of mindfulness meditation.

In the late 1970s Dr. Brown became interested in the study of trauma and abuse largely through peer collaboration with Sarah Haley, one of the founding members of the International Society for the Study of Traumatic Stress.

In the 1980s Dr. Brown served as Director of Training and then as Chief Psychologist at The Cambridge Hospital. He helped develop a clinical psychology internship and postdoctoral training program to provide the best young talent in psychology the opportunity to work with a disenfranchised inner city chronic mental health population. He also developed and directed the Behavioral Medicine Program, a joint venture between psychiatry and primary care medicine.

In the early 1990s Dr. Brown became interested in the topic of memory for trauma and abuse. His textbook, *Memory, Trauma Treatment and the Law*, co-authored with D. Corydon Hammond, PhD and Alan W. Scheflin, is the recipient of awards from 7 professional societies, including the 1999 Manfred S. Guttmacher Award given jointly by the American Psychiatric Association and the American Academy of Psychiatry and Law for the "outstanding contribution to forensic psychiatry."

Dr. Brown served as an expert witness or consultant on trauma and memory in over two hundred lawsuits, including testimony before the International War Crimes Tribunal for the prosecution of war criminals of the former Yugoslavia. He also worked on behalf of clergy abuse clients in Louisiana for 17 years with Roger Stetter, author of *In Our Own Words: Reflections on Professionalism in the Law*, which the Louisiana Bar Foundation distributed to every lawyer and judge in Louisiana.

Mr. Stetter said, "Dan was a brilliant guy and all of my clients thought the world of him. It became clear from my conversations with people in Newton, where he lived, that everyone there loved him as well. I think it was Dan's combination of brilliance and modesty that made him so special. He almost never talked about himself. His life was about helping others, showing respect and genuine concern for their welfare.

Dr. Brown also served on the Harvard Medical School faculty for nearly four decades, where he co-directed and taught courses on hypnosis, trauma, meditation, peak performance, and attachment. He worked to stay abreast of the latest scientific developments in assessment and treatment, and use these findings to offer clinicians practical, state-of-the-art methods to upgrade their standard of care.

Larry Lifson, director of the Continuing Education Program of the Department of Psychiatry at the Beth Israel Deaconess Medical Center, a major teaching hospital of Harvard Medical School, wrote that "Dan Brown was not only an enormously gifted clinician and highly esteemed teacher, he also was a beloved mentor to so many of his students."

Most of his clinical writing and teaching from the 1980s and 1990s focused on treatment for complex trauma disorders. He co-authored two books on developmental psychopathology—a book on affect development, *Human Feelings*, and a book on self-development from a cross-cultural perspective, *Transformations of Consciousness.*

In the 2000s Dr. Brown began to study adult attachment and received intensive training in the Adult Attachment Interview. His research focused on the relative contribution of early attachment pathology to the development of personality and dissociative disorders in adulthood. He is the senior author, with David Elliot, of a major textbook on the treatment of attachment disorders in adults, *Attachment Disturbances in Adults.*

Dr. Brown taught hypnotherapy for 38 years and wrote several important books on hypnosis, including Hypnotherapy and Hypnoanalysis with Erika Fromm, PhD, a noted hypnoanalyst who served as his primary clinical mentor—a relationship that spanned 35 years.

Dr. Brown's interest in meditation started while at grad school at University of Chicago. During that time, he also studied Tibetan, Sanskrit, and Pali in the Buddhist Studies Program at the University of Wisconsin in Madison. He spent ten years translating meditation texts for his doctoral dissertation on Tibetan Buddhist Mahāmudrā meditation.

Dr. Brown studied many forms of meditation practice over the course of his life, including Patanjali's Yoga Sutras with Mircea Eliade and Dr. Arwind Vasavada, and Burmese mindfulness meditation with Mahāsī Sayādaw and Achaan Cha.

Dr. Brown first learned Indo-Tibetan concentration and insight meditation with his root teacher, the Venerable Geshe Wangyal. He studied meditation practices from the Mahāmudrā, Nyingma Dzogchen, and Bonpo Dzogchen lineages with numerous Tibetan lamas, including H.H. The 14th Dalai Lama and H.H. The 33rd Menri Trizin, the spiritual head of the Tibetan Bon religion.

Dr. Brown also spent 45 plus years translating meditation texts from Tibetan and Sanskrit, and is the author of *Pointing Out the Great Way: The Stages of Meditation in the Mahāmudrā Tradition* (2006, Wisdom Publications) based on his doctoral dissertation of twenty-five years earlier He taught meditation retreats internationally for over 30 years, often in collaboration with Tibetan meditation masters including Denma Locho Rinpoche, Rahob Tulku Rinpoche, Tenzin Wangyal Rinpoche. Dan taught in the spirit of the ecumenical Rime movement, synthesizing the "greatest hits" of meditation instructions from various lineages to develop a comprehensive and precise path from ordinary dualistic consciousness to full enlightenment.

The latter part of his life was devoted to his goal of leaving behind a complete set of instructions to guide Western meditation practitioners along this path.

He was known for his unique integration of contemporary Western research on peak performance and positive psychology with the classical Buddhist meditation lineage traditions.

He spent 10 years conducting outcomes research on beginning and advanced meditators, and led the only scientific study identifying the neurocircuitry of the meditative experience of the awakened mind. He was especially interested in meditations designed to stabilize awakening in everyday life and to bring about the flourishing of positive qualities of mind.

Brown met his wife, Gretchen Nelson, in 2007 at a meditation retreat he was teaching in California. They began teaching meditation retreats together in 2007. They were married in 2010, by Rahob Rinpoche, and besides his wife, he is survived by two sons, Gabriel and Jeremy.

Dr. Brown was held in the highest esteem by his professional colleagues, yet he was perhaps even more deeply loved and appreciated by the many clients and students whose lives he profoundly touched. As prolific as he was, he had a way of making each individual he worked with feel deeply seen and respected for who they were and what they were capable of. His relentless commitment to helping others experience their true potential was unparalleled.

While any single one of Dan's many accomplishments would have made for a life well-lived, Dan never lost touch with his humble roots, and was known for enjoying good food, fishing and football with his friends and family.

Daniel P. Brown, PhD
CURRICULUM VITAE (abbreviated)

Part I. General Information
Date Prepared: July 16, 2024
Date of Birth: September 11, 1948
Place of Birth: New Bedford, MA
Date of Death: April 22, 2022

Education:
1971 B.S. University of Massachusetts, Microbiology
1973 M.A.University of Chicago, Religion & Psychological Studies
1981 Ph.D. University of Chicago, Religion & Psychological Studies

Training:
Internships:
1975-1976 Psycho-diagnostic Clerk and Clinical Extern, Psychosomatic and Psychiatric Institute, Michael Reese Medical Center, Chicago
1976-1977 Clinical Psychology Intern (APA-approved), McLean Hospital, Belmont, MA
1977-1981 Clinical Fellow in Psychology, McLean Hospital, Belmont, MA
Research Fellowships:
1978-1980 Research Fellow in Social-Behavioral Science, Harvard Medical School
Licensure and Board Certification:
1980 Licensed Psychologist, Massachusetts, #2399-PR
1990 Diplomate, American Board of Psychological Hypnosis, #209
Member, Executive Board, ABPH
Other Training & Certification:
2002 Certified Consultant, American Society of Clinical Hypnosis.2006
Successfully completed training in administration & scoring of the Adult Attachment Inventory; passed full 30-case reliability testing at high reliability level. AAI training with Deborah Jacobvitz, Ph.D. Reliability testing with Mary Main & Erik Hesse.

Academic Appointments:
1975-1976 Instructor, Religion and Psychological Studies, The University of Chicago
1980-1990 Adjunct Assistant Professor, The School of Social Work of Simmons College
1990-1991 Adjunct Associate Professor, The School of Social Work of Simmons College

1991-2006 Adjunct Professor, The School of Social Work of Simmons College

Hospital or Affiliated Institution Appointments:

1981-1986 Instructor in Psychology, Harvard Medical School at The Cambridge Hospital

1986-1990 Assistant Professor in Psychology, Harvard Medical School

1993-1997 Lecturer, Dept. of Psychology, Boston University

1990-2006 Assistant Clinical Professor in Psychology, Harvard Medical School

2006-2022 Associate Clinical Professor in Psychology, Harvard Medical School

Other Professional Positions and Visiting Appointments:

1974-1975 CIC Visiting Scholar, Dept. of Asian Studies, University of Wisconsin, Madison, WI

Hospital & Health Care Organization Service Responsibilities:

1977-1978 Staff Psychologist, Department of Mental Health, The Commonwealth of Massachusetts, Westboro State Hospital, Cambridge/Somerville Unit, Special Dual Diagnosis Treatment Team.

1978-1979 Psychology Associate, Highland Counseling Associates, Athol, MA

1980-1986 Supervisor, The Psychotherapy Center, The Cambridge Hospital, Cambridge, MA.

1980-1982 Director of In-Service Training, Department of Psychiatry, Central Hospital, Somerville, MA

1981-1985 Associate Director of Psychology, Department of Psychiatry, The Cambridge Hospital, Cambridge, MA.

1982-1983 Director of Hypnotherapy Service and Training, Department of Psychiatry, The Cambridge Hospital, Cambridge, MA.

1983-1992 Director of Behavioral Medicine Services, The Department of Psychiatry, The Cambridge Hospital, Cambridge, MA.

1985-1987 Director of Psychology Training and Clinical Services, The Department of Psychiatry, The Cambridge Hospital, Cambridge, MA.

1987-1990 Chief Psychologist, Department of Psychiatry, The Cambridge Hospital

1984-2000 Director, Daniel Brown, Ph.D. & Associates, The Center for Integrative Psychotherapy, 75 Cambridge Parkway, Cambridge, MA 02142

2000-2020 Director, Daniel Brown, Ph.D. & Associates, 796 Beacon St. Newton MA 02459

Major Administrative Responsibilities & Committee Assignments:

National/International:

2007 Chairman, Task Force, Division 56 American Psychological Association Liaison to DSM-V on Trauma-Related Disorders

2006 Executive Committee. Division 56 Psychological Trauma. American Psychological Association.

2006 Chairman, Task Force on Hypnosis and Memory, American Society of Clinical Hypnosis.

1998 Consultant, Expert Witness, United Nations, Office of the Prosecutor, International War Crimes Tribunal for the Former Yugoslavia, The Hague, Netherlands. Helped establish standard of evidence for what constitutes reliable memory in victims of severe war atrocities—standard upheld in two appeals

1998-2022 Member, Task Force on Hypnosis and Memory, APA-Division 30 (Psychological Hypnosis)

1998-2002 Executive Board, American Board of Psychological Hypnosis

1986-1990 Director, U.S. Center, Sino-U.S. Qi Gong Health Sciences Development Center, The Cambridge Hospital, Cambridge, MA and The Beijing College of Traditional Chinese Medicine, Beijing, P.R.C. Organized and led a delegation of scientists from HEW and the AIDs U.S. National Commission to China to educate the Chinese on stopping the spread of AIDs in China.

1989-1990 Vice President, World Academic Society of Medical Qi Gong

1987-1991 Association of Psychology Internship Centers (APIC), Post-Doctoral Membership Committee

1989-1991 Chairman, Post-Doctoral Training Site Membership Committee (APIC)

1988-1990 Education Committee, Division 30, APA

1980-1982 Occasional consultant on cross-cultural sensitivity for the Health Services Division, World Bank, Washington D.C.

Hospital:

1983-1990 Education Committee, The Cambridge Hospital, Cambridge, MA

1986-1990 Executive Committee, The Cambridge Hospital, Cambridge, MA

1986-1988 Executive Board, The Erikson Center, Cambridge, MA

Professional Societies:

American Psychological Association—-Divisions 30, 38, 41

American Society of Clinical Hypnosis (Fellow)

Society of Behavioral Medicine

International Society of Traumatic Stress Studies

International Society for Mental Training & Excellence

For a complete version of Dan's CV, please visit www.danielpbrownphd.com

APPENDIX 2

Daniel P. Brown, PhD Bibliography

Books/Monographs:

Wilbur, K., Engler, J. & Brown, D. 1985. T*he Transformation of Consciousness: Conventional and Contemplative Developmental Approaches.* Boston: New Science Library (Shambala/Random House).

Brown, D. & Fromm, E. 1986. *Hypnotherapy & Hypnoanalysis*, with a forward by Ernest R. Hilgard. Hillsdale, New Jersey: Lawrence Erlbaum Associates.

Brown, D. & Fromm, E. 1986. *Hypnosis and Behavioral Medicine*, with a forward by Gary Schwartz. Hillsdale, NJ: Lawrence Erlbaum Associates.

Fass, M. & Brown, D. 1990. *Creative Mastery in Hypnosis and Hypnotherapy*, with a forward by Martin Orne. Hillsdale, NJ: Lawrence Erlbaum Associates.

H.H. The Dalai Lama, Goleman, D., Brenman-Gibson, M., Brown, D., Bolen, J.S., Engler, J., Levine, S., & Macy, J. 1992. *Worlds in Harmony: Dialogues in Compassionate Action*. San Francisco: Parallax Press.

Ablon, S., Brown, D., Khantzian, E. & Mack, J. 1993. *Human Feelings: Explorations in Affect Development and Meaning*, Hillsdale, NJ: The Analytic Press.

Brown, D. & Scheflin, A.W. (Guest Editors). Summer, 1996. Special issue on the false memory controversy. The Journal of Psychiatry and Law, 24, 137-338.

Brown, D., Scheflin, A., & Hammond, C.D. 1997. *Memory, Trauma Treatment and the Law*. New York: Norton.

Goleman, D., (Ed.) with H.H. The Dalai Lama, Brown, D., Davidson, R., Kabat-Zinn, J., Salzberg, S., Valera, F. & Yearley, L. 1997. *Healing Emotions: Conversations with the Dalai Lama on Mindfulness, Emotions, and Health*. Boston: Shambhala.

Brown, D. & Scheflin, A.W. (Guest Editors) Fall-Winter, 1999. Special issue on interrelationship between factitious behavior, dissociative disorders, and the law, The Journal of Psychiatry and Law, 27, 363-706.

Brown, D. 2006. Forward by R. Thurman. *Pointing Out the Great Way; Meditation Stages in the Tibetan Mahāmudrā Tradition*. Boston, MA: Wisdom Publications.

Brown, D. 2009. *The Pointing Out Style of Indo-Tibetan Buddhism; A Guide to Awakening. Volumes 1-3.* Boston, MA. Private, publication manual, restricted access only to previous students and teachers of this style of meditation.

van der Linden, J., Brown, D. 2012. *Dissociation et memoire traumatique*. Dunod: Paris, France.

Brown, D., Elliott, D. et al. 2016 *Treating Attachment Disturbances in Adults; Treatment for Comprehensive Repair*. New York: Norton.

Bru rGyal ba g.Yung drung. 2017. Geshe Sonam Gurang and Brown, D. (Trans.). Translated under the guidance of His Holiness Menri Trizin. Pith Instructions for the A Khrid rDzogs Chen [Bon Great Completion Meditation]. Translated for the Pointing Out the Great Way Foundation.Occidental, CA: Bright Alliance.

Geshe Sonam Gurang and Brown, D. 2019. Translated under the guidance of His Holiness Menri Trizin. *The Three-fold Embodiment of Enlightenment; The Bon Yogi Texts of the Path of Liberation of Shar rDza bra' shis rGyal mtshan*. Occidental, CA: Bright Alliance.

Geshe Sonam Gurang and Brown, D. 2019. Translated under the guidance of His Holiness Menri Trizin. *The Twenty-One Nails, According to the Zhang Zhung Oral Transmission Lineage of Bon Great Completion*, Root text by Taphiritsa and Gyer spungs sNang Bzher Lod Po. Occidental, CA: Bright Alliance.

Geshe Sonam Gurang and Brown, D. 2019. Translated under the guidance of His Holiness Menri Trizin. *The Six Lamps, According to the Zhang Zhung Oral Transmission Lineage of Bon Great Completion*, Root text by Taphiritsa, auto-commentary attributed to Gyer spungs sNang Bzher Lod, Po, three additional commentaries, and Pointing Out the Six Energy Drops, transcribed by gTsang pa Bye Bral. Occidental, CA: Bright Alliance.

Geshe Sonam Gurang and Brown, D. 2019. Translated under the guidance of His Holiness Menri Trizin. *Heart Drops of Kuntu Zangpo*, by Shar rDza bra' shis rGyal mtshan. Occidental, CA: Bright Alliance.

Bissanti, M., Brown, D. & Pasari, J. (2020) *The Elephant Path: Attention Development and Training in Children and Adolescents*. Occidental, CA: Bright Alliance.

Geshe Sonam Gurang and Brown, D. (2021) translated under the guidance of His Holiness Menri Trizin. *The Precious Treasury of the Expanse and Awakened Awareness: The Ornaments of the Definitive Secret*, by Shar rDza bra' shis rGyal mtshan, Occidental, CA: Bright Alliance.

Bru rGyal ba g.Yung drung. (2022) Geshe Sonam Gurang and Brown, D. (Trans.). Translated under the guidance of His Holiness Menri Trizin. *Pith Instructions for the A Khrid rDzogs Chen [Bon Great Completion Meditation]*. Translated and revised for the Pointing Out the Great Way Foundation. Occidental, CA: Bright Alliance.

Chapters in Books and Other Monographs:

Brown, D. (1984) "A model for the levels of concentrative meditation," In D.H. Shapiro & R. Walsh (Eds.) *Meditation: Classic and Contemporary Perspectives,* 281-316, New York: Aldine.

Maliszewski, M., Twemlow, S.W., Brown, D.P. & Engler, J.E. (1981). "A Phenomenological Typology of Intensive Meditation: A Suggested Methodology Using the Questionnaire Approach", Revision, 4: 3-27.

Fromm, E., Boxer, A.M. & Brown, D.P. (1985) "Representations of Self-Hypnosis in Personal Narratives," In D. Waxman, P.C. Misra, M. Gibson & M.A. Basker (Eds.) *Modern Trends in Hypnosis*, pp. 215-222, New York: Plenum Press.

Brown, D. & Engler, J. (1984). "A Rorschach Study of the Stages of Mindfulness Meditation," in D. Shapiro & R. Walsh (Eds.) *Meditation: Classic and Contemporary Perspectives,* pp. 232-262, New York: Aldine.

Brown, D. (1988) "Hypnotic treatment of asthma," Advances, 5: 15-29.

Brown, D. (1990) "Erika Fromm: An intellectual history," In. M.L. Fass & D. Brown (Eds.), *Creative mastery in hypnosis and hypnoanalysis: A festschrift for Erika Fromm*, pp. 1-29, Hillsdale, N.J.: Lawrence Erlbaum and Associates.

Brown, D. (1990) "The variable long-term effects of incest: Hypnoanalytic and adjunctive hypnotherapeutic treatment," In. M.L. Fass & D. Brown (Eds.), *Creative Mastery in Hypnosis and Hypnoanalysis*, pp.199-229, Hillsdale, N.J.: Lawrence Erlbaum and Associates.

Fromm, E. & Brown, D. (1991) "The Hypnoanalytic Treatment of Unconscious Traumatic Memories and Developmental Deficit Caused by Early Incest," In. O. van der Hart (Ed.) *Trauma, dissociatie en hypnose*, pp. 221-248, Amsterdam: Swets & Zeitlinger, Publishers.

Brown, D. (1993). "Clinical hypnosis research in the past five years," In E. Fromm & M. Nash (Eds.). *Contemporary perspectives in hypnosis research.* New York: Guilford.

Brown, D. (1993). "Affective development, psychopathology and adaptation," In S. Ablon, D. Brown, E. Khantzian & J. Mack (Eds.). *Human feelings: Explorations in affect development and meaning.* Hillsdale, NJ: Analytic Press.

Brown, D. (1993). "Stress and emotion: Implications for illness development and wellness," In S. Ablon, D. Brown, E. Khantzian & J. Mack (Eds.). *Human feelings: Explorations in affect development and meaning.* Hillsdale, NJ: Analytic Press.

Brown, D. (1993). "The path of meditation: Affective development and psychological well-being," In S. Ablon, D. Brown, E. Khantzian & J. Mack (Eds.) *Human feelings: Explorations in affect development and meaning.* Hillsdale, NJ: Analytic Press.

Brown, D. (1995). "Types of suggestibility and their applicability to memory distortion in trauma treatment," In J. L. Albert (Ed.), *Delayed Memories of Abuse*, (pp.61-100) Northvale, NJ: Jason Aronson.

Brown, D., Scheflin, A.W., Frischholz, E.J. & Caploe, J. (2002). "Special methodologies in memory retrieval: Chemical, hypnotic, and imagery procedures," In R. I. Simon & D.W. Schuman (Eds.). *Retrospective assessment of mental states in litigation; Predicting the past.* (pp. 369-423) Washington, D.C.:American Psychiatric Association Press.

Brown, D. (2003) "The evolving standard of psychological testing in forensic evaluations," In. R.I. Simon & L.H. Gold (Eds.). *A textbook in forensic psychiatry: Guidelines for assessment.* (pp. 601-635) Washington, D.C.: American Psychiatric Press.

Brown, D. (2009). "Assessment of attachment and abuse history, and adult attachment style," In C. Courtois & J. Ford (Eds.). *Complex traumatic stress disorders: An evidence-based clinician's guide.* (Pp. 124-144) New York: Gulford.

Axelrad, D., Brown, D., Wain, H. (2009; 2016). Hypnosis, In. H.I. Kaplan, A.M. Freeman & B.J. Sadock, (pp. 2804-2832). C*omprehensive textbook of psychiatry.*

Brown, D. (2015). "Body meditation in the Tibetan Buddhist and Bon Traditions," In G. Marlock & H.C. Weise (Eds.) (pp.921-928) *Handbook of body psychotherapy and somatic psychology*. (2nd. ed.).

Brown, D. (2016) "Afterward". In A. Raz & M. Lifshitz (Eds.) (pp. 449-458) H*ypnosis and meditation.*

Steele, H., Brown, D. Sinason, V. (2017). "Bindung und complexes trauma" [Attachment and complex trauma: Essential conditions for treatment of survivors of child abuse]. In K.H. Brisch (Ed.). (pp., 92-112) *Bindungs-traumatisierungen: Wenn bindungspersonen zu tatern warden [Treating attachment disorders—Conference proceedings].* Munich, Germany: Klett-Cotta.

Journals:

Krippner, S. & Brown, D. Field Independence /Dependence and Electrosone 50 Induced Altered States of Consciousness, J. Clin. Psych., 1973, 29: 316-319.

Krippner, S. & Brown, D. Altered States of Consciousness and Mystical-Religious Experience: Methodological Perspectives, Research J. of Phil. & Soc. Sci., 1975, # (1): 39-76.

Brown, D. A Model for the Levels of Concentrative Meditation, Int.J. of Clin. & Exp. Hypnosis, 1977, 25:236-273.

Brown, D. & Fromm, E. Selected Bibliography of Readings in Altered States of Consciousness (ASC) in Normal Individuals, Int. J. of Clin. & Exp. Hypnosis, 1977, 25: 388-391.

Brown, D. & Engler, J. The Stages of Mindfulness Meditation: A Validation Study, J. of Transpersonal Psychology, 1980, 12: 143-192.

Fromm, E., Brown, D., Hurt, D., Oberlander, J., Boxer, A., & Pfeiffer, G. The Phenomena and Characteristics of Self-Hypnosis, Int. J. of Clinic. & Exp. Hypnosis, 1981, 29:189-246.

Shapiro, D., Shapiro, J., Walsh, R. & Brown, D. The Effects of Intensive Meditation on Sex-Role Identification: Implications for a Control Model of Psychological Health, Psychol. Reports, 1982, 51: 44-46.

Brown, D., Forte, M., Rich, P. & Epstein, G. Phenomenological Differences Among Self Hypnosis, Mindfulness Meditation & Imagining, Imagination, Cognition & Personality, 1983, 2: 291-309.

Brown, D.P. & Engler, J.E. An Outcome Study of Intensive Mindfulness Meditation, J. Psychoanalytic Study of Society, 1984, 10: 163-225.

Klagsbrun, J. & Brown, D. Getting the Picture: The Use of Imagery to Clarify Therapeutic Impasses, Psychotherapy: Theory, Research & Practice, 1984, 21: 254-259.

Brown, D.P., Forte, M. & Dysart, M. Visual Sensitivity and Mindfulness Meditation, Perceptual and Motor Skills, 1984, 58: 775-784.

Brown, D., Forte, M. & Dysart, M. Visual Sensitivity Differences Among Mindfulness Meditators and Non-Meditators, Perceptual and Motor Skills, 1984, 58: 727-733.

Brown, D. Hypnosis as an Adjunct to the Psychotherapy of the Severely Disturbed Patient: An Affective Development Approach, Int. J. of Clin. & Exp. Hypnosis, 1985, 33:281-301.

Forte, M., Brown, D.P. & Dysart, M. Through the Looking Glass: Phenomenological Reports of Advanced Meditators at Visual Threshold, Imagination, Cognition & Personality, 1984-1985, 4 (4): 323-338.

Forte, M., Brown, D. & Dysart, M. Differences in Experience Among Mindfulness Meditators, Imagination, Cognition & Personality, 1987-88, 7 (1), 47-60.

Brown, D. Pseudomemories, the Standard of Science and the Standard of Care in Trauma Treatment, American Journal of Clinical Hypnosis, 1995, 37, 1-24.

Scheflin, A.W. & Brown, D. (Summer, 1996). Repressed memory or dissociative amnesia: What the science says. The Journal of Psychiatry and Law, 24, 143-188.

Brown, D., Scheflin, A.W., & Whitfield, C.W. (Spring, 1999). Recovered memories—the current weight of the evidence in science and in the courts, The Journal of Psychiatry and Law, 27, 5-156.

Brown, D. & Scheflin, A.W. (Fall-Winter, 1999). Factitious disorders and trauma-related diagnoses, The Journal of Psychiatry and Law, 27, 373-422.

Brown, D., Frischholz, E.J., & Scheflin, A.W. (Fall-Winter, 1999). Iatrogenic dissociative identity disorder–An evaluation of the scientific evidence, The Journal of Psychiatry and Law, 27, 549-638.

Scheflin, A.W. & Brown, D. (Fall-Winter, 1999). The false litigant syndrome: "Nobody would say that unless it was the truth," The Journal of Psychiatry and Law, 27, 649-705.

Brown, D. (2001). (Mis)representations of the long-term effects of childhood sexual abuse in the courts, Journal of Child Sexual Abuse, 9, 79-107.

Van der Hart, O., Nijenhuis, E., Steele, K. & Brown, D. (2005), Trauma-related dissociation: Conceptual clarity lost and found, Australian & New Zealand Journal of Psychaitry.

Brown, D. (2007). Evidence-based hypnotherapy for asthma: A critical review, Special Edition on Evidence-Based Hypnotherapy. International Journal of Clinical and Experimental Hypnosis, 55(2), 1-30.

Brown, D. (2009). The energy body and its functions: Immuno-surveillance, longevity, and regeneration, New York Academy of Sciences, 1172, 312-337.

Brown, D. (2009). Mastery of the mind East and West; Excellence in being and doing and everyday happiness, New York Academy of Sciences, 1172, 231-251.

Baker, R.L. & Brown, D. (2015). On engagement: Learning to pay attention. Special edition on "Balance in Legal Education Symposium" University of Arkansas Law Review, 36, 337-385.

Schoenberg, P., Ruf, A., Churchill, J., Brown, D. & Brewer, J. (2018). Mapping complex mind states: EEG neural substrates of meditative unified compassionate awareness, Consciousness & Cognition, Jan, Vol 57, pages 41-53.